James Fredrick McCurdy

History, Prophecy and the Monuments; or, Israel and the Nations

Volume III

James Fredrick McCurdy

History, Prophecy and the Monuments; or, Israel and the Nations
Volume III

ISBN/EAN: 9783337088163

Printed in Europe, USA, Canada, Australia, Japan

Cover: Foto ©ninafisch / pixelio.de

More available books at **www.hansebooks.com**

HISTORY, PROPHECY

AND

THE MONUMENTS

HISTORY, PROPHECY

AND

THE MONUMENTS

OR

ISRAEL AND THE NATIONS

BY

JAMES FREDERICK McCURDY, Ph.D., LL.D.

PROFESSOR OF ORIENTAL LANGUAGES IN
UNIVERSITY COLLEGE, TORONTO

VOLUME III

COMPLETING THE WORK

New York
THE MACMILLAN COMPANY
LONDON: MACMILLAN & CO., Ltd.
1906

TO
DAVID BENTON JONES
AND
THOMAS DAVIES JONES
IN REMEMBRANCE OF
PRINCETON, 1872-1876
AND BEYOND

PREFACE TO VOLUME THREE

It is now over four years since the publication of the second instalment of the present work. The completion of my task has been retarded by many interruptions, of which the most serious came from the necessity laid upon me of preparing a somewhat lengthy biography of a deceased friend. Of the scope and subject-matter of this volume little needs to be said. The importance attached to the Hebrew prophecy of the period is justified when one considers how greatly the inner as well as the outer life of Israel was affected by other nations and peoples. Moreover, the essential character of prophecy is still misunderstood by most educated people, and in the popular exposition of the prophets little attention is paid to the permanent and essential elements of their unique discourses. The best way to begin the study of the prophets is to learn how their word and work are interwoven with the life and history of their times. I have also made an attempt to connect the non-prophetic and indirectly prophetic literature of Israel with its historical occasions or antecedents, though in this region of inquiry we tread upon much more uncertain ground.

I have again to express my gratitude for the kindness with which the two earlier volumes have been everywhere received. For several corrections in matters of fact and of opinion I have to thank those eminent specialists who have honoured the work with their notice. Of non-specialist critics a very few have been unfair; and two of these, in spite of the warning of my first preface, have indulged in anonymous scurrility. These, however, were writers for the London *Saturday Review* and the Edinburgh *Scotsman*.

The volume closes with the end of the Babylonian exile, and thus rounds out the period during which the contemporary monuments illustrate the history and prophecy of Israel. This epoch is also a turning-point in the career of the Hebrew people, so that the subsequent times must be treated from a different point of view.

J. FREDERICK McCURDY.

Toronto,
 November 24, 1900.

CONTENTS OF VOL. III

Book IX

HEBREWS AND EGYPTIANS

CHAPTER I

The Kingdom of Judah under Josiah. § 835-841. P. 1-5

§ 835. Special place of Israel in the closing Assyrian period — § 836. Relations with the Eastern powers — § 837. The forward outlook and the part played by Egypt — § 838. Effect of international relations on the inner life of the people — § 839. Political relations of Judah at the accession of Josiah — § 840. Prophetic policy of acquiescence in Assyrian rule — § 841. Religious reform favoured by freedom from Assyrian influence

CHAPTER II

The Great Reformation. § 842-864. P. 6-18

§ 842. The reform of Josiah in spirit and purpose — § 843. Its chief leaders — § 844. Little told us of antecedent movements or of popular feeling — § 845. How the party of reform regained power — § 846. The finding of the "book of direction" — § 847. What this book was, and how it was found — § 848. Its probable history — § 849. The mandate of the book and its effect on Josiah — § 850. A commission of inquiry — § 851. Resort to a prophetess — § 852. A convocation and covenant — § 853. Specific objects of the reform — § 854. Unspiritual worship of Jehovah — § 855. Worship of old Canaanitic deities — § 856. Assyrian (Babylonian) cults — § 857. Immoralities fostered by impure religions — § 858. Popular superstitions; divination supplanted by the word of prophecy — § 859. A reformation of morals involved in that of religion — § 860. Abolition of local shrines, and its motive — § 861. The centralization of worship in Jerusalem — § 862. Transference and transformation of the feasts — § 863. Levitical priests — § 864. Widening out of our inquiry

CHAPTER III

DEUTERONOMY AND HEBREW LITERATURE. § 865–945. P. 19–80

§ 865. Importance of Deuteronomy in the literature of Israel — § 866. Vantage-ground for a survey of earlier literary history — § 867. Salient points of literary progress — § 868. Difficulties of tracing the history of Hebrew literature — § 869. Principles and facts to be kept in view — § 870. Characteristics of Old Testament composition — § 871. Conditions of its rise and growth — § 872. Acquisition by the Hebrews of the art of writing — § 873. Egypt probably not the source of the Phœnician alphabet — § 874. Presumption in favour of Mesopotamia — § 875. Evidence of invention by Aramæans — § 876. Presumption of a Babylonian basis and material — § 877. Whence and when did the Hebrews acquire the art of writing? — § 878. Writing universal among early Semites — § 879. Testimony of Jud. v. — § 880. Israel before Moses partook of the culture of Canaan — § 881. Literary bearings of the question only indirect — § 882. For what purposes writing was employed successively — § 883. Periods of Hebrew literature up to the Exile — § 884. Distinction in modes of origination — § 885. Earliest stories of Genesis — § 886. Distinction of motives in their composition — § 887. How they came to be preserved — § 888. Poetic national memorials easily remembered — § 889. The Song of Lamech — § 890. The Song of Miriam — § 891. The desert journey and the Mosaic legislation — § 892. The Decalogue — § 893. No surviving literature of the desert wanderings — § 894. "Book of the wars of Jehovah" — § 895. Other Pentateuchal poems of later origin — § 896. Fragment of the "Book of Jashar" — § 897. The Song of Deborah — § 898. Lyric tradition maintained : David's lament over Saul and Jonathan — § 899. Collections begun for an interested community — § 900. Effect of national unity — § 901. Influence of professional scribes — § 902. Motives and themes of new compositions — § 903. Origin of literary interest in the fates of individuals — § 904. Solomon's reign more favourable to collection than David's — § 905. The "Blessing of Jacob" — § 906. Compilation of the two oldest poetical books — § 907. The reign of Solomon the end of a period — § 908. Remaining quotations in the earlier literature — § 909. Religious poems ascribed to David — § 910. What sort of "proverbs" are appropriate to Solomon — § 911. Absence of the ethical and spiritual in this early period — § 912. General characteristics of its literature — § 913. Its vital and potential element — § 914. Next period marked by the division of the kingdom — § 915. In how far the Hebrew literature was "national" — § 916. Inference from the general facts — § 917. The heroic narrative of Judges — § 918. Period of "heroic prose" and its conditions — § 919. Narratives of Saul and David — § 920. First "Book of the Covenant" — § 921. Earlier and later sections of the book — § 922. The non-practical portions the later — § 923. Character of the "prophetic histories," J and E — § 924. The scope and purpose of these works — § 925. Summary of the contents of J and J E — § 926. The principal contents of E — § 927. Characteristics of J — § 928. Characteristics of E — § 929. Both J and E composite works — § 930. E composed in northern Israel, probably about 770 B.C. — § 931. J written in the kingdom of Judah — § 932. Possibly near the close of the eighth century B.C. — § 933. The motives of its composition — § 934. The compilers compared with the prophets — § 935. Succeeding literary productions — § 936. Relation of written prophecy to the earlier literature — § 937. Unknown colleagues and helpers of the prophets — § 938. Prophetic writing shows the oratorical style — § 939. The manner of Amos implies earlier prophetic writing — § 940. Occasions and effects of public speaking — § 941. Need of a new and living word during the Assyrian period — § 942. Prophetic literature held the field alone for a whole century — § 943. Progress from the historians, through the earlier prophets, to Deuteronomy — § 944. Decisive practical advance made by the Deuteronomist — § 945. Close organic association of J E and Deuteronomy

CHAPTER IV

RELIGION AND MORALS. § 946-1018. P. 81-125

§ 946. Religion as a main factor in the moral history of Israel — § 947. Estimate of the morality of the individual in earlier times — § 948. Conditions of patriarchal morality — § 949. Classes of moral acts — § 950. How the will of the community determined the moral standard — § 951. Obedience to the claims of the deities — § 952. Reliability of our sources of information — § 953. Deceit in primitive life — § 954. Comparison with other virtues — § 955. The record of patriarchal fraudulency — § 956. Relations of the sexes — § 957. Violations of chastity — § 958. Altruistic virtues — § 959. Generosity and magnanimity — § 960. Joseph's character in connection with his history — § 961. Distinctive traits of the patriarchs — § 962. Moral quality of their adherence to Jehovah — § 963. Heroic and semi-barbarous virtues of the age of the judges — § 964. Treachery and tribalism — § 965. Prevalent unchastity — § 966. Influences for and against the altruistic virtues — § 967. The rise of the kingdom distinguished by patriotism — § 968. Potential value of the central sanctuary — § 969. Personal prowess and self-devotion among the chiefs — § 970. Veracity still unfashionable — § 971. Sexual irregularities — § 972. Generosity varied by cruelty and wrongs — § 973. Explanation of tribal morality — § 974. The need of public teachers supplied by the prophets — § 975. Moral censorship a secondary matter in the ministry of Samuel — § 976. The significance of Samuel in Old Testament morals — § 977. Advance shown in Nathan's rebuke of David — § 978. Prophecy in abeyance under Solomon — § 979. Prophetic encouragement of the revolt of the "Ten Tribes"— § 980. Moral effect of the dread of Jehovah — § 981. The moral crisis under Ahab — § 982. How the royal crime awakened the popular conscience — § 983. Prophetic morality as representing a cause and a party — § 984. Conditions of moral progress — § 985. Advance in the conception of the character of Jehovah — § 986. Intelligent inward rejection of idolatry and its accompaniments — § 987. A new conception of the religious community — § 988. Necessity of a self-sacrificing struggle — § 989. Moral results of national unification — § 990. Industrial and commercial progress — § 991. Effects of the schism between rich and poor — § 992. Concentration of national worship — § 993. A system of moral education — § 994. Moral and spiritual contrasts in the closing days of northern Israel — § 995. The party of Jehovah in Judah ; Isaiah's disciples — § 996. Helpers and comrades of the prophets in the whole course of prophecy — § 997. Periods of moral and religious history from Hezekiah to the death of Josiah — § 998. Germinal ideas and progress in the time of Isaiah and Micah — § 999. First necessary limitation : the localizing of Jehovah's influence and interest — § 1000. Second limitation : corporate or representative character of moral responsibility — § 1001. Third limitation : lack of proportion in estimating moral qualities — § 1002. Significance of the reforming period of Hezekiah — § 1003. The third period, the time of Manasseh, a preparation for the reforming period of Josiah — § 1004. This third period determined the final issues — § 1005. Parallel with earlier seasons of degeneracy — § 1006. Earnestness of the worshippers of Molech — § 1007. Reaction in favour of Jehovah — § 1008. Effect of religious and moral antagonisms on belief and doctrine — § 1009. Nature and consequences of the conception of the holiness of Jehovah — § 1010. Results in the development of moral individuality — § 1011. The ideas of sin and forgiveness — § 1012. Preparation for Deuteronomy and the Reformation — § 1013. Moral influence of the priesthood — § 1014. The priests as securing divine favour for their clients — § 1015. Priests in Israel as intercessors and counsellors — § 1016. Moral helpfulness of the priestly profession — § 1017. Reforming and literary work of the priests — § 1018. Moral and religious influence of men unknown to history

CHAPTER V

THE REFORMATION IN EFFECT. § 1019–1026. P. 126–131

§ 1019. Reforms accomplished during the lifetime of Josiah — § 1020. Obstacles hard to overcome — § 1021. Inherent difficulties — § 1022. The corporate unity of the nation the strength and weakness of the movement — § 1023. The ethical and the ritual element compared — § 1024. Deuteronomy and the truer national life — § 1025. Its preparation for individualism — § 1026. Effect of the prescribed ritual system

CHAPTER VI

THE EGYPTIANS IN PALESTINE. § 1027–1044. P. 132–142

§ 1027. Military strength of Josiah's administration — § 1028. Fateful results of a warlike movement — § 1029. Change in Egyptian policy — § 1030. The new dynasty of Sais — § 1031. Enterprise of Pharaoh Necho — § 1032. Revival of foreign ambitions — § 1033. Prospects of an invasion of Western Asia — § 1034. Josiah and Necho at Megiddo — § 1035. The mourning for Josiah — § 1036. Influence of his oath to Assyria — § 1037. Explanation of his antipathy towards Egypt — § 1038. The Egyptian occupation — § 1039. Accession and captivity of Jehoahaz — § 1040. Eliakim (Jehoiakim) the vassal of Egypt — § 1041. Character of the Egyptian régime — § 1042. The Babylonian Nabopolassar — § 1043. The Egyptians succumb to young Nebuchadrezzar — § 1044. Judah a dependency of Babylon

Book X

HEBREWS AND CHALDÆANS

CHAPTER I

BABYLON AND NEBUCHADREZZAR. § 1045–1064. P. 143–159

§ 1045. Scope and duration of Babylonian influence — § 1046. Interest of the story of the Chaldæans — § 1047. Résumé of their earlier history — § 1048. Their devotion to Babylon — § 1049. They combine Assyrian and Babylonian types of character — § 1050. They made few great changes in the Semitic world — § 1051. Nabopolassar and his plans — § 1052. Character of Nebuchadrezzar — § 1053. His religious spirit — § 1054. Purity of his religious feeling — § 1055. Point of view in our study of Babylon — § 1056. Greatness of the city — § 1057. Description by Berossus — § 1058. Situation and defences of Babylon — § 1059. Streets, bridges, quays, and river traffic — § 1060. The temple of Merodach and its belongings — § 1061. The tower of Babel — § 1062. The new royal palace — § 1063. Borsippa, its temple of Nebo and its tower — § 1064. Life of the people of Babylon

CHAPTER II

SILENCES OF PROPHECY TILL THE CHALDÆAN EPOCH. § 1065–1074. P. 160–166

§ 1065. Prophetic silence during the Deuteronomic period — § 1066. Why the work of the preaching prophets was non-official — § 1067. Jeremiah takes no part in the measures of reform — § 1068. His indifference towards ritual and ceremony — § 1069. He had no official dealings with Josiah — § 1070. The prophets stood in advance of as well as aloof from the king and his officers — § 1071. Symptoms of this radical separation — § 1072. Why prophecy concerned itself with international affairs — § 1073. Were prophets or priests concerned in Josiah's fatal campaign? — § 1074. The Chaldæan era and public prophecy

CHAPTER III

JUDAH'S VASSALAGE TO THE CHALDÆANS. § 1075–1081. P. 167–171.

§ 1075. Process of subjection of Syria and Palestine — § 1076. Attitude of Nebuchadrezzar towards Judah — § 1077. Expected help from Egypt an encouragement to revolt — § 1078. Repression of the rebellion and death of Jehoiakim — § 1079. Young Jehoiachin and his surrender — § 1080. Treatment of the conquered people — § 1081. Fate of the king and the exiles of the first captivity

CHAPTER IV

JEREMIAH AND THE COMING OF THE CHALDÆANS. § 1082–1127
P. 172–209

§ 1082. Jeremiah almost wholly a prophet of the Chaldæan period — § 1083. Date of his first great discourse, 605 B.C. — § 1084. His previous silence and his sudden prominence — § 1085. Political occasions of the opening prophecies — § 1086. Composition and occasion of the first discourse — § 1087. National trouble after the death of Josiah — § 1088. Second condition: conflict at Carchemish — § 1089. The battle-song of Jeremiah — § 1090. His forecast of the Chaldæans — § 1091. Third condition: the expected invasion from the north — § 1092. Dramatic scene at its announcement — § 1093. Jeremiah and his professional rivals — § 1094. Modes of false and true worship — § 1095. Crime and punishment of Tophet — § 1096. Exile and outlawry of souls — § 1097. Falsifying revelation — § 1098. The prophet's mood of grief and vexation — § 1099. The Old Testament Confession — § 1100. Punishment for the broken Covenant — § 1101. Attempt at assassination — § 1102. Lesson from the potter's art — § 1103. Attitude of the priests and prophets — § 1104. Mutual hostility and Jeremiah's maledictions — § 1105. Aggravations of his wrongs — § 1106. His blame for loyalty to Jehovah — § 1107. The problem of his suffering — § 1108. Jeremiah the representative of a class — § 1109. The supreme trial prepares him for conflict — § 1110. The potter's vessel and the valley of Tophet — § 1111. Official punishment of Jeremiah — § 1112. His inward conflict and victory — § 1113. Vindication of his attitude toward the Chaldæans — § 1114. Moral necessity of national chastisement — § 1115. He plainly announces Nebuchadrezzar — § 1116. Jeremiah interdicted; his message committed to writing — § 1117. Literary form of the discourses — § 1118. Time and place of Baruch's public reading — § 1119. Consequences of the lecture — § 1120. Burning of the roll by Jehoiakim — § 1121. Execution of Jeremiah threatened — § 1122. Character and policy of Jehoiakim — § 1123. The attitude of the politicians — § 1124. Interval of political quiescence — § 1125. Jeremiah and his rivals during the great drought — § 1126. The prophet comforted and encouraged — § 1127. Jeremiah's vicarious ministry of suffering

CHAPTER V

HABAKKUK AND THE CHALDÆANS. § 1128–1139. P. 210–219

§ 1128. Characteristics of the book of Habakkuk — § 1129. Parallel with Nahum — § 1130. The Chaldæans as scourges of Israel — § 1131. Why are the Chaldæans not themselves punished? — § 1132. The prophet on his watch-tower — § 1133. His answer of faith triumphant — § 1134. Futility of the Chaldæan régime — § 1135. The moral case against them and their merited doom — § 1136. Meaning of Hab. iii. — § 1137. Date of the prophecy — § 1138. Progress from Zephaniah to Habakkuk — § 1139. Habakkuk and Jeremiah

CHAPTER VI

JEREMIAH AND THE FIRST REBELLION. § 1140–1147. P. 220–226

§ 1140. Prophecies of the first rebellion — § 1141. The Rechabites — § 1142. Lessons for Israel — § 1143. Prophetic laments over Jehoiachin — § 1144. Reminiscence of his fate — § 1145. Harshness of the language explained — § 1146. Misfortune as a measure of sin — § 1147. The actual fate of Jehoiachin

CHAPTER VII

JEREMIAH AND JUDAH'S LAST PROBATION. § 1148–1173. P. 227–244

§ 1148. Zedekiah as a Chaldæan vassal — § 1149. Situation of Jeremiah — § 1150. An epoch in his public and literary career — § 1151. Zedekiah, his ill-fortune and his weaknesses — § 1152. His people after the deportation — § 1153. Effect of the changes of fortune — § 1154. Their troubles as payers of tribute — § 1155. Their religious sentiments — § 1156. Effect upon their political views — § 1157. Movement towards revolt; how met by Jeremiah — § 1158. Encouragement to sedition by the prophet Hananiah — § 1159. Spectacular close of the controversy — § 1160. The fate and case of Hananiah — § 1161. Counsel for Zedekiah — § 1162. Indictment of the rival school of prophets — § 1163. Oracle concerning Edom — § 1164. The prophet's care for the exiles in Babylon — § 1165. Prophetic hopes centred in them — § 1166. Parable of the figs — § 1167. Embassy from Zedekiah to Babylon — § 1168. Jeremiah's letter to the captives — § 1169. His opponents in Babylonia — § 1170. The intrigue of Shemaiah and its failure — § 1171. Zedekiah's journey to Babylon and renewed submission — § 1172. The message of Babylon's final doom — § 1173. End of Jeremiah's rôle as Babylonian prophet

CHAPTER VIII

Ezekiel in Exile and the Home-land. § 1174–1206. P. 245–267

§ 1174. Ezekiel the priest-prophet — § 1175. His style and teaching — § 1176. His interest in the home-land and its people — § 1177. Limitations of his prophecies relating to them — § 1178. Siege of Jerusalem symbolically portrayed — § 1179. Horrors of the siege symbolized — § 1180. Representation of the subsequent fate of the people with bitter denunciations — § 1181. Effect of Ezekiel's visions on the leaders of the people — § 1182. Vision of Jehovah's glory and the contrasted "jealousy-image" — § 1183. Vision of primitive beast-worship — § 1184. The weeping for Tammuz — § 1185. Illustration from Babylonian literature — § 1186. Explanation of the myth — § 1187. Its religious motive — § 1188. An image of a world-wide tragedy — § 1189. Its moral danger — § 1190. Historical illustration of the evil — § 1191. A vision of sun-worship in the temple — § 1192. The saving mark on the forehead — § 1193. Vision of the firing of Jerusalem — § 1194. The doom of the plotters of sedition — § 1195. The restoration and the change of heart — § 1196. The city as forsaken by Jehovah — § 1197. A vision of sudden flight — § 1198. Current fallacies due to false prophecy — § 1199. Evil work of false prophetesses — § 1200. The people themselves ready to be deceived — § 1201. They are not to be saved by the righteousness of others — § 1202. Parables of the character and fate of Israel — § 1203. Ezekiel's preaching intermitted — § 1204. The responsibility of the individual — § 1205. How the exiles reasoned about their fate and its cause — § 1206. Discourse to the deputation of elders

CHAPTER IX

Rebellion, Siege, and Fall of Jerusalem. § 1207–1239. P. 268–295

§ 1207. Change of rulers in Egypt — § 1208. Egypt encourages revolt in Judah — § 1209. Allegory of the two eagles, the cedar, and the vine — § 1210. Nebuchadrezzar consulting the oracles — § 1211. The mode of divination — § 1212. Parable of Judah's relations with foreign peoples — § 1213. Expedition against Palestine — § 1214. Process of the siege of

Jerusalem — § 1215. Zedekiah's appeal to Jeremiah — § 1216. The doom of Zedekiah and its mitigation — § 1217. Treatment of the slaves in Jerusalem — § 1218. Their temporary release and their reënslavement — § 1219. Jeremiah's indictment of the offenders — § 1220. Jeremiah predicts the return of the Chaldæans — § 1221. Arrest and imprisonment of Jeremiah — § 1222. Retreat of the Egyptians and resumption of the siege — § 1223. Mistaken heroism of the defenders — § 1224. Interview with Zedekiah; Jeremiah in the royal courtyard — § 1225. Property in Anathoth transferred to Jeremiah — § 1226. The prophet's hope of future restoration — § 1227. He is thrust into an empty cistern — § 1228. The king persuaded to rescue him — § 1229. Last interview between Zedekiah and Jeremiah — § 1230. End of the siege: the breach in the wall — § 1231. Flight and capture of the royal party — § 1232. Treatment of the conquered city — § 1233. Methods of devastation — § 1234. Deportation of citizens — § 1235. Fate of the king and the leaders of the revolt — § 1236. The siege of Jerusalem in Hebrew literature — § 1237. Authorship of the Lamentations — § 1238. The poems set forth historical situations; do not relate the facts of history — § 1239. Kindred literature probably of a later time

CHAPTER X

The Remnant in Palestine and Egypt. § 1240–1262. P. 296–312

§ 1240. Condition of the remnant of Judah in Palestine — § 1241. The Babylonian policy towards them — § 1242. Gedaliah, Jeremiah, and the captain of the guard — § 1243. Formation of the new settlement — § 1244. Jeremiah and the services of religion — § 1245. Ishmael the traitor — § 1246. His murder of Gedaliah — § 1247. His other atrocities — § 1248. Surprise and escape of Ishmael — § 1249. Panic and southward flight of the Judaite chiefs — § 1250. Deportation of the remainder — § 1251. The desolation of Judah — § 1252. Jeremiah resorted to as counsellor — § 1253. He gives an oracle dissuading from flight to Egypt — § 1254. His counsel disregarded: the march to Egypt — § 1255. Symbolical action of the overthrow of Pharaoh Hophra — § 1256. Worship of the "Queen of Heaven" — § 1257. Jeremiah's last denunciation and his martyrdom — § 1258. His prophetic genius and its decisive test — § 1259. Illustration from modern conditions — § 1260. The prophet's vision and the national fiction — § 1261. Our modern prophets and our national fiction — § 1262. Meaning of Jeremiah's life for humanity

CHAPTER XI

The Exile as an Epoch. § 1263–1267. P. 313–317

§ 1263. Paradox of the results of the exile and its antecedents — § 1264. Problem of causes and effects — § 1265. Questions suggested by the Babylonian residence — § 1266. Need of a particular inquiry — § 1267. Historical clearness promoted by the exile

CHAPTER XII

The Deportations. § 1268-1271. P. 318-320

§ 1268. Preponderance of the deportation of 597 B.C. — § 1269. Inferences — § 1270. Various classes of the deported people — § 1271. Condition of the exiles on the journey

CHAPTER XIII

The Hebrew Settlement in Babylonia. § 1272-1289. P. 321-334

§ 1272. Region of the principal settlement — § 1273. Local distribution of the exiles — § 1274. How their employments were determined — § 1275. Their antecedent occupations in Palestine — § 1276. Agriculture, trade, industrial and other arts in Babylonia — § 1277. A time of opportunity for settlers — § 1278. Social and business conditions; status and treatment of slaves — § 1279. Classification of Babylonian slaves — § 1280. Distinctive advantages afforded by the Babylonian system — § 1281. Freedom of movement possible to the higher order of slaves — § 1282. The conditions summed up — § 1283. Importance of agriculture in Babylonian life — § 1284. The country round about Nippur — § 1285. Effect of the rise of Babylon and of the Kasshite dynasty — § 1286. Later vicissitudes; disfavour of Nebuchadrezzar — § 1287. The business functions of the temple and the priests — § 1288. Source of their influence upon the progress of the country — § 1289. Nebuchadrezzar's displeasure towards them connected with the settlement of the Hebrews

CHAPTER XIV

Employments of the Exiles in Babylonia. § 1290-1306 P. 335-349

§ 1290. What water was to Babylonia — § 1291. System of canalization east of the Euphrates — § 1292. Condition of the region enjoying the water supply — § 1293. How the Euphrates itself was affected with its affluents; modern illustration — § 1294. Recent illustration east of the Euphrates — § 1295. The general condition of the country characterized — § 1296. The exiles to be restorers and repairers of wastes and ruins — § 1297. Agreement with the policy of Nebuchadrezzar — § 1298. Summary of the situation — § 1299. The canals that gave the water supply — § 1300. Modern canals of this region — § 1301. Occupations of the colonists after the settlement — § 1302. Extension of their avocations — § 1303. Improvement of the land: its productions — § 1304. Need of vigilance against constant dangers — § 1305. Uses of the Kebar for navigation — § 1306. What became of the Hebrew artisans?

CHAPTER XV

THE EXILES AS A COMMUNITY. § 1307–1312. P. 350–353

§ 1307. Relations with the central government — § 1308. The king's interest in the principal colony — § 1309. Solidarity of the exiles — § 1310. Simple organization of the colonies — § 1311. Administration of family heads and elders — § 1312. Leadership and general oversight

---

BOOK XI

HEBREWS, CHALDÆANS, AND PERSIANS

CHAPTER I

MORALS AND RELIGION OF ISRAEL IN EXILE. § 1313–1349. P. 354–379

§ 1313. The true Israel revealed and on trial in captivity — § 1314. The physical environment as affecting mind and temperament — § 1315. New conceptions of life and history awakened — § 1316. A change of political ideals fostered — § 1317. General conditions of social progress — § 1318. Great determining moral factors — § 1319. Importance of business relations — § 1320. Effect of business on character — § 1321. Careful protection of business interests in Babylonia — § 1322. Hebrew business antecedents and principles — § 1323. Babylonian rules and procedure — § 1324. Dealings in agricultural business — § 1325. The moral discipline for Israel — § 1326. How slaves and servants could better their condition — § 1327. Qualifying observations — § 1328. Limitations of the moral influence — § 1329. Paramount importance of religious and moral issues — § 1330. Danger and evil of unchastity — § 1331. A one-sided restriction — § 1332. Encouragement of sacred prostitution — § 1333. How the Hebrews regarded it — § 1334. Their repugnance to idolatry in an alien land — § 1335. Better opportunities for the prophetic teaching — § 1336. Religious dilemma: question as to the power of Jehovah — § 1337. Could Jehovah actually be and have control in Babylonia? — § 1338. Effect on prevailing conceptions of God — § 1339. Earlier progress in religious individualism — § 1340. Effect of the scattering of the nation — § 1341. Jeremiah's conception of the new Covenant — § 1342. Ezekiel's denial of imputed guilt — § 1343. Ezekiel as continuing the spirit of Deuteronomy — § 1344. Summary of Ezekiel's later teaching — § 1345. The permanent elements of the religion of the exiles — § 1346. The Sabbath as a Babylonian institution — § 1347. Advantage of a stated day of rest — § 1348. Mourning and self-abasement of the religious meetings — § 1349. Effect of the sifting and purifying process

CHAPTER II

HEBREW LITERATURE OF THE EXILE. § 1350–1363. P. 380–388

§ 1350. Internal causes of the literary activity of the Exile — § 1351. Outward conditions, especially Babylonian influences — § 1352. Effect upon form and style — § 1353. Examples in post-exilic writers — § 1354. Increased employment of symbol and allegory — § 1355. Increase of historical interest — § 1356. Effect of Deuteronomy in a one-sided view of historic principles — § 1357. The books of Kings and the national cultus — § 1358. References made to earlier sources — § 1359. Narrative additions to the annals of the kings — § 1360. The probability of two revisions — § 1361. Revision and reshaping of Deuteronomy, Judges, and Samuel — § 1362. Ritualistic work; the Law of Holiness — § 1363. Psalm composition

CHAPTER III

THE CHALDÆAN DOMINION. § 1365–1372. P. 389–394

§ 1364. General policy of Nebuchadrezzar — § 1365. Siege of Tyre and campaigns in Egypt — § 1366. Prophecies of Jeremiah and Ezekiel concerning Egypt — § 1367. Ezekiel's discourses on Tyre and Sidon — § 1368. The closing stage of the Chaldæan empire — § 1369. Evil-Merodach — § 1370. Neriglissar and his short-lived son — § 1371. Accession and character of Nabonidus — § 1372. His policy toward the provincial cities

CHAPTER IV

CYRUS AND THE PERSIANS. § 1373–1389. P. 395–407

§ 1373. The Iranians — § 1374. Iran and the westward migrations of Medes and Persians — § 1375. The Iranian communities — § 1376. Their religion — § 1377. Its contrast with Semitism — § 1378. Early history of the Persian branch — § 1379. Conflict and compromise of the Medes and Lydians — § 1380. Forecast of consequences — § 1381. Cyrus in myth and legend — § 1382. Cyrus as conqueror of the Medes — § 1383. He thus rids Mesopotamia of the Scythians — § 1384. Were the Scythians then in control of Media? — § 1385. Explanation of the submission of the Medes to Cyrus — § 1386. Rapid organization of a Medo-Persian empire — § 1387. Invasion of Median territory by Crœsus of Lydia — § 1388. Conquest of his kingdom by Cyrus — § 1389. Annexation of the Greek colonies and of eastern Iran

CHAPTER V

CYRUS KING OF BABYLON. § 1390-1399. P. 408-414

§ 1390. Happy fortune of Cyrus — § 1391. His delay in marching upon Babylon — § 1392. Misgovernment and folly of Nabonidus — § 1393. A divine commission to right the wrongs of the Babylonians — § 1394. Change in the policy of Nabonidus — § 1395. The campaign against Babylon in the Inscriptions — § 1396. The connected story — § 1397. Babylonia made a Persian kingdom — § 1398. The native religion retained and patronized by Cyrus — § 1399. Liberation of foreign slaves and exiles

CHAPTER VI

PROPHETIC IDEALS. § 1400-1420. P. 415-431

§ 1400. Occasions of a new literary epoch — § 1401. The Medes and the doom of Babylon — § 1402. Picture of the fallen oppressor — § 1403. The Medes in Jer. l., li. — § 1404. Persia and Media in Isa. xxi. 1-10 — § 1405. Isaiah II: his training and outlook — § 1406. His genius for expression: parallel with Vergil — § 1407. The prophet, his pupils and coworkers — § 1408. How deliverance should be effected — § 1409. The vision of Cyrus and his unknown Leader — § 1410. The prophet sees results in conditions — § 1411. The prophetic view of Cyrus, and its implications — § 1412. The reputation of Cyrus — § 1413. His moral statesmanship — § 1414. His treatment of subject states — § 1415. The restoration of captives — § 1416. The religion of Cyrus — § 1417. The unfulfilled ideal of his deeds and character — § 1418. The unfulfilled vision of prophecy — § 1419. Its larger realization — § 1420. Regenerative ideas of prophecy

ADDITIONAL ABBREVIATIONS

ATR. = R. Smend, *Lehrbuch der alttestamentlichen Religionsgeschichte*, 1893.

BA. = *Beiträge zur Assyriologie*, edited by Delitzsch and Haupt.

CIS. = *Corpus inscriptionum Semiticarum*.

DB. = *Dictionary of the Bible*, edited by James Hastings.

EB. = *Encyclopædia Biblica*, edited by T. K. Cheyne and J. S. Black.

Einl. = C. H. Cornill, *Einleitung in das Alte Testament*, 4th ed., 1896.

HA. = J. Benzinger, *Hebräische Archäologie*, 1894.

Her. = Herodotus.

Kosmologie = P. Jensen, *Kosmologie der Babylonier*, 1890.

MVG. = *Mittheilungen der vorderasiatischen Gesellschaft*.

Nab. *annals* = Annals of Nabonidus, § 1382.

Neb. = Inscription of Nebuchadrezzar II. in IR, 53–58.

Nippur = J. P. Peters, *Nippur, or Adventures and Explorations on the Euphrates*, 2 vols., 1897.

PCT. = *Babylonian Expedition of the University of Pennsylvania; Cuneiform Texts*, vol. IX, 1898.

RBA. = M. Jastrow, Jr., *The Religion of Babylonia and Assyria*, 1898.

SBOT. = *Sacred Books of the Old Testament*, edited by Paul Haupt.

Book IX

HEBREWS AND EGYPTIANS

CHAPTER I

THE KINGDOM OF JUDAH UNDER JOSIAH

§ 835. The fortunes of Assyria as the controlling power of the Semitic world have been followed until the empire and its capital ceased to exist. We have also traced the slow but steady revival of Babylonia under Chaldæan leadership and in a general way described the condition of the wide region once subject to the rule of Nineveh (§ 821). The survey of our field was, however, not quite complete; a special place is demanded for the people of Israel during the closing years of the Assyrian régime. To help to an understanding of the affairs of the kingdom of Judah during this and the following period up to the Exile, we may again refer to the normal political relations between Palestine and the dominant powers of Western Asia.

§ 836. From the beginning of recorded history until Alexander the Great brought the forces of Europe into play, the fate of Palestine and Syria was controlled from the banks of the Tigris or of the Euphrates. If at any time a change took place in the general situation, it was brought about by the restless endeavours of Egypt to gain a footing in Asia, whenever the dominant Asiatic power was crippled for a time or was slowly making way for its successor. We may recall the era of the domination of the separate states in old Babylonia, as the now long-forgotten cities of the lower Euphrates valley came each in turn to exclusive power. We next bring to mind the political and intellectual supremacy of Babylon itself in Syria and Palestine, followed by the precarious Egyptian occupation, after Assyria and Babylonia had begun their long contention. Then comes before us the epoch of Israel in Palestine, with the episodes of the border wars and the rise of Damascus, all made possible by the inaction of the eastern powers whose strength was being wasted upon one another. We next pass in review the era of Assyrian aggression, its slow but certain acquisition of the Syrian and Palestinian states, the subversion of Damascus, the conquest and captivity of northern Israel, the vassalage, the rebellion, and the chastisement of Judah.

§ 837. If from the same historical standpoint we now look forward instead of backward, we shall see the same parts still being played by the leading actors in the drama. The decline of Nineveh and the withdrawal of its garrisons afford Egypt the opportunity of grasping again at Asiatic dominion, and even of masquerading awhile as the heaven-sent ruler of Palestine (2 K. xxiii. 34), and once more her fond illusion of an Asiatic empire is dispelled by an older and stronger claimant from beyond the River. Nineveh is gone, but Babylon remains and revives. The Chaldæans succeed to the empire and the traditions of Assyria. Egypt is extruded from her brief occupancy of Palestine, and the old problem of Hebrew independence or subjection is worked out as before, only now Nebuchadrezzar is the controlling factor instead of Tiglathpileser or Sargon. Such are the main outward conditions of the kingdom of Judah in the days of King Josiah and his ill-fated house.

§ 838. My readers do not need to be reminded that the domination of Assyria and Babylonia in Palestine involved much more than mere political results. But its religious and moral consequences have not as yet been so obvious, because they are not immediately suggested by the outward events that more obviously mark the progress of history. Yet it is in the movements of the inner life of a people that we can best find out the sources and the process of its development, as the qualities of a soil are tested by the upturnings of the plough. The whole period in the history of Judah from Josiah to the Exile is one of those seasons of startling self-revelation which come to nations no less than to individuals, and in studying it we must not lose sight of this secondary aspect of international relations. For the time of Josiah itself, which now more immediately concerns us, we have ample evidence, often indirect but none the less clear and strong, as to the internal condition of the kingdom, most of it drawn from the literature of the most instructive religious movement of pre-christian antiquity.

§ 839. The reign of Josiah was indeed almost wholly occupied with domestic concerns. When he came to the throne (639 B.C.) at the age of eight years, peace prevailed, as far as we know, throughout the dominion of Assyria. Egypt had been lost to the empire about six years previously (§ 768). But the Scythians had not yet begun their ravages (§ 811), and the empire was otherwise intact. The great insurrection had been quelled, and no spirit was left in the subject states for further revolt. And when the collapse of the empire had begun, and that process of degeneration was going on which preceded dissolution (§ 820 ff.), Josiah, the young monarch now come to his majority, had little inducement to strike for independence. All the freer was he, therefore, to engage in that moral and religious work which has given him a unique distinction among the kings of the earth.

§ 840. The reforming party in the state, under whose fostering care the young king spent the years of his minority, had learned well the principles of the foreign policy maintained by the prophetic teaching throughout its history — to respect the oath of allegiance to the suzerain, to engage in no international intrigues, and to rest quietly and confidently in the protection of Jehovah. Only thus, they rightly insisted, was it possible to secure the peace and tranquillity necessary for the worship and the practice of religion. There was thus no inclination to revolt, even when the chances of success were better than ever before. Nor was there temptation to unite with any of the feeble surviving communities of Palestine so as to form a strong independent power. Thus the party of reform did not fear any interruption in their task from partisans of disorder and sedition. It is significant, however, of the freedom of action which Judah claimed for itself that the district of Bethel, which was a part of the Northern Kingdom, was now claimed by the king at Jerusalem and made the object of his reforming zeal, along with the cities of Judah proper (2 K. xxiii. 15 ff.).

§ 841. While Josiah did not formally renounce his allegiance to the moribund kingdom of Assyria, there were unmistakable evidences that the bond was morally dissolved. It is in this very sphere of religious reform, which is the distinction of Josiah and his epoch, that the virtual independence of the nation is most plainly marked. It is one of our cardinal principles (§ 299) that among the ancient nations of the East political subjection was, by moral necessity, followed by religious dependence. The attentive observer will find this nowhere more clearly exemplified than in the history of Israel in its vassalage to Assyria. As in the days of Ahaz (§ 640), so in the times of Manasseh, during most of whose reign all opposition to the Assyrian domination had ceased, the worship of Israel bore in its most conspicuous features the stamp of Babylonian or Assyrian influence. The situation gives a valuable suggestion as to the external conditions under which religious and moral progress was possible in the kingdom of Judah. It was impossible, as we have just seen, while foreign influence was irresistibly strong. It was equally impossible during the political confusion attending the intrigues and revolts that marked the reigns of the latest kings. The most favourable occasions were offered when the pressure of the suzerain state was withdrawn. Such was the case in the later times of Hezekiah (§ 796) and such also in these days of Josiah.

CHAPTER II

THE GREAT REFORMATION

§ 842. Since no important movement religious or political could be undertaken without the formal sanction and direction of the king, the reform which goes under the name of Josiah, though long prepared for, could not be put in operation until he assumed the direct control of the government. This reform aimed to be radical and complete. It was, moreover, no mere fierce intolerant iconoclasm. It was essentially a positive propaganda resting on profound and well-considered views as to the right object and mode of worship, and — what was most significant of all — as to the necessary association of religion and morals.

§ 843. It was a noble band of devoted servants of Jehovah who, after being silenced by Manasseh and Amon, reappeared to oppose the whelming tide of idolatry and corruption in Jehovah's land. We know the names of a few; but they were necessarily the representatives of a like-minded community. Of these the king's chief counsellor was Shaphan, the state secretary or chancellor, the founder of a worthy line of patriots (see 2 K. xxv. 22; Jer. xxvi. 24; xxix. 3; xxxvi. 10 ff.; xxxix. 14; xl. 5, 9, 11; xli. 2). He had perhaps been the guardian of the king's tender youth, and was at any rate retained in the highest place in the government on account of his years and fidelity. Already his son Ahikam was bearing part of his burdens (2 K. xxii. 12). Next to him was Hilkiah the priest, also well advanced in life.

§ 844. Such were the men whom we find to have been Josiah's trusted counsellors when his public career began.

As in the other reigns described in the books of Kings, there was here a large background of action and movement which does not appear in the word-pictures that serve for historical records. The change in dominant opinion that marks the transition from Amon to Josiah is as significant as it is obscure. Religious sentiment especially was hard to move, and we must beware at the outset of assuming that among the people at large it was greatly moved. In the very nature of the case only moral causes working through social conditions were sufficient to bring about such a change,[1] and these are always difficult to ascertain and to trace. The attitude of the leading men is more clearly revealed, and in the present instance it is quite fully described.

§ 845. Under what influences did the chief men of Josiah's time become so imbued with the theocratic spirit? In the time of Hezekiah, Israel's vantage-ground was hardly and slowly won. It was more than lost in the days of Manasseh. How was it recovered? Negatively, by the absence of noxious foreign influence (§ 840 f.). From the positive and more important side a complete answer is probably beyond reach. Some help may be gained by following up the course of the literary and moral development of Israel; and this we shall attempt later (§ 865 ff.). Meanwhile we can do little more than remind the reader that the events recorded must have had an adequate cause. And we must also repeat the reminder that Hebrew narrative is extreme and one-sided from the modern occidental point of view. Under Manasseh not merely a few devotees but a substantial party of Jehovah must have kept their ranks unbroken, so that when the favourable time arrived decisive action could be taken. The circumstances attending the violent death of Amon

---

[1] It is scarcely necessary to remind the reader that a "good" reign was much more of a phenomenon in Israel than was an evil reign. The king was ultimately the product of the people, and the popular religion was mixed with heathenism during the whole duration of the kingdom.

and the succession of his infant son are unknown; but we may take for granted that the theocratic party availed themselves of the occasion to secure control of young Josiah. It was the Jerusalem priests alone who had the opportunity, through organization and official prestige, to gain such an advantage. And since, as we have just seen, a sort of priestly aristocracy was in control at the time of the reformation, we may conclude that this powerful body had been brought into line with a movement which, though rudely checked, was neither dead nor sleeping during the oppression of half a century.

§ 846. The story of this movement as brought into effect may be written somewhat as follows, on the basis of 2 K. xxii., xxiii. (cf. 2 Chr. xxxiv., xxxv.). In the eighteenth year of Josiah, when, as we may assume, the serious work of his reign had been long begun, the business of repairing the temple was being undertaken after the old-fashioned method of first securing by free-will offerings the money wherewith to do it[1] (cf. 2 K. xii. 4 ff.). When a considerable contribution had been made, Josiah sent his secretary, Shaphan, to Hilkiah to notify him that he might now count and disburse the money. In the course of the interview Hilkiah informed his visitor that he "had found the book of direction in the house of Jehovah." The book was handed to the secretary, who, having read it, returned to the king, gave an account of his errand, and having produced the book read it aloud to him.

§ 847. Here an explanation is needed. What was the book of direction? and how did it come to be found in

---

[1] The fact that Josiah repaired the defects in the temple is of itself no proof that it had been neglected in the preceding reigns. As in Assyria and Babylonia, where every king made it his boast in his memoirs that he repaired the temple of his favourite god, it was doubtless a matter of principle with the kings of Judah to keep the sacred places in order. Yet so much had been added for the purposes of heathenish worship that it is perhaps fair to assume that during the long reign of Manasseh less attention had been paid to the temple proper than to certain chambers and annexes (2 K. xxiii. 4, 7, 11 f.), where, as in the next generation (§ 1183 ff.), some of the idolatrous rites were observed.

the temple? The former question is easily answered. The book was a new and enlarged edition of the "Book of the Covenant" (§ 920, 943 f.) prepared for the need of the times. It comprises substantially the legal portion of Deuteronomy (chs. xii.-xxvi.), to which the hortatory preface (chs. v.-xi.) was probably added somewhat later. This legislative code is thoroughly interspersed with arguments and appeals for a purer faith, a stricter ritual, and a more spiritual habit of life.[1] The second question has perhaps created more serious difficulty of another kind, the ground of which is that the book, being almost or quite a contemporary production, could scarcely have been lost in the temple. The difficulty is in part removed when we observe that the narrative says nothing of the book having been lost. All that is necessarily implied (xxii. 8, 13) is that Hilkiah lighted in some way upon the book.[2] What is harder to explain is the definite phrase "the book of direction," which points to some book known as at one time existing, and from which, since Josiah was apparently unaware of its contents, it may be inferred that the book had not been in circulation among his contemporaries.

§ 848. The probable explanation is that the former "law-book," which we now know as the first "Book of the Covenant," and whose existence was a matter of notoriety in Israel, had never been in force as a statute-book,

---

[1] Perhaps the whole of chs. i.-xi. was added by the same hand, i.-iv. 40 being a review of the history of Israel from the Exodus to the settlement east of the Jordan, placed in the mouth of Moses just before his death, followed by a solemn appeal to serve and obey Jehovah. Ch. xxviii. was probably the original conclusion of xii.-xxvi., ch. xxvii. having been interpolated to connect its subject (the curses and blessings on Ebal and Gerizim) with the similar ideas of ch. xxviii. Chs. xxix. and xxx. are apparently a hortatory continuation of xii.-xxvi; xxviii. by the same hand as i.-xi. Chs. xxxi.-xxxiv. are from several sources, and did not belong to the older Deuteronomy.

[2] The word (אצמ) in all the Semitic languages has the same meaning of attaining or acquiring. For the Hebrew cf. Gen. xxvi. 12; 2 Sam. xx. 6. Our English *find* is identical with Latin *peto*. The meaning of *invenire* is similarly developed.

and had been almost forgotten, kept as it was during the unsympathetic régime of Manasseh in the hands of a small theocratic circle; and that it was now reproduced in an expanded form, with the hortatory and minatory additions which greatly impressed King Josiah. The work of preparing the book having been done under priestly auspices and perhaps within the precincts of the temple itself, the volume might very well have been "found where it was not lost." That there was a certain amount of conscientious finesse in the business is, however, quite apparent, though in this quality it has been outclassed by many of the ecclesiastical intrigues of our better Christian times.

§ 849. To realize the effect of the reading of the book upon the susceptible soul of Josiah we must read it ourselves, that is, read over Deut. xii.–xxvi., and imagine what a pious king in old Jerusalem must have felt in hearing for the first time a divine revelation of such tremendous import. The book contained explicit directions as to worship and conduct, and as the penalty for national disobedience decreed the loss of home and country, the sentence of the offenders was cumulative. For many generations warnings and precepts had been alike neglected, and when the day of doom should come, the sins of the fathers also would be visited upon the children. Could the doom be averted by speedy and complete obedience and penitence?

§ 850. Hilkiah himself was summoned and appealed to. He was unable or unwilling to answer. A commission of inquiry was then appointed by the king, of which Hilkiah was the head, and which besides included the state secretary Shaphan and his son Ahikam, Achbor, one of the royal council, and Asaiah, "the king's servant."[1] To them the charge was given: "Go and inquire of Jehovah on my behalf and on behalf of the people and on

---

[1] For this peculiar title see Stade, GVI. I, 650, and the illustration inscribed there and in Benzinger, IIA. p. 258 (cf. p. 310). Stade's conjecture that the chief of the eunuchs is meant is unnecessary. The officer had apparently to attend to the special personal business of the king, while the other officials were servants of the state.

behalf of all Judah, concerning the words of this book that has been found; for great is the wrath of Jehovah that has been kindled against us, because our fathers have not obeyed the words of this book, to do what has been enjoined upon us" (xxii. 13).

§ 851. The deputation, under the lead of Hilkiah, sought a prophetic not a priestly oracle (xxii. 14). This was the fitting course in every way, particularly in an emergency, and when the interests of the community were at stake (cf. § 589 and note). Resort was had, however, not to a prophet, but to a prophetess named Huldah, wife of the keeper of the wardrobe. She is the only prophetess of the Old Testament belonging to the higher prophetic era,[1] when "direction" implied a differentiation of the spiritual from the civil or judicial function.[2] The action was strictly regular. It has been asked why some outstanding prophet like Jeremiah was not appealed to. But the question implies a misconception of the function of the great prophets of the Old Testament. They did not belong to the prophetic guilds, nor had they anything to do with the "directing" or with the official oracles, while Huldah was a member of an inner circle of professionals (§ 1066). Her answer as far as it is reported was wholly in accord with the movement for reform. It was to the

---

[1] Of Noadiah (Neh. vi. 14) we know only the name. The context would suggest that she was a degenerate.

[2] A development from the lower rudimentary function of Miriam and Deborah. Comp. Professor I. J. Peritz, "Woman in the ancient Hebrew cult," in *Journal of Biblical Literature*, 1898, p. 142 ff. The subject is still somewhat obscure, but there seems to be no reason why we should make the prophetess a development independent of the prophet. Both really belonged to one system, but the prophetess was a rarer functionary and therefore all the more suited for appeal in a critical time, as carrying exceptional inspiration. Moreover, we can hardly exclude the idea that, as in the case of the Pythia, the Sibyl, the Witch of Endor, and others, the power of divination was ascribed to woman when she assumed the prophetic rôle, cf. Ez. xiii. 17 ff. (§ 1199). That Huldah was a member of the professional circle is made still more clear by the fact that her place of residence is specially mentioned, since the professions occupied severally streets or quarters of the city by themselves (cf. Jer. xxxvii. 21).

effect that the penalty annexed to disobedience would certainly be inflicted, but not in Josiah's day, since he had humbled himself before Jehovah (xxii. 14–20).[1]

§ 852. Josiah immediately called a general assembly of the people at Jerusalem, their elders and the orders of priests and prophets taking the responsible places as representatives. To them he read the book, and bound himself and them by a solemn oath and covenant to obey its precepts and carry out its requirements (2 K. xxiii. 1–3). The fulfilment of this engagement was the great work of reform.

§ 853. Since our present concern is with the reform as it affected the policy of the kingdom and the condition of the people as a whole, it will suffice to point out in a general way its purpose as bearing (1) upon the mode and form, (2) upon the place, of worship. As to the first object, the reformers were to extirpate the foreign non-Israelitish rites and observances, and to rid the worship of Jehovah of everything sensuous and material. As to the second, no place of worship was to be tolerated except the temple at Jerusalem. That this work was associated with an ancient "law-book," revised, enlarged, and adapted to present occasions, grew out of the fact that it was intended to vindicate, reëstablish, and develop whatever in belief and practice was rooted in the truest faith and teaching of Israel's past history.

§ 854. The religious abuses to be rooted out may be grouped as follows: (1) The unspiritual worship of Jehovah. The adoration of Jehovah in a symbolic material form was never so great a danger in Judah as in

---

[1] Huldah concluded by saying (v. 20) that Josiah should be gathered to his tombs (*i.e.* added to those already in the family tombs, cf. Job xvii. 1) in peace. On this point her oracular inspiration failed. Stade (GVI. I, 652) thinks that the oracle, as we have it, is a substitute for the original, which must have been a command to go on with the practical fulfilment of the injunctions of the book. The whole of the answer may not be given in the text, though what is given has the air of being expanded and elaborated.

Israel. Idolatrous worship of Jehovah in the strict sense perhaps never existed in Jerusalem. Indeed, the only public authorized image appears to have been the brazen serpent destroyed by Hezekiah (2 K. xviii. 4). But it was inevitable that the rites of Jehovah in an unspiritual age should degenerate by association with any one of the various popular idolatrous symbols, from the comparatively innocent stone-pillars, with their traditional suggestion of the presence of the deity, and the *asheras* or conventionalized sacred trees beside the altar of Jehovah, to the grosser symbols of imported foreign cults. The radical remedy was the obliteration of all outward symbols or accompaniments of worship according to the direction of Deuteronomy (xii. 3; xvi. 21 f.); and such was the work of the reformation (2 K. xxiii. 14 f.).

§ 855. (2) There was the worship of old Canaanitic deities. This was one of the most noxious and persistent of unlawful cults. Not that any distinct personal Baal was adored in Judah after the downfall of Athaliah and her Phœnician ritual (2 K. xi.). It was rather the intrusive revival in times of laxness and infidelity of the cults of the local deities, the "baals" of the several cities or sacred places of ancient Canaan. The syncretism of Jehovah and Baal worship was aggravated by the fact that Jehovah was naturally and innocently called the "Baal" or "Lord" of his people. Yet it seems open to question whether there was not at least in Jerusalem a generalizing of the old local Baal worship in one collective image which was abolished in this reform by Josiah (2 K. xxiii. 4). There had been also the cult of the Phœnician Ashtoreth (Astarte) introduced by Solomon, the last trace of which was now effaced by Josiah along with the former shrines of Chemosh of Moab and Milcom of Ammon[1] (xxiii. 13). It was the "high places" that

---

[1] A pantheon was the natural accompaniment of the little world-monarchy of poor Solomon. That it was revived under Manasseh indicates the inveterate inclination of old Israel to diverse worship (see Deut. xiii.).

particularly promoted all such degradation of the service of Jehovah. To the category of Canaanitic deities must be assigned the Molech (or more properly *Melech*) to whom children were offered by fire in the time of Manasseh (2 K. xxi. 6; cf. Mic. vi. 7). The mound of Tophet in the valley of Hinnom where this most horrible of rites was practised was destroyed by Josiah (2 K. xxiii. 10). For prohibitions in the "law-book" see Deut. xii. 29–31; xviii. 10.

§ 856. (3) More imposing and more influential among the ruling classes were the special modes of worship borrowed from Assyria and Babylonia (§ 841). What had been introduced by Ahaz in consequence of his subjection to his Assyrian patron (§ 640) was now supplemented by a complete priestly service. There were utensils for sacrifice to the host of heaven in the temple itself, which were burned by Josiah along with other idolatrous appliances on the bottom flats of the Kidron valley (2 K. xxiii. 4). There were priests who burned incense to the sun and the moon, and the signs of the Zodiac, and all the host of heaven (Deut. xvii. 2–7), who were got rid of by Josiah (xxiii. 5; cf. xxi. 3; Jer. viii. 2). There were the horses which the kings of Judah had dedicated to the "Sun," and to which a place had been assigned on the west side of the temple (cf. 1 Chr. xxvi. 18), and which were now removed by Josiah, who at the same time burned the chariots of the sun with fire (xxiii. 11). There was on the roof of the cupola of Ahaz an astrological observatory which Josiah broke to pieces (xxiii. 12). Add to these the adoration of the "Queen of Heaven," who was made the consort of Jehovah[1] (see Jer. vii. 18),

---

[1] In the same way as the Babylonian *Anu*, the highest heaven-god, was provided with a consort *Anat* (Jastrow, RBA. p. 153); compare *Bêl* and *Bêlit* ("Beltis"). The impersonal, indefinite character of the western or Canaanitic Baal is illustrated by the fact that there was no corresponding feminine deity, Ashtoreth (Babyl. Ishtar) being a mere female analogue and not a companion or mate.

a cult which persisted even to the time of the Captivity (Jer. xliv. 17 ff.).

§ 857. (4) The most virulent of the evil practices of the time, in large measure promoted by a perverted religious feeling and even made a religious institution, was sexual indulgence, the universal attendant upon nature worship in the ancient East (§ 1188 f., 1330 ff.). The ministers of these obscene rites within the very precincts of the temple were expelled by Josiah, and their apartments were razed to the ground (2 K. xxiii. 7 ; cf. Deut. xxiii. 17 f.).

§ 858. (5) Finally there were superstitious beliefs and customs, partly native to the soil, partly inherited from the old nomadic life of Israel, and partly imported from abroad — above all from Babylonia, where sorcery and magic had long been a science and an art (cf. Isa. xlvii. ; § 1329). All such usages and their professors Josiah put away, "that he might make good the words of direction which were written in the book that Hilkiah the priest found in the house of Jehovah" (2 K. xxiii. 24; cf. Deut. xviii. 10–14). The object of divination and necromancy was to ascertain the will of the higher powers. Instead of this the will of Jehovah was to be followed and might be ascertained. For this end was issued the great proclamation of the prophetic word, of its authenticity and its sufficiency (Deut. xviii. 15 ff.).

§ 859. The foregoing may suffice as a representation of the religious evils and abuses which abounded in the early days of Josiah and in those of his predecessors. It was characteristic of this great movement that it was the first attempt on a large scale to remove not only religious but moral evils, and that on the ground that the one class was necessarily involved or rather included in the other. In the account of the reform in Kings (cf. 2 Chr. xxxiv. f.) no mention is made of the purification of justice and of the redress of social wrongs. For this we must turn to the "book of direction," which was incidentally and yet virtually a hand-book of ethics for the people of Jehovah. Besides inculcating justice in all the walks of life, it breathes a lofty spirit of humanity and of regard for the needy, the suffering, and the oppressed. Save on the one point of intolerance toward the enemies of Jehovah, it stands in these aspects almost upon a New Testament level. The central and controlling idea in the book is, however, that which was asserted in the reforms of Josiah, the doing away with all modes of false worship, and the exclusive establishment of a spiritual worship of Jehovah. In other words, the book is primarily and fundamentally formal and ritualistic.

§ 860. To secure this great end, however, it was not enough that all the opposing or competing modes and forms of worship should be prohibited and abolished. Image-breaking would not cure idolatry. Idolatry was mainly fostered not by image-worship, but by the conception of the local manifestations of Jehovah. Idolatry is inevitable if God exists or appears in many forms. In other words, the unity of God secures his spirituality. In every local shrine or "high place" (*bāmā*) there were, to be sure, seductions to mixed or debased forms of worship. That was a great evil, but by care and watchfulness it might be kept down. What could not be quenched in the popular mind was the persuasion that every shrine had its own type or manifestation of Jehovah. The result was the prevalence of practical polytheism with its attendant symbolism and image-worship. Hence the revolutionary idea of abolishing all the high places, except the central shrine of Jerusalem.[1] The attempt had been made by Hezekiah, but it failed,

---

[1] This idea was perhaps first suggested by Isaiah, the prophet of "Zion." But Hezekiah, if we may judge from Isaiah's own teaching, probably did not attempt the thorough-going abolition of local worship aimed at by Josiah (cf. Isa. xix. 19, 21, and i. 29). At any rate the age was not then ripe for the revolution, though outward circumstances were favourable. The difference between the reform of Hezekiah and of Josiah is discussed by W. R. Smith, OTJC.[2] p. 355 ff., and more skeptically by Smend, ATR. p. 268 f.

in spite of the prestige that came to Jerusalem through its great deliverance (§ 796). The idea, however, with the purpose was not extinguished. It worked in the faithful theocratic party all through the dark days of Manasseh and Amon. It naturally proved a chief motive of Deuteronomy, placed at the opening of the "lawbook" (Deut. xii. 1–28), repeated and reiterated throughout the work, and realized in the active measures of Josiah.

§ 861. Hand in hand with the zeal of the reformers for the purity of Jehovah's worship went their desire for the aggrandizement and sanctity of Jerusalem as the exclusive seat of that worship. Centralization was for Israel as desirable and as inevitable in the religious as in the political sphere. But for a religion such as that of Jehovah it was far more difficult to realize. For it was in Jerusalem itself that the gravest obstacles to purity of worship were found, as the account of the attempted reform will show (2 K. xxiii. 4 ff.). Thereafter, however, Judah was more and more absorbed in Jerusalem, for good or for evil.

§ 862. Two far-reaching measures in the line of the general purpose of the reform contributed to the centralizing movement. One of these was the enhanced religious value and dignity given to the great annual feasts: the feast of unleavened bread, the feast of weeks, and the feast of ingathering. These were agricultural feasts, long cherished among the people as celebrations of the chief events of the year, the first attending the barley harvest, the second the wheat harvest, and the third the fruit harvest. These had always a religious character, for every feast was a religious service (§ 499). But if they could be wholly detached from traditional half-heathen associations with the powers and processes of nature, they might be made to subserve instead of impairing the true worship of Jehovah. Hence it was ordained that they should be held only in Jerusalem at the temple. Each of them, moreover, was invested with a deeper and higher religious meaning. The first and the greatest of them at the beginning of the year was especially honoured and indeed transfigured for all coming ages. With it was united the closely following ceremony of the offering of the firstlings of the flock born in the springtime. Hence the full significance of the combined feast of unleavened bread and the passover. The celebration of this festival was made the occasion of the ratification of the work of reform; "and the king commanded all the people, saying, Keep the passover unto Jehovah your God, as it is written in the book of the covenant" (2 K. xxiii. 21; cf. Deut. xvi. 1–17).

§ 863. Yet another decisive movement marked this momentous religious epoch. The Levites had long been the proper holders of the priestly office, though not always the only sacrificers (Jud. xvii. 5 ff.; 2 Sam. xv. 24). for sacrifices could be offered by a man of any tribe, as by a house-father for his household, or by a king for his people. But now the order of the priesthood was made strict and exclusive: only the descendants of Levi could be priests, and all the members of the tribe were to have part in the office (Deut. xviii. 1 ff.). Now as all the sacrifices were to be performed at the sanctuary in Jerusalem, this priestly system came to minister to the greater glory of the central shrine, having all the political force of a close corporation and all the religious prestige of a divine institution.

§ 864. Such was the great Reform in intent and warrant. What it was in effect we shall see somewhat later (§ 1019 ff.). It behooves us now to inquire into the history of the ideas and principles upon which it was based. This inquiry will lead us (1) to trace the growth and estimate the character of the literature which led up to Deuteronomy; and (2) to follow the progress of moral and religious feeling and practice up to the era of the Reformation.

CHAPTER III

DEUTERONOMY AND THE HEBREW LITERATURE

§ 865. Deuteronomy was not the work of a day or a year. Much less was it the unaided work of those who composed it. Its roots were struck deep and wide into the moral and religious history of Israel. In substance, far more than in form, it is an exhibition of the development of the national religious thought and life. It is, moreover, so comprehensive and far-reaching as to be central and fundamental for the Old Testament Revelation. It is indeed itself a perpetual revelation, a challenge to each succeeding age to consider the depth and breadth and length of the process of the religious education of the race, as startling to each new inquirer as it was to Josiah and his ministers. As the counterpart of the obscure yet active and affluent historical period in which it saw the light, we must resort to it if we would find the key to the literature of ancient Israel. From the point of view of literary history, it is of special importance because it is essentially an expansion and adaptation of earlier documents (§ 943 ff.), and also because the same school of reformers and writers that produced it continued their work in editing the earlier historical books of the Old Testament, thus giving form and colour to a great portion of the sacred writings.

§ 866. We are thus at length in a position to review the earlier literature of the Hebrew people. It is not our province to give an analysis of the writings which comprise this literature. For this we must refer the reader to modern works too well known to require special mention. Still less are we called upon to settle the questions of date, authorship, and composition of the sacred documents whose discussion forms the staple of present-day criticism of the Old Testament. Fortunately, there is now general agreement among scholars as to at least the principal components of the body of the literature which was in the possession of the Hebrews up to the end of the seventh century B.C. It is more properly the duty of the historian to show how the literature of the several epochs of the people's history is an expression of the national life, and illustrates its progress and vicissitudes. So far as most of the prophetic writings are concerned, we have been able, as we have been compelled, to do this from the beginning. They are, in fact, contemporary historical documents indispensable to the understanding of their times. But other literary movements, including, strangely enough, much of the so-called historical narrative, do not fit in so readily with the ascertainable course of history. Their relations to one another and to the Old Testament as a whole cannot be understood until we reach some turning-point in the nation's career with some great clarifying work as its literary record. Such a period is that of Manasseh and Josiah, and such a work is Deuteronomy.

§ 867. In a sense Israel as a nation was never without a literature. From a time at least as early as the Exodus heroic poems and popular traditions were in circulation. Historical records were not made till the time of the kingdom; and it was late in monarchical times before these were systematically compiled. All the literature that could serve the purposes of a moral movement was for ages based upon the principles announced by Moses. It is to these principles that we must trace the development of a code of morals resting upon the nature and the claims of Jehovah, and of a system of civil law in conformity therewith. But such productions could not have been highly elaborated apart from a society prepared to receive them and to put them in practice. Such a society was first developed through the ministry of the prophets. Yet the prophetic writings did not wholly precede this moral and legal literature; for the preaching prophets had a literary influence before the literary prophets began their work. Such influence was mainly exerted upon the priestly order, out of whose ranks came some of the prophets. Under its auspices much of the book of Deuteronomy was gradually compiled and collated before its publication as a separate work; for the priests were practically concerned in the preservation of their religion as a system, and for this a ceremonial, judicial, and ethical code was indispensable. What was essentially new and original had come, however, from Amos and his school, and the era of the spiritual empire of Israel dates from the apostle of Tekoa, in whose hands prophecy first took the form of literature.

§ 868. The difficulties of writing a history of Hebrew literature[1] are very great. Some of them are: the length of time covered by the production of the literature; the obscurity surrounding the lives and persons of the authors; the lack of obvious relation between much of the literature and any known period of the nation's career; our imperfect knowledge of much of the inner and outer history of the people; the intellectual interval between modern critics and ancient Hebraic writers and speakers, and still more that between the authors and the later Jewish editors and compilers: the lack of literary self-consciousness on the part of the authors, and their anonymousness; their ignoring of second causes and human agencies, leading

---

[1] Apart from the suggestions and germinal ideas found in the epoch-making works on the religion and history of Israel the most directly instructive writings on the literary history of the Old Testament are W. R. Smith's OTJC., Stade's GVI., Book I, and Kautzsch's *Abriss der Geschichte des alttest. Schrifttums*, appended to ATU., and now translated into English. An outline of recent conclusions is given in Bennett, *Primer of the Bible* (1897). very handy, but almost too concise.

them to omit from their chronicle subordinate events and occasions; their dynamical rather than chronological conception of the process of history, making it natural for them to transfer the thoughts of one age or person to another with which they were providentially associated; their imperfect mechanical methods and appliances, leading to errors of omission, addition, or transposition, and occasioning the combination of separate compositions on one roll of manuscript; uncritical theories and principles of later scribes and compilers, creating confusion in the arrangement of the books.

§ 869. To understand the words and thoughts of another age or people than our own, we need knowledge and intellectual sympathy. Modern criticism seeks the one while it cultivates the other. Not content with learning what preceding generations have thought and asserted about the Old Testament writings, we examine the sources themselves directly, in the light of contemporary monuments, and with the established methods of historical research according to the well-ascertained laws of mental and moral, political and social evolution. Some of the most serious of the above-named difficulties may thus be overcome as soon as we have learned sufficiently the genius and bent of the people, and the character of their changing, as well as their permanent environment. Some things we may be sure of in their literary history as characterizing the early stages of the development of all civilized ancient nations; some other things we may infer from the knowledge to be gained of their own peculiar institutions. Certain factors conditioning the course of their literature stand out as of supreme importance. Such are the spirit and habit of their nomadic life and tribalism; their ancestral and primitive memories and traditions; their fortunes in war and migration; their religious institutions, especially the priesthood and prophecy, and above all the character of their God or gods; the religious and political habits and disposition of the influential neighbouring peoples; the character and aims of parties or communities within the nation; the principles and beliefs of the party or community which became the true or surviving Israel within Israel.

§ 870. It would thus appear that we have to interpret the Old Testament both as a history and as a literature. Literary criticism is an adjunct and instrument, almost a sub-department, of historical research, because (1) the literature is a product of the history; and (2) because we need the results of literary criticism to check and control our scheme of the facts of history, and sometimes even to explain the facts as ascertained. In this auxiliary use of literary interpretation it is of the first importance that we know the characteristics of the Old Testament writers and writings: their mode and style of narrative and description; their use of figures of speech, especially of synecdoche and hyperbole in longer or shorter passages; their notions of time, space, and number; their conceptions of the world and of events as related to human and extra-human forces and powers; their views of their own and their nation's position and destiny, of their relations to their God, of life and duty, of the state of the dead to whom they were gathered.

§ 871. The conditions under which literary composition was promoted in Israel are partly general, prevailing wherever an indigenous literature has been cultivated, and partly peculiar to the genius and history of Israel itself. The former may be taken to include: 1. Universal and necessary factors. These have, perhaps, been best set forth by Taine as "race, environment, and epoch, or the permanent impulse, the given surroundings, and the acquired momentum."[1] 2. Those conditions which are found to have attended the beginnings of every ancient national literature. These may be summarized as follows: (1) The occurrence in the young community

---

[1] *Littérature anglaise*, Intr. § V.

of memorable events, such as victories, deliverances, new settlements, new social institutions. (2) Stated tribal or national gatherings, gradually forming an interested body of speakers and hearers. (3) The rise of a profession or guild of bards, minstrels, reciters, narrators, who perpetuate and give shape to the traditions of the eventful past. These conditions have prevailed in most ancient nations, and yet few nations have given birth to a great or lasting literature founded upon such beginnings. All depends upon the special conditions. What these were in the case of Israel will appear in the course of the inquiry. But there is one factor which has been so much misunderstood and is of such prime importance, that it demands a separate discussion at the outset. It is often brought before us by questions like these: When did the Hebrews learn the art of writing? Is it possible to trace the conditions under which the earliest writers found their materials or did their work?

§ 872. That the art of writing was in vogue among the Hebrews, even at the time when the oldest surviving records were penned, is very probable, apart from the value of the direct Biblical testimony. The notion now widely prevalent that it became known to them only after their establishment as a nation is a hasty assumption which, however, deserves consideration. In the first place, it has been held as a dogma that the knowledge of the so-called "alphabet" came to the Hebrews from the Canaanites (Phœnicians) after the settlement in Palestine, and these Phœnicians in their turn are supposed to have adapted the characters from the Egyptian hieroglyphics.

§ 873. Both of these positions are, however, somewhat doubtful. The latter in particular is becoming continually more precarious.[1] What once gave it almost exclusive cur-

---

[1] The reader has an opportunity of seeing a summary presentation of the evidence in favour of the Egyptian origin in DB. under "Alphabet," where Mr. Isaac Taylor adds nothing to the evidence formerly published by himself and others. Not more than one-third of the whole list of signs

rency was an assumption that the Phœnician letters must have arisen from the Egyptian: otherwise whence could they have come? Nothing was then known of any other ancient system of writing than the Egyptian, and it seemed to be morally necessary to derive the later system from the earlier. Since then it has come to light, (1) that the Egyptian language and writing never had any footing in Asia: (2) that the Babylonian language and writing were in common use in Syria and Palestine for centuries before the Phœnician alphabet was introduced to the world; (3) that at the time when circumstances most favoured the introduction of Egyptian letters into Western Asia, namely, the days of the Egyptian occupation of Palestine and Phœnicia by the kings of the nineteenth dynasty, the Babylonian language and writing were used for ordinary purposes in these countries and even in correspondence addressed to Egyptians residing in Egypt (§ 148 ff.). Hence, apart from the fact that an obvious resemblance is lacking between most of the Phœnician letters and any selected list of hieroglyphs, no historical basis existed for the adoption by Asiatics of the writing of the alien and self-centred Egyptians.

§ 874. A survey of the known conditions may perhaps warrant the conjecture that the "Phœnician" alphabet came into general use after the disuse of the Babylonian script, in consequence of the gradual withdrawal of Babylonian influence from the West-land under the Kasshite dynasty (§ 120 ff.). It is probable that it was devised in the centre of the western Semites, and not among the people of the Mediterranean border-land, whose business dealings were mainly with non-Semites. Hence not Phœnicia, but Mesopotamia, the centre of the land traffic, should be looked upon as the region of its origin. The great emporium, Charran (§ 141), a home of learned priests, and

---

resemble the corresponding Egyptian letters, which, moreover, are chosen from forms which had gone out of use long before the Phœnician characters came into existence.

one of the greatest resorts of travellers and merchants in Western Asia, may possibly have been the city where it was mainly elaborated.[1]

§ 875. Though direct evidence is wanting, certain specific considerations tell in behalf of an Aramæan origin: (1) The language and writing of the Aramæans took the place of the Babylonian in the active business life of the whole region west of the lower Euphrates and the Tigris; their language was the language of business and diplomacy (2 K. xviii. 26), as the Babylonian had been. (2) Historically the common alphabet changed far more among the Aramæans than among the Phœnicians.[2] It was from the former that the Hebrew "square" characters were derived. What can thus be traced in surviving monuments suggests that before the earliest period of which we have written record the same sort of activity went on among the Aramæans. (3) In the eighth and seventh centuries B.C. the Aramæan language and writing were frequently used in Assyria and Babylonia along with the native cuneiform.[3] They thus pen-

---

[1] Its growth was of course gradual, like every other system of conventional signs. Its main motive and occasion were commercial, but its complete elaboration involved the art and skill of the student, since it was an almost perfect representation of the north Semitic sounds. Circumstances were favourable to the production of an improved method of writing. As long as the Babylonian language was used for political and commercial notes and correspondence, the cuneiform characters were employed with it. Even non-Semitic languages were written in cuneiform (§ 150, 154, 256). Its inadequacy to express the gutturals must have contributed, with other occasions, to its abandonment when the Babylonian language was crowded out of Syria, first by the Hettite speech and writing, and later permanently by the Aramæan.

[2] The relative rate of change may be followed in Euting's table of the Semitic alphabet in Bickell's *Hebrew Grammar*, tr. by Curtiss (1877), or in his latest presentation in Zimmern's *Vergleichende Grammatik der semitischen Sprachen* (1898). An excellent exhibit is made in Stade's *Hebr. Grammatik* (1879) in Plate I appended, where the course of the "western development" and of the "eastern development" is made plain to the eye by sufficient examples.

[3] See III R. 46; CIS. Part II, vol. i., Plates 1–14, 15 ff., 73 ff. These inscriptions are found on the signet-rings of citizens, on weights in-

etrated into the private and public life of the people, their daily business and civic affairs. The characters are practically identical with the contemporary Phœnician. On the supposition that alphabet-making began with the Phœnicians and spread eastward, it is not easy to understand how the Aramæans (who were in any case familiar with the Babylonian script formerly in universal use) and Assyrians with them should have employed such a Phœnician alphabet, and especially that in their hands it should have diverged so little from the Phœnician type. If, however, the alphabetic system originated with the Aramæans, the facts are readily explained. (4) The Aramæans did most to spread the knowledge of the alphabet throughout Western Asia. From the eighth century B.C. onward their inscriptions are found from Northern Syria to West-central Arabia, and from Egypt to the banks of the Tigris. This does not exclude the possibility of a borrowing; but, taken with what has been said, it makes it improbable. (5) The names of the letters, as far as they can be understood, point to their production among a people familiar with nomadic and pastoral usages. Such names as "camel" (*Gimel*), "tent-pin" (*Wau*), "ox" (*Aleph*), and "ox-goad" (*Lamed*)[1], would hardly have been thought of by the maritime Phœnicians. The Aramæan settlements were everywhere centres of nomadic and pastoral life and traffic. (6) The names of the letters adopted by the Greeks from the Phœnicians have nearly all the Aramaic definite ending $\bar{a}$.[2] In fine, the historic rôle of the

---

spected by public censors, and as dockets to business contracts drawn up by clerks. Cf. de Vogüé in CIS. *ibid.* p. vi.

[1] Stade, *Hebr. Grammatik* (1879), p. 25, note 7, observes that the oldest forms of the letters *Beth* and *Daleth* correspond to the shapes of the tent and the tent-opening rather than to those of a "house" and a "house-door."

[2] It should be noticed with regard to the guttural letters א, ה, ח, and ע, changed into *Alpha*, *Epsilon*, *Eta*, and *Omikron* respectively, that the way must have been already prepared for this transfer by the pronuncia-

Aramæans, played during the formative era of the alphabet, their function as intermediaries and negotiators, and their geographical distribution, seem to have predestined them to devise a more fitting medium of expression and communication than that employed by their Babylonian and Hettite predecessors.

§ 876. It is useless to speculate upon the forms and modes of writing that immediately preceded the alphabetic. Documents may yet be unearthed which will settle the essential questions. Meanwhile, it is natural to assume that the Aramæan "inventors"—if one may use such a misleading term—received suggestion and stimulus both from the Hettite and from the Babylonian system, mainly from the latter. The "invention," though of such tremendous consequence, was not in itself a very wonderful feat. Its difficulty has been exaggerated through the consideration that the Egyptians and Babylonians, peoples more civilized and literary than the early Phœnicians or Aramæans, did not progress from the ideographic or syllabic to a completely alphabetic system. But the Egyptians did actually devise a partial alphabet, and the Babylonians were within reach of it at any time. It may be said that if the decisive transition had really been so simple and obvious, the Egyptians and Babylonians would surely have made it. Those who offer this plea may be referred for an answer to the opponents of reform in English spelling. With every conceivable motive to adopt a purely alphabetic method, we adhere to a mixed system somewhat analogous to the Egyptian [1]

---

tion of the trading Phœnicians themselves, who notoriously dropped their gutturals all along the shore of the Mediterranean. The popular saying that the Phœnicians brought the alphabet to Greece means that the Greeks learned the alphabet from them in the intercourse of trade. How important the naming of the letters was may be inferred from the fact that the Greeks learned in addition to the signs, their Phœnician (Aramaic) names.

[1] For example, the spelling *though*, which expresses two simple sounds by six distinct signs, is more hieroglyphic than alphabetic.

and much less consistent than the Babylonian. It would seem that the business of simplification could be done only by a people familiar with imperfect modes of writing, yet not wedded to them by the force of literary tradition and sacred custom; in other words, a people like the practical ubiquitous Aramæan pupils of the Babylonians.[1] Future discoveries may lead to exact inductions.[2]

---

[1] How simple the process was may be shown as follows: According to the cuneiform system, a series of signs were read and pronounced, *ba, bi, bu, ab, ib, ub, da, di, du, ad, id, ud*, and so forth through the consonants. The Babylonians, among whom were ardent grammarians, knew as well as we do that it was possible to analyze and classify the sounds thus indicated, and they did, in fact, represent the vowels by special signs. But they did not go any farther, even after the alphabetic Aramæan was used in their midst, because they already had a system sufficient for their purposes, and sacred to them as being the gift of Nebo (I R. 35, nr. 2, line 4). The Babylonian signs were essentially combinations of strokes like the Aramæan and Phœnician. Moreover, the signs had names given to them, as the letters of the alphabet also had.

[2] The literature on the ancient alphabet is large, but not very important. The elaborate treatises for the most part maintain an Egyptian origin, and are antiquated through the fact that the material for study and comparison has of late years greatly increased and is still increasing. The best known to English readers is that of Isaac Taylor, *The Alphabet*, 2 vols. 1883; notable are Wuttke, *Die Entstehung der Schrift*, 1872; Lenormant, *Essai sur la propagation de l'alphabet phénicien dans l'ancien monde*, 1872; Brugsch, *Ueber Bildung und Entwickelung der Schrift*, 1868; Berger, *Histoire de l'écriture dans l'antiquité*, 1891. A good statement of the history of opinion is given by Stade, *Hebr. Grammatik* (1879), p. 23 ff., cf. Nowack, HA. I, 279 ff.; and (more independent) Benzinger, HA. p. 278 ff. Deecke (DZMG. xxxi. 107 ff.) propounded the hypothesis that the Semitic alphabet was derived from the cuneiform Assyrian. It was impossible for him, however, to demonstrate the transition stages, and the historical considerations were not fully available even as late as 1877. Stade (*l.c.*), who rightly observes that the old Babylonian is to be thought of in any case rather than the Assyrian type of cuneiform script, objects to the theory generally upon the following plea among others: "that in the older time the Semitic peoples had much more active, friendly intercourse with Egypt than with the lands of the Tigris and Euphrates." This odd remark is repeated by Nowack in a slightly altered form (p. 282). Hommel, GBA. p. 50 ff., adduces strong arguments for the view that the Semitic alphabet is of Babylonian origin. Meyer (GA. § 197) thinks that the Hettite writing had a decisive influence upon the system. This is doubtful.

§ 877. The other point involved in the preliminary question of the age and mode of writing among the Hebrews (cf. § 872) has to do with the time when and the source from which they derived this important aid to literature. The opinion, now so generally accepted, that the Hebrews had no acquaintance with the art until they settled in Palestine after the conquest, is based upon a manifold misconception. Its possibility may be admitted, but not its probability. This opinion is thus stated by a recent writer : [1] "If — and this is a matter as to which we have no certain information — the Israelites during their nomadic life in the desert used any sort of writing, this was without doubt in the lowest grade of development, that is to say, a stage in which no syllable signs, much less letters, were employed, but only mnemotechnic signs or picture writing, such as at the present day the Bedawin possess (*wasm*), with which they brand their cattle, or put marks upon rocks and other available objects. The Israelites became acquainted with alphabetic writing, as with civilized life generally, only when they came into contact with the Canaanites in the West Jordan or possibly in the East Jordan country." To the same effect another writes : [2] "When we consider that the old Hebrew alphabet is identical with the Phœnician, that the Moabites had the same alphabet as the Israelites, and

---

[1] Benzinger, HA. p. 288.
[2] Nowack, HA. I, 288 f. Kautzsch writes more generally in *Abriss der Geschichte des alttest. Schrifttums* (ATU., Appendix), p. 136 ; "The conditions under which alone a real literature can at any time arise — above all, the wide extension of the art of writing and *reading*, a settled mode of life and comparative national prosperity — did not exist for Israel till toward the end of the period of the Judges at the earliest, and not during the wilderness journey or in the time of the continual struggle for existence of the tribes after the entrance in Canaan." This judgment, perhaps too sweeping, does not exclude the *use* of writing. Cornill remarks sensibly (*Einl.*[4] 1896, p. 8) : "The Tell el Amarna discoveries of 1887 have opened up to us wholly unimagined perspectives. In view of such facts, there is no ground whatever for denying to Moses a knowledge of writing."

that the Canaanites in many things were the teachers of the Israelites, it is natural to conjecture that the Israelites learned from them the art of writing."

§ 878. The solution of the problem is not, however, such a simple matter. It is not certain that Israel was never in Canaan before the final settlement. But granting that the Israelites led wholly a wilderness life before the occupation, it does not follow that they knew nothing of writing. To affirm that they must have been ignorant of the art shows a misconception of the character of ancient Semitic civilization. Because the Semites did not attain to such a culture as that of the Greeks, it has been assumed that they were essentially a barbarous people. The " Phœnician " letters have been regarded as the sole and exceptional means of culture, because of the commercial enterprise of that offshoot of the race, and because it was from them that the Greeks learned the alphabet. This view we now know to be erroneous. Whatever we may think of the kind and degree of the culture of the ancient Semites, they seem to have been everywhere and at all times writers. It was therefore not at all necessary for Israel to have occupied Palestine in order to learn this art. There is, as we have seen (§ 875), no evidence either that the Phœnicians were the first to use the letters called by their name, or that it was from them that the other inhabitants of Palestine received the alphabet. In any case the universal prevalence of writing before Israel's final settlement made it quite possible for them to learn to write, even apart from the special opportunities open to favoured members of the race in Egypt. Wherever trade was carried on within the vast region between Egypt, South Arabia,[1] and Babylonia, there accounts were

---

[1] The facts about the Minæan kingdom of South Arabia and its trade relations northward are not quite clearly made out. It is probable that this people, whose inscriptions are numerous, had close commercial relations with North Arabian tribes. The influence of Minæan culture and writing has, however, been greatly exaggerated.

cast up, contracts made, and records kept. It is therefore without warrant that writing has been denied to Israel during the Mosaic epoch.

§ 879. But let us look at the question from another point of view. In the ode of Deborah (Jud. v.) we have a document of about 1120 B.C.,[1] which presupposes writing as a thing long established. In one passage (v. 14) it is said,

" From Machir there came down the troop-leaders.[2]
And from Zebulon those that march with the baton of the captain."[3]

The names of the officers, meaning originally "engravers" and "scribes," taken in connection with the whole of the splendid poem, throw a flood of light upon the culture of early Israel. They demonstrate that Hebrew was the language of Israel before the Exodus, for such a mastery of it for the highest literary purposes could not have been acquired in a single generation, at least not by a race of untutored nomads. The inferences are of decisive importance. (1) The Hebrews in Egypt spoke Hebrew. They could have learned it only in Palestine, for it is "the language of Canaan" (Isa. xix. 18). (2) Israel in Egypt was an exile from Canaan, and the settlement was a return homeward. Placing these facts along with the

---

[1] It is useless to attempt to make out a chronology of the Judges from the biblical numbers. The Exodus is now admitted to be fixed at about 1200 B.C. — rather later than earlier than that date (§ 167). The first inroad of the tribes into Canaan having been made about 1160, not much more than a generation was required to bring about the state of things described in Jud. iv. and v.

[2] Literally, "prescribers, ordainers" (cf. Isa. x. 1; Prov. viii. 15). Our word "prescribe" has had an analogous history. The word meant first to engrave, then to write down (naturally with a small graving-tool or stylus), and lastly, from the fact that regulations were specially written down, came the sense of ordaining.

[3] Literally, "the scribe," i.e. the man who kept the muster-roll, who was in this rudimentary military system the commander of his troop. "The poet evidently seeks changing expressions for the often recurring idea, chiefs" (Moore, Commentary on Judges, 1895, p. 151).

evidence for Hebrew settlements in Canaan about 1500 B.C. (§ 369, note), and the still later proof that there was a considerable settlement of Hebrews there shortly before the Exodus, in the days of Merneptah,[1] we reach the conclusion that while the story of the patriarchal settlement in Canaan has a substantial basis, the account of the residence in Egypt and of the events till the occupation is only a part of the total history.

§ 880. The special matter before us, however, is the early acquaintance of Israel with the art of writing, and this is clearly proved by the history of the terms used in the above extract. Etymological inference is sometimes precarious, but here it is certain and unmistakable. Writing was such an old national habit among the speakers of Hebrew that words designating it had taken on secondary and ulterior meanings, implying a long process of institutional development. This process, however, as linguistic comparison shows, was undergone in Canaan and not elsewhere; and we must therefore assume that Israel partook of the culture of that country from the days of the Babylonian occupation onwards. There can therefore be no question as to the external facilities for literary composition at the disposal of the Hebrews in the days of Moses.

§ 881. The knowledge and practice of writing, however, only made a written literature possible; it did not necessarily imply its existence. Writing, even alphabetic writing, was often, perhaps usually, employed among ancient Semites by communities which had no literature at all, since its motive and object were practical, not sentimental (see § 899). On the other hand, a literature, or at least its materials, existed usually independently of and sometimes previously to the practice of writing. The foregoing discussion has therefore merely served the pre-

---

[1] According to the now famous hymn celebrating the power of that Pharaoh, and discovered by Professor Petrie in 1895. Near the end it contains the line, among others referring to his conquests in Palestine, "Israel has been torn out without offshoot."

liminary though important end of helping to clear the way for the settlement of the matter in hand and determining its conditions. We may, besides, learn by analogy what place was occupied by a written literature in the cultural development of such a people as the Hebrews. Conclusions may be drawn from the literary monuments of ancient peoples taken along with the ascertained laws or gradations of their social and political evolution.

§ 882. The following summary may serve to show the purposes for which writing was employed successively in a typical community of the ancient East. We may, I think, say that writing was used (1) for business purposes, such as trading accounts, notes of bargains or of formal contracts, registration or indentures of slaves or hired labourers, the defining of boundaries and sites of buildings; (2) for lists of men liable to serve in war or upon actual service; (3) for civil contracts, trading or manufacturing rights guaranteed to guilds of skilled workmen, charters to privileged tribes or cities; (4) for family records, chiefly genealogical; (5) for songs and poems of the deeds of the great of old or of former tribal leaders; (6) for special statutes based on legal decisions or "judgments"; (7) for official records usually if not entirely of a larger or smaller "kingdom"; (8) for traditions and legends running back to prehistoric ages connecting the national history with the remotest past.

§ 883. The development of an actual literature has also a periodicity of its own, and the observed progression of other literatures is helpful for our study of the Hebrew. Literature may be broadly defined as the published[1] productions of the human mind. In an ancient national literature we can, of course, deal only inferen-

---

[1] Published, that is, by word of mouth or by writing or printing. The dictionary definitions confine literature to what is written or printed. This excludes the vast body of compositions which preceded and conditioned the *Iliad* and *Odyssey*, the Vedas, the old songs of Israel and of every people that has developed a national literature.

tially with what has passed out of the sight of men, which is in most if not in all instances larger than what has been preserved. Taking into view all the conditions and the available evidence, we may distinguish the successive stages of Hebrew literature, up to the Exile, as follows: (1) the poetical heroic or epic ballad; (2) the prose heroic or epic narrative; (3) the historical or national narrative; (4) the oratorical or prophetic.

§ 884. For modes and directions of literary activity we are thrown back upon the surviving literature itself. The first question is: Are there among the extant Hebrew writings any which plainly indicate that they originated in the early days of the historic Israel? We have, moreover, to distinguish between literature which was promoted and maintained by oral transmission, and that which was committed to writing soon after its origination.[1] In these days of critical rearrangement it will be a comfort to many to be assured that the opening chapters of the Old Testament are also the oldest, in as far as they contain the oldest materials of Hebrew literature.

§ 885. Such are the venerable relics that are enshrined in the stories of the creation of the world and of man, of the earliest history of mankind, of the flood, of city building, of Babylonian civilization, and of the dispersion of races. Not all, however, of the traditions that went to the making of Gen. i.–xi. are of Hebrew origin. One of the two writers[2] who contributed to our present

---

[1] From the standpoint of the historical student intellectual and moral movements are of more importance than editorial activity. Hence the origin of the various portions of the Hebrew literature is of more concern to us than questions as to the occasions of their assuming their present form.

[2] Since critical analysis is not our present object, and in any case established conclusions must be taken for granted, I shall continue to refer to the documents which make up the historical or historico-legal books by the usual marks: D = Deuteronomist; E = Elohist; H = Law of Holiness; J = Jehovist; P = Priestly narrative. Explanations and particulars the educated reader may find in Driver's *Introduction*, or more readily in Bennett's *Primer of the Bible* (1897), not to mention other well-known books.

Bible this introductory section (P or the priestly narrator) may have drawn most of his materials relating to these events directly from Babylonia. These presumably non-Hebraic elements are the account of the creation of the heavens and the earth (as distinguished from that of the world of men by J or the prophetic narrator) comprised in Gen. i. 1–ii. 3, and the longer systematizing, statistical account of the deluge (as distinguished from the more poetical and anthropomorphic story by J) in Gen. vi. 9–22, vii. 6, 11, 13–21, 24; viii. 1, 3–5, 13–19. The basis of the remainder, that is the material used in the narrative of J, was thus the oldest genuine Hebrew literature.

§ 886. There can be no reasonable doubt, however, that, directly or indirectly, the germinal portions of both narratives came from Babylonia. The important question not easily solved is, What portion of these stories formed the actual elements of ancient tradition or, in the wide sense, of Hebrew national literature. We at once perceive that two motives have been at work in the narrative, the one aiming to perpetuate the original material, more or less changed in the transfer from mouth to mouth, and the other seeking to make the recital a vehicle of the conceptions proper to the religion of Israel. It is the additions and modifications made from the latter motive that have really given to these chapters the character of biblical literature, just as it is the poetic and mythological setting of the corresponding Babylonian legends[1] which have given to them their place among the world's literary monuments. But the earliest period of religious reflection, such as is implied in the theological cosmogony of Genesis, is later than that of the first literary activity. Hence it is only for the popular traditional

---

[1] For descriptions and analysis of the Babylonian creation legends see especially Jensen, *Die Kosmologie der Babylonier* (1890); Gunkel, *Schöpfung und Chaos* (1895); Delitzsch, *Das babylonische Weltschöpfungsepos* (1896); and Jastrow, RBA. (1898).

elements of the stories that we can claim the greatest antiquity. Moreover, we have these only in a modified and eclectic form, such portions being selected as lend themselves best to the scheme of interpretation.[1] Further help in the difficult task of distinguishing the popular from the theological elements in these chapters is gained by noting the points which the Babylonian and the Hebrew versions of the creation and the deluge have in common.[2]

§ 887. But how has it happened that this unsystematized and fragile literary material had in primitive days such vitality and persistency? We may answer this question at least in part : (1) The subjects of the traditions were intensely fascinating to men of all grades of culture.

---

[1] So also in the Babylonian epic. Jastrow, RBA. p. 409.

[2] It is unnecessary to show in detail that it is in Babylonia that we are to seek for the originals of at least the principal of the earliest narratives of Genesis, those of the creation and the deluge. Though many attempts have been made to show close analogies between the Genesis story of the flood and the legends or traditions of many other peoples in all parts of the world, the best practical proof that these identifications are baseless is furnished by the fact that no systematic comparison can be made between them, while, on the other hand, scholars of the highest eminence since the era of George Smith's "Chaldæan Genesis" (1875) have been busy in comparing the details of the Hebrew accounts with those of the Babylonian. Possibly there was at one time a body of common north Semitic popular traditions, and it is unfortunate that the Phœnician legends are accessible only in a late and fragmentary form. Apart from striking resemblances in details of plot and incident the Hebrew and Babylonian accounts are alike in making the sinfulness of men the occasion of the deluge and their destruction its object. For the question of the Israelitish character of the Bible tradition as a whole the most significant facts are (1) that conclusive evidence points to Babylonia as the ultimate home of all the traditions ; (2) that the narrative of P containing elements different from those of J probably owes its materials to the post-exilic residence of Israel in Babylonia ; (3) that the style and plan of P reveal the influence of Babylonian education ; (4) that nevertheless J. which was composed not later than the eighth century B.C. (§ 932), has in its flood story, at least, more resemblances to the Babylonian versions than are exhibited in the narrative of P. A rational reconstruction of the early history will make it very probable that the ancestors of the main stock of Israel were in a position to bring with them from Babylonia the oldest elements of the national literature.

(2) It is very probable that these traditions were never quite disconnected. Even in their popular form they very early made part of schemes of cosmology which gradually became highly refined and elaborate with the progress of knowledge and reflection. Thus it is certain that the material which was taken over from the Babylonians by the Hebrew writers had already been worked up into lengthy compositions of wide currency. (3) Almost from the first these traditions were circulated and transmitted from generation to generation in rhythmic or poetic form.

§ 888. So much for these ideas or conceptions symbolized in concrete form which furnish the motive of the opening chapters of the Bible. But it was also this poetic shaping and moulding which, more than anything else, helped to preserve almost the exact words of other early compositions. I refer particularly to memorials and recollections of tribal or national achievement. Such *memorabilia* thus framed strike the imagination, and by reason of the parallelistic mode of expression and the continual reshaping into concise and telling periods, sink deep into the memory.

§ 889. A unique example is the song of Lamech, of which a fragment has been preserved by the Jehovist in his earliest narrative of human fortunes (Gen. iv. 23, 24). This mere remnant paints with Hebraic vividness the titanic and pitiless temper of primitive tribalism. But how much of both the earlier and the later history of our race is summarized in this earliest war-song, in its stern exultation over the dead and conquered foeman, in its glorifying of revenge as the business and the joy of life! And this most human of passions, as old as sin and death, and as new as the last anniversary of Sedan or of Majuba, how shockingly vulgar it appears here in its essential savagery! And how this old barbarian of the song strips our militarism of its gaudy trappings, showing it, in its essence, to be mere manslaughter, and tenfold more murderous than the vengeance of Cain! The very primitiveness and unconventional frankness of this old ballad are proof of its remote antiquity. On this, as well as upon other and more obvious grounds, we must assign to it the rank of one of the oldest extant Hebrew poems, though it would be vain to seek for the original author or even the age to which he belonged.

§ 890. The survival of such a poem of strife and victory gives a suggestion as to the kind of composition which first became, in the strict sense, literature, irrespectively of the time when it was committed to writing. It was national, or rather tribal, perils and triumphs that were first commemorated in enduring verse. The first purely Israelitish poem is very probably the song in Ex. xv. Not that the whole poem is of contemporary origin, for important additions were apparently made by the author of the work in which it is found (E). The characteristic portion, however, or the first two-thirds of the whole, is genuinely antique, and must go back to the earliest period of the national existence. Archaisms abound, even more exceptional than those of Jud. v. (§ 894). Such are archaic inflectional forms (*e.g.* in vs. 2c, 5a, 6e), archaic usage of words later employed otherwise (vs. 2b, 4a, 6b, 7a). Equally striking are the primitive religious conceptions such as that of Jehovah as a "man of war" (v. 3) with the parallelism that "Jahwè is his name." As a matter of fact, not literary but historical considerations have convinced critics that the whole poem is of later origin. Now that fuller light is breaking in upon the history of Israel and its relation to the culture of the times, a more conservative attitude toward such questions as are here raised may be fairly expected to prevail.

§ 891. It is significant, however, that for the period intervening between the Exodus and the close approach to the eastern border of Canaan, there is little or no representative literature. Doubtless a tradition of many incidents that occurred during this interval was maintained for several generations, until the documents were drawn up which idealized them into close coördination with the later religious history. Notes of the several stations of the wilderness journey, of the conflict with Amalek, the rendezvous with Jethro, and other decisive events, may well have been made by the great leader (cf. Ex. xvii. 14). But these are scarcely the material of literary composition. There is, however, one transcendent occurrence, of which, at first sight, there seem to be copious literary memorials. The sojourn at Sinai plays a more prominent part in the current theory of the development of the nation than any other event not excepting the Exodus itself. The narrative testifies to the consciousness of the new epoch in Revelation. It is not merely that Moses is here a legislator. That has already been emphasized in Ex. xviii., which gives a picture of his activity true to the life. Such a picture, however, might be the later expression of a traditional conception, though none the less authentic on that account. But in the Sinai narrative the very contents of his inspired legislation are given. Of this whole body of commands the three component parts are strikingly dissimilar to one another. These are the Decalogue (Ex. xx. 1–17), the Book of the Covenant (Ex. xx. 23–xxiii. 19), both in E, and the Priestly Legislation, giving directions concerning the tabernacle, the priesthood, sacrifices, purifications, and atonement, vows and tithes (Ex. xxv.–xxxi., xxxv.–xl., and all Leviticus), along with miscellaneous laws mainly relating to the organization of the tribes in view of their desert journey, the duties of the Levites, the maintenance of ceremonial purity, and the administration of the tabernacle (Num. i.–x.).

§ 892. In the last-named large and varied body of ordinances it is probable that some of the simple directions relating to the life and conduct and practical management of the tribesmen are embodied. But the whole legislative *corpus* is plainly an idealizing system, the product of much later days, and it would be vain to seek in it for literary material of the date of the sojourn in Sinai. The other two stand in closer relation to the early times of Israel. The chief difficulty in the way of ascribing the laws of the Book of the Covenant to Moses directly and in their present form is the fact that they imply a long period of settled agricultural life with a corresponding social and political development. In itself it seems reasonable that the lawgiver should have sought to educate his people for their residence in Canaan as actual proprietors of the soil in view of the enormous moral and economic difficulties of such a social and industrial revolution. And, therefore, there can be little doubt that the spirit if not the actual words of his teaching pervades this most influential of all ancient law-books. The preceptive portions of the Decalogue, as distinguished from the prefatory sentences, which are still further expanded in a later rendition (Deut. v. 6–21), are Mosaic in spirit and possibly in language. Their antiquity is proved by the sure tradition of their inscription on the tablets of stone that were placed in the ark of the Covenant. It is remarkable that there is another decalogue (Ex. xxxiv. 17–26, from J) whose ten enactments contain precepts found both in the Book of the Covenant and in the Decalogue proper. It is impossible that the larger documents could have been expanded from this smaller one. The smaller is therefore an independent selection from the materials which lay at the basis of the larger. Hence it brings us even less near than the Decalogue of Ex. xx. to the fountain of tradition.

§ 893. The period between the encampment at Sinai and the final march upon Canaan is to be estimated according to the principles already indicated. Except probably in the names of the stations, the scanty materials supplied by tradition have been expanded and modified to answer to the idealistic conceptions of a later age. But when we come once more within the domain of stirring events, we are greeted with outbursts of national feeling of an originality and freshness that attest their antiquity and genuineness. Here again, as at the Exodus, we have that intense life and energy of a common struggle and a common triumph, which in a gifted and patriotic community is sure to find expression in popular song.

§ 894. Such are the fragments of the poems preserved by E (§ 923 ff.) and contained in Num. xxi. They are all extracted from a lost work of the early days of the kingdom, entitled the "Book of the Wars of Jehovah," to which the first is expressly assigned (vs. 14, 15). It is a mere topographical fragment, but is put into genuine poetic form, and shows minute power of observation, combined with an appreciation of natural scenery rare and unexpected :

"The declivity of the valleys
Inclining to the dwelling of Ar
And leaning upon the border of Moab."

This poem is thus seen to be nearly or quite contemporaneous with Israel's march along the region thus described; for such language is the reminiscence of an eyewitness. The next fragment is the famous "Song of the Well" (vs. 17, 18), which also is probably, though less certainly, an actual reminiscence. The third and longest is not quite intelligible. It may, as Meyer maintains,[1] have had reference originally to a victory gained by Northern Israel over Moab, and have been transferred by E through a misunderstanding to the Mosaic period. The history of the first two fragments, at all events, seems to have been as follows. They were composed by poets or minstrels of the time. They were recited by rhapsodists till, at some unknown date, perhaps in the time of David, they, with other poems of the early wars of Israel, were collected into a "book." Next they were incorporated by E into his historical work. Characteristic of their time

---

[1] ZATW. I, 130 f. (1881).

of production is the title of the last collection of the period when Jehovah was a "man of war" (§ 890; cf. 1 Sam. xviii. 17; xxv. 28).

§ 895. The remaining poems and poetic fragments contained in the Pentateuch have little or no material of Mosaic times. The prophecies of Balaam (Num. xxiii. and xxiv.) are of admirable dramatic effect as placed in the mouth of a heathen seer of Pethor; but they no more lend themselves to a theory of literal interpretation than does the psalm of Jonah, composed according to the rules of Hebrew rhythm and parallelism in the "sheol" of the great fish. They were, moreover, a striking lesson to outside nations, as well as to Israel, of the guardian care of Jehovah over his own people in spite of all the forces that threatened to destroy them. The whole story is the outcome of various traditions based upon an historical episode (Mic. vi. 5) of which the central feature was that the king of Moab unsuccessfully appealed to an alien soothsayer[1] to bring misfortune upon Israel during its march upon Canaan. The character of the poems themselves indicates that even the oldest stratum (xxiv. 17-19) can scarcely have originated before the time of David, who was the conqueror of both Moab and Edom.

§ 896. We naturally look for some contemporary record of the struggle of Israel for the possession of Canaan. But at least the early history of that struggle has left no direct literary memorial, with the exception of a brief poem or poetical fragment placed in the mouth of Joshua in connection with his great victory over the five kings of the "Amorites" (Josh. x. 12). That this adjuration to the sun and moon, or its substance, was uttered during some noted encounter with formidable enemies is made probable by the fact that it was misunderstood by its later editors, and interpreted to mean that the sun and

---

[1] That the narrative is composite and assigns more than one residence to Balaam is now generally admitted. For details of criticism see the article "Balaam" in EB. and the literature there cited.

moon actually stood still until the issue of the battle was decided.[1] According to the context of a later date the verse is taken from the "Book of Jashar" (§ 906 f.).

§ 897. Of the later stage of the conflict with the Canaanites a memorial has been left which is at the same time one of the gems of all Oriental literature. The "Song of Deborah" (Jud. v.) is by many critics thought to be the earliest Hebrew composition extant. Though so much as this cannot be conceded, it will be agreed that it bears more numerous marks than does any supposed earlier composition of being the work of an eye or ear witness. Its relation to the political and social development of Israel has already been dwelt upon (§ 479 f.), and it has also been shown (§ 879) how it throws light upon the cultural progress of the people as well. From the point of view of literary history, it is clear that it obviously cannot be the first important production of its kind, much less the first considerable poem generally. In it we see the lyric poetry of war and patriotism brought to perfection. Its treatment of the theme from so many standpoints and with reference to so many national interests is of itself a mark of long ex-

---

[1] The mistake was due, in part at least, to a misinterpretation of דמם, which does not mean "stand still," but "be silent," then "cease" (Lam. ii. 18; Ps. xxxv. 15), here naturally to cease shining. The Hebrews were praying for darkness, not for light; and the prayer was answered by the coming on of a great tempest (v. 11). It may be added in support of this view (1) that both sun and moon are appealed to, of course as representing the light-giving forces generally; (2) that the staying of the moon would not add to the light of any day, however much prolonged; (3) that the appearance of the moon in the heavens with the sun is an exceptional occurrence. We have to deal here not with meteorology or astronomy, but with popular poetry. How natural this metaphorical use of being "silent" is may be seen in *Samson Agonistes*, l. 86–88:

> "The sun to me is dark
> And silent as the moon
> When she deserts the night,"

a passage imitated by Milton from Dante, *Inferno*, I. 56: "Where the sun in silence rests," and V. 30: "Where light was silent all" (Cary).

perience in literary composition. The song is, in fact, a literary consummation, like the poems of Homer. Here we may learn too that we are to judge of ancient society by what it has itself to tell us of its possibilities and achievements, and not according to criteria drawn from the more familiar conditions of modern life. Thus we see that a people may have developed itself greatly along certain lines of art and reflection, while it may be very rude and backward in other matters which seem to us to be the first essentials of morals and civilization.

§ 898. Having learned that the period of the judges was not much more than a century in duration, we find that there was no long abatement in the cultivation of lyric poetry. In the restless, unsettled times that intervened till the accession of David, there was nothing to provoke any other sort of composition, and in the events of the period there was much to encourage the continuance of an art and habit already become national. Nothing composed before the death of Saul and Jonathan has been preserved; but the essential thing is that the poetic tradition was maintained. Indeed, it was impossible that it should die out as long as there were sacred festal assemblies, gatherings of the clans, and yearly family reunions, with their minstrels and bards. Hence we cannot consider David's elegy over the dead king and his much-loved son (2 Sam. i. 19-27) as anything singular of its kind. Its preservation indeed implies that it was but one of a class of compositions prized and cherished by the people at large. In a word, this poem, with its symmetrical structure and fine sense of proportion, introduces us to an established poetical literature.

§ 899. David's lament brings us, indeed, very near to the time of the first self-conscious literary movement, resulting in the collecting and editing of poems already current. In his time there first came a direct provocation to this epoch-making enterprise. We may explain by referring once more to the art of writing. As we have said (§ 881), its use, even when widely extended, does not make a literature, because literature does not imply writing, but merely circulation. Business documents may and usually do exist mainly for individuals. They are mere memoranda, whose use and reference lie outside the writings themselves. But the material of literature, whether poems or national records, has its interest in itself. We are taken by it out of the region of calculation and routine, into the world of sentiment and reflection, from the outward adjustments of society to the movement and expression of its inner life. And the interest in it is not that of individuals or parties, but of a community. In a word, literature is publication, and publication implies a public. The first condition then is that there must be a considerable circle of people interested in the matter in hand; that is to say, a circle wider than and somewhat different from the gatherings which were wont to be entertained by the reciters of songs or "sayings" (המשלים Num. xxi. 27).

§ 900. How was such a public created? Obviously by those events and ideas which left the deepest and most permanent impression, or, in other words, which were felt to have most to do with the vital interests of Israel. Whatever commemorated these events and ideas became precious and inalienable. The more closely the clans and tribes were drawn together and became animated by a common cause and a common impulse, the more they learned to prize and cling to the traditions and monuments of their common history. Chief among these memorials were the songs and stories of the eventful past, and it is to what was inspiring in them, by being genuinely and passionately Israelitish, that their preservation was due. They were thus at once bonds and symbols of a growing nationality. But as long as there was division of interest or action, with a multiplicity of sanctuaries and other trysting places, popular tales and poems were not apt to circulate widely and thus become the common property of many people. Hence it was that only what was strongest and best, and but little of that, survived the strife and separation of the days of the judges or the unsettlement and confusion of the transition period of the early monarchy. But with the consummation of a united Israel, under the sway of David, came not merely the opportunity, but the inner necessity of a publication in documentary form of those traditions which consciously and in a very real sense justified the claim of Israel to be the chosen people of Jehovah.

§ 901. Add to this that in David's time there was introduced the practice of official and professional writing which must have greatly promoted the collection of literary relics. The king's secretaries now for the first time registered contemporary events of national significance (§ 522). What more natural than that another guild of scribes should grow up whose task it was to engross and preserve the records of the past? Not only so, but the same writers would soon be employed to indite and transcribe the original utterances of the singers and orators of the time and whatever contemporary production was thought worthy of preservation. Between the professional minstrel, if we may use the term, and the professional chronicler and poet, there must needs intervene the professional scribe.

§ 902. Nor was there any lack of material. A gifted people just arrived at national self-consciousness, and with an inspiring poetic tradition behind it, could not fail to give proof of its new attainments and powers, as the tree must attest its maturity by the bearing of fruit. Fresh subjects suggested themselves as the themes of poetry. Even the new kingly order in the state deepened the significance of Israel's vocation. Such a tragedy as the life and death of Saul and Jonathan could not have been enacted before on any arena of Israel's history, and its catastrophe must have moved many susceptible souls to pity and terror, of which the deepest and strongest expression has survived in David's lament. Then there were the great events of the time, transacted on a scale such as Israel never knew before or after the redemption of the land from the Philistines: the reunion of all Israel under the warrior-statesman-poet who had long been the hope of the nation; the submission of the neighbouring peoples; the promise, however illusory, of lasting prosperity and peace. And the very troubles that dashed the fair horizon with a gloom that was never lifted impressed the imagination and moved to utterances of sympathy and grief. Of such a kind was the rebellion of Absalom and his death, which again evoked a lament from David (2 Sam. xviii. 33), whose distinction it was to pronounce the most moving of all elegies over the noblest of friends and the most ignoble of sons.[1]

§ 903. The mention of David's elegies suggests cultivation of a type of composition previously unknown. I mean that which dealt with the fates of individuals instead of the fates of the nation or of the community. It was again the institution of the monarchy which prepared the way for this enrichment of the literature of Israel with the oldest and most essential portions of Judges and Samuel. The fortunes of no man less than a national leader could excite an interest wide enough to create for itself the public which is necessary for a literature. It is this that has given its special interest to the parable of Nathan with regard to the appalling, yet kingly, crime of David (2 Sam. xii. 1 ff.). Observe, moreover, how many features and standpoints of interest are presented in the personal history of David and his court, which did not fail to play their part in the narratives of a somewhat later time, the prose epics of ancient Israel (§ 918 f.).

§ 904. We can scarcely suppose, however, that the actual collecting of writings on any large scale began

---

[1] Compare also the pathos of his poetical lament over Abner (2 Sam. iii. 33 f.). Translate freely: "Should Abner die an ignoble death?"

under David. Collection follows publication, and there was then hardly enough of the latter to suggest the necessity of gathering up and arranging the various compositions of that and the preceding ages. This is, properly speaking, editorial work, which also involves a comparison of texts and the addition or subtraction of inherited materials. The beginning of such a work must be assigned to the more expansive and leisurely time of King Solomon. There all the conditions favourable to such an enterprise were present. A new institution was the temple with its services. Everywhere among Semitic peoples a great sanctuary was a centre of intellectual life and interest. In Jerusalem it never became in this way what it was in Babylonia; but we are more apt to underrate than to overrate its significance and that of the priests, who through it became a guild of collectors and compilers. Yet their influence was for a time less direct than that of the poetical school. Tradition ascribes to Solomon himself the authorship of lyric poems as well as of proverbs (1 K. v. 12, or EV. iv. 32). But this is merely an Oriental way of saying that he took the lead among a school or circle of poets who were an ornament as well as an appendage of his court, and by whom much of his own reputed wisdom was loyally contributed. Thus there is every reason to believe that in the Jerusalem of his time there was much intellectual activity, stimulated by growing knowledge of the world without, attained chiefly through Phœnician and Egyptian trade and alliance.

§ 905. It is probable that something of the original thought and speech of this era has been preserved to the latest times. We have already alluded to the nucleus of the prophecies of Balaam (§ 895). Far more important is the great historical poem known as the "Blessing of Jacob," a survey of the tribes of Israel in their final settlement in Canaan, placed in the mouth of the patriarch dying in Egypt (Gen. xlix.). The description is, from a literary point of view, quite unique. It is a sort of character study, inasmuch as it gives a résumé of the achievements of the respective tribes, and connects their fortunes with their outstanding characteristics severally. That it belongs to the time of the undivided kingdom is reasonably certain. It cannot be earlier, because, while the tribes are all mustered and dealt with as individuals, they yet form one whole, at peace with one another and prosperous. Moreover, the supremacy of Judah (vs. 8-12) was not gained till the time of David. It cannot be later, for such a poem is inconceivable after the schism, and especially after the outlying tribes had been in whole or in part lost to Israel.[1]

§ 906. It is also probable that we owe to Solomon's scribes the compilation of the two books already cited, the "Book of the Wars of Jehovah" and the "Book of Jashar," the one being apparently a collection of poems celebrating the triumphs of Jehovah the "man of war" (§ 894) as champion of his people Israel, up to the entrance into Canaan, and the other a selection of national poems of more general character, composed after that event[2] (§ 896).

§ 907. The last quotation made from the book of Jashar belongs to Solomon's time,[3] and there is nothing of the sort of a later date. The fact is significant. It is noticeable that with the book of Samuel the poetical quotations end. The explanation is that with the establishment of the kingdom under David and the unification of the tribes, the period of personal and family adventure, the age of Hebrew romance and chivalry, comes to an end,

---

[1] Contrast the "Blessing of Moses" (Deut. xxxiii.; § 935).

[2] "Jashar" is an honorific name of Israel, of which "Jeshurun" (Num. xxiii. 10 as amended; Deut. xxxii. 15, xxxiii. 5, 26; Isa. xliv. 2) is a diminutive. Both words were of course originally appellatives: "the upright," or rather the "right," or well pleasing (to Jehovah), or, which is the same thing practically, the successful, victorious one.

[3] According to the Sept. of 1 K. viii. 53, which has a reference to the book in the reading ἐν βιβλίῳ τῆς ᾠδῆς. This has been conjectured to stand for בְּסֵפֶר הַיָּשָׁר, the last word having been turned into הַשִּׁיר. So Wellhausen in Bleek's *Einleitung* (4th ed.), p. 236.

and with it minstrelsy and rhapsody decline. Hence, when the historical compilers, working at a later time, gave extracts from these books, and quoted other fragments of popular songs and sayings, they placed none of them later than the days of Solomon.

§ 908. Besides the poems and poetic fragments and sayings above noticed, quite a number of others are quoted in the earlier canonical books. Thus we have the fine parable of Jotham (Jud. ix. 7–15), which itself contains expressions in poetic or rhythmic form; the lament of Jephthah (Jud. xi. 35); the riddle of Samson and its pendants (Jud. xiv. 14, 18); his exultation after victory (Jud. xv. 16); the song of Hannah (1 Sam. ii. 1–10); Samuel's denunciation of King Saul (1 Sam. xv. 22–23); the popular song of David's prowess (1 Sam. xviii. 7; cf. xxi. 11, xxix. 5); David's lament over Abner (2 Sam. iii. 33 f.); David's great triumphal song (2 Sam. xxii.; cf. Ps. xviii.); and his "last words" (2 Sam. xxiii. 1–7).[1]

§ 909. Of these quotations some are obviously genuine; others are clearly the product of later times, such as the song of Hannah, and Samuel's denunciation. Others are less clearly so, David's great psalm and his "last words." It is with reluctance that any good son of the church relinquishes the belief in Davidic psalms. But many considerations combine to make such a belief impossible. (1) Those Psalms which are held to be most certainly Davidic show traces of a later age. Some reserve to David this same Ps. xviii. (2 Sam. xxii.) alone. There is much in this sublime poem to remind us of David's spirit; but if the spirit is David's, the words and the elaboration are scarcely his. A theophany worked out in detail (vs. 7–17), is a prophetic idea (Mic. i.; Hab. iii.; Ps. l.) to which David and his age were incompetent. The self-approbation of vs. 19–26 is inappropriate to David,

---

[1] Add the sayings of 1 Sam. x. 12 (xix. 24), xxiv. 13, and the obscure proverb of 2 Sam. v. 8.

who with all his faults was not ignorant or forgetful of them. (2) The Psalms throughout are not merely religious, but spiritual; David was religious but, so far as we know, he was not spiritual. His habit of life (§ 970 ff.) was unfavourable to piety. The "last words" (2 Sam. xxiii. 1–7), which are not a "psalm," being too individual or autobiographical, are more in keeping with David's character, and the personal groundwork is undoubtedly his. It is touching in its naïveté, and the unadorned ruggedness of the style gives it a flavour of originality, in contrast with the smoothness and harmony of most of the Psalms, which are the work of trained disciples of various schools. It may have received its present form as part of the collection which contained the song of Hezekiah (Isa. xxxviii. 10–20) of three centuries later. (3) The time of David was unfavourable to psalm-making. Even if "psalms" were the natural expression of David's soul and heart, he could not have written the canonical Psalms in the age in which he lived, any more than Homer and his colleagues could have written the *Prometheus Vinctus* or the *Antigone*. A great poet, such as David was, may create a literary style, but he cannot create a literary atmosphere, much less a world of action and emotion which it envelops. The ruling ideas of the Psalms are such conceptions of spiritual needs, and of Jehovah's power to satisfy those needs by his various and abounding grace, as the religious people of David's time, from lack of education and experience, could not have cherished. (4) There is really no biblical tradition to the effect that David was a psalm writer, the titles to the Psalms being unauthentic. Historically we know of him as a lyrical poet indeed, but as a poet of his time and circumstances, especially moved by love and friendship, and also as a minstrel and a patron of minstrelsy (Amos vi. 5).

§ 910. The case would seem at first to be somewhat different with Solomon and the Proverbs. Apophthegms, parables, pregnant witty sayings, were indigenous in Israel, and even apart from the evidence of the book of Proverbs, it is doubtful whether any national literature is so rich in such utterances as is the Bible. This gift of proverb-making was shared by several peoples more or less nomadic to the south and east of Palestine (cf. Prov. xxx. and xxxi. and 1 K. iv. 30 f. EV.), whose genius must have influenced that of the poets and sages of Israel. The age of Solomon was, however, not the time of the " Wisdom " school of Biblical literature, which combined religious and ethical earnestness with philosophic reflectiveness. No one of these qualities is to be expected from Solomon and his colleagues, who appear to have been chiefly distinguished for practical sagacity and worldly shrewdness. Collections, oral and written, of wise and witty observations, of parables like that of Nathan, and of fables like that of Jotham, were doubtless made in Solomon's time; and the first collection of proverbs having borne his name, all subsequent ones, of which it was the nucleus and the occasion, received a similar honour. Yet we must beware of imagining that very many utterances of Solomon and his associates have been transferred to the book of Proverbs. The Hebrew *māshāl* is just as comprehensive a term as is our "proverb," and not every *māshāl* was religious or ethical in its purpose. On the other hand, since a good deal of Proverbs is non-religious and non-ethical, and so out of harmony with the object of the final collection, it is probable that some of the sayings of this more secular age were borne along by mouth or pen to the latest days.

§ 911. This distinction between the secular and the religious in the development of Hebrew thought and life is fundamental to any rational conception of the history of biblical literature. The antithesis, as thus made, is of course purely modern and critical. The Hebrews of these times were not conscious of it. The sphere of religion, that is, of association with Jehovah, was universal within the limits of Israel. His operation and influence extended to every domain of thought and action. Hence, Jehovah was supposed not merely to give oracles on the outcome of human enterprises: He was also the giver of wisdom and of all the endowments of the seer, the poet, the warrior, and the ruler.[1] A very sane and wholesome belief, it will be agreed; but the point now to be made is that the men to whom canonical literature of a high spiritual order is ascribed do not appear to have lived within that sphere of religious experience with which this literature is conversant. The time came at length when the best minds[2] in Israel received, enjoyed, and illustrated the truths that nourish the life of the spirit, and they were the authors of that which really makes the Old Testament what it has been to the world.

§ 912. With the reign of David and Solomon the first stage of Hebrew literature reaches its close. This we have called (§ 883) the period of heroic poetry, or of the epic ballad. The reader may now see in how far the term is justified. It will be observed that though the subjects of the compositions are somewhat varied, they all fall under the one head of heroic tradition. Hence, also, there is here no artistically developed epic[3] like the *Iliad*, the *Odyssey*, or the *Æneid*. Yet there is what may be called a rudimentary epic, a body of epical germs and materials,

---

[1] Compare Cheyne, *Jewish Religious Life after the Exile* (1898), p. 131 f.

[2] We do Nathan and other contemporaries of David and Solomon injustice if we assume that the latter were the highest religious spirits of the time. It cannot have escaped attention that David and Solomon, the first successful kings of Israel, were the only kings to whom any large portion of the literature is ascribed. Is not this to be explained by the fact that their successors, men like the rest of their kind, lived in the clearer light of history?

[3] Of the higher epic there is no genuine specimen in Semitic literature. The Gilgamesh ("Nimrod") epic of the Babylonians is the nearest approach to it. But there is abundance of the ballad epos, which, if the artistic genius had been present, might have been organized into a commanding epic poem. Cf. R. G. Moulton, *Literary Study of the Bible* (1898), p. 229 f.

chiefly in the form of the heroic ballad. There is thus a true epos in the earliest Hebrew literature, though it has not been unified and coördinated so as to illustrate a single great theme. We may sum up here by recalling the characteristics of the literature of this period. Unlike that of subsequent stages, it was mainly, if not wholly, circulated by word of mouth. Another distinction is that it was very fragmentary. Characteristic also is the conspicuous absence in it of spiritual religion as a motive power in life and conduct.

§ 913. This last-named distinction would seem to mark a cardinal defect. And yet, from the earliest known beginnings, there was in Hebrew literature, as in the Hebrew community, the germ of the most powerful religion which the world has felt and known, an intellectual and moral impulse, a master idea destined for the uplifting and propelling of the race. Since no epoch in history or literature is cut off from a preceding epoch, and no people develops except from itself, the later Israel which we know of must have drawn some deep inspiration from this first long period of its life and thought. And that which we find in it, fitful and spasmodic, it is true, — like the fortune of the tribes and the nation, — and yet a vital and inextinguishable force, is Israel's sense of Jehovah's guardianship and of its own destiny. Hence, we shall not go far astray in holding the most precious of the poems and the sayings of the olden time to have been the "Song of the Exodus," the "Song of Deborah," the "Book of the Wars of Jehovah," the "Book of Jashar," and the "Blessing of Jacob."

§ 914. To show how this sentiment shaped itself towards worthier ends, how it gradually came to be cherished in its most vitalizing and potential form, with an elevating and inspiring view of Jehovah's character, is the task of the historian of Hebrew literature. Here it must suffice to point out when and how the successive literary periods were introduced. The next determining event was the division of the kingdom. This catastrophe and the political condition of the time generally were unfavourable to poetical composition. But there was much to suggest the employment of the new art of prose writing in preserving the traditions of the tribal and national heroes of the times nearly preceding.

§ 915. To appreciate this new development we must make an important distinction with regard to the useful, but easily misunderstood term "national" literature. While the whole of the early literature may rightly be called national, the inspiration of nationality as derived from the united kingdom of David and Solomon (§ 900) was rather that of an ideal than of an accomplished fact. As has been shown already (§ 526 f.), it was only under David that a real union of the tribes was officially fostered, and even then nothing more was actually realized than a coalescence of the northern and southern divisions. There was, indeed, for a time a national aspiration. But as far as it was a political sentiment it was an outgrowth of the pre-regal rather than of the regal period. And after the division whatever there was of patriotic feeling was nourished only by the common worship of Jehovah among the children of Israel, which was always the chief unifying force throughout Hebrew history.

§ 916. Hence we find (1) that in the subsequent literature the history of Israel is viewed from different standpoints, according as the writer belongs to the northern or southern kingdom; (2) that much of the history-making consists of reminiscences of tribal or sectional conditions; (3) that when the undivided kingdom bulks largely in the literature it is more or less idealized; (4) that the national idea, if cherished at all, is cherished by those who are most concerned for the religion of Jehovah, the God of the whole of Israel; (5) that the insistence on this idea necessarily involves the idealizing of the kingdom as it was once united under David — hence the beginning of the Messianic hope and ideal.

§ 917. We are now introduced to the first consecutive prose writing that has been preserved in the canonical books. There can be little doubt that the central and earliest portion of the book of Judges (ii. 6–xvi.)[1] was the product of a time not much later than the disruption. It gives an account of the deeds of the local rulers who kept order, in their several districts, between the time of the settlement and the kingdom (§ 187 ff.). The recollections of their actions are, for the most part, clear and vivid. There is least adherence to the literal style of narrative in the history of Samson (ch. xiii.–xvi.), which is a separate, elaborate story of the purely heroic type. This circumstance alone would suffice to show that the tales were gathered and published in the northern kingdom, remote from the scene of Samson's exploits. But the way in which Judah is elsewhere ignored, and is here referred to only as contributing a single champion,[2] puts the matter beyond a doubt. We may well suppose that the popular stories of David's career, which were so greatly to the advantage of the kingdom of Judah, were matched by the collectors of traditional tales with reminiscences of the great deeds of the northern leaders.

§ 918. That the composition of these stories in their first published form is separated by a considerable interval from that of the preceding cycle, appears plainly from the fact that they are written in simple prose, and that

---

[1] That is, apart from the song of Deborah (§ 897) and the phrases introductory to each section, with other additions by the Deuteronomic compiler (§ 1361), for whose agency here see Driver, *Intr.*, and Moore, *Commentary on Judges*, pp. xix ff., and the authorities quoted in these works. Moore dates the older of the two sources, which he identifies (after Schrader, Stade, and Budde) with J and E respectively, in the first half of the ninth century B.C. This is probably too late to afford a connection with the stream of living tradition which comprises the narrative of the greater judges.

[2] Perhaps the story of Samson is introduced from the desire to give some place (cf. iii. 31) to the wars with the Philistines, which were so important in Israel's history, and in which the northern tribes played no very distinguished part.

the style is already that of classic narrative Hebrew. From the nature of the subject and the heroic style generally we must, however, assign this main part of Judges to the period of the prose epic or "heroic prose" (§ 883). That a prosaic garb was adopted instead of a poetical was due to the fact that the age was prosaic. The land was troubled; but it was not excited, only perplexed and baffled. The old ideals were shattered; and, especially in the northern kingdom, pressing problems of rehabilitation and readjustment left no room for the play of the genius of romance. We may infer from the fact that the song of Deborah alone is given in the poetic form[1] that the narratives were of later composition.

§ 919. Of kindred style and origin is the story of David's reign and his personal life as king, which was composed in Jerusalem, perhaps at a somewhat later date than the tales of the judges. This narrative embraces almost all of 2 Sam. v.–vii. and ix.–xx. It is an extraordinarily faithful and vivid picture of one of the most interesting and memorable kingly lives. A distinct work is the history of Saul (1 Sam. ix., x. 1–16, xi., xiii., xiv.). Some uncertainty hangs over the time and place of the origin of this section. Yet the freshness and naturalness of the narrative, and its presentation of the older view of the establishment of the kingdom, that it was a necessary movement approved by Jehovah (ctr. 1 Sam. viii. and xii.), point to a comparatively early date. More doubtful is the position of the remainder of the history of David, within which the Jerusalem court history has been imbedded, the whole running from 1 Sam. xvi. to 2 K. ii. The reference to "kings of Judah" in 1 Sam. xxvii. 6 would seem

---

[1] The sayings of Samson (Jud. xiv. 14, 18; xv. 16) are merely incidental to the narrative. Yet they are significant as illustrating the point made above as to the special character of the tradition and story of Samson. It is to be noted that it is only in the old heroic epos that the characters speak poetically. So in the wisdom fables of India, (Hitopadeça, Panchatantra, etc.), the narrative is prose, while the speakers talk in verse.

to bring the time pretty well down below the disruption. It has also been argued that the absence of partiality for either of the kings or for the institution of the kingdom points to a later period. We must content ourselves meanwhile with claiming for the first half century after the schism the history of Saul and the Jerusalem biography of David as king. Of somewhat later date is the story of the fortunes of the Ark (1 Sam. iv.–vi.), centering in Shiloh and its sanctuary, and composed in northern Israel.

§ 920. We have now to deal with a different order of composition, the first "Book of the Covenant," contained in Ex. xx. 22–xxiii. Most critics assign the work to the great E document (§ 923 ff.). But E was probably not its first compiler: it bears the mark of a prior juridical codification. Much of its contents, therefore, is of older date, how old we cannot say. In any case it is a mistake to make the time of David the absolute *terminus a quo;*[1] for the period of the judges was one in which the establishing of precedents ("statutes") for new conditions and emergencies was an absolute necessity. The laws represent the growth of a simple pastoral and especially agricultural jurisprudence, and the absence of regulations concerning the special relations of city life show that the bulk of them were formulated, or at least practised, before the monarchy. They are of priceless value, not simply for the legislation itself, but also for the proof they afford that Israel was not a wholly ill-regulated society under the judges.[2] Now, if such laws existed long before their final compilation, should they not be treated like the heroic poetry as the literary records of earlier times? No; for

---

[1] As is done by Cornill, *Einl.*[4] (1896), p. 69.

[2] The book of Judges is a reminder that the Hebrew historical narrative is selective and dramatically one-sided and extreme. Critics have thought that in my sketch of a well-to-do householder of the later period of the judges (§ 503 ff.) I have transferred to this time the conditions of a later age. But I avowedly chose a favourable specimen of his class, and his environment is not pictured in the brightest colours.

laws were not "literature" (cf. § 899). They were not published even by word of mouth at the time of their first observance (cf. § 882). They were customs, usages, prescriptions, which for ages needed no outward authentication. The several courts which put them in force, whether of elders, judges, or priests of the local sanctuaries (§ 486 ff.), were themselves the embodiment of law or "direction," as representatives of Jehovah; and it was only some higher or wider necessity that led to their collection and publication.

§ 921. Moreover, the laws are, in the strict sense, a digest or abstract of the best rules of procedure written in the terse and business-like form that befits an age devoid of preachers and moralists, and thus distinguished from their successor, the Deuteronomic code. Yet we must make a distinction. Those laws that were really practical and operative do not occupy nearly all of the document. There is at least one other large element comprising principles and appeals in the guise of ordinances. Thus we have the commands not to wrong or oppress a "stranger" (xxii. 21; cf. § 552), not to afflict a widow or orphan (v. 22), followed by reasons grounded in the will (or the character) of Jehovah (cf. vs. 26 f.); and these are not coördinate with the preceding enactments. They are rather of the tone and spirit of the long hortatory appendix (xxiii. 20–33).

§ 922. This combination is striking. What does it imply? Two general explanations are possible. The object of the publication was either literary and educative or else it was intended as an authoritative manual with official sanction. In the one case the compiler and editor was one of a guild or class of thinkers and writers imbued with high patriotic and religious aims. In the other case the instigators were the king and nobles. At first sight the latter view is the more plausible, for the aim of the publication seems a practical one. On account of the apparent influence of E, we then actually think of the northern kingdom (§ 930); and the era of reconstruction and readjustment under Omri (§ 212) seems a suitable occasion.[1] But a closer view makes the other hypothesis seem more tenable. Taken as a whole, the work is too advanced ethically and religiously for that era or any proximate date. Making all due allowance for the defective character of the narrative accounts of these times, it remains certain (cf. § 979 ff.) that the religion and morality of the leading men in either kingdom were still below the stage of theory and propagandism; and the publication of the code in its complete form under their auspices is therefore highly improbable. On the other hand, the sentimental, non-practical sections were superadded for a purpose. They are already beyond the scope and intent of the effective statutes which, as has been shown,[2] are merely the best jurisprudence of a simple, half-patriarcha society, and not necessarily the outcome of exceptiona. moral and religious sentiments. In fact, as will appear in the more obvious case of Deuteronomy, the Old Testament legislation as published never had statutory validity or a directly practical purpose. It was intended to connect the highest law and justice of the day with the fountain of law and justice, Jehovah the true God of Israel. Hence we have not yet arrived at the all-important point where we can find the higher principle of life and thought in active operation. For this we must turn to the two great works J and E.

§ 923. J and E are the somewhat vague and mystical, but convenient designation of the remains of two documents found interwoven with one another in the Hexateuch. They were, when complete, two histories (to use the modern term) of Israel, from the earliest times till the settlement in Canaan. Neither of them appears to have been originally a single composition, and each of them

---

[1] Or, if the treatise be assigned (less reasonably) to J and the kingdom of Judah, we will naturally think of the reformation of Asa (1 K. xv.).
[2] See W. R. Smith, OTJC.² p. 340 ff.

shows evidence of growth and of internal combination and adjustment. Moreover, each of them had taken up into itself, at least by the time it assumed its final form, some of the compositions already mentioned in our survey; thus it is probably E that contains the first "Book of the Covenant" just spoken of; while J has, among other things, the oldest traditions of Israel and the race generally. They were, however, combined in one complete and separate work (J E) before the publication of Deuteronomy. They are marked off by striking characteristics from P, with which they have many topics in common. More properly, P is marked off plainly from them as the product of a different movement and stamped with the impress of a much later age. J and E have strong mutual resemblances and, although produced within different environments, are evidently the result of the same or closely associated literary and religious impulses. Yet the differences in points of view and in purpose are so real and important that no single term, except the very general phrase "prophetic histories," has been devised to describe them. This designation distinguishes them from the priestly document (P), and also implies that they were completed, if not entirely compiled, in the age of the great prophets, and embody some distinctively prophetic ideas.

§ 924. J, however, is so deeply imbued with the prophetic spirit that the name is sometimes applied to it alone. Its chief outward mark is its use of the name Yahwè (Jehovah) for the Divine Being from the beginning, while E is equally consistent in the employment of Elohim; hence the term Yahwistic or Jehovistic applied to the document and the writer as distinguished from Elohistic. To the combined history in the Pentateuch drawn from J, E, and P,[1] J furnishes the most continuous

---

[1] Naturally authorities differ with regard to the assignment of many passages to their sources, but these passages are seldom of great length or importance, and a presentation of the results of criticism is quite feasible and very helpful. A detailed exhibition by chapter and verse of the

story. There are, indeed, no important breaks in his narrative, as far as the career of the main characters and of the nation as a whole is described, though significant facts are supplied by E, even more than by P, which bulks so much more largely and deals more with institutions and their founders. E, indeed, although an original document of immense importance, performs in our present text a function mainly supplementary. It does not begin till Gen. xv. Its most valuable contributions relate to the legislative history and material.

§ 925. A fairly good idea of the contents and spirit of J and E may be gained from the statement of some of the topics dealt with by each of them exclusively. Thus from J, as already indicated (§ 885), we have the account of the creation of the world of men (as distinguished from that of "the heavens and the earth" by P). From him alone proceeds the story of the probation and fall of "the man" and his "helpmeet," of the first sacrifice, the first murder, and the career of Cain and his descendants (Gen. ii. 4–iv.). To the accounts of the Flood, the promise to Noah, the national or racial genealogies (Gen. vi.–x.) J and P have both contributed; but the settlement of Babylonia (x. 8–12) and the dispersion thence of the human race (Gen. xi. 1–9) are described only by J. From him, too, we have the whole narrative of the relations of Abraham with Lot and the cities of the Plain (Gen. xviii., xix.), the romantic story of the quest of a wife for Isaac (Gen. xxiv.), and nearly all that is told of the earlier life of Jacob and Esau (most of Gen. xxv.–xxvii.), the episode of Judah's family history (Gen. xxxviii.), and a large portion, partly duplicated with E, of the story of Joseph, particularly the actions and con-

---

respective contributions of J, E, and P to the Pentateuch appears in Cornill, *Einl.*[4] (1896), p. 19 f. The analysis of Genesis, Exodus, and Numbers, with a discussion, is given by Driver, *Intr.*[6] (1897), pp. 14–17, 22–24, 28–32, 60–69. Leviticus is universally given entire to P, and nothing of Deuteronomy is credited to any of the three.

versations in which Judah takes part. The Blessing of Jacob (Gen. xlix. 2–27) was inserted by J (§ 905). In Exodus, as a whole, J is less prominent than either E or P. He is most largely represented in the account of the preliminaries to the migration from Egypt, and of the flight.[1] But in Numbers, which is mainly an institutional and statistical book, both J and E are overshadowed by P. When they appear it is usually difficult to distinguish the parts of the combined narrative (J E). From them come the most interesting sections of Numbers: Hobab's guidance of Israel, the murmuring of the people at Taberah, the appointment of seventy elders, and the complaint of Aaron and Miriam against Moses (chs. x. 29–xii.)[2] and the strictly historical or narrative portion of the book between the departure from Kadesh Barnea to the settlement of the two and a half tribes east of the Jordan, including the extracts from ancient poems and the episode of Balaam (chs. xx.–xxv. 6, and most of ch. xxxii.).[3] In the book of Joshua, which, as part of an original Hexateuch, is properly an appendix to the Pentateuch, and in which the distinction of the sources is very difficult to make,[4] J E is to be taken as practically one document, comprising most of the story of the conquest of Canaan (chs. i.–xii.),[5] while the account of its allotment among the tribes (chs. xiii.–xxiv.) is chiefly the work of P.

§ 926. The most important contributions of E may be summarily indicated: an essential part of Abraham's vision of Israel's possession of Canaan (Gen. xv., not easily separable from J), the exposure of Sarah at Gerar, the expulsion and relief of Hagar, the covenant at Beersheba, the trial of Abraham's faith (Gen. xx.–xxii.),

---

[1] See below (§ 926) what is said of E in this connection.

[2] Ch. xii. is generally thought to belong to E.

[3] Ch. xxiv. probably belongs mainly to J, and chs. xxi.–xxiii. to E.

[4] Cf. Cornill, *Einl.*[4] p. 80 f.

[5] Very important, however, are the Deuteronomic additions, comprising the whole of ch. i. and frequent later insertions; see Driver, p. 104 ff.

Jacob's vision and vow at Bethel (Gen. xxviii. 11 ff.), the ascription of Jacob's prosperity to divine providence, the flight of Jacob and his wives from Laban, and the covenant between Jacob and Laban (most of ch. xxxi.), Jacob's renunciation of "strange gods," and his second visit to Bethel (Gen. xxxv. 1-8), and the death of Rachel (Gen. xxxv. 16-20), large portions of the story of Joseph,[1] Jacob's blessing of Ephraim and Manasseh (Gen. xlviii.), Joseph's formal forgiveness of his brethren, and his death (Gen. l. 15 ff.). In Exodus comes first E's version[2] of the events leading to the departure from Egypt, apparently resting on a distinct tradition and enhancing the providential character of the deliverance by emphasizing the feebleness and dependence of Israel and the haughty sternness of Pharaoh. E inserts, also, the song of the Exodus (§ 890). He alone tells of the contest with Amalek (ch. xvii.) and the attempt to organize the tribes on an administrative principle (Ex. xviii.; cf. § 455 ff.). He is the principal source of what is told of the primary Sinaitic legislation — its preliminaries (ch. xix.), the Decalogue (ch. xx.; § 892), the first Book of the Covenant (chs. xxi.-xxiii.; § 920), the narrative of the golden calf, and the appointment of Joshua as minister to Moses (chs. xxxii. 1-xxxiii. 11).[3] Of E in Numbers and Joshua enough for our present purpose has been said in the last paragraph, but we must not overlook the poetical extracts in Num. xxi. (§ 894) or the "Blessing of Moses" in Deut. xxxiii. (§ 935).

---

[1] For a skilful exhibition of the points of difference, with a citation of the passages assignable to each of the sources, see Driver, pp. 17-19.

[2] Developed by Bacon in *Triple Tradition of the Exodus* (1894), following up his articles in the *Journal of Biblical Literature* (1890-1893). His analysis shows the antithesis between J and E to be much greater than had been supposed. J, for example, makes Israel in Egypt to have been prosperous, socially important, and numerous.

[3] The remainder of this legislative section (xxxiii. 12-xxxiv. 28) is an intricate combination of J and E, except perhaps the "Little Book of the Covenant" (xxxiv. 11-28), which is by most critics assigned to J.

§ 927. A glance at the passages above cited will reveal the main characteristics of J and E. J is the story teller and the dramatist of the Old Testament. For vividness, selective and graphic skill, and touching simplicity, he is unsurpassed in any literature. He is at once the most realistic and the most sympathetic of narrators; witness the trembling of Isaac, the cry of Esau (Gen. xxvii. 33 f.), and the appeal of Judah (Gen. xliv. 18 ff.). Nothing human is alien or repulsive to him (Gen. xxx. 14 ff.; xxxviii.); and he is equally at home with the divine. Thus he is the most anthropomorphic of Old Testament writers in his representations of the Deity. "He *fashions, breathes* into man the breath of life, *plants, places, takes, sets, brings, closes up, builds,* etc. (Gen. ii. 7, 8, 15, 19, 21, 22), and even *walks* in the garden (iii. 8). He *comes down* to see the tower built by man and to confound their speech (Gen. xi. 5, 7; so xviii. 21; Ex. iii. 8), *visits* the earth in visible form (Gen. xviii., xix.), *meets* Moses and seeks to slay him (Ex. iv. 24), *takes off* the chariot wheels of the Egyptians (xiv. 25)."[1] His moral and religious teaching is well characterized by Dillmann:[2] "He is distinguished by the abundance of choice and instructive thoughts, of weighty ethical and religious truths, which he knows how to breathe into his legendary stories, or rather to draw from them, without detracting from the poetic flavour and childlike simplicity of expression which they carry with them from their currency upon the lips of the people. Among the three narrators he shows the deepest knowledge of the nature, origin, and progress of sin among mankind, of God's counteracting work, of his plan of salvation (Gen. iii. 15 f.; v. 29; viii. 21 f.; ix. 26 f.; xii. 2 f.; xviii. 19), of the choice of God's chosen instruments and their education towards

---

[1] Driver, *Intr.*⁶ pp. 9, 121. The italics are our author's.

[2] *Die Genesis erklärt* (4th ed.), p. xiii. See also the more detailed analysis by Dillmann, in his *Numeri, Deut. und Josua* (1886), p. 629 f., quoted by Driver, p. 120.

faith, obedience, and rightful living, of the destiny of Israel to bring about the saving of the nations."

§ 928. E has not the literary charm and power wielded by J, though he is not deficient in narrative skill (Gen. xxii.). He has a fondness for details; uses freely the names of persons and places. He does not so much try to tell a story as to keep alive the occasion and the remembrance of beliefs and traditions. Hence, he is specially attracted by the ancient sanctuaries, particularly those of the northern kingdom, and at the same time gives a chief place to the laws and customs that have grown up under the theocracy. Thus, while J is most deeply concerned about the ideas or principles of Jehovah's government and revelation, E is set upon exhibiting the various forms and modes in which God rules and manifests himself to his people. On the one hand we have from him the history of national organization and legislation (Ex. xviii.-xxiii.), and on the other a record of the indirect disclosures of dreams and visions of the night and voices from heaven (Gen. xv.; xxii. 11, 15; xxviii. 11 ff.; xxxvii. 5 ff.), as contrasted with the bodily appearances of Jehovah set before us by J. Though not so deeply imbued with the prophetic spirit as J, he represents the progress of institutional religion up to the highest pre-Deuteronomic level. In his story of Jacob he speaks of the patriarch erecting a pillar as a Bethel [1] or "residence of God" (Gen. xxviii. 18, 22) on the site of the most important sanctuary of the northern kingdom; yet he records, also, how Jacob put away the "alien gods" from his household (Gen xxxv. 2 ff.; cf. Josh. xxiv. 14 ff.). Abraham is to him a "prophet" (Gen. xx. 7), though of a very unspiritual type; while in his sketch of the career of Moses the prophetic ideal is more nearly reached (Ex. xxxiii. 11; Num.

---

[1] Greek βαίτυλος and βαιτύλιον, a sacred stone (in Damascius and others), came from Canaanitic Phœnicia. On the worship of sacred stones, see especially W. R. Smith, RS.² p. 207 ff. The literature of this aspect of "Bethel" is given in DB. I, 278 note.

xii. 6 ff.). Above all, he is concerned to set forth God's providential guidance and control of his people.

§ 929. J is a composite work. This is not the place for the proof of this position by a detailed analysis,[1] but considerations of a broader kind may be urged: (1) There is evidence of divergent views in J on matters of fact. Among the instances are the following. In Gen. ix. 18 f. Shem, Ham, and Japhet are the ancestors of all succeeding mankind, while in vs. 25-27 Canaan, as son (or representative) of Ham, is coördinated with Shem and Japhet, as the head of a distinct people. In Gen. iv. 20-22 contemporaries of the writer seem to be descended from Cainites, and therefore not from the sole survivors of the Flood. This with the survival of *Nephilim* (Num. xiii. 33, J E; cf. Gen. vi. 4) seems to show that an authority was used by J who did not take account of the destruction by the Deluge. (2) Such a startling break in continuous discourse as is shown in Gen. xxxviii. indicates a direct secondary contributor to J's narrative of the patriarchs. This is not a case of the insertion of older compositions, such as those frequently found in E or such as the Blessing of Jacob in J himself. The material has been adapted by the hand of the responsible writer of the book. (3) This instance suggests a more general observation. The moral and sentimental interval between Gen. xxxviii. and the history of Joseph in the context is but one of many apparent literary inconsistencies in the work. What is the explanation? Not merely that J was a realistic writer of wide human sympathies (§ 927), but besides that the materials

---

[1] See the *résumé* in Cornill, *Einl.*[4] pp. 42-46, tracing the brief history of the question, and cf. Kautzsch, *Abriss*, p. 153 f. The inquiry so far has been systematically pursued only in connection with Genesis. Budde's *Biblische Urgeschichte* (1883) has given the strongest impulse to the discussion. See König, *Einleitung* (1893), pp. 197-200, for a conservative view. Agreement as to the sections and their limits has not been reached. Driver, in his *Intr.* (p. 123), scarcely touches the subject. The question is one of importance from its bearing on the history of prophetic ideas.

of his book came from different sources in different regions of Palestine, and also from different ages. It may be said that no writer would introduce into his work what was not in harmony with his own ideals, and that such scruples, if justified, should also throw doubt on the final unity and completeness of the work. Not necessarily so; for the Old Testament compilers habitually made use of various traditions which attained a certain canonical standing through venerable age and ancestral associations, and what the later Jehovistic circle might not have appropriated from current literature it adopted and utilized from the old.[1] The composite character of E, though extremely probable, is more difficult of proof;[2] nor is the question of such biblical importance as that of the composition of J. It is understood that E has transferred bodily much older literature, chiefly poetical and legislative (§ 894, 925 f.); but the narrative portion does not lend itself to obvious partition.

§ 930. It is the unanimous opinion of critics that E was composed in the northern kingdom. The prominence of Joseph, Ephraim, and Reuben (as contrasted with Judah in J), and such sacred places as Bethel, Shechem, and Beersheba (cf. Am. v. 5; viii. 14; 1 K. xix. 3), with many other indications, point surely to this conclusion. Nor can the approximate time of composition be a question of much uncertainty. (1) E's religious position is far beyond that of the time of the early kings, while there is no evidence that the author had come under the influence of either Amos or Hosea. Thus the time would not be later than 770-760 B.C. (2) The early turbulent

---

[1] This is little to be wondered at when Samson is cited as one of the ancient worthies even in the later New Testament times (Heb. xi. 32). Have we not also our "Saint" David?

[2] Cornill, *Einl.*[4] pp. 39-41, following in the main the lead of Kuenen, approves of a division into E[1] and E[2]. So far there has been no general acceptance of Kuenen's results, though his discussion has opened a promising field of inquiry.

times of the kingdom are past; their history lies before the writer; the traditions have been gathered up and are grouped around definite persons and places; legislative digests have been made. The date therefore is probably after the Syrian wars. (3) There is in the book a consciousness of national strength and achievement with no note of trouble to mar the harmony of the retrospect. The decline of the kingdom had therefore not begun. All this points to the first part of the reign of Jeroboam II. (4) While linguistic marks in general are not obvious, there is one of high significance. In Genesis E uses "Yahwè" for the Deity not at all, and even after the declaration of Ex. iii. 14 f. very sparingly. Whatever may have been the motive of the preferential use of "Elohim,"[1] there is no doubt that an age of theological reflection had been reached; and that while the book may have been composed by a single writer, he was a member of a sort of Elohistic school. Taken all in all, the evidence points to very nearly 770 B.C.

§ 931. Similar questions relating to J are not so easily disposed of. While the majority of inquirers hold that the work proceeded from the southern kingdom, a few critics of weight, such as Reuss, Kuenen, Schrader, pronounce in favour of the northern, on the ground that no Judaite would have given prominence to the northern shrines of Shechem, Bethel, and Peniel (Gen. xii. 6; xxviii. 13 ff.; xxxii. 30 f.). This phenomenon has given rise to the hypothesis[2] that the foundation of the work ("J¹"; cf. § 929) was laid in the northern kingdom, while the later form of the book is a Judaite recension. But such a supposition appears unnecessary when we consider that the prophets of Judah were patriotic Israelites and held

---

[1] It is conceivable that in the struggle waged by the prophetic party in northern Israel against false worship, the use of Elohim as a singular (with a plural verb in Gen. xx. 13, xxxi. 53) was encouraged as an effective protest against the plurality of deities.

[2] See Kautzsch, *Abriss*, p. 154.

fast to all the treasures of common ancient tradition. On the other hand, the association of Abraham and Jacob with Hebron, and the prominence given to Judah, the head of the tribe, as well as the subordinate place assigned to Joshua, are explicable only on the theory of a Judaite origin.

§ 932. To fix the date of J, that is, the date of the finished work, is not easy. There are no allusions to historical events that justify a certain inference.[1] General considerations may, however, be presented: First, the manifold geographical and ethnological knowledge shown by J points to a stage of culture not earlier than the days of Uzziah. Notice particularly the accurate transcription and grouping of Babylonian and Assyrian (Gen. x. 11 f.) and of south and east Arabian names (vs. 26 ff.). Secondly, there are strong indications of Assyrian (Babylonian) influence in J's primitive history. While it is in every way probable that the earliest traditions of Genesis came to J by direct tradition (§ 886), the details of the setting of the creation story (Gen. ii.) and of the dispersion (Gen. xi.) were evidently due to contemporary information. In other words, the acquaintance with Babylonia shown by J was acquired through direct knowledge of the country itself or of its literature. Such advantages were possessed by Judaites only after the reign of Ahaz, to whose initiative it was due that Assyrian and Babylonian worship and manners became fashionable in Jerusalem (§ 640, 856). Thirdly, the advanced stage of theological reflection shown in the profound conception of human nature and its moral tendencies and possibilities (Gen. ii.-iv.), and of the inner

---

[1] It has been supposed that a *terminus a quo* is given in Gen. ix. 25 f. in an allusion to the servitude of the Canaanites, which is thought to have been realized in the days of Solomon (1 K. ix. 21). But the reference is too general to be of value. At any rate, it cannot be seriously held that any essential part of the work was written as early as the time of Solomon.

conditions of righteousness (Gen. xv. 6), place J not only in advance of E but also on a level with the literary prophets. It was therefore quite probably toward the close of the eighth century B.C. that J was composed.

§ 933. We cannot conjecture the motive that prompted the composition of the earlier stratum, or strata, of J. But the book, as it has come to us, may perhaps be accounted for as follows. It was not written from the Judaite point of view alone, as opposed to that of the northern kingdom, but rather from the standpoint of Judah as representing the whole of the true Israel. This is shown by its impartial reference to places and persons of common ancient tradition (§ 931). Hence it can scarcely have been written while the northern kingdom, with its religious and (from 734 B.C.) political rivalry, was still in existence. But after the downfall of Samaria (722-1), E being in the hands of the prophetic party in the southern kingdom as a literary and spiritual legacy, what more natural than to set forth, in a work of similar scope and plan, that all things from the beginning of the world were under Jehovah's control; that his was a world-religion; and that the type of worship and belief cherished in Judah and Jerusalem was that of the patriarchs? Why the theme was not pursued further, why neither J nor E systematically continued his narrative beyond the settlement in Canaan, may be understood in the light of the fact that histories of the judges and the early kings were already in circulation (cf. § 917 ff.).

§ 934. Another observation may be allowed. It may seem unfitting that J should be placed on an ethical and spiritual level with the early literary prophets, in spite of the inequalities and the *chiaroscuro* colouring of his work. But we may remember that we have here to do with Hebrew "historical" writing, which, while it is true to the past as far as manners and customs are concerned, also idealizes the past and invests its characters with the glamour of that quality which we may call the traditional heroic (cf. § 929). We must, in all fairness, judge of such an author by his best; and this best is no whit below the moral and spiritual heights attained by the prophets of the eighth century B.C. Yet we must beware of classifying J, or the compilers of the "prophetic histories" generally, with the literary prophets, or the reforming, preaching prophets, who preceded them. They were pupils, while the prophets were the masters. They were not public men, but quiet observers and students. They were not originators but conservators of truth. Hence only the best that they preserved to us can be compared with the genuine prophetic revelation. Their strength lay partly in this discipleship, and partly in a literary brotherhood or guildhood, to which the spirit and habit of the inspired prophets were altogether alien.

§ 935. But these great works do not make up the total literary history from 900 B.C. (cf. § 919) to the flourishing period of literary prophecy. J and E were themselves united into one work (J E) soon after the completion of J. The "Blessing of Moses" (Deut. xxxiii.), preserved in E (§ 926), was perhaps written in the period of the revival of Israel under Joash and Jeroboam II (§ 262). As contrasted with the "Blessing of Jacob" (§ 905), of which it is an imitation, we observe that now the tribe of Simeon does not appear, that Reuben is near its end, and that Levi has gone over wholly to sacerdotalism. The centre of the poem is the exaltation of Joseph and Ephraim (v. 13–17), and this is significant for the date of its composition. From northern Israel came, also, the stories of Elijah and Elisha (1 K. xvii.–xix., xxi. and 2 K. ii.–ix.), with the historical notices included. The career of Elijah probably formed at first a special work, as did also that of Elisha, while the historical records were of course added by the compiler from special sources. Finally, that account of the history of Samuel and Saul which emphasizes the evils and perils of the institution of the kingdom (cf. § 919), along with the associated narratives (1 S. i.–iii., viii.; x. 17–24; xv.; xvii.–xix.; xxi.; xxii.; xxvi.),[1] is, perhaps, to be assigned to an Ephraimitic writer living in the declining period of northern Israel.

§ 936. Of the writings of the prophets up to the time of Josiah a summary has already been given in connection with the domestic and international events that affected their ministry. Thus, we have passed in review Amos and Hosea in northern, and Isaiah and Micah in southern Israel. Two things are yet lacking for the proper historical treatment of their prophecies. We should show how the most essential elements in their teaching were related to the antecedent thought and life of Israel; and we should, also, try to account for their writings as literary productions. The former question is one that may be more suitably discussed in connection with the development of religion and morals (§ 946 ff.). On the latter topic a few words should be said here.

§ 937. Amos of Tekoa made an epoch (§ 867), one of the greatest in the history of our world. But he did not create the epoch. There were prophets of his own class before him. Those to whom he refers as his colleagues (iii. 7; cf. ii. 11 f.) were not professionals who followed the business merely to earn their bread (cf. vii. 12). Whether, like him, they were born outside of the prophetic guilds or not, they as well as he had something to "prophesy," that is, to speak out spontaneously, as the word literally means. They were of the school of Elijah, who, passing beyond the function of seer[2] and of court counsellor (Nathan, Gad), became a preacher. It was

---

[1] I give this list of passages tentatively from Kautzsch, *Abriss*, p. 157 f. Cf. Budde, *Die Bücher Richter und Samuel* (1890), and *The Text of Samuel*, in SBOT.; Driver, *Intr.*; and Cornill, *Einleitung*, on the chapters in question. The subject is difficult, but a comparatively late date must be assumed for at least most of the material indicated here.

[2] See 1 Sam. ix. 9, where the consciousness of the distinction between the seer and the later prophet is significant for the date of that section of the book (cf. § 919).

these unordained and itinerant preachers that turned the ancient world upside down. Their theme was righteousness and justice, urgently demanded for the pleasing of Jehovah and for the saving of the state. Their commission was simply to have heard the word of Jehovah (Am. iii. 8).

§ 938. As they heard, so they spoke (Num. xxii. 8, 18, 38; xxiii. 3, 12, 26; Am. vii. 15 ff.; Isa. vi. 9 ff.; Jer. i. 7; *et al.*). Yet Amos and Isaiah and Jeremiah had each a well-defined language and style of their own, and these were the result of education and training. But what is more important for our present purpose, there was a characteristic prophetic manner from the beginning. Both in matter and form the discourses of Amos reveal to us a mature and finished work. There is structural completeness in the parallelism of the more strictly poetic portions, and the author has everywhere a command of those rhetorical figures that give grace and form to a masterly oration. But there is, besides, a distinct manner of address and argument which is characteristic of all written prophecy. It is the style of classical Hebrew oratory, and we may call this stage of Hebrew literary development the oratorical period.

§ 939. We have, however, no verbatim reports of the extant prophetic speeches. They have come to us in a form more or less condensed, and in some cases the addresses were never delivered at all. We have to feel our way through them for impressions of the living voice, of the place and the time and the hearers. Much more difficult is it to catch the voices of which the words of the earliest prophecies are the echo. By what intellectual discipline, by what favouring occasions, through what stimulating influences, — apart from moral and religious motives, — was the prophetic type of literature developed? Of one thing we may be certain. The book of Amos was not the first written composition of its kind. Practice in speaking alone cannot account for the concentrated force of expression,[1] the lucidity of order and reasoning distinctive of a work which, in nine short chapters, gives the substance of a score of sermons, which is itself a handbook of social ethics, which gives a survey of the nations, and minutely describes the moral and religious condition of a kingdom. Much practice in writing upon kindred themes must be assumed as an antecedent. This habit of writing, however, was secondary, and was not always, perhaps not often, the business of the prophets themselves. Moreover, the written memorials were sometimes composed much later than the spoken discourses.

§ 940. We shall not, then, go far astray if we regard the practice of public speaking as the chief external stimulus to prophetic composition. Properly considered, Old Testament prophecy, as distinguished from the private or official revelation of the seer, is essentially oratory,[2] the addressing of an assemblage or a community. The occasions were doubtless furnished mainly by the popular gatherings at feasts and for worship at the favourite shrines. Amos himself spoke at Bethel (Am. vii. 10, 13), and the language of the indignant chief priest of the sanctuary implies that the prophet was out of order only because he had inveighed against the royal proprietor of the sanctuary. The roll of Jeremiah was read (Jer. xxxvi. 9 f.) on a great fast day before the temple in Jerusalem. But before the Deuteronomic revolution (§ 860–862), both in northern Israel (Am. v. 21; Hos. ii. 13; EV. 11) and in the kingdom of Judah (Isa. i. 13 f.), festal gatherings were frequent at the principal shrines. The keen interest which the prophets took in them shows that they made them a chief occasion of their

---

[1] Condensation was favoured by the scarcity and costliness of writing materials, just as conversely the average book of the present day mainly consists of cheap stationery. Fancy Amos turning over the pages of his commentators!

[2] It is probable that נטף, a synonym for "prophesy," meaning to "drip," and causative, to "drop" (e.g. Am. vii. 16), is in some way connected with the oral delivery of prophetic messages.

utterances. Thus the part played by popular assemblies in stimulating the earliest literature of Israel (§ 871, 898) was now reënacted on a higher plane in the making of "some better thing," apart from which the older revelation could "not be made perfect."

§ 941. In this communication with the people through the living voice of the prophets there was a vitalizing principle; the same, indeed, as that which, as a saving element, informed the whole of the Old Testament literature. What gave a more than Promethean fire and potency to prophecy was this, that it seized upon and was possessed by living issues of eternal moment. The prophets were the messengers and organs of the ever living God, and hence they found their work and its joy in the present, — in its duties, its hopes, its possibilities. The previous literature had now done its part. The stories of the fathers, the struggles and triumphs, the failures and sins, of the generations that were gone, had linked Israel with a God of revelation and providence, of holiness and faithfulness. But a new order of things had begun. Egyptians and Canaanites and Philistines were no longer dreaded. They were like the Rephaim, huge but impalpable shades. Even the Syrians no longer inspired Israel with terror. But a greater foe was to come, as yet hardly seen except from afar. And who would abide the day of his coming? It was not clear that Jehovah himself would then save and defend his people. Nay, he would turn to be their enemy and would fight against them. For they had forsaken Jehovah, and despised the Holy One of Israel (Isa. i. 4). The very "day of Jehovah," for which they looked, would be "darkness and not light" (Am. v. 18, 20). Only a new and living word could guide and comfort in the gathering gloom. And this was the word of the prophets, a word of light and life.

§ 942. A clear century of literary history, from J E to Deuteronomy, was occupied by prophecy and the prophetic lyrics alone (§ 605 f.). The fact is eloquent of the originality, force, and timeliness of the prophetic word. The literature up to the middle of the eighth century B.C. had dealt with the old order of things that ended with the establishment of a lasting peace and a vigorous government under Jeroboam II and Uzziah. The motives and the progress of the long antecedent history, with the lives of the founders of Israel and the checkered career of Israel itself, had been set forth at large. The fundamental institutions, legal and moral, that were the guardians of its past and seemed to guarantee its future, were written up. But this could not of itself avail to guide and steady the people of Jehovah in the confusion and disorder, international and domestic, of the new Assyrian times. Men who are in an underground labyrinth may see around them by the light of a candle, but only the inbreaking light of the sun can guide them to the upper day. Such, in its way, was the "sure word of prophecy" to all who would heed and follow.

§ 943. And what of the next great event, the publication of Deuteronomy? It was in the true line of evolution of the ancient literature, as it had been deflected by the prophetic movement. Deuteronomy was essentially a completion of the old histories in the spirit and under the impulse of prophecy. J and E showed, in the motive of their composition, that they were looking toward the goal aimed at by the prophets who took their place in the order of revelation. But what to them was an aspiration and an ideal became to the prophets the very breath and bread of life. Where they ended their work, the prophets began theirs. The historians gave the facts of history and of providence. The prophets brought these into vital relation with present issues. They showed that the past, present, and future of Israel were determined by the God of the whole earth, who adjudged the fate of his people according to the laws of his own moral nature. Then came the Deuteronomist, who revived and reinforced the old rules of life and conduct by the application to them of these prophetic principles, thus bringing both the rules and the principles into active operation. J E was a book of institutions and ordinances and of the leadings of Providence (§ 924 ff.). How closely Deuteronomy is connected with it appears from a comparison, which shows that "the laws in J E form the foundation of the Deuteronomic legislation."[1]

§ 944. Thus, Deuteronomy took a practical step beyond J E and the earlier prophets, though still in the same line of development; for it showed that the spirit of obedience to Jehovah and the moral purpose of the former revelation alike required that there should be, on the part of the people, a more complete surrender of the heart and life to his service. To secure a fuller consecration and a purer worship new enactments were made, broader and stronger, dividing sharply between the holy and the unholy, the sacred and the secular, the lawful and the proscribed. Hence Deuteronomy was not merely a repetition of the ancient law: it completed it; it justified it; it spiritualized it. The old historians and seers built an ark of safety for Israel. The prophets guided it through the swelling waters and drifting wrecks of the national deluge. The Deuteronomist took possession of the devastated land, settled it anew, and rededicated it to Jehovah. And with the reënactment of the Covenant (Gen. ix. 13; Deut. v. 3) a bow of promise was seen for a moment in Israel's troubled sky, the storm-cloud of judgment blending with the sunshine of mercy, and showing how earth might be reconciled to heaven.

---

[1] I quote from Driver, to whose useful comparative table of the laws of the Pentateuch (*Intr.*[6] p. 73 ff.), I would refer the reader for further details. A general division of Deuteronomy having been given in § 847 and note, no further analysis need be attempted here, especially as the book is of simple structure, and the recent literature is in every respect adequate. Among special works, the commentaries of Driver (1895) and Andrew Harper (1895) are to be particularly recommended.

§ 945. Here we must close our historical survey of the literature that culminated in Deuteronomy. What specially distinguishes that profound and far-reaching work is the spirit and the sanctions of its teaching and its commands. To appreciate this more subtle quality of the book we need to follow closely the development of moral and religious principles and ideas, as shown in the life and thought of the leading men in Israel's history.

CHAPTER IV

RELIGION AND MORALS

§ 946. Our review of the inner history of Israel (Book VII) has taught us that it was religion that made the deepest lines of cleavage between parties in society and in the state. As far as public policy was concerned, the "Opposition" was normally composed of religious puritans. Civil broils had as their chief exciting cause religious discontent, and the determining if not always the primary political issue in both kingdoms was the question whether Jehovah was to be honoured by a pure and exclusive worship, or whether his rites should be adulterated with those of inferior and discredited deities. Still more profound was the social schism that resulted indirectly from the predominance of the party of religious compromise. It was the partisans of Jehovah who took the side of the suffering and the oppressed, and with their wrongs and their vindication the cause of Jehovah was identified (§ 597, 602). Naturally, it is the political antagonism that is noted in the historical records, and the social strife that finds expression in the reflective literature (§ 598 ff.). It was these political and social crises that led to the composition of the classical writings on the subject; and the movements or events connected with such crises furnish us with our data for an estimate of religious forces and religious progress.

§ 947. We thus see that the great moral issues in Israel were practically religious issues as well. We cannot, however, determine directly the course of moral progress in Israel from the history of its worship and beliefs. We must rather test the genuineness, depth, and power of religion by the moral conduct of its professors. Our earlier studies upon the "society morals and religion" of Israel up to the fall of Samaria and the accession of Hezekiah (§ 539 ff.) dealt mainly with the question of social morality, since the inner development of the people could best be traced in the progress of the community as a whole. Now that we are confronted with the problem of the results of prophetic teaching as tested by the great reformation, we must examine the prevailing types of individual morality in the preceding times. Our inquiry will show that before the prophetic era the morality of the best men in Israel was as a rule both rudimentary and partial. A personal conscience seemed scarcely yet awakened. The higher modes of life and conduct seemed unknown. Such virtues as were practised were of that coarse and robust kind which belongs and is indeed necessary to primitive society.

§ 948.[1] We have to begin with the so-called patriarchal epoch. Before Abraham there is no Bible history in any true sense of the term; and where there is no history there is no morality that can be tested and described. Morality is always much of a social matter, especially among primitive peoples. What the community is in the habit of doing is in general the norm and guide of individual conduct. The practical limits are set on the one side by what the community tolerates, and on the other by what it desires. Further, we know the facts of ancient tribal life only from the record of the deeds of the leaders, in which the figures of Abraham, Isaac, Jacob, and the Twelve stand out in solitary relief.

§ 949. In reading the story of the ancient patriarchs, we must be at once struck with the apparent freedom

---

[1] The substance of § 948–993 is taken, by permission, from my article, "The Moral Evolution of the Old Testament," in the *American Journal of Theology*, I, 658 ff.

and breadth of movement and action which it reveals, the absence of moral restraints, the self-impulsiveness, so to speak, of moral choice. This phenomenon has, to a large extent, its explanation in the conditions of the nomadic life. We have to make, in any case, a distinction between classes of moral acts. There are some deeds which are wrong in the very nature of things, while there are others which are wrong because they are injurious to our fellows or to society. The latter class may at one time be permissible and at another reprehensible. A monumental instance is the discrimination made by Jesus between the ideal marriage bond and the loosening of the relation tolerated in an earlier stage of the history of Israel. Polygamy also is now regarded as immoral in civilized states. But it was sanctioned by high example in ancient Israel. The same is true of slaveholding. Indeed, slaveholding was not, and could not be at any time, interdicted in ancient society. Yet the abuse of the relations thus tolerated or approved was always reckoned an offence. Harsh treatment, either of a wife or a slave, was always wrong. Thus social institutions, themselves subject to change and readjustment, may within their proper spheres raise or lower the conditions and standards of moral obligation.

§ 950. The fundamental consideration in such variable cases is the interest of society. Not that this was a matter of agreement or of contrivance in any way. It was simply the unconscious adjustment of the community to its necessities. Society has progressed mainly by the suppression or gradual abandonment of habits and customs which have been found to be injurious. It is an important and difficult question, how far we are to distinguish between the evils which are in themselves wrong and those whose culpability varies with the requirements of society and its consequent varying moral standards. If we go far enough back in social history, we shall come to a stage where almost any sort of action is justifiable under given circumstances. The decisive sanction was the will of the community; in other words, the usages and customs which formed the basis and bond of union. In ordinary cases individual choice was overborne by the interests of the clan or the family. A striking instance is afforded by the difference of treatment accorded to kinsfolk and clansmen, on the one hand, and to aliens, on the other. Kindnesses, or even the ordinary offices of humanity, would by usage, that is upon principle, be withheld from the latter. What would be counted a crime done to a tribesman was sometimes a meritorious and even an obligatory act when done to an outsider. For the avenger of blood there was no punishment, but rather approbation, since the duty to take up the cause of a kinsman, even if he were in the wrong, was paramount (§ 398). Thus no claim of compassion could avail even in behalf of one who had unwittingly provoked such corporate resentment. It is difficult to see how social morality, which rests essentially on the equal claims of all men for justice if not for mercy, could flourish in these primitive communities. The matter was aggravated by the fact that the sole judge of the avenger was the family or tribal head. It would be strange, indeed, if the common virtues were maintained in the stress and strain of daily life when the vendetta was kept up by the community from a sense of right. When individual action was subordinated to the claims of the community there was little room for that spontaneous choice between opposing courses which is at once the test of moral quality and the basis of moral discipline. Qualities of mind and heart essential to the moral life of the individual were, in the very nature of the case, not yet evoked, since in that stage of society the solidarity of the social unit was a much more obvious thing than the individuality of its several members. Indeed, the notion that the members of the family or kin formed by themselves an undivided life lies at the very foundation of tribalism.

§ 951. Another great moral determinant was the claim of the deities upon the obedience of their followers. We may say in general that in the primitive tribal condition the obligations of a man to his deity are analogous in some respects to those which bind him to the usages or behests of his community. In a very profound sense the same ties united the members to one another and to their common divinity. Even if we do not accept the view that most tribal religion was based upon ancestor-worship, we must concede that the tribesmen regarded themselves as being akin to their gods, as in fact sharing with them a common life (§ 397). This was certainly one of the sources of the power wielded over them by the objects of their reverence and homage. There were two principal ways in which such power was exercised. One was connected with sacred places, the proper seats of the gods, where the rites of their worship were performed, and whose sacredness conferred a special sanctity or immunity upon special things or actions. Another was associated with the declared will of the gods, which was made known through various channels, but mainly by the domestic or communal priests, who ministered within the family or family group, or in the common sanctuary of the tribe.

§ 952. We revert now to the moral standards and ideals of the so-called patriarchal society among the Hebrews. The subject has already been glanced at in connection with the moral inferiority of some portions of J E. This was explained on the ground that the biographers had faithfully recorded the traditions of the fathers which did not stand on the ethical level of the prophetic times (§ 929, cf. 934). We have thus obtained an incidental guarantee of the accuracy of the pictures of ancient life found in the book of Genesis. Such accuracy is, moreover, generally conceded, since the narrative answers to any fair test that may be applied by archaeological and sociological criticism. The question before us is the relation in point of morality between the Israel of tradition and the Israel of later history; and there can be no doubt that with the stories of patriarchal life we stand at the fountain head of an unbroken stream of national tradition.

§ 953. Moral actions may for convenience be divided into those which spring from ordinary human relations and those which have a special religious motive or warrant. Of the former class the most prominent offences are deceit and fraud. Oriental deception has been notorious chiefly because the civilization of Western Asia has been specially unfavourable to the promotion of veracity and justice. These virtues are seldom highly developed in communities of low political organization. That men are naturally liars is a fact of anthropological science as well as of biblical and historical observation. It is only by slow gradations of self-discipline that truthfulness has been established anywhere as an attribute of individuals or communities.

§ 954. It would therefore naturally be expected that the virtues of sincerity and rectitude would be rudimentary or wanting in nomadic or semi-nomadic peoples. The foundation of such qualities is the sense of responsibility for one's acts to God or to man, or to both. But when religion consists mainly of ceremony or ritual, there is little chance for the evoking of the former. And when property is attached so precariously to the individual, no large issues or powerful motives are present that might arouse and foster the latter. When the individual subordinates his personality to the interests of his tribe, the demands of conscience are weakened, or rather, the sense of moral obligation cannot be developed. At the same time other virtues may be conspicuous which are in a line with the surrender of oneself to the cause of the community. Thus it happens that the early age of great races is an age of heroism, and that we find among them well-grounded traditions of noble deeds of courage and devotion that serve as an inspiration to all later generations.

In some such way must we represent to ourselves the earliest or patriarchal age of ancient Israel.

§ 955. Of the propensity to deceive and cheat, the recorded habits of the three great patriarchs may be taken as fairly representative. Very ancient must be the social laxity exhibited in Abraham's betrayal of his wife (Gen. xii. 10 ff. in J; Gen. xx. 1 ff. in E) and Isaac's duplication of the crime (Gen. xxvi. in J). A more normal type of deception is exhibited in the career of Jacob, which illustrates, on the one hand, the advantage of family leadership and the ancestral blessing, and, on the other, sets forth the means that might be resorted to in order to secure these priceless gains. I do not dwell at length on the lessons of the story, which was made entirely true to life and which, at the same time, seems in every instance to show that dishonesty is the best policy. A larger idea may have inspired this cherished national tradition, which we may express as follows after the manner of the modern Jacob: The outcome of the self-aggrandizement of Jacob, from the time when, under the guidance of his crafty mother, he cajoled Esau out of the blessing till his permanent settlement in Canaan, was a better thing for Israel and humanity than would have been his discomfiture by his rivals; just as, at the present time, the success of the policy of Cecil Rhodes and the vindication of his "personal honour" are better for England and mankind than the continued possession by a kindred but unprogressive community of an auriferous territory and of its birthright of freedom. Even from the industrial and cultural points of view, not to speak of the spiritual interests ultimately involved, it was better that the higher and more progressive type of man should have the promise and the possession of Canaan, than that the lower and undeveloped type, the huntsman of the wilderness, should be the heir of the "father of the faithful." This conception of history is, we may say, hardly on a level with the true prophetic (*e.g.* Jer. xvi. 13) or Christian spirit. But by the time when the tradition was embodied in the record (§ 923 ff.), it had become the valid interpretation of the original story. The narrative of the fact has already been dealt with (§ 929).

§ 956. We may now briefly examine the moral conduct and standards of the ancestors of Israel in the equally fundamental matter of the relations of the sexes. At the outset we may say that in such a society as theirs there is no question of extreme grossness or utter self-abandonment to revolting vice. Their life was on the whole simple and moderate. It was, speaking generally, life in cities which promoted institutional vice, if the term may be permitted. And to this stage the early Hebrews had not yet become accustomed. Vices associated with the worship of those deities which were regarded as the type of the procreative or sexual instinct naturally flourished where great temples were erected and maintained to their honour. Thus it came to pass that that passion of human nature, whose unbridled indulgence has tended more than anything else to demoralize society and to bring about the destruction of families and nations, received, so to speak, an apotheosis in the transition from nomadic to city life (see § 1184 ff., 1332 f.).

§ 957. We have, accordingly, to deny to the most ancient of the Hebrews any form of rank sensuality. On the other hand, polygamy, intermarriage of near relatives, and the still more debasing practice of concubinage were freely tolerated. Yet we must take into account the effect on the whole social fabric of the institution of slavery, the most important factor in ancient life and manners (§ 539 ff.). A notable secondary result of the system was the custom which accounts for the pathetic story of Gen. xvi. In general, the inferiority of the wife as part of the property of the house-master (§ 412) had the consequence that the freedom which was granted to him was denied to her, that the dismissal of a wife was customary and easy, while that of a husband was unknown.

The conception of "adultery" in such a society was, accordingly, quite different from ours: the infidelity of a husband involved no separation from his wife, while that of the wife or betrothed maiden might be a capital offence, according to the decree of the head of the family (Gen. xxxviii. 24). As to the prevalence of adultery in this semi-historic period we are not informed. We can speak with more definiteness as to the relations of people unmarried or unbetrothed. These were, as a rule, tolerably innocent, as is usually the case among a nomadic people of long endurance and established fame. There would otherwise have been no guarantee of purity of race, the first essential of tribal stability. It is a pleasing feature of the oldest Hebrew society, as also of the oldest Arabian, that young men and women were at liberty to consort freely with one another — a thing impossible were sexual irregularity either approved or frequent. It is quite another question how sexual vice was regarded from the moral point of view. That professional harlotry was not unknown to the earliest Hebrew society we have abundant proof, though we have no direct evidence that any member of the degraded sisterhood belonged to the community of Israel. But the institution of sacred prostitutes was prevalent among the Canaanites of the time, according to the stories of Genesis. Significant is the matter-of-fact way in which the notices are recorded. The action ascribed to Judah on the way to Timnah (Gen. xxxviii. 15 ff.) is mentioned as the most natural thing in the world.

§ 958. We have now to look at the Hebrew patriarchal society from a point of view which more nearly approaches the altruistic. This convenient term comprehends the various sentiments and impulses that provoke to deeds of self-sacrifice in any form — magnanimity, generosity, compassion, self-denial. It suggests directly the essential basis of morality, which in all ages and places rests fundamentally upon the giving up of self. For these primitive ages, however, the two qualities already discussed are much readier tests of moral progress than those about to be considered. Veracity and chastity are virtues which presuppose not merely a strong personal self-discipline, but also a public or social sentiment which is attained only after a long period of education and cultivation has gradually raised the moral standards of the community. If, therefore, there is any such thing as moral progress in human history, these later virtues must be given a higher place than the more primitive. Qualities which are more elementary still, such as endurance and courage, we do not need to discuss at all. They are found in all kinds and stages of society, and, in fact, may be said to be a necessary condition of the survival of any society whatever. Indeed, they are so far from being criteria of moral progress that they are not even exclusively human. In civilized human society their real significance does not consist in their exercise or display by itself, but only in the occasion or issue that has called them forth.

§ 959. Instances of generosity and magnanimity are frequent in the patriarchal history. In the character of Abraham these virtues are perhaps the most distinguished traits. He is the type of an enterprising chief formed to be a leader of men and the pioneer of a great enterprise. It is a true instinct which associates these qualities with such an epoch-making man. Of the moral character of Isaac we know almost nothing. He is represented as being largely under the control of his cunning Aramæan wife. He is evidently intended, however, to be merely a connecting link between Abraham, the head of the race, and Jacob, the head of the nation. Of the last-named we cannot find any positively meritorious trait recorded. The meaning of this seems to be that while his story is true to patriarchal life, it is also a reminiscence of the successful endeavours made by "Israel" to gain a footing among the nations (cf. § 955). Thus he is a type of the national advancement generally. —

Tantæ molis erat Judæam condere gentem.

The only sort of nobleness of which the family of Isaac could boast is to be credited to the wild and passionate hunter Esau, the type of laggard races.

§ 960. The character of Joseph presents the highest type of ancient Hebrew morality. His story is remarkable from several points of view. But its most remarkable feature is the grandeur and symmetry of the moral portraiture of its hero. His would be a great character in any age; but the marvel of it is that it exhibits a life lived in that primitive stage of social development which, as we have already seen, is most unfavourable to the manifestation of high moral qualities. Fidelity, honour, sense of personal responsibility, ideal chastity, magnanimity, — not of the pagan, not of the Old Testament, but of the Christian type, — these are some of the traits of the favourite son of the subtle and selfish Jacob. The easiest solution is that the story is an idealizing parable drawn for the instruction of a later reflective age of Israel's history. And yet, however the narrative may have assumed its present literary garb at a later date, the events recorded are not impossible. The two most prominent features of Joseph's character are his fidelity in service and his self-repression. But he was invested with responsibilities beyond those possible in the semi-nomadic environment of his early days. Trained in this school, he meets the supreme temptation with an answer which shows that he feels himself to be a moral trustee (Gen. xxxix. 8).

§ 961. With Joseph there is a still more solemn restraint: "How can I do this great evil and sin against God?" Nothing shows more clearly than this the exceptional place in the patriarchal history held by Joseph. The others are typical of their time and place. But such an appeal to divine authority in matters of moral conduct stands alone in the early Hebrew history. There is much said of religious acts on the part of the patriarchs and of their fidelity to Jehovah. Their faith in Him determined also their course in important matters. But we do not find that it determined them strongly and steadily toward righteousness and mercy. What, then, is their significance in the history of morality? They were men of large, original genius (§ 445, 447). True, we cannot but oppose the view that sets them in the category of Old Testament saints and moral exemplars. Yet we must admire the independence, enterprise, and success with which these early leaders of the race broke through the force of tradition and custom and hewed out new paths for themselves, thus becoming the prototypes and forerunners of the religious leaders who gave character to the later Israel. And this they did most conspicuously in their faith and worship. If they were historical characters, Jehovah was their God, or at least their supreme divinity. The narrative is consistent in showing how they came to discard ancestor-worship and strange deities generally (Gen. xxxv. 2 ff.).

§ 962. Such adherence to Jehovah did not of itself constitute morality. It was merely a ceremonial, and, as it would appear from the history of Jacob, sometimes a purely selfish form of primitive religion. But we are not seeking merely for evidences of high moral sentiment and achievement. What we desire is an explanation of the morality afterward characteristic of Israel. And here, as it would seem, we have an essential antecedent. While it is questionable whether in any age, or under any form of civilization, a deep and true morality can be developed except upon the foundation, or with the aid, of a religious sanction, it is certain that among a people such as ancient Israel religion is the only basis of any morality worthy the name. Where industrial pursuits were maintained systematically, if at all, by exclusive hereditary guilds; where commerce was confined to travelling merchants and occasional caravans; where no political system above the assembly of the elders had ever been devised, the industrial, or commercial, or political morality that has formed the precarious support of the great western civilizations was beyond attainment, as it was beyond imagination.

To either national or individual morality a long antecedent process of discipline is a prerequisite. To Israel such a discipline could only come through the religion whose feeble yet sure beginnings were made by the fathers before the perilous adventure was made of the migration to Egypt. The strenuous adherence, even by a half-blind and groping instinct, to Jehovah as the tribal God was of itself an inward exercise that had a moral quality of its own. So true is that saying which has transfigured the primitive and rudimentary faith of the founder of the race: "And he trusted in Jehovah, and he reckoned it to him as righteousness" (Gen. xv. 6).

§ 963. What do we find to be the moral features of Hebrew society in the period of the judges? Did any decisive changes take place in the community of Israel which would tend to develop the national and individual conscience and make it a controlling force in speech and act as between Hebrew and Hebrew, and Hebrew and foreigner? Were the three prime qualities, rectitude, chastity, and magnanimity, largely exemplified? How did the occupations of the people and their general social environment affect them? It must be confessed that the virtues most likely to be encouraged were those of the heroic or semi-barbarous type. Courage, endurance, fidelity to clan, family, and companions in arms, must have been often and signally displayed. The long struggle with the native Canaanites, over wide areas or in isolated holdings, for the possession of fortresses, fertile valleys and plains, vineyards and olive groves, or with various swarms of foreign invaders, played a principal part in moulding the Hebrew temper into strength, elasticity, and hardness. It was this discipline that gave to Israel the resisting and recuperative power which was and is the marvel of the ancient and modern world.

§ 964. Not very much can be said of influences favourable to the development of the rarer and more precious moral endowments of a people. In a community trained to irregular warfare, swift reprisal, deadly revenge, little stimulus could be afforded to any latent or incipient openness or candour which might have been educed in the more peaceful occupations of earlier days. Ehud (Jud. iii.) can be a moral hero only to those who hold that no means are reprehensible which can secure a desirable end. Like his, but much more treacherous, was the act of Jael, the wife of Heber the Kenite. In it we have not only gross deception, but a violation of the laws of hospitality, which, when it has once been freely offered, is inviolable, according to all inter-tribal usage. The outrage was heightened by the circumstance expressly recorded (Jud. iv. 17) that an alliance actually subsisted between the half-Israelitish Kenites and the followers of the Canaanitish king. Moreover, the splendid lyric which celebrates the triumph of Israel over the last great combination of the Canaanites counts Jael blessed above all women who dwell in tents (Jud. v. 24), because she had come to the help of Jehovah (cf. v. 23) by deluding into fatal security an enemy of his people.

§ 965. Such cases are characteristic of the times and the people, and so stand out boldly in the record. How was it in this period with the virtue of chastity? A sample or two will suffice to show that the standard of morals had not been raised during this later period. Gideon, one of the best-approved leaders of Israel, had not only many wives, but a concubine as well. What we call lust in Mohammed we can only extenuate in Gideon on the ground that he lived in a remoter age. Jephthah was the son of a harlot. Samson resorted to harlots as a matter of habit. Delilah, in spite of her Hebrew name, may have been a Philistine. But the Baal worship which was rife in most of Israel during this whole period must have brought with it its due measure of licentiousness more or less professional. Concubinage was but one remove from harlotry (Jud. xix. 1 ff.). A still darker shadow is seen to rest upon at least a portion of the land in the prevalence of the worse than bestial crime in the city of Gibeah (xix. 22). Israel, as a whole, was at last shocked into horror and indignation. But the succeeding narrative, ending with the rough and ready method of securing wives by capture (xxi. 21 ff.), recalls vividly the essential spirit of the people and the age, their primitive habits and manners, and their rudimentary conception of the saving virtues of society.

§ 966. An aspect scarcely more favourable is presented by the practice of the altruistic virtues. At least, the book of Judges gives no suggestion of their prevalence. It is to be admitted that allusions to the gentler side of life and conduct are hardly to be expected in the memorials of a rude and warlike age, which naturally record only extreme instances. And among the larger households in the more settled districts, particularly in the later days of the judges, there were doubtless many manifestations of neighbourly kindness and perhaps even of chivalrous generosity. The institution of the *goël* especially gave scope and occasion for actions of the latter class. While in the rudeness and savagery of the times the services of the protector of kinship were perhaps most frequently in demand as an avenger of blood (Ex. xxi. 12 ff.), the necessities of unfortunate kinsfolks, particularly of widows and orphans, must have evoked innate feelings of compassion and sympathy in many a heart. Such a traditional picture as that which is presented at the close of the book of Ruth can scarcely represent an isolated instance. It is not to be supposed, however, that this is an indication of the prevailing type of manners.

§ 967. It was scarcely possible that any essential change in the national morals could take place during the historical period immediately following the judges. Yet the early vicissitudes of the kingdom had a great deal to do with building up the national character. And it was especially the new spirit infused into the people by the personality and achievements of David that prepared the way for that larger nationalism which made possible an historic Israel and is even yet not extinct in Judaism. The predominant note of the rise of the monarchy is patriotism. The deliverance of the individual family groups, the first thought of the beleaguered clansmen, was found to depend upon common action against the Philistines. The idea of a united Israel was first realized under Saul at the instance of the prophet-priest-judge Samuel. The rising tide of loyalty to Jehovah and his cause, as against the aliens and their gods, swelled by the first successes of Saul and still more by the heroic daring of Jonathan, was checked by the king's mental and moral collapse; it retreated with the defection of David and the ensuing intestine strife; it fell to its lowest ebb with the tragedy of Gilboa. The accession of David to the tottering throne, and his steady advance to preëminence, first within Israel itself and thereafter in Palestine and the whole of the West-land, were the real making of Israel into a nation. No later failures or disgrace or ruptures could efface the memory of this triumph; nor could any subsequent national success rival it as an ideal of kingly achievement or as a measure of Israel's greatness.

§ 968. There was now wanting but one deep common source of inspiration, one cardinal element of national solidarity, — a central, dominant sanctuary. This idea, cherished so fondly by David, was realized in the temple of Solomon. Thus were established at last the main outward conditions of a permanent state under the most potent of guarantees. But of far more enduring importance than the promise of political stability, soon to be so rudely disturbed, was the foundation then laid for progress in morality and for the practice of a religion which should be something more than ceremonial formalism. The larger relations of political, business, and social life then inaugurated gradually brought with them a sense of responsibility which must have sobered and steadied the new self-conscious community. The oath or the vow made before Jehovah became more binding with the recognition of his enthronement for righteousness upon Mount Zion, the place where he had chosen to set his name. It is not necessary to inquire now how and when such claims were ignored or weakened. We may content ourselves with remarking that while these were conditions essential to moral advancement, they might naturally be expected to be only slowly operative, finding their true scope and vindication in a later time. What, however, we wish particularly to know is the actual moral standing of the best men of Israel in this age of the early or undivided monarchy. Examples here crowd upon us, and we must limit ourselves in the choice.

§ 969. Again, we have to emphasize the prominence of the military or heroic virtues. This is, in fact, preeminently the heroic age of Israel. Physical courage was universal, as befitted a people engaged in a protracted life and death struggle. Not to lack of bravery, but to want of discipline, to the decline of the kingly qualities in the monarch, to the effect of panic fear in a superstitious age, are to be ascribed the half-heartedness and the frequent retreats of the armies of Israel during the régime of Samuel and Saul. Of individual prowess every leader gave proof during the whole of the period. David's worthies (2 Sam. xxiii.) were a product of the spirit that was now moving in Israel like a long pent-up flood. They were the flower of that age of Hebrew chivalry. Nor was there lacking that self-devotion which in the undisciplined warfare of a struggling community is really more heroic than the most gallant charge of a regular army. No deed of daring done by David's men, inspired by his example, could surpass the brilliant achievement of Saul's knightly son at Michmash. A nation which bred such heroes could scarcely hereafter be utterly ignoble. And in these actions, the theme of song and legend till the latest generation, were indirect occasions of nobler manners and purer motives throughout the moral realm.

No man can risk his life non-professionally in a worthy cause without being stirred to the depths of his soul by an electric thrill which reacts by moral sympathy through his whole spiritual nature. The clods, once disturbed by celestial fire, were henceforth magnetic and responsive to the touch of spiritual forces which else had found and left them useless and dead.

§ 970. But these secondary movements had as yet scarcely begun; and it is a sad descent that brings us to the level of the everyday morals of the early monarchy. The virtue of veracity seems especially wanting in the make-up of the men of the period. For the sake of brevity we shall confine ourselves to the career of David. We are at once struck with the fact that whenever any danger threatened, if a falsehood served his turn it was immediately employed (1 Sam. xix. 13 ff.; xx. 5 ff.; xxi. 2; xxvii. 10 ff.; 2 Sam. xv. 34). He deceived friends and enemies indifferently. It was especially in his relations with the Philistines that deceit was systematically practised, ranging from simple disguise to the grossest of falsehoods. His affair with his faithful servant, Uriah the Hettite, shows him at his worst. There is probably no record of treachery and lying consistently pursued that surpasses this in remorseless cruelty and moral baseness. If the narrative contained all that we know of David, the deed would have been universally regarded as one almost unequalled in the foul and blood-stained annals of kingly rule. We may at any rate say this about the matter, that it belonged to the stage in David's life when he was as yet untouched by any deep religious feeling.

§ 971. In the relations between the sexes we see at best no marked advance. Not to speak of polygamy, concubinage was fashionable in the best families. The promptness with which David, the outlaw chief, espoused the wife of the newly dead Nabal, and with which David, the king, made a lawful wife of the widow of the murdered Uriah, speaks plainly of the subserviency of well-born women. The act of Absalom, by which he proclaimed to all Israel his usurpation of his father's rights (2 Sam. xvi. 21 f.), does not appear to have shocked the moral sensibilities of his fellow-citizens, or even of the "elders of Israel" (2 Sam. xvii. 4), who still adhered to his cause. In the more enlightened time of Solomon, the increase in outward prosperity and the glamour of a brilliant court were the accompaniment of gross and unbridled sensuality. David's harem, extensive as it was, could not compare with that of Solomon. And one knows little of social history, or of human nature, if one supposes that the evil of excessive self-indulgence was confined to the recreant who sat on the throne, and who in these vital matters was a law unto himself. Courtiers and nobles, and the wealthy and fashionable generally, were as certain then as they are now to imitate and rival the sins and follies of a prince. Nor was sexual vice confined to the legalized license of polygamy and concubinage. The worship of the foreign deities introduced by Solomon along with his heathen wives of necessity included religious prostitution. True, we still have no reason to suppose that many daughters of Hebrew families gave themselves to this or to any form of illegitimate vice, "for no such thing ought to be done in Israel" (2 Sam. xiii. 12). But Ashtoreth, the goddess of the Sidonians or Phœnicians (1 K. xi. 5), could not enjoy the royal patronage without enforcing the usages inseparable from her debasing cult.

§ 972. What shall be said of the practice of the altruistic virtues during the earlier times of the monarchy? The imagination summons up at once the figure of the heroic and magnanimous Jonathan. An age which produced a man so unique in nobility of soul should not be called quite morally barren. We are seeking, however, for cases of sympathy with the poor and oppressed, the friendless and the weak, and of the relaxation of the pitiless code of revenge upon family, or personal, or national enemies. Of what was done in private we know little. The temper of representative men may best be judged of by their conduct toward their rivals or foes. David's treatment of the Moabites (2 Sam. viii. 2) and of the Ammonites (2 Sam. xii. 31) was a war measure, and was neither better nor worse than that which the Assyrian kings before and after his time boasted of inflicting upon obstinate rebels. The claims of blood revenge were enforced as remorselessly as in the days of Gideon (Jud. viii. 18 ff.). The circle of leading men that stood nearest to David suffered particularly from the law of reprisal. To his account must be reckoned the pitiful fate of Rizpah, the daughter of Aiah, and of her innocent children, done to a shameful death as the victim of a blood feud. True it is that repentance here again manifested itself, and that he sought to quiet the soul of the comfortless mother, and to reunite in Sheol the distracted ghosts of the family he had supplanted (2 Sam. xxi. 11 ff.).

§ 973. It is now time, however, to draw some general conclusions as to that portion of Israel's history which we have been permitted to survey. In the first place, we see how morality still moved and worked its way within the sphere of the family, the clan, and the tribe. Its sanctions sprang from the beliefs of the community rather than from the independent conviction of the individual; custom ruled rather than conscience, prescription rather than self-impulsion. One essential ground of the limitation is obvious. Duties and employments were few and simple. These were prescribed by paternal injunction; and when spontaneously assumed they created no new conditions that would bring intelligence into play and so evoke the moral sense through the balancing of conflicting claims. Secondly, the most striking apparent exceptions to this general fact were the leaders of the people, who seemed to strike out new paths for themselves, or were commissioned to fulfil higher functions than any yet known to the nation.

§ 974. But we have now to take account of a moral factor of the first importance: I mean the public teachers. The great popular leaders from the time of the earliest judges till the end of the undivided kingdom, had very little to do with the moral education of the nation. The judges themselves appear to have done little to rectify popular misconduct. Nor were the priests, whose duties included also the judicial function (§ 585 f.), conspicuous for their high sense of moral obligation. The sons of Eli and the sons of Samuel, who came into office as a matter of course by hereditary succession, are much more likely to have represented the average priest and judge than their fathers, who are singled out for special distinction. What we learn of the influence of the religious officials comes out naturally in their bearing toward the leading men of the time. In this matter two interesting points declare themselves. First, we notice that no interference is made with the conduct of any influential man till the time of the kings. Second, it is a new order of men who attempt a reformation in public morals. These men were the prophets.

§ 975. What, then, was the character of this epoch-making intervention by the prophets? The first instance is that of Samuel in his rôle of mentor and censor to King Saul. And here we are surprised to find that he does not appear to have intervened in questions of morality at all. His only recorded protest against Saul's conduct is made on the ground of disobedience to an arbitrary command (1 Sam., chap. xv.). When Saul spared Agag and the best of the spoil, it cannot be maintained that he did what was wrong in itself. Unfortunately we can, on the other hand, hardly visit with stern condemnation the terrible war of extermination waged by Israel. Such conflicts— blood feuds on a larger scale—were the order of the day among the neighbouring peoples of the time, and Israel had suffered more than Amalek in the long series of reprisals. Nor can we put Saul's comparative moderation to the credit of his humanity. His preservation of Agag was too much a departure from the prevailing usages of war to have been intended for more than a temporary purpose. On the whole, it would appear that the rebuke to Saul, and the terrible penalty annexed thereto, were inflicted not on the ground of the inherent wrongfulness of his acts, but because he had not deferred to the prophetic word.

§ 976. Samuel's significance generally, in the history of Old Testament morals, may be thus stated: He is the first in the long list of the leaders of Israel whose conduct in fundamental matters of morality is brought directly into view (1 Sam. xii. 3). The last of the judges, he is the first the character of whose administration of justice is spoken of at all. He tolerated the institution of the monarchy, but made it the prime essential of the character of the king that he should bow to the will of Jehovah, and to his representative, the prophet-priest. He virtually founded the prophetic guilds, the chief conservative influence in the life of northern Israel. His services to morality were great, but mainly indirect and potential.

§ 977. A distinct advance along one line was made by the next kingly mentor, the prophet Nathan. His rebuke of David for his most atrocious crime goes to the foundation of the moral principle of conduct. As his parable shows, it looks at David's sin in the light of his relation to his environment; it shows the disturbance (or wrong) thereby occasioned in the system of which he was the moral centre. To stigmatize a sin as a sin on account of its selfishness was something new in the recorded history of the world. True, the outrage was so obvious that it could not well escape challenge; but it is just one of the providential occasions of moral evolution that men and communities should be startled into a sense for better things by a sudden revelation of the effect of their offences. Such a case is isolated, to be sure, in the moral ministry of the prophets of the time. But the crime was rank and grievous, and as it struck at the sanctity and peace of the home of the common man in Israel it was made monumental. The rule that the sins and follies of a monarch excite emulation rather than repulsion, finds in this instance, at least, a wholesome exception.

§ 978. It is remarkable that no prophet appears as a censor of morals till the time of the divided kingdom with the exception of Gad, who acted as the minister of Jehovah in connection with David's ambitious scheme to take a census of Israel. On the other hand, we find in the person of Nathan the prophetic influence wielded in behalf of the cruel and treacherous intrigue through which the rivals of Solomon were put out of the way (2 K. i.). The moral paradox is solved when we consider that the paramount interest was the preservation of the state, in the furthering of which the individual was made of little account. Thereafter Solomon seems to have dispensed with prophetic help and guidance. His only religious achievement, the building of the temple, being an affair of worship and ritual, was done under the auspices of the priests. On the whole, his reign was probably more harmful to public and private morals than that of any other king of either Israel or Judah, with the possible exception of Manasseh.

§ 979. It is significant, however, that the secession of northern Israel was instigated by a prophet of Jehovah (1 K. xi. 29 ff.). Among the considerations that impelled him was doubtless the fact that Solomon's extravagance and exactions were injuring Israel as a whole and making the predominance of Judah a national curse.[1] He thus follows in the line of Nathan and Gad (§ 977 f.). But what Judah thus lost in moral character and prestige as compared with the "Ten Tribes," it more than made up finally through the possession of a temple free from image-

---

[1] Notice also that Ahijah was of Shiloh, in the very heart of the territory of the rival and much-wronged tribe of Ephraim.

worship; while the semi-idolatry instigated by Jeroboam I, and the political unsettlement of his kingdom,[1] with its accompaniment of intrigue, proscription, and murder, defeated the worthy ends aimed at in the revolution.

§ 980. We thus see a growth in moral sensibility among the religious leaders of Israel, and we also discern the principle of its development. It was the harm done to the people of Jehovah which awakened a sense of the wrath of Jehovah himself. This can hardly be called as yet a genuine sense of sin; for in the first place, the feeling aroused was fear rather than sorrow, and, in the second place, it was as members of the community rather than as individuals that the responsibility was felt. Yet here was the germ of spiritual morality, and this was the region in which it unfolded itself, for only thus could that consciousness of wrong-doing be awakened which is of the essence of the saving repentance that seeks and gains forgiveness. But the story is a long one, and we must be content if we can follow its leading motives.

§ 981. Our next glimpse of moral progress in Israel is gained from the memorable reign of Ahab. The tumultuous times of the first dynasties were over, and Omri had made himself strong at home and abroad (§ 212). His son came to the kingdom as a matter of course, and the sense of power without responsibility (1 K. xxi. 7), the typical Oriental absolutism, bore its natural fruits. There was nothing upon which he might not lay his hand, not even the patrimony of one of the people of Jehovah. When he seized the estate of Naboth the wrong was irreligion, and therefore immorality. Jehovah was the owner of the land, and Naboth was his tenant (§ 580). Besides, the patrimony was a sacred trust for his family (xxi. 3), where rested the dust of his ancestors under the guardianship of Jehovah.

---

[1] Cf. Montefiore, *Hibbert Lectures* (1892), p. 85 f.

§ 982. Very probably this act of oppression and profanation did not stand alone in the reign or time of Ahab. But, like the great transgression of David, it was because it ended in an appalling tragedy that it became monumental. The vengeance denounced against the offender is a measure of the offence. This is a rare historic occasion. It makes us feel at one with the outraged people of Israel. As we shudder with their horror at the deed, we follow them with eager sympathy in their gradual appreciation of its essential wickedness. Indignation at the conspiracy, the judicial murder, the robbery, was followed by a moral revulsion at the enormity of the misdeed. It was the crime against the community which stirred the common heart. Every freeman in Israel was for the moment a Naboth in imagination, at the mercy of a rapacious king and a cruel, lustful queen. Ordinary petty wrongs done to persons or to property were a matter of course from the days of old. They were the mere trickling of a mountain stream. This was the breaking up of the fountains of the great deep. The sense of being wronged grew into the sense of wrong, and the offence against Israel was felt to be a sin against Jehovah. It was the word of the great prophet that startled the true Israel into a knowledge of itself. The message came in thundertones, and between the strokes gleamed the lightning-flashes of revelation. It was not a very clear or sustained illumination, but it served God's turn and man's need.

§ 983. With Elijah prophecy enlarged its range and its depth. The prophet was no longer a mere seer or oracle or mentor of princes. He was the guardian and censor of national morals; in short, a preacher and teacher. But, what is even more important to observe, there was a corresponding advance among the best minds and spirits of his people. Let us learn, once for all, that the prophet never stood quite alone, and that he was, apart from his special commission, merely a foremost representative of a class or society or school. We are warned of the danger of overlooking this obvious sociological and psychological principle by the reminder which was addressed to Elijah himself at the very opening of this new era of prophecy (1 K. xix. 18).[1] The essential thing for the future was that from this time onward there was a worthy common cause and common interest, and a party in the state that stood for the rights of the defenceless and the oppressed on the ground of religion and justice, and in whose consciousness the practical conflicts of rights and wrongs wrought out a sense of the necessary antithesis of right and wrong.

§ 984. The fortunes of this class or party in their relation to society and public life have already been sketched (§ 597 ff.). The perpetual antagonism and ever widening chasm between the rich and the poor, the oppressor and the oppressed, the wicked and the pious, are depicted in letters of flame by Amos, Hosea, Isaiah, and Micah, and here we need not reproduce the familiar picture. What concerns us now is to see how the idea of moral responsibility, once awakened, was developed up to the time of Josiah. For this end we cannot do better than sum up the essential conditions of moral progress, giving first those which are inward or subjective, and then those which are subjective and external. The summary necessarily consists in part of a résumé of previous observations.

§ 985. 1. A purer and loftier conception of the character of Jehovah. Morality has never progressed in any community without the stimulus of a religious sanction. Men have looked to their gods or God as requiring from them the most solemn duties of their lives. Moreover, something besides mere ceremonial service is always thought to be demanded. Even where the crudest forms of faith and worship prevail, and where morality in the

---

[1] "Seven thousand" is merely a very general number, and possibly stands here for a much larger sum of faithful adherents of Jehovah.

positive sense can hardly be predicated of the votaries, such duties as are incumbent on them (that is, whatever has the character of solemn obligation, the motive of all moral action) are regarded as the will of the supernatural being who is the head and patron of the community. And among the Semites deference to the will of the deity is usually absolute. As their vocabulary indicates, they had really no " will " of their own : the only real agents in the world were their divinities. This conception is both cause and effect of their singular religiousness. It explains also their exclusiveness, their fanaticism, their deadly persistency. Given a wrong or debasing view of the desire of the deity and they are the most hopelessly intractable and noxious of mortals. Given a lofty and inspiring view of the deity and they become the elect of their species. This is a master-key to Hebrew Prophetism, Christianity, and Mohammedanism. Hence in proportion as the conception of the character of the presiding and informing deity is raised and refined the nature of his requirements is correspondingly purified and exalted. That is, moral motive and conduct change for the better.

§ 986. 2. A divorce between the worship of the single and only true God and the adoration or service of any and all other objects of devotion. This is only accomplished as the individual learns by experience the emptiness and spiritual unsatisfactoriness of false worship — not merely the helplessness of the false gods ; because to a people gradually emerging from superstition such a fact is not so easily demonstrated. With this experience goes the practical observation that God does not always punish his enemies directly, but that he does reward those who fear him and do his will : the sense of the חֶסֶד and the אֱמֶת of Jehovah ; the completion of the formula, " Surely God is good to Israel," by the addition, " to such as are pure in heart " (Ps. lxxiii. 1).

§ 987. 3. In this way a new and higher conception of society is eventually gained. The ideal of the social order is no longer the family, the clan, the tribe, or even the organized nation, but the people of Jehovah. A new community arises from the riving of the old, containing the germs of indefinite progress and expansion.

§ 988. 4. On the side of conduct there must be a practice of the common virtues which are at once the mainstay of the social order and the expression of the will of Jehovah: honesty, chastity, mercy, and helpfulness. These and other essential virtues can only be maintained along with the vindication of the lofty character and the pure worship of Jehovah. This vindication can be accomplished only after and through an inevitable prolonged struggle between parties in the community and the state. Only by suffering, discipline, and the enduring of wrong can the principles of a party of righteousness be put to the proof and finally secure a moral triumph: —

> "There is no gain except by loss,
> There is no life except by death;
> There is no glory but by shame,
> No justice but by taking blame."

By adherence under stress of trial to the true worship of Jehovah and the practice of "righteousness," which is the obligation and test of his service; and, on the other hand, by an observation of the lives and fates of the opposing party in church and state, idolatry or mixed worship *plus* immorality — luxury, greed, sensuality, cruelty — is continually made more odious and disreputable.

§ 989. Some of the accompanying or coöperant external conditions are: 1. National unification. This was in a measure secured by the kingdom. Only by some such assimilation could the tribal habits, restricted views of obligation, local prejudices and antipathies, arbitrary administration of justice, be to any considerable degree done away. Terrible evils came with the kingdom. But by it the necessary antithesis of good and bad, pure and impure, righteousness and injustice, was brought to self-consciousness in an influential party loyal to Jehovah and his cause.

§ 990. 2. Industrial and commercial development. This undoubtedly fosters the greed and selfishness of the grasping and covetous. On the other hand, no community becomes honest and veracious unless by business training it is made to realize as a people the advantages of honesty and veracity, and the evils of cheating and crookedness in matters of bargain and sale. How greatly such convictions were needed may be suggested by the business habits of any nomadic or semi-nomadic community in the East. The Hebrews did not have this aid to morality in full measure till the Babylonian exile (§ 1319 ff.). A concomitant advantage is the possession of fixed property, which develops character by the responsibility of ownership and trusteeship, and steadies the practical purpose and endeavour of business life.

§ 991. 3. Social changes, resulting in the creation of privileged classes of the rich and powerful, including kings and nobles. Everywhere, but especially in Oriental countries, such changes develop the worst passions and instincts of human nature — selfishness, cruelty, self-complacent indifference to suffering and wrong. These classes also adhered to and patronized the forms of false and mixed worship which minister to lust and fashionable vices and pleasures. On the other hand, the plain-living votaries of Jehovah had their numbers chiefly augmented from the ranks of the poor and the oppressed. The gulf between the two classes became steadily wider and deeper. The true nature, the essential character, of the antithesis became better appreciated. Vague and abstract conceptions of the relations of Jehovah to his people were replaced by a concrete realization of his power to help, to sustain, to uplift. Blind reliance upon, or dread of, his power was mitigated and neutralized by the consciousness of his love and grace. The prosperity of the wicked, accompanied as it was by hateful and injurious conduct, was now less envied. Jehovah put gladness into the heart of his followers more than others had when their corn and their wine increased (Ps. iv. 7).

§ 992. 4. *A concentration of the national worship.* The essential evil of the local sanctuaries was that the " high places " were infected with nature worship in one or more degrading forms; and that such associations, based on tradition and habit, and falling in with natural inclination, were ineradicable. In northern Israel such a centralizing system was never accomplished. In Judah it was favoured by many circumstances, and when secured by a reforming monarch the prestige of the central sanctuary made it perpetual. Thus, in spite of frequent and gross debasement of the national worship, a solidarity of sentiment, a community of belief, a coöperation in policy and action were promoted which were essential to the progress of the cause of righteousness.

§ 993. 5. *An educative system.* This was mainly supplied by the genuine prophets of Jehovah. Ritual and ceremony were needed; and in Israel they were not always unspiritual. But the priests as a class were incompetent and mechanical, though there was no enmity between the two orders, and the priesthood contributed signally to the ranks of the prophets, as well as to the outward reformation of the state. It was the line of the prophets that received and kept the saving truth and " passed from hand to hand the torch of life." From simple and rude beginnings, at the opening of Israel's career as a nation, they maintained the one essential principle of fidelity to Jehovah, growing steadily in inspiration, insight, and devotion. Thus they became the light of Israel and the world. But, as educators of their people, they secured no permanently effective agency till they created a literature under Amos and his successors, or, what is much the same thing, until they reached intuitions and conceptions of God and duty which were worthy of permanent record.

§ 994. The highest and most spiritual of these conditions were slow and tardy in coming into play, and Israel's moral progress during this prophetic period may be very summarily stated. For the northern kingdom, besides the indirect testimony of J E (§ 926, 930), the principal evidence comes from Amos and Hosea. Of the nation as a whole, no favourable judgment can be formed. But for purposes of moral history discrimination is necessary. The chief obstacle to reformation was the perpetuation of the local shrines, and this for the reason that the remnant of the faithful had little community of worship, in spite of the sacred feasts, the new moons and sabbaths, and other feast-days (Hos. ii. 11). That some were found true we learn from the wonderful though obscure personality of Hosea. While, like Amos, he draws prophet-wise a picture wholly dark of the times and the people, he himself, as revealed in his writings, is a proof of the existence of a small but intrepid band of pure and loyal souls. A life like his, whose very breath was love and faith, demanded spiritual fellowship for its nurture and its daily sustenance. That his followers and supporters were a very small company we can scarcely doubt. But they were necessarily a power as well as a witness for righteousness, even in the evil times of Samaria's downfall. Nor did they altogether perish with the going down of the kingdom. It was not in the nature of such a society to dissolve and cease, even with the extinction of the nation. They were not a forlorn hope, losing all for which they fought and died. They were rather a hard-pressed army of patriots who cut their way through their foes to join their allies across the frontier, whom they reinforced and inspired to victory.

§ 995. The party of truth and righteousness in the kingdom of Judah was in the line of true succession to this heroic, prophetic band. It was in the very centre of the moral struggle in Jerusalem, and with the fall of Samaria in view, that Isaiah gathered his disciples about him. Far from the riot and ribaldry of voluptuaries, and the taunts of frivolous sceptics, and the intrigues of false and seditious politicians, he discoursed to them of the one sure foundation-stone on which the community could rest its hopes, of the "overwhelming scourge" which should come upon those who had made lies their refuge and hidden themselves under falsehood, of the hail-storm which should sweep away the refuges of lies. He declared that everything must bide the test of the measuring-line of justice and the plumb-line of righteousness, and that a divine ordinance, fixed and inviolable, determines the application of the rule (Isa. xxviii. ; cf. viii. 6 ff.).

§ 996. With this revelation we are brought close to the fountain of Old Testament morality. We see running here in its early course that stream of ethical thought and sentiment that swells and broadens to all eternity. Here we have the explanation of the prophetic life and work, the key to the history of prophecy itself. It is not Amos and Hosea and Isaiah and Micah and Habakkuk and Jeremiah, alone, but they and their teachers, and their disciples, that raised the walls of the spiritual temple upon its unseen, immovable foundation-stone. Their principles, their endurance, their successes and defeats, their own spiritual progress, give unity and consistency as well as motive and meaning to the inner history of Israel. We think of the profound prophetic conceptions in the Jehovistic history (§ 931 ff.). We do not forget the other forces that wrought for the purification of the state, which we may call for convenience the reforming priestly party and the reforming court party, and of these we must take serious account in our study of moral progress under the monarchy. But much of their inspiration they owed to the genuine prophetic influence, and, being essentially official and professional, they were more easily reformed from without than from within.

§ 997. To trace that history in broadest outline up and through the great Reformation is now a comparatively simple task. Like all spiritual processes this, the most decisive movement of the ancient world, was a matter of personal experience. Hence the outward events are little known and of little direct importance until the conflict with the party of repression and moral reaction became public and national. We may conveniently make four periods. The first reaches to the deliverance of Jerusalem from Sennacherib; the second to the death of Hezekiah; the third to the accession of Josiah; the fourth through the Reformation till his death.

§ 998. In the first period we observe the moral arraignment of the civil and religious evil-doers brought to a climax by Isaiah and Micah. The excitement caused by the denunciations of Micah is attested by their being called to mind at a critical period more than a century later (Jer. xxvi. 17 ff.). That Isaiah had a wider outlook and did a greater work is partly due to his position in the capital, and to his skill and sagacity in keeping in touch with the leading people of the state, and at length carrying them along with him — a class of people who would have been alienated by the indiscriminate bitterness of his provincial colleague. The most obvious outward mark of the success of this double prophetic vocation was the partial reform instituted by Hezekiah (§ 795 f.). A more permanent result was the increase of attachment to Jerusalem as the centre of national hope and worship, due on the one hand to Isaiah's doctrine of the inviolability of Zion, and on the other to the dread of the desolation predicted by Micah. Still more potential morally was Isaiah's conception of a community of Jehovah's worshippers, which was partly realized in his own little circle, and which kept itself intact in the darkness of the following generation. Of this community the lineal successor is the church of God, and its literary monument is the Old Testament.

§ 999. With all the strength and nobleness of the germinal ideas of this splendid prophetic era, it was marked by the limitations incident to its stage of moral development. It is the gradual emancipation from these trammels that distinguishes the comparative spiritual freedom attained during the Exile. First, there was the notion that the presence of Jehovah and the benefits of worship were confined to his own land and people and his special seat. This conception was not merely a necessity in the evolution of religious thought, but it was also a saving practical doctrine, as it served to discourage the abounding nature-worship and superstitions of the local shrines. From the point of view of religious truth, however, it manifestly tended to narrowness of view, intolerance, self-sufficiency, and formality.

§ 1000. Second, the view still prevailed that Jehovah had an interest in the people as a whole rather than in individuals. Hence the responsibility for good and evil was rather national than personal. It is true that the antithesis between the righteous and the wicked was bound ultimately to make clear the principle of personal responsibility. Indeed, the fundamental doctrine of prophecy, that sin is a defiance of the will of Jehovah and goodness a compliance with his will, implied freedom of choice on the part of the individual. But these Hebrew seers were not logicians or psychologists. They concerned themselves more with the effect and issue of sin than with its cause and origin, and it was a work of time for them to break entirely with the traditional conception of men as having a corporate rather than a personal existence. Hence the sinner was one of the community, a class of "sinners"; and the righteous man in the same way was one of the community of the "righteous" or the "pious." So persistent was the inherited tribalistic notion (§ 397) that a single life resided in the clan and was shared by its members, whose patron god was at the same time its ultimate ancestor or life-giver. The power of this inwrought idea could only be broken when a sense of moral obligation was awakened in such men as Jeremiah and his pupils. But at this stage, when the party of Jehovah or of righteousness was formed, the antithesis was still felt to be between two communities and not between two associations of individuals.

§ 1001. A third limitation was the lack of proportion and consistency in the prophetic estimate of virtues or moral qualities. What affected the claims of Jehovah and what touched the life of the community was of cardinal importance. Hence to those prophets the great transgression was the mixed or hypocritical or merely formal worship of Jehovah; and next to it in impiety was the oppression or robbery of Jehovah's wards, the poor and humble. Thus is to be explained the fact that the most obnoxious sets of people were the rich (§ 598) and the priests. What we miss the most is the virtue of charity and tolerance and a regard for man as man. The persecuting and vindictive spirit and the threats of destruction were not due, however, to *odium theologicum*, but to the higher motive of indignation for wrong perpetrated against Jehovah and his suffering people.

§ 1002. The preservation of Jerusalem from the armies of Sinacherib (see § 704 ff.) introduced a second period, which was, however, very brief, as it lasted only till the death of Hezekiah. It was marked by an increased regard for the prophetic word on the part of king and people, as well as more earnest efforts to put down the Canaanitish modes of worship with their Babylonish accompaniments, which had been fostered by Ahaz. The disturbed condition of the country (§ 791) must have greatly obstructed the moral and spiritual progress which the prophetic party had hoped for. It is impossible, however, to get definite information as to this obscure period generally, or even to infer anything from subsequent conditions.

§ 1003. Nor can we learn anything at first hand of the devoted followers of Jehovah during the third period, the cruel times of King Manasseh. But we know that this was a time of intense occupation with the ideas and aims of the faithful community. Only so can we explain the strength of the reforming movement under Josiah, and, what is more significant still, the ethical wisdom and depth of the book of Deuteronomy. Thus the fourth period (that of Josiah's régime) from the point of view of moral and religious development, really forms one great epoch along with the third, from which it differs so greatly in all external features. In the later time we see the embodiment of the ideas of the earlier, the execution of its plans, and the fulfilment of its hopes.

§ 1004. We have here a rare opportunity to balance the opposing claims of the two communities thus engaged in a struggle upon whose outcome depended the fate of the world. Nowhere else were the true character and tendency of the forces arrayed against prophetism so clearly displayed. Just as signally revealed were the aims and methods of the party of progress and reform. Moreover, the issue of the conflict was then virtually determined, or at least conditioned, since it was at this stage that a movement was made all along the line through which at last the conquered party became the conqueror. Hence the very situation challenges our inquiry into the merits of the contest. We ought to discover what was saving and permanent in the contentions and principles of the party of progress and reform.

§ 1005. There were two outstanding features in the religious policy of Manasseh and his ministers. First, he made a systematic effort to repeal the reforming measures of Hezekiah, and to substitute for his plain, unsymbolizing worship of Jehovah a more imposing cult, which should enthrall the multitude and extinguish religious puritanism. Second, he took active measures against the reforming party, which culminated in persecution to the death. The situation is obviously similar to that of the reign of Ahaz, and also reminds us in several respects of the religious strife of the days of Ahab and Elijah. In both cases the adoration of strange deities was superadded to the symbolical image-worship of Jehovah and to the old Canaanitish demonology. As Ahab had been led by the prestige of the Tyrian alliance to enter upon the service of the Phœnician Baal, so the glamour of the victorious gods of his suzerain impelled Manasseh to the erection of shrines for the celestial pantheon of the Assyrians (§ 856). Under both Ahab and Manasseh violence was resorted to for the suppression of the pure religion of Jehovah. The parallel is made more striking still by the sequel of both administrations. When Jehu and Josiah came to power, they alike retaliated in kind against the votaries of the alien worship. Still more striking than these parallels is the contrast shown in the fact that while the forms of worship promoted by Manasseh showed little or no moral advance over those favoured by Ahab, the type of religion and morals exhibited in Deuteronomy is far higher than that exemplified or tolerated by Elijah, Elisha, and Jehu.

§ 1006. One moral distinction, however, must be granted to the religious practices of the time of Manasseh. I mean their intense earnestness and profound sincerity. The variety of cult and ritual which they exhibited, far from being an indication of spiritual frivolity, was rather a proof that every possible effort was made to conciliate the native deities of Canaan and the powerful gods of Assyria and Babylonia. The pathetic appeals for light on the dark and urgent problems of worship and sacrifice, which in Mic. vi. 6-8 are put into the mouth of a pious contemporary, show that even a votary of Jehovah could be tempted to offer to Him that form of oblation which was most horrible, and at the same time most fascinating, in the heathen rites of his time and people. To offer up one's own offspring to Molech was the acme of Canaanitish self-devotion, and that Israelites could bring themselves to it shows a religious desperation that could only be quelled by revolution.

§ 1007. The ethical character of the prophetic religion was promoted by the antagonism which sprang up on this crucial question and other practical issues in the religious life of the nation. The revolting cruelty of the deity who could require such sacrifices could be easily learned by all except misguided fanatics. A recoil was inevitable in favour of Him who proclaimed to men baffled and disheartened by the tyrannical claims of rival ceremonial systems: "What doth Jehovah require of thee but to do justice and to love mercy and to walk humbly with thy God?" True, the yoke of bondage to rites and ceremonies could not be thrown off, and indeed it soon had to be tightened in the interest of that very religion to which it was essentially alien. The prophetic note, as often afterwards, sounded far above the practical reason of those who were charged with the offices of religion.

§ 1008. But the ruling classes and the majority of the people, both in and outside of Jerusalem, continued to follow an organized system of heathen and half-heathen worship, of which the most repulsive of practices were a customary adjunct. Hence to the faithful minority everything in the popular religion which detracted from purity of thought and worship became more repugnant, along with everything in practical life not in accord with justice, mercy, and submission to the will of Jehovah. The effect on belief or doctrine was necessarily intense and lasting. Never is feeling so quickly crystallized into an article of faith as in times of religious hardship and conflict. To speak of dogma in the modern metaphysical sense as an expression of the Old Testament spirit would be, it is true, an impertinence almost amounting to blasphemy. The prophetic word, the basis of all pre-Christian teaching, was not logical or philosophic statement, but a revelation of concrete facts as to the nature of Jehovah and the duty of men. And such a communication of new truth had not only an outward form but also an inner history that was human and personal. The truth itself, as far as known, was the resultant of manifold forces, social and individual, working under the impulse and direction of the inscrutable divine spirit in the souls of those through whom the message came. All teaching was at once spontaneous, subjective, and concrete, based in its substance and expression upon the experience and aspirations of men who had the gifts of feeling, seeing, and speaking. Hence abstract dogmatic statement was inconceivable and unimaginable, apart from the fact that the language was incapable of being used for the purpose.[1] Yet doctrines and principles may exist without and before dogmas and maxims, and faith without and before either.[2] These doctrines and principles were propounded and practised in those days of storm and stress with a conviction and energy of which philosophizing and critical peoples and times can have no conception.

§ 1009. Such a doctrine was the holiness of Jehovah. His sanctity had been always admitted. But it was a new experience to preach and believe that He was both righteous in action and essentially pure in character. The name of Jehovah came to include holiness in this twofold aspect; and as the word (שם) implies, it was his "mark" — that by which He was known. The foregoing observations have led up to the conclusion that such a knowledge of Jehovah was, in part at least, the outcome of moral and religious antagonisms. The effect of such a belief upon the character of the believer was regenerative. The conception worked by reflex influence. To adapt the old

---

[1] Even such familiar New Testament expressions as "God is Light," "God is Love," are foreign to Hebrew conception and linguistic usage. It is scarcely necessary to remind the reader that the most abstract of the doctrines of Jesus are given in concrete form; for example: "*I am* the Way, the Truth, and the Life."

[2] "Faith" is never mentioned in the Old Testament, though it is there throughout in the form of "trust." Such is the faith that is even ascribed to Abraham (§ 962), who had neither doctrines nor principles. And the Roman centurion, who showed greater faith than any in Israel (Luke vii. 9), had principles and no doctrines.

saying: as a man's God is, so must he himself be. But the converse also holds: what a man is, that his God must also be. God, however, is an ideal, and man, essentially a mere animal, but with head aloft and gazing into heaven,[1] normally aspires towards that ideal. He can never become as great and good as his visions. Yet it is only by straining that he rises at all. It is the pure in heart who see God (Matt. v. 8) and "he that hath this hope in him purifieth himself even as He is pure" (1 John iii. 3; cf. § 994).

§ 1010. Observe also how this clarified notion of Jehovah's character tended to develop moral individuality (cf. § 1000). The knowledge of his holiness could come through personal experience alone. Whatever else was a matter of traditional belief — his faithfulness to Israel, his swiftness to punish his own and his people's enemies, his readiness to accept a sacrifice — this vitalizing conception at least was a matter of conviction, and could be certified to the individual soul alone. All that it implied and all that it brought with it served to confirm and deepen a personal relation with Jehovah.

§ 1011. The most potent consequence was a new idea of sinfulness and the results of forgiveness. Upon this I need not here enlarge. What is of importance, however, is to see how the condition of the feeble and struggling minority loyal to Jehovah favoured these spiritualizing ideas. Necessarily its members were excluded from the services of the sanctuary (cf. § 609). How such a privation tended to refine and ennoble the believer is shown in one of the most beautiful and artistically perfect of sacred poems (Ps. xlii., xliii). Spirituality always costs, and it was a heavy price that was paid for the blessing. But the gain was worth more than all that was suffered. Precious above everything else was the dis-

---

[1] According to the well-known line of Ovid: "Os homini sublime dedit cœlumque tueri," *Met.* i, 85.

covery anticipated by earlier prophets (Amos v. 21 ff., Hos. vi. 6, Isa. i. 11 ff., *et al.*), but now for the first time verified by a community of separate worshippers, that after all a sanctuary and its propitiatory sacrifices were not necessary for the essential exercises of religion or for pardon and peace with God. None the less did they yearn for the renewal of those outward communications with Jehovah which Old Testament saints always regarded as channels of grace and help. And perhaps they themselves scarcely realized that greater blessings came through the discipline of loss and separation than through the enjoyment of the unbroken privileges of the sanctuary.

§ 1012. Thus the national and official degeneracy of the period of Manasseh reacted according to sure moral laws upon the chosen spirits from whom came the words and the deeds that were to save Israel and the world. Practically the effect was seen most clearly in the period of Josiah and Deuteronomy. But the reaction of unfettered freedom did something more and something less than fulfil the moral promise of the years of repression and discipline. It invaded the spiritual sphere proper to prophetic thought and activity, and it fell below the prophetic ideal in laying excessive emphasis upon law and ritual. The compromise was, however, inevitable. The drafting of the reforming principles and methods came into the hands of professionals, and the carrying out of the reforms into the hands of politicians. On the whole they did better for their time than the prophets alone would have done in their place, for practical men "are wiser for their own generation" than idealists, and are saved by a marvellous instinct from apprehending more of new and saving ideas than they themselves are able or willing to put into practice.

§ 1013. It will be remembered that the reform of Josiah was conducted under the auspices of the priests. Their interest in the matter requires that a few words should be said of the part played by them in the moral and religious education of Israel,[1] especially that it may be seen whether or not it was purely formal. This vital point may be decided by observing the tendency of their official work to affect the character of their clients.

§ 1014. To begin with, the primitive man felt that he was completely under the power of his God or gods. It was this power that gave him thriving cattle or fertile fields or a prosperous family, or, peradventure, scattered his flocks, blighted his grain, or sickened or slew his children. But such curses or blessings might be arbitrary and inevitable. It was a decisive advance when a causal and necessary connection between them and the character of the individual was established; in other words, when some sense of moral responsibility was created in his mind. Here the institution of propitiatory sacrifice played a preliminary and auxiliary but most important part. The matter of first consequence always was that the deity should be conciliated. Even when national issues were hanging in the balance, he might not always intervene, for he might be indifferent or angered toward the people. The business of the priests was to secure his continual interest and favour. At first they interceded or sacrificed for the community, then for its representative, above all the chief or king, then for individuals in proportion to their prominence or the value of the offerings presented at the shrine. Individuals also might present their supplications or their *piacula*, the fruits of the field or the firstlings of the flock. But this they did in connection with sacred places and, if possible, through sacred persons.

§ 1015. In the Hebrew community, even before the rise of prophecy, the conditions were peculiarly favourable to the development of an individualistic or spiritual idea of religion in connection with ceremonial worship. First, there was the prime advantage that in Israel after

---

[1] Supplementing what has been noted of their judicial work in § 488 ff.

the time of Moses there was very seldom a multiplicity of coördinate deities to distract the worshipper or to weaken the religious sentiment. What was most seductive was the degradation of the worship of Jehovah by a sensuous symbolism, and the survival or revival of ancient popular superstitions. The purification of the worship of Jehovah was, therefore, of itself a distinct gain for the religious consciousness of the nation. Secondly, there was the fact that the priests, the active and moving religious force of the community, the mediators between Jehovah and the people, were also counsellors and mentors in the place of God (Ex. xxii. 7 f.; Deut. xxxiii. 9 f.) as givers of oracles and decisions in matters of dispute. They thus associated the life and conduct of their suppliants with their religious services (§ 488 f.). So essential was "direction" or "judgment" to the priesthood that the very last of the Old Testament prophets, while indulging in a pathetic reminiscence of the lost ideal, gives an exhaustive definition of this most spiritual of the priestly functions as follows : " Trustworthy direction was in his mouth, and unrighteousness was not found in his lips : in innocence and in uprightness he walked with me, and many did he turn away from iniquity. For the lips of a priest should guard right knowledge, and men should seek direction at his mouth, for a messenger of Jehovah of Hosts is he " (Mal. ii. 6 f.).

§ 1016. But in the very nature of things such offices could not be a permanent attribute of the priesthood. They could in truth only be duly fulfilled in an elementary stage of society. Partly on account of their abuse, (cf. § 490) and partly on account of the gradual and permanent restriction of the priests to intercessory and sacrificial work, their judicial and oracular functions fell into abeyance and were taken over by the prophets, or in more businesslike fashion by the local elders (§ 486). It is impossible to say how far the public or the individual conscience was affected by this ministry of the priests. Probably their influence for good was mainly conservative, preventing a relapse of the unstable society of the times into social anarchy and strife, depredations and reprisals. Yet we may be sure that their work was of positive benefit in two directions. When honest and faithful, they encouraged a spirit of justice and toleration among their clients. What was perhaps of more potential value, they, in their own persons, familiarized the people with the fundamental principle that their common life was religious throughout, and consisted of something more than religious service; that their ordinary duties had a religious sanction; that their obligations rested upon the behest of a supernatural power, who was also the head of the whole community. The consciousness or subconsciousness of this relation to supernatural powers gave of itself no ethical quality to an action, but it furnished a basis upon which the prophets raised the structure of spiritual morality, thus taking up the higher work which an official priesthood was incompetent either to apprehend or to achieve.

§ 1017. Thus neither the work nor the word of the priests, as far as it was official and professional, could aid directly in the moral and spiritual elevation of the individual, since it did not operate in the realm of conscience. But their indirect influence for good upon individual life was immeasurable. Not only, as we have seen, did they keep Jehovah before the mind of Israel in the twilight of its reason and faith, but the larger ministry into which they grew with the increasing complexity of both religious and civil life made provision for ever enlarging and real needs of worship and ritual. Ceremonial religion could not, it is true, renew the individual heart and life; its abuse could and did induce in the worshippers arrogance, hypocrisy, and the exclusion of God himself by means of the very symbols of his presence; the unfaithfulness, venality, and sensuality of many of its ministers drew upon them bitter and persistent prophetic denunciations[1] (*e.g.* Am. ii. 8 ; Hos. v. 1 ff. ; Mic. iii. 11). Yet this very priestly guild, when in harmony with the true prophets, wrought salvation in Israel in critical times, instigated all the reforms in worship, collected and guarded both the civil and ceremonial law of the nation, preserved the continuity of religious thought and knowledge in the long dark ages of Israel's history, and edited large and indispensable sections of the Old Testament.

§ 1018. When we see how little the literary prophets of the time had to do with the so-called "legislation" as given in Deuteronomy, and, on the other hand, keep in mind those who were in most sympathy with its special enactments, we gain an insight into the conditions of moral and religious progress that is quite invaluable. We are apt to suppose that it was the great prophets and well-known guides of the people who had most to do with epoch-making moral and religious movements that have left their mark in the literature of the Old Testament. The present instance shows plainly that this was not necessarily the case. It indicates besides that a great deal of the work which lay behind the moral, ceremonial, and civil law of the Hebrews was done by obscure priests and by disciples of the prophetic school (§ 937) in periods of history which we usually regard as religiously dead and unproductive. The growth of Deuteronomy, not merely as a literary, but as a moral and religious achievement, is proof of this. We know who the men were that were concerned in bringing this book to light and in securing its practical validity. We have no record of the epoch-making men who were concerned in its production.

---

[1] In degenerate times false prophets leagued themselves with recreant priests, a combination which virtually included the professionals of both orders. It was then that the true prophets were most outspoken against both. The dark picture is completed by Jer. v. 31, vi. 13, viii. 10, xxiii. 11, 34 ; Zeph. iii. 4 ; Ezek. xxii. 26. Cf. § 1066.

CHAPTER V

THE REFORMATION IN EFFECT

§ 1019. Of the details of the work of reformation we are not informed beyond the overturning of the abuses in worship already noted (§ 854 ff.). There can be little doubt that uniformity of religious service was secured during the rest of the life of Josiah, that the high-places were dismantled, that the idols disappeared from view, and that resort to the central sanctuary at the stated feasts was general and regular. Jerusalem itself was thoroughly cleared of ceremonial and moral impurities, and the ritual worship of Jehovah gained a dignity and prestige which it never wholly lost. Among the various adjustments of the new system special difficulty must have been felt in settling the cases of the deposed guardians of the local shrines. The provision whereby the priests were brought to Jerusalem and maintained there (2 K. xxiii. 8 f.) must have been, if persistently carried out, a heavy burden on the sacred revenues, as well as socially injurious. Equal difficulty must also have attended the organization and settlement of the whole body of the Levites at Jerusalem (Deut. xviii. 1 ff.). Practical obstacles must indeed have rendered this special legislation to a great degree ineffective.

§ 1020. The new programme had a fair trial. It was maintained for twelve years, and during that time it had behind it the official force of the kingdom, with the king's authority and active support. A fair measure of success attended it as far as it interfered with established usages which were the vehicle and support of the popular religion. But the enforcement of the ethical provisions of the "book of direction" was a task beyond legislation and its executive processes. The evils were inveterate and virulent; native to the soil (§ 495); the long habit of the nation; bound up with the practice of the great world, Hebrew and Gentile, outside the coterie of prophets and priests in Jerusalem, whose zeal must have been regarded by many as an outburst of intolerance, and by many more as a tumult of utopian folly. It was easier to break down an altar than to set free a family enslaved for a petty debt; to dismiss an idolatrous priest than to bring down from his place of power and pride a grandee grown rich by oppression and usury, or a judge in league with him through bribery and perjury (Mic. vii. 2 f.).

§ 1021. There were insuperable difficulties in the very nature of the case. First, there was an inner contradiction between the principles of the reform and its methods. Its moral groundwork, and its pleas for repentance, trust, and submission of the heart and life, were inconsistent with the notion of physical compulsion. The due effect of the appeals to the spiritual nature of the people was to create an ideal of religious service which must have been impaired by the drastic measures adopted to secure an external reformation. Thus was presented, as in the book of Deuteronomy itself, so in the system of conformity and uniformity which it prescribed, that practical antithesis between prophetic ideals and administrative necessities (cf. § 1012), and the far more profound antithesis between zeal for truth and zeal for a system, which have both sustained and marred the historic churches of Judaism and Christendom. Accordingly, while the ideal of Deuteronomy was to be at some time realized in the world, it was impossible to accomplish by force what could be effected only by moral influence and by the slow inducements of Providence within the souls of men.

§ 1022. Again, a fundamental and necessary defect of the movement lay in the fact that while Deuteronomy and its crusade appealed to Israel as a whole and as a corporate entity, its arguments and exhortations could properly affect only the individual heart and life. And yet, on the other hand, Deuteronomy had to hold fast to the idea of the solidarity of the community, not merely because it was a traditional conception, but because nearly all the pleas for a more spiritual religion and a nobler mode of life were based upon it. It was upon the ground of the common relation to Jehovah that the unity of the nation was felt and recognized, and it was upon the same ground that a common worship and loyal obedience were claimed for Him, and that help for the poor and unfortunate, and redress of all the wrongs within the community, were made a matter not merely of sentiment but of practical legislation. Thus this dominant conception was at once the strength and the weakness of the reforming cause.

§ 1023. But it is easy to make a radical mistake in summing up the effect of the Reformation and of the manual of reform which an eminent critic has adjudged to be "perhaps the most influential and far-reaching book that was ever written."[1] We must not suppose that the whole matter is settled by saying that on the one side there were mere external regulations that rested on force, and on the other a proclamation of principles that appealed to the heart and conscience. It is not to be assumed that ritual was wholly an outward thing. We must, in the first place, distinguish according to their nature and history between the ethical and the ritual in revelation and religious usage. Each of them must be regarded as a product of the higher religious life of Israel. They were not antagonistic, though they were antithetic (§ 1021). They ran from the beginning along parallel

---

[1] Cornill. *Der israelitische Prophetismus* (2d ed. 1896), p. 91.

lines. The one was mainly impelled by prophetic inspiration and direction; the other sprang from the necessities and proprieties of formal worship. The one was the free and untrammelled outcome of reflection and discourse; the other was the result of official deliberation and agreement, arrived at from time to time and finally embodied in rule and statute. Both are rooted in the same great dual motive, to secure the holiness of Jehovah's people and the purity of his worship; a motive working in long lines of historic development, beginning with the first prescriptions of Moses and ending perhaps in eternity. But, looking at the inherent force and potency of the two elements of Deuteronomy, we see that the ethical is both before and after the formal, the restrictive, and the punitive, because it is inward "in the heart" (Deut. xxx. 14), because it is spontaneous and unforced, because it is self-attesting and self-justifying. The one is like the cosmic influences, silent, sure, and constant, that "preserve the stars from wrong" and that give us the sunshine and the seasons. The other is like the terrestrial forces, irregular and uncertain, that bring us clouds and rain, lightning and tempest. The one, like the air of heaven, is the very breath and life of soul and spirit. The other, like the wind that bloweth where it listeth, is often boisterous and harsh; yet it keeps the moral atmosphere pure and sweet, and bears the voyager safe over life's treacherous sea.

§ 1024. The ethical and spiritual ideas of Deuteronomy have given dignity and immortality to the book because they inspired and vitalized its rules and ordinances and because in themselves they have been among the chief of all historic forces and agencies. Notice their adaptation to the most urgent needs of the Hebrew community of the time. We are impressed by the patriotism of the book, as being of the deepest and truest sort. To the people of Israel, denationalized as they were by foreign customs as well as by long servitude to foreign potentates, the doctrine was asserted and reiterated, that the land was Jehovah's, and that they were the tenants of it as Jehovah's people. "The land" or "the rest and the inheritance" (xii. 9) or "thy gates" (*i. e.* thy city, xvi. 5) "which Jehovah thy God giveth thee," is a standing phrase (cf. § 580 f.). This notion has ever since inspired the most fervent and steadfast patriotism known to the world, from ancient Palestine to modern South Africa. Jehovah's service by Jehovah's people in Jehovah's land may be taken as the theme of Deuteronomy. See how even the formal prescriptions of the religious life are permeated by the spirit of this threefold conception: "And now, behold, I have brought the first of the fruits of the ground, which Thou, Jehovah, hast given me!" (xxvi. 10). Such Deuteronomic sentiments must needs spiritualize and purify from pride and selfishness the feelings cherished by men everywhere for home and family and country.

§ 1025. Even the conception of the corporate unity of Jehovah's people, which has been noticed as a necessary defect of the book in its practical enforcement (§ 1022), became in the hands of the writer an actual preparation for the later and truer principle of the relation of the individual to God. For the obedience and worship and love of the heart, which were demanded upon the ground of the common union with Jehovah, were bound at length to manifest themselves as a personal experience and privilege, known besides to God himself alone. But we must leave the subject here, content to have merely pointed out some of the ethical treasures that lie on the surface of the book, or at a little depth below the surface.

§ 1026. And yet in the book as it stands the purely spiritual and ethical elements are secondary, introduced for the purpose of upholding and commending a thorough and rigorous system of ritual observance (§ 860 ff.). They are the pillars of a great structure, strong and stately, but still in this building only pillars. The consequences of the ritual system itself may be summarized as follows:[1] (1) The old religion of Israel found God everywhere in the Holy Land, revealing his power by various tokens: hence the multiplication of shrines and images. The reformers, by abolishing images and sanctuaries, left the common man outside of Jerusalem, the favoured shrine, without the manifest signs of God's presence, and therefore in a sense without God, since they had not arrived at the conception of the divine omnipresence. (2) Religion in the old time had been a matter of course and a constant element of everyday life. Every meal was in fact a sacrifice. With the restriction of the Israelite to the three great feasts and to worship at Jerusalem alone, he was led to think of and to pass through life in a great measure without religion, which had shrivelled up to the observances of these three festal seasons. (3) In the olden time every man was a priest in his own house, and sacrifices were offered by many besides the priests. Now, with the exclusive concentration of the priesthood in the tribe of Levi, the distinction between clergy and laity was created. At the same time the priestly function was modified. The priests, instead of being counsellors and givers of oracles at the local sanctuaries, became expounders of the written law. (4) Deuteronomy also created the distinction between church and state. Formerly the king and the government cared for and administered the affairs of religion. Now all this was in the hands of a caste or order distinct from nobles and people alike. Thus it was made possible for Israel, through this churchly system, to survive the destruction of the state. (5) Now for the first time religion was grounded upon a book, and became itself a system of statutes or a "law." And thus the doctrine of a Holy Scripture and its inspiration is to be traced finally to Deuteronomy.

---

[1] In what follows of this paragraph I have done little more than abridge the observations of Cornill in p. 84 ff. of his admirable little book, *Der israelitische Prophetismus* (2d ed. 1896).

CHAPTER VI

THE EGYPTIANS IN PALESTINE

§ 1027. Outward conformity to prescription was at best of little significance for the ultimate fate of the people. The chances of a single life were all that lay between it and a revulsion which might more than undo all that had been effected at so great a cost. But thirteen years of the new religious régime had passed when that life came to an end, and in a way which seemed to belie the promise of a happy reign. During the years of Josiah's maturity his people must have increased in numbers, wealth, and outward strength. Assyria having relaxed its hold upon the district of Samaria, a portion of the country to the north of the old boundary of Judah must have been annexed, if it were only to secure protection against bands of marauders from the other provinces of Assyria now left without a settled government (cf. § 840). Josiah had excellent business men about him to administer the revenues of his kingdom. He was a strong ruler, and his virtual independence increased his interest in the development of his country. He had a loyal army which was ready to follow him even in hazardous enterprises. Hence when it was thought necessary to attack a foreign invader, the superiority of the enemy was not sufficient to prevent his taking the field against him.

§ 1028. The conflict with this trespasser upon the soil of Palestine brings the Hebrew people again upon the arena of a world-moving struggle. It was the singular distinction of this little community to be perpetually involved in movements that turned the channels of human history. When it was at peace, it was creating and working out the conditions of moral and religious progress that were to be the example and the inspiration of all coming time. When it was at war, it took a part far beyond its relative political importance in those international contentions which decided the fate of the most powerful of ancient empires. Now, after many years of profound internal repose, it dashed, all of a sudden, into a conflict on which depended the fortunes of the two great civilizations of Oriental antiquity.

§ 1029. Of the reigns of Esarhaddon and Asshurbanipal, not the least important events were the Assyrian conquest of Egypt under the former king, and its reconquest and final abandonment by the latter (§ 756, 764 ff.). Among other interesting matters was the great enlargement of international relations (§ 768, 775). The liberation of Egypt from the Assyrian yoke was due in large measure to mercenary troops of Ionians and Carians sent to the support of Psammetichus I by Gyges, king of Lydia. This dependence of the ruling dynasty upon the most available foreign support continued to be a feature of Egyptian history. The Ethiopian dynasty had been crushed by Assyria. It had been self-reliant, patriotic, and unbending. Necho I, the prince of Sais in the Delta, was a favourite of the Assyrians (§ 766); and to them he owed not only pardon and reinstatement after rebellion, but support during the rest of his life. His son Psammetichus was fortunate in securing the aid of foreigners, who demanded only their pay and rations, in driving out another set of foreigners, who strove for dominion, homage to their gods, and unfailing tribute.

§ 1030. This dynasty of Sais grew in power and in largeness of aim and outlook. Sais, the capital, throve apace, though Memphis, the old-time northern seat of empire, was also patronized. The name of another city, Thebes, or No-Amon, recalls a calamity that thrilled with its horrors the lands across the Isthmus (§ 770) and reminded the world that the glory of Upper Egypt had departed. The seat of power was permanently fixed in the Delta, and the old sacred cities on the undivided Nile took their place among the numberless monuments of the past. Sais became one of the world's centres of influence. Greek mercenaries and Tyrian merchants, both of whom were granted settlements in the Delta, spread the fame of the reviving empire of the Pharaohs among the nations. The reign of Psammetichus, remarkable in so many ways, was distinguished also for its duration. He was prince of Sais in 664 B.C., deliverer and undisputed ruler of Egypt in 645, and died about 610.

§ 1031. Necho II, the Necho of the Bible, continued his father's general policy and sought to surpass his achievements. The encouragement of foreign soldiers, sailors, and traders brought with it an astonishing spirit of commercial enterprise. He attempted to restore the old Suez Canal, but the work was too heavy, and he was compelled to desist.[1] Herodotus[2] informs us that Necho had fleets of triremes in the Red Sea as well as in the Mediterranean. His statement[3] that this Pharaoh sent Phœnician ships from the Red Sea, which sailed around Africa ("Libya") and returned through the straits of Gibraltar in the third year of their voyage, is now accepted as true, being confirmed by the report of the mariners that during the trip they came to a stage where the rising sun was on their right hand; that is, they turned to the north after sailing to the south.

§ 1032. Of more direct concern to us is the new departure of Pharaoh Necho in foreign political relations. His father had spent his chief energies in building up and securing the kingdom which he had freed, and had fortified his frontier cities south, northwest, and northeast.

---

[1] This must be the real meaning of the exaggerated story of Herodotus, II, 158.

[2] Book II, 159.   [3] *Ib*. IV, 42.

Yet Herodotus[1] tells of his having taken Ashdod after a long series of campaigns, ending perhaps about 615 B.C. It is doubtful if this conquest was maintained, but it shows how eager the Egyptians were to secure a base of operations in Asia against Assyria. When Necho came to the throne, that empire had been shorn of its power, stripped of its possessions, and dethroned from its supremacy. The lion was no more king of the forest, but was at bay in his lair (Nah. ii. 11 f.), and was being pressed hard by the hunters, furious at the loss of the choicest of their flock. Now at last Egypt seemed to have her opportunity. It was long since she had ruled in the Westland of Asia. For centuries she had played a waiting policy, acting on the defensive, except when she was herself a subject state of the hated Assyrian.

§ 1033. It was in Necho's third year (608 B.C.) that he brought his motley army across the Isthmus. Nineveh had not yet fallen and had still a name to live, but now there was none to defend the rich provinces of Mesopotamia and Syria, whence her garrisons had been withdrawn. Visions of a larger Egypt rose before the Pharaoh's imagination, an empire unrestrained by the desert, of which Tyre, the market-place of the world, should be the centre. The conquests of Thothmes and Rameses, immortalized in papyrus and stone, should be outdone by his achievements. When he took the fateful step, crossed the River of Egypt and entered the Philistian plains, he looked to meet with such a welcome as that which, a century before, had greeted from afar the expected march of Egyptian armies! Then Egypt was the hope of the desperate communities of Palestine, goaded to madness by Assyrian extortion. Egypt was the traditional ally of the oppressed peoples all along the line of march. They will, he thinks, make no opposition to

---

[1] *Ib.* II, 157. Jeremiah xxv. 20 speaks of "Askalon, Gaza, and Ekron, and the remnant of Ashdod."

him now, and perhaps some sturdy bands of shepherds or hunters will join his ranks for pay or the hope of plunder. He does not dream of an attack from the only self-contained nation this side of the Euphrates. He knows, to be sure, that Josiah had sworn fealty to the king of Assyria; but that was thirty years ago, and who, in any case, would keep faith with a moribund oppressor! He passes the slopes of Judah and Benjamin and Ephraim. He will not enter their territory now, or even negotiate with the king of Judah. But on his return, victorious over Nineveh and lord of Western Asia, how eagerly will the remnant of Israel come forth to offer him homage!

§ 1034. He enters the plain of Jezreel, so full of names that recall the old-time glories of the Pharaohs. Here he becomes aware of an enemy on his flank. It is none other than Josiah of Judah, who undertakes to cut off his march and challenges his right to pass through the limits of ancient Israel. Necho sends him a friendly message. He is anxious to conciliate him, in view of the great business now in hand. "What have I to do with thee, thou king of Judah? I am not against thee this day, but against the (kingly) house with which I am at war" (2 Chr. xxxv. 21). But Josiah will not listen. The armies come together at Megiddo, at the first available point after the plain of Esdraelon (Jezreel) had been entered from the southwest by the pass that leads from the vale of Sharon.[1] Josiah is hard pressed by the archers and

[1] See the beautiful map in HG. Plate VI. Professor Smith argues rightly against the supposition of Herodotus (II. 159) that Necho sent his troops by sea to the coast and then followed the land northeastward, and remarks that in that case he would have landed at Akko and not marched as far south as Megiddo. The ἐν Μαγδόλῳ of Herodotus points to a confusion of Megiddo with the frequently occurring "Magdala." The site of Megiddo is the modern *Lejjun*; see HG. p. 385 ff. The Κάδυτις which Herodotus mentions as a large city of "Syria," captured by Necho after the battle, cannot be Gaza, as some suppose, much less Jerusalem (קדש; *el Kuds*). It is probably an Egyptian reminiscence of Kadesh on the Orontes (§ 162 f.). The allusion in Jer. xlvii. 1 may perhaps be explained as an episode of the expedition of 587 (xxxvii. 5).

"sore wounded" (2 Ch. xxxv. 23). He is transferred by his men to a "second chariot," and over the hills of Ephraim he is brought home to Jerusalem to die.

§ 1035. The calamity was great and irreparable, and the grief of the people of Judah could not be restrained. "And all Judah and Jerusalem mourned for Josiah. And Jeremiah lamented for Josiah. And all the singing men and singing women celebrate Josiah in their dirges until this day. And they made them a custom in Israel, and behold they are written in the dirges" (2 Chr. xxxv. 24 f.). But no lamentations could bring back the good king to the land that he alone could rule aright; or to his boys, who were exposed by his death to dangers and temptations from without and within; or to the work of Jehovah, which none of his kingly successors had the grace or the power to continue.

§ 1036. But to the stricken people the folly was not so obvious as it is to us. Let us see what Josiah's motives must have been. We may well suppose that he was influenced by his oath of allegiance to Assyria. We know what the prophetic view of this relation was. In the solemn adjuration it was not simply the gods of the suzerain whose vengeance was invoked upon the recreant, but the God of his own land also, who was held to have abjured his prerogative, and to have placed his subjects at the disposal of the servants of Asshur (cf. 2 K. xviii. 25; § 290, 700). And in proportion to the piety and fidelity of Josiah must have been his sense of the obligation to keep faith with his superior. Josiah's compact with Assyria doubtless also included the obligation on his part to protect, as far as possible, the whole of Palestine, over which the empire of the Tigris had held direct sway for more than a century.

§ 1037. However we may regard this aspect of the situation, we would in any case find a justification for the aggressive action of the king of Judah, in the Egyptian invasion of his northern border. Egyptian success in

Syria meant the certain subjection of Judah, the exchange
of a nominal vassalage to Assyria for assured submission
to Egypt. How abhorrent this must have appeared to a true
servant of Jehovah we can readily imagine. Among other
evils it might involve the addition of African deities to the
mixed and impure worship which had just been suppressed
but not extirpated. A student and disciple of the prophets must have borne in mind their warnings against an
Egyptian alliance, and their denunciations of Egypt itself.
In the impending struggle Judah must be either an ally
or an enemy of Egypt; and the choice made by Josiah
was not unworthy of a kingly soul, desperate as was his
march to the fatal plain of Megiddo.

§ 1038. Thus Judah came, for the first and last time,
under Egyptian control. But the badge of servitude was
not at once affixed. Assured of the ultimate acquisition
of Jerusalem, Necho continued his northward march till
he reached a point whence he could direct operations
simultaneously against both northern and southern Syria,
and at the same time prevent an uprising in Palestine
itself. It was at Riblah on the Orontes route to the
Euphrates (§ 202) in the northern portion of Cœle-Syria,
that he fixed his camp — a station which remained the
headquarters of great foreign armies of occupation till the
end of the Judaite monarchy [1] (§ 1213).

§ 1039. Meantime the inevitable revolution took place
in the little kingdom thus bereft of head and hope. As
often happened in an ancient Oriental state suddenly left
kingless, two parties were formed. The one counselled
submission to Egypt. The other, consisting of the "people
of the land" (§ 806), stood for patriotic independence. The

---

[1] It is interesting to observe how the general conditions of warfare in
the Westland had changed since the days of Tiglathpileser III. Then
the great vantage points were Arpad, Hamath, and Damascus (§ 294,
307, 335). Now from one central rendezvous the whole of Syria and
Palestine could be overlooked and controlled; so much had the Assyrian
arms and government and military routes unified the lands and the
peoples.

sturdy freeholders, who had begun to feel the blessings of a long peace and righteous administration, foreboded impoverishment from the Egyptian yoke with its fines and tribute, and set upon the throne Josiah's son Jehoahaz (2 K. xxiii. 30). Of his unfortunate young life only shadowy recollections were left even to his own and the next generation. We are not quite sure what place he held in the family of Josiah.¹ It is probable that he was the second son and that the older, Jehoiakim, being favourable to Egyptian rule (cf. 2 K. xxiii. 34), was put aside by the independent faction. His given name seems to have been Shallum (Jer. xxii. 11). Of his general character we have little or no indication. The poetical sketch by Ezekiel (xxi. 3), which is identical with that drawn of Jehoiakim (xix. 6), is nothing more than a characterization of the average king of Judah. His reign of three months was, indeed, too brief to leave any definite impression. Courage, at least, was shown by his defiance of the Egyptian king and army. The next step was the natural sequel to the overthrow of Josiah. A force was sent against Jerusalem. The city was besieged and soon capitulated. Jehoahaz was dethroned and brought in

---

¹ According to 2 K. xxiii. 31, Jehoahaz was twenty-three years old at his accession, and according to xxiii. 36 his brother Jehoiakim was twenty-five. Hence we would infer that Jehoahaz was the second in age. But the list of the sons of Josiah in 1 Chr. iii. 17 f. (in which the Lucian Sept. reads correctly "Jehoahaz" instead of the unknown "Johanan" of the received text) declares him to be the eldest. What is still more extraordinary, the same list, giving four sons, calls the youngest "Shallum," the name by which Jehoahaz is known to Jeremiah (xxii. 11). From this one might be tempted to infer that Jehoahaz was really the youngest son, whom the landholders had enthroned as a mere lad and as thus being more likely to yield to their purposes; that "Johanan," the eldest, had died in infancy; and that the "twenty-three" of 2 K. xxiii. 31 (copied in 2 Chr. xxxvi. 2) is an error. More likely is it, however, that the compilers of the list of sons, overlooking the identity of Jehoahaz and Shallum, found a place for the latter name by putting it at the end of the group. Again, it is quite possible that the same compilers, taking account of the fact that Jehoahaz was the first to ascend the throne, assumed that he was the eldest.

chains to Pharaoh in his northern encampment. His fate was such as in those days befitted a rebel of the first degree. He was carried away to Egypt (2 K. xxiii. 34) with every mark of ignominy (cf. Ez. xix. 4 and § 802). With him were deported a considerable number of the people, who formed a sort of colony for a few years at least (Jer. xxiv. 8). There he remained a prisoner, and no man knows when death released him from that ancient "house of bondage." Though little trace is left of him in the records of history or in human memory, certain words uttered concerning him, more perhaps in sorrow than regret, are unforgetable.

> "Do not weep for the dead,
> And do not mourn for him;
> Weep sore for him that goeth away,
> For he shall never more return,
> And see the land of his birth.[1]

"For thus saith Jehovah as to Shallum, son of Josiah, king of Judah, who reigned instead of Josiah his father, and who went forth from this place: He shall not return thither any more. For in this place whither they carried him captive there he shall die, and this land he shall see no more." (Jer. xxii. 10 f.; cf. § 1143.)

§ 1040. Eliakim ("Whom God establishes"), presumably the eldest son of Josiah, was now placed upon the throne by the Egyptian invader to advertise to the world his own supremacy in Palestine, and to impress upon the people of Judah their change of masters. Pharaoh modified his name[2] to Jehoiakim ("Whom Jehovah estab-

---

[1] Cf. § 801, and the article, "What Exile meant to Israel," in the *Sunday School Times*, Sept. 9. 1899.

[2] There was no usage among ancient Orientals more expressive than the giving of personal names. The name was not a label, as it is with us, but a characteristic. In Hebrew phraseology it is sometimes even equivalent to the person himself, as "the name of Jehovah." Among other relations it specially indicates that of dependence, above all when it is "theophorous," or bears the name of a deity (cf. § 407. In the present case Necho would not alter the essential meaning of the name, for

lishes"). A fine of one hundred talents of silver and one talent of gold was levied directly upon the land, and this amount was duly exacted from the baffled freeholders (2 K. xxiii. 33).

§ 1041. Jehoiakim had as king a difficult task to fulfil, and neither his mental nor his moral endowments were equal to his responsibilities. His character will require our attention later, as a matter of Biblical interest (§ 1122). We are now more directly concerned with the events of his reign. For three years and longer the Egyptian yoke was worn by the people of Judah. Probably a reasonable autonomy was granted them. Egypt's best policy was to make the dependence as little galling as possible; for, though rebellion was certain to be unsuccessful, the hands of the Egyptians were tied by the necessity of guarding the eastern frontier of their newly acquired possession. And ere long their light-hearted campaign was completely frustrated by the Chaldæan conqueror, who had already claimed the Assyrian realm as his inheritance and was steadily advancing to the realization of his purpose.

§ 1042. The reconquest of the Assyrian provinces of the West was, however, not to be the achievement of Nabopalassar himself. According to the account which we get from Berossus by way of Josephus, the Chaldæan leader remitted this arduous task to his son Nebuchadrezzar, who was said to have borne an important share in the conquest of Nineveh. He had had a busy life, spent in the slow process of building up his native state till it could divide with the aggressive Median power the sovereignty of the richest portion of the world. He had now spent two years at least (cf. § 827) in the business of introducing law and order into his eastern provinces. But it was a matter of time to win over the country between

---

Judah was still Jehovah's land. But the very slightest change in the form would imply his authority as the namer, and therefore the master, of the subject prince. At the same time the term chosen would indicate his patronage of the local religion of Jehovah.

the Rivers to the new régime, and to adjust so many unsettled districts to the new government.

§ 1043. It was, accordingly, not till 605 that young Nebuchadrezzar was ready to cross the Euphrates. His encounter with the Egyptians must have seemed a predestined success. Pharaoh Necho, in spite of his years of occupation, soon realized how insecure was his tenure of the old Egyptian possessions (§ 1033). He did not dare to meet the advance of the Chaldaeans on the east of the River, but made his stand at Carchemish (Jer. xlvi. 2), the famous old fortress and emporium on the western side. The defeat of the Egyptians was followed by their retreat and their eventual abandonment of their Asiatic dominions. Thus the futility of Egypt as a military power was once more demonstrated, and its fondest hopes of an Asiatic empire shattered forever.

§ 1044. The kingdom of Judah fell in due course to the victorious Chaldaean. The fate of the Hebrew people was henceforth for nearly ninety years bound up with the policy and fortunes of the Babylonian empire. Our interest in their outer and inner history becomes more intelligent when we remember their wider relations. Whether at home as a subject state, or in exile as a band of slaves, the Hebrew community was but one of a number which owned the sovereignty of Babylon, and played their parts in the world under its protection and surveillance, and under the external conditions which it imposed. We must therefore try to get some tolerably correct notion of the genius and scope of this later Babylonian régime, and of the policy of the ruler who made so deep an impress upon his own and later times.

Book X

HEBREWS AND CHALDÆANS

CHAPTER I

BABYLON AND NEBUCHADREZZAR

§ 1045. We have now arrived at one of those turning-points in the affairs of Israel and of the world, which may well make us pause for a brief retrospect. There is a widespread impression that ancient Semitic history, in contrast with that of the Western lands, is monotonous and lifeless, devoid of a continuous purpose and of great inward motives. One of the aims of the present work is to rectify this error, and to show to what great issues the history of the North Semitic communities continually and coherently tended. Next to Israel itself the most potent factor in this process of the ages was Babylonia. The significance of some of the very earliest movements in the valley of the lower Euphrates has been already foreshadowed (§ 93, 116, 291), and will soon appear more clearly in the unfolding of the decisive events. Even the history of the Assyrian empire, involving the fate of Israel and of Western Asia during its critical epochs, was but a side-current in a larger stream, fed at the beginning, and ever and anon replenished, by Babylonian thought and endeavour.

§ 1046. From the political and moral standpoint none of these movements was more important than the latest of the Babylonian revolutions — that which made the Chaldaeans leaders of the Semitic world. Apart from the essential significance of this movement there attaches to the story of the Chaldaeans a romantic interest but seldom awakened by the achievements of Oriental communities. The nearest parallel is that afforded by the history of the rise of Judah to predominance among the tribes of Israel. But in the vicissitudes of the Chaldaean princes there is even more of heroic and patriotic achievement than that which has made so illustrious and fascinating the career and adventures of David. Their efforts to expel the Assyrians from Babylon, and to secure for themselves the dominion which they alone had the genius and the courage to administer, lasted for a century and a half, and was carried on during most of that period against fearful odds.

§ 1047. To recall to the reader their deeds and their fate I need only refer to the earlier passages in this work devoted to their commemoration. Under their own proper name they come first into view in the ninth century B.C. (§ 223). For a hundred years they submit with but little resistance to the Assyrian kings. Next we see their tribes resisting in common the Assyrian encroachments, and showing on their own part an equal and unique aggressiveness. Then we find them during the reigns of Sargon and Sinacherib under the leadership of the great Merodach-baladan aspiring to the possession of Babylon itself, and maintaining there an intermittent authority, fraternizing with the patriotic party throughout Babylonia, winning over for a time the all-powerful priestly interests, and when forced to retreat to their native haunts by the sea, proving themselves to be almost an invincible foe. The persistent onslaughts of Sinacherib kept them in the background, and thereafter till the end of the Assyrian empire they were forced to content themselves with reprisals and precarious alliances with the foes of the oppressor. The leaders of the Chaldæan uprising were hunted down and exterminated to the third generation by the last of the great Assyrian kings. But the overthrow of his dynasty and the destruction of his empire soon followed as the Nemesis of this and kindred atrocities, and swift as was Assyria's decline and fall, swift also was the rise of the Chaldæan power.

§ 1048. Obscure as is the origin of these adventurers from the "Sea-land," their national character and political methods are unmistakably clear. Though their antecedents seem unfavourable to such an historical rôle, they were genuinely Babylonian in their spirit and aims, and completely identified with the old Babylonian policy in church and state. Nor was this attachment to Babylonian things and ideas a mere result of their acquisition of the city of Babylon with its imposing institutions and inspiring traditions. From the earliest time of their appearance in history they show evidence of a certain community with the very locality which afterwards became the centre of their dominion. Their favourite objects of worship, as we learn from the naming of their children, were precisely those deities which were honoured above all in Babylon and Borsippa, the gods Merodach and Nebo. This coincidence, with the fact that they seemed to claim a certain right to rule and protect the city of Babylon, suggests that whatever may have been the origin of the bulk of the population (cf. § 223), at least the ruling class were of Babylonian origin in the strictest sense of the term. They were possibly a colony driven southward by the Kasshite invaders (§ 120 ff.).

§ 1049. Along with these tendencies the Chaldæan empire established by Nebuchadrezzar exhibited a genius for centralizing government which was distinctively Assyrian. The new establishment, standing as it did in the direct line of imperial development which culminated in the Roman empire (§ 6), naturally enough assimilated the antecedent political and national types. The temper of the Babylonian people, encouraged by the religious and mercantile habit, was politically too inert to secure the supremacy or even the continued liberty of the state. Assyria, on the other hand, had perfected a military and political system, which if imitated with moderation and caution, might well be expected to endure in peace and safety. It is this synthesis in the Chaldæan monarchy of the Babylonian and Assyrian types of national spirit and purpose which has given such significance to the closing epoch of the ancient Semitic régime. But of this later on. We are now to see how Nebuchadrezzar the Chaldæan dealt with the old subject states of the West.

§ 1050. Though the Chaldæan type of government had such a general resemblance to its predecessor, the process of erecting the new empire upon the ruins of the old almost seems to have violated a necessary law of Oriental history. Nineveh had fallen; but would not the victor ruling in Babylon continue the policy and the methods of the Assyrian empire in all their rigour? Western Asia had never known such a stern regimen as that which was wielded from the banks of the Tigris, nor was any such to be henceforth known in that ill-fated land, until Tartar cruelty and Muslim intolerance were made secure by "Christian" diplomacy, until Assyrian paganism was outdone in savage lust by a system which follows up conquest with devastation, and prolongs the horrors of war in official rapine and murder. In the remaking of the nations, after the collapse of Assyria, there was something new under the sun. It had been the standing order of the ancient world that one form of tyranny over feeble states should be superseded by another equally galling, that the resettlement of affairs in the subject territory should involve the turmoil and bloodshed of a tedious reconquest. Such was not the fate of the lands that had owned the sceptre of Nineveh. The reason was, in part, that they were weary of resistance and of strife, and were ready to accept any rule that would not press too heavily. The work of subverting the nations had been done by the Assyrian once for all. No subjugation in detail was needed by Chaldaean or Persian or Macedonian or Roman. Hence the wonder of the Chaldaean revolution. Momentous as was the effacement of the first empire of the world, the establishment of the second, under a new autocrat, did not reverse the political fortunes of the dependent peoples. With them the decisive question was whether the Assyrian should have an imperial successor. When this issue was fully decided, the affairs of the Semitic world resumed their normal course, with Babylon at the helm instead of Nineveh. Syria and Palestine were longer disturbed than the other old dependencies of Assyria, but the distortion was soon set right again.

§ 1051. This freedom from disturbance was also due, in large measure, to the character of the first two rulers of the new empire, who were men remarkable for energy and wisdom. The earlier career of Nabopalassar (625–605 B.C.)[1] has already been described. His breadth of view was shown by his alliance with Cyaxares of Media, and by his plans for the organization of the dominion that fell so suddenly into his hands. The allotment of the respective spheres of control, which eventually became, in both cases, actual possessions, was made on the simple and

---

[1] Of this epoch-making prince something more personal is known from his own inscriptions. He appears as the devout restorer of the temple of Merodach, "the temple of the foundations of heaven and earth" in Babylon, and of the temple of Bêlit (Beltis) at Sippar. His care for Sippar is also shown by his having built a canal for restoring the deflected waters of the Euphrates to that ancient city (§ 94). These acts indicate his desire to make northern Babylonia, which had been longest under Assyrian control, more surely Chaldaean. The Merodach temple inscriptions are published by Strassmaier, in ZA. iv. 129 ff., with translation (for which cf. KB. iii, 2, p. 2 ff.), and, after a more complete copy, by Hilprecht, in OBT. I, pl. 32, 33 (transcribed by D. W. McGee, BA. iii, 525 ff.); those relating to Sippar, by Winckler, in ZA. ii, 69 ff., 145 f., and 172 f. (cf. KB. iii, 2, p. 6 ff., and BA. iii, 527 f.).

obvious basis that the Medes should have the highlands and the Chaldaeans the lowlands of Western Asia. Each people thus chose according to its previous habit of life and native preference, and upon the lines thus indicated each advanced till the limit of extension was reached.[1] Hence the Chaldaean realm embraced nearly all that the Assyrians had succeeded in organizing and controlling — a territory thus made ready for a new imperial administration. Assyria proper (§ 74) was itself divided. The northern portion lying on the mountain slopes fell to Media, which thus kept guard over Nineveh, while that which lay to the south of the Lower Zab became Babylonian. The boundary lines, defined by nature, were, as far as we know, always settled amicably, in spite of the expansion of the two empires along contiguous lines. Moreover, the Medes became indirectly protectors of Babylonia. The chief danger which had long threatened the Semitic country, and which contributed greatly to the ruin of Assyria, was the incursions of mountain tribes from the north. These were kept in hand by the Medes, who made them either allies or subjects.

§ 1052. Only two years of life remained to Nabopalassar after the fall of Nineveh, and it was reserved to his illustrious son to give its permanent character to the Chaldæan name and empire. Nebuchadrezzar II (*Nabū-kudur-uṣur*, "Nebo, preserve the boundary," 604–562 B.C.), though the heir of the Assyrian monarchy, was a genuine Babylonian in spirit and temper. He is, indeed, the representative Babylonian, as Tiglathpileser III is the representative Assyrian. With him conquest was not the occupation nor dominion the end of the life of a monarch. These were a part of his responsibilities as successor to a line of warriors and world-rulers; but his real interest was the worship of

---

[1] It is noteworthy that the Medo-Persian expansion under Cyrus (§ 1386 ff.) continued in the same direction, the Babylonian empire remaining intact long after Cyrus had subdued the whole of the highlands as far as the coast of the Ægean.

his gods, the care of their temples, and the upbuilding of Babylonia, especially of its capital city. As the head of an empire he stood midway between the Assyrian and the Persian types: he did not harass and ravage his subjects like the former, while he did not study local interests like the latter (see § 1414). He cannot fairly be called an aggressive ruler. His general policy was rather to keep the empire intact, according to its Assyrian limits, than to extend its boundaries. Hence, as a rule, he avoided aggressive war throughout his long reign. His slowness to undertake suppressive campaigns, and the freedom he allowed his vassals, as in the case of the kings of Judah, were due to his tolerant and generous disposition, as well as to his preoccupation with his beloved Babylon (§ 1055). He reminds us somewhat of Esarhaddon (§ 762) in his largeness of view and goodness of heart. Of Nebuchadrezzar also it can be said that, while stern toward the leaders of a rebellion, the mass of the offending community were treated with consideration — a fact to which the people of Judah owed their survival.

§ 1053. Under the old Semitic type of government a strong monarch literally made the kingdom or the empire (§ 51, 534). The importance of Nebuchadrezzar for the history of Israel and of Revelation makes it fortunate that he is one of the few ancient Orientals of whose personality we can gain some knowledge. There are two aspects of his character which specially reveal the source of his influence. In one of these he appears as a religious man and in the other as a patriot.[1] Strictly

---

[1] It is only these aspects of his character that are illustrated in his numerous inscriptions so far discovered. Like other Babylonian kings, he describes his temples, palaces, and public works, and ignores his military and political achievements. The principal published inscription is that in the possession of the East Indian Office in London, in archaic characters, I R. 53–58 (in cursive or modern Babylonian, 59–64). I R. 65 f. also gives the cylinder inscription first published by the famous Grotefend in 1848, and a few shorter ones appear in I R. 51 f. Since the date of I R. (1861), several others have been found and published. See the transcrip-

speaking, the religious sentiment explains most of his public actions. Babylonian kings generally, as compared with those of Assyria, showed their devotion to the gods by preserving and beautifying their sanctuaries rather than by subduing the nations in order to increase the number of their votaries. How much more highly he estimated his favourite form of practical religion is evident from the tenor of his principal inscription, in which he makes almost the only allusion to his warlike achievements found on his monuments. In this passage,[1] which merely forms part of an introduction to the story of his works of piety at home, he speaks of having subdued many countries near and far in the service of Merodach.

§ 1054. The inscriptions of Nebuchadrezzar are not singular in being full of devout expressions. What we observe in him is the concentration of his devotion upon a few gods of the Babylonian pantheon, especially Merodach, the healer and protector of mankind, and his son Nebo, the god of revelation and knowledge. These were, to be sure, the tutelary deities of Babylon and the surrounding region, so that he would worship them chiefly in any case. But it is the kind of worship paid to any deity that indicates the character of the worshipper. Now what is conspicuous in Nebuchadrezzar is the purity and self-abandonment of his adoration, as contrasted with the self-laudatory grandiloquence of the Assyrian kings. Indeed, there was none among all the ancient Semites whose recorded utterances are so little unlike those of the worshippers of Jehovah. The follow-

---

tions and translations by Winckler in KB. iii, 2, pp. 10–71, forming a valuable handbook of the monuments of the great Chaldaean. There nearly all the published inscriptions are given except Pognon's *Inscriptions babyl. de Wadi Brissa* (§ 1211 note). A long inscription in fine preservation has been obtained by the Pennsylvania expedition. Brief inscriptions, at least, he must have written about other matters, for a fragment much mutilated tells of an expedition to Egypt in his thirty-seventh year. See Pinches, in TSBA. vii, 210 ff., and Tiele, BAG. 435 f.

[1] Neb. II, 12 ff.

ing is a prayer to Merodach: "Everlasting ruler, lord of all that is, the king to whom thou hast given a name well-pleasing to thyself, make thou him[1] to prosper and lead him upon a plain path.[2] I am the prince obedient to thee, the creature of thy hand; thou hast created me and hast allotted to me the dominion of the whole race of men. According to thy grace, O Lord, which thou hast made to pass over them all, let me love thy glorious dominion; let the fear of thy god-head dwell in my heart; grant what seemeth good to thee, O thou who hast created my life."[3] Such was the religion of the Chaldæan "servant of Jehovah" (Jer. xxv. 9.). Thus were fulfilled the pious hopes of Nabopalassar, who has left on record[4] that in restoring the great temple of Merodach in Babylon, he himself and his two sons joined in the tasks of the workmen (cf. § 749), and that he bade the older lad carry mortar to the walls and bring offerings of wine and oil.

§ 1055. In his patriotic endeavours to build up and strengthen Babylon, the main motive was also religious.[5] Indeed, every public work was a religious performance. Moreover, the temples and the priestly organization held such practical control that no business interest was untouched by them. But the reader should have a clearer idea of the city and the country which made a second home for Israel during so many years. Of the plans for developing the country at large, we can speak better when we come to describe the Hebrew colony on the Kebar (§ 1272 ff.). The Babylon of the time, where some of the exiles dwelt, and which was virtually a creation of the Great King, may here be very briefly described.

---

[1] Literally, "his name." (Cf. § 1410 note.)
[2] Ps. xxvii. 11. The words for "plain" in the two prayers are from the same root יָשָׁר.
[3] Neb. I, 55 ff.; II, 1.
[4] Inscription for the temple of Merodach, II. 69 ff.
[5] This had the result of undue care for Babylonia, at the expense of the interests of the subject states; cf. § 1152.

§ 1056. The Bible student and the student of history are equally moved by the name of Babylon.[1] It is perhaps our most familiar type of fallen and desolate grandeur. Complete as is its present desolation, its former glory was equally conspicuous. Oriental antiquity had nothing to equal it, and to the western world it long remained the ideal of human magnificence. It was the immemorial capital of a great community, to which, above all other nations, ancient traditions were precious and sacred. In it were gathered the treasures of the literature, science, and art of a people among whom knowledge and skill were always appreciated and always progressive. It was the emporium, the workshop, and the university of Asia. It was the survivor and the heir, not merely of many opulent cities, but even of old superseded civilizations. It was now prosperous as never before. The time, too, was propitious. The Semitic world was enjoying the blessings of peace, after the downfall of the Assyrian disturber and the tumults and strife of many centuries. The Chaldæan

---

[1] Any description of the Chaldæan Babylon must still be very general. Since the era of modern rediscovery, the native records have given us the first authentic accounts (see note to § 1053). But from the point of view of the writers, the details are necessarily selective rather than descriptive, and valuable information is to be gained from classical writers, especially Herodotus (I, 178 ff.), who personally viewed the city about 450 B.C. The account of Ctesias (in Diodorus Siculus) is somewhat less reliable. Very important, though scarcely more than panoramic, are the statements of Berossus (in Josephus against Apion, I, 19, § 1057), himself a resident of Babylon. One of the best modern descriptions is that of Tiele (BAG, pp. 441–454), and there is a good, though too reserved, discussion by Pinches, in EB., art. "Babylon," with a plan. In both of these essays the observations of the modern travellers — Rich, Taylor, Ainsworth, Loftus, Rawlinson, Layard, and others — have been taken into account. Dr. D. W. McGee, lecturer in University College, Toronto (drowned in 1895 at the age of twenty-three), had nearly completed a treatise, *Zur Topographie Babylons auf Grund der Urkunden Nabopalassars und Nebukadrezars*, which is now in course of publication in BA., edited by Professor Delitzsch. The present excavations by the German expedition under Koldewey promise to clear up many unsolved difficulties of the gravest kind.

princes had brought Babylonia to its own again. With the inspiration of a swift and splendid access of freedom and power, they were eager to repair the former devastations (§ 740, 783), and make the resurgent capital the centre of the world. And stronger than mere political motives in the new kingly line was a holy jealousy for the name and dominion of Merodach and Nebo. Rival deities must abdicate their thrones in the many-templed cities of Babylonia for the greater glory of the gods of Babylon. What was their loss was the gain of Merodach and Nebo and of the city of their love and choice. Merodach, indeed, had always been greater than any single name could express. As patron of Babylon the great, he was invested with the attributes of the old Babylonian Bēl. Thus Bēl, once worshipped at Nippur, the most ancient centre of the Semitic religion, was now resident in the seat of the world's empire as Bel-Merodach.[1] Thus it was that in the phrase of a Hebrew prophet (Isa. xiii. 19) Babylon became "the glory of kingdoms, the proud adornment of Chaldæa."

§ 1057. Speaking of Nebuchadrezzar Berossus says: "He adorned the temple of Belus and the other temples in an elegant manner out of the spoils he had taken in this war.[2] He also rebuilt the old city and added another to it on the outside, and so far restored Babylon that none who might besiege it after that time should be able to divert the river, so as to make an easier entrance into the city. And this he effected by building three walls about the inner city and three about the outer. So

---

[1] Cf. Jensen, *Kosmologie*, pp. 134, 307; Jastrow, RBA. p. 54 f., 145 ff. The identification of Bēl and Merodach was as old as the political supremacy of Babylon under Chammurabi (§ 117); but the absorption of Bēl by Merodach, with a complete interchange of names, is characteristic of the Chaldæan era. The indirect effect upon Israel of this depreciation of Nippur and its "Bēl" will be pointed out later (§ 1285 f.).

[2] That is, the early campaign in the West, interrupted by his father's death, which Berossus (or Josephus) combines in one description with the later operations in the West.

when he had fortified the city with walls and adorned the gates magnificently, he added a new palace to that which his father had dwelt in, close by it also, but loftier and more splendid. . . . Immense and magnificent though it was, it was finished in fifteen days. In this palace he erected very high promenades supported on stone pillars : and by planting what was called a hanging garden, and replenishing it with all sorts of trees, he made it resemble exactly the scenery of a mountainous country. This he did to please his queen, because she had been brought up in Media, and was fond of mountainous surroundings."

§ 1058. The above may serve as a vague outline to which some definiteness may be given by details from other sources. First, as to the general situation of the city. It lay mainly on the east or left bank of the Euphrates, the most thickly settled portion occupying a space of about four miles across from north to south within the irregularly bending course of the river, which turns south-west, south, and east, and then runs due south for five miles, the modern village of Hillah being three miles south of the easterly bend. The features of most interest and importance were the walls, the canals, the temples, and the palace. The outer wall was of enormous extent. According to Herodotus, the city was 480 stadia or 55 miles in circumference, and this wall 80 feet wide. Alongside of it ran a moat so broad that no arrow could be shot over it.[1] Above its wide summit stood dwellings of officials, and between them lay a street where chariots might run. This wall, said to be mountain-high, was the greatest structure known to antiquity. It was the work of Nebuchadrezzar and his men, devised to make the defences of the city doubly sure. It was pierced with "a hundred" gates of bronze. This was, however, not the outermost obstacle to a possible invader. Eastward still was dug an immense

---

[1] There were enclosing walls for this moat, which may explain the reported statement of Berossus, quoted above, that there were three walls around the outer city.

artificial lake supplied by an overflow of the Euphrates and by diverted affluents of canals. Four thousand cubits inward from the outer wall stretched the rampart *Nēmitti-Bēl* ("The station of Bēl") and the inner wall *Imgur-Bēl* ("Bēl is propitious").[1] This immense intervening space was occupied with fruit and vegetable gardens, groves, suburban residences, brick-kilns and other factories. The rampart and the inner wall had been begun by Nabopalassar and were now finished by Nebuchadrezzar. The numerous gates in both of these walls leading to the city proper were inlaid with bronze and splendidly ornamented. Between Nēmitti-Bēl and Imgur-Bēl lay a moat, itself enclosed with walls of no mean altitude, and having its slopes completely bricked.

§ 1059. In the city itself the numerous streets ran at right angles to one another, as in the most modern of our own towns. At the ends of certain principal streets the moat was bridged over, and bridges also spanned the chief canal east of the Euphrates, which ran from north to south through the city. On both banks of the Euphrates long lines of quays received the merchandise of the world, and the river between was thronged with boats and barges of every description known to inland navigation (cf. § 1305). The Euphrates formed the main western defence of the city proper, but doubtless the smaller city on the right bank of the river had its own system of fortification.[2]

§ 1060. A colossal temple and the royal palace crowned the work of the Great King within the walls. The great temple, known in the artificial priestly terminology as

---

[1] Besides Nebuchadrezzar's own inscriptions, see II R. 50, 20. 21. *a. b.* It was in Babylonian surroundings that a Hebrew prophet said of the ideal restored Jerusalem, "Thou shalt call its walls 'Salvation,' and its gates 'Praise'" (Isa. lx. 18).

[2] In the time of Herodotus there was a considerable portion of the city on the west of the river (I. 180). Berossus (Josephus against Apion, i, 20) seems to imply that new walls were erected in the reign of Nabonidus. But the inscriptions of Nabonidus say nothing of this.

Esagila ("the lofty house"),[1] was a very ancient structure and it was the pride of all the kings of Babylon to keep it in repair and beautify it. This temple and the shrines of which it was composed he adorned with lavish generosity and unrivalled elegance and splendour. The temple proper resembled in arrangement and functions the temple in Jerusalem,[2] but some of the features which were distinctly Babylonian were also of great importance for the history of Oriental religion. We can only remark here the threefold division of a vestibule, a long inner court, and a most holy place or oracle, entered every New Year's day (the first of Nisan) to know the will of Merodach. Of the appliances of the temple we note particularly the chief altar in front, two large columns at the entrance to the court,[3] a large basin or "sea" (*apsū*), and a ship, adorned with precious stones, in which Marduk was carried in festal procession.[4]

§ 1061. Most characteristic of the chief Babylonian temples was a four-sided building called a *zikkūrat* ("high tower"), which was separate from the main structure, though an essential part of the whole sanctuary. It was at Babylon and Borsippa of seven stages corresponding to the seven planets: Sun, Moon, Mercury, Venus, Mars, Jupiter, Saturn. Originally, however, it was merely an erection of indefinite height upon a mound or terrace — the "high place" of primitive worship. While in Israel and elsewhere the temple was a development of the high place and its shrine, in Babylonia, with its complex sys-

---

[1] Assyr. *bīt elū* (§ 117).
[2] See the summary of the parts in Tiele, BAG. p. 444, and, for the whole subject of Babylonian temples, Jastrow, RBA. p. 612 ff.
[3] Found at Nippur and Lagash, and doubtless a feature of Babylonian temples generally, apparently a survival of a gateway. See RBA. p. 625 f.
[4] This was a prominent feature of the Babylonian cult. Each god had his own vessel, which had a special name given to it. The custom was a survival from the times when the chief cities lay on the Persian Gulf. See RBA. p. 654 f. May it not also symbolize the belief that the ocean was the ultimate source of the divine beings?

tem of worship, this storied tower was the direct evolution of the high place itself, the other structures being developed from the shrine and its belongings. This tower of gradually narrowed stages was the most imposing single feature of the whole sacred establishment.[1] To relieve its monotony enamelled bricks of gorgeous colours were employed for many, at least, of the rows. This lofty structure had also numerous shrines attached to it, and the space between it and the temple proper was the gathering place of votaries, where stood the chief altars, and where offerings were presented. Perhaps in the same region were the tables of the money-changers, with their constant noisy traffic. Within the sacred precincts were also many chambers and separate buildings in which was transacted the business, sacred and secular, of the vast institution (cf. § 1287). The whole temple area was enclosed by a wall, which thus, in Babylonia at least, embraced a city within a city.

§ 1062. To match the grandeur of the city and temple of Merodach, and to further protect Imgur-Bēl, the king erected a new palace alongside of Nēmitti-Bēl and between the two walls, probably to the north of the temple area. A terrace of 490 cubits in length was prepared, and in fifteen days the actual building of the palace was completed.[2] It was protected by a double wall of brick

---

[1] At Borsippa (§ 1063), where the ruins are best preserved, Sir Henry Rawlinson reckoned its height at 140 feet, the first stage being 272 feet square and the seventh 20 feet. In most ruined cities the remains of these structures are the most prominent object. The minor temples had no such storied towers, since each of these originally marked the site of a separate city, the founding of which was an act of worship (§ 498). On the symbolical idea of the structure, see *Kosmologie*, p. 255; RBA, p. 614 ff.

[2] This is the statement of the king himself (Neb. VIII. 64 f.): "In fifteen days I completed its construction." Thus the account of Berossus (§ 1057) is confirmed. The site of this most renowned of ancient palaces, where Nebuchadrezzar lived, where Cyrus held court, and where Alexander died, is generally held to be *el Kasr*, "the palace," the central mound of the city proper (cf. Her. I. 181). See the plan in EB. by Mr. Pinches.

and stone. The gates were inlaid with bronze, bordered with gold and silver, and inlaid with precious stones. This palace he then connected with the old palace of his father. What he himself thought of the structure we learn from his own words: "That house I made an object of admiration to be gazed at by all mankind. I decorated it splendidly. With a prodigality of strength and with the awe of my majesty its walls are compassed round. No evil or unrighteous man doth enter it. The attack of the hostile and the unsubmissive[1] I have kept far from the sides of the citadel of Babylon. The city of Babylon I have made as strong as a wooded mountain."[2]

§ 1063. A word must be said of the neighbouring city of Borsippa, to the south, but on the western side of the Euphrates. This was not, as was formerly thought, enclosed within the outer wall of Babylon, from which its own outer wall must have lain at least four miles distant. Its sacredness to Nebuchadrezzar was due to its being the proper seat of Nebo, who shared with Merodach, from the remotest times, the divine sovereignty and protectorate of the district of Babylon or Babylonia proper. Its temple town *Ezida* ("the enduring house")[3] we have already spoken of (§ 1061. note). The king restored the decayed temple of Nebo and his consort Nanā, renewing also the temple tower with great magnificence and majesty. This famous structure, "the house of the seven lights of heaven and earth" (the planets, § 1061), can hardly have been the "tower of Babel" (Gen. xi.). This phrase seems to be a generalized expression for a great city foundation, of which "Babel" was the type. The tower of Babylon itself (*Esagila*, "the lofty house"), which was probably, at least, as large as that of Borsippa,[4]

---

[1] *lā bābil pāni*, "who does not present the face," *i.e.* refuses to appear before the king and do homage.

[2] Neb. VIII. 29–44. [3] Assyr. *bīt kēnu* (§ 117).

[4] The "tower" of Sargon at Khorsabad (§ 667) was of about the same elevation as that of Borsippa. The identification of Borsippa with the

is more naturally to be understood. Borsippa was also strongly fortified, the king's concern for it being scarcely less than that which he felt for Babylon.

§ 1064. To get a more adequate conception of Babylon as the Hebrew exiles saw it, we must think of the manifold occupations and employments carried on in the city. We must imagine the warehouses filled with the products of Europe, Asia, and Africa. We must picture to ourselves the manufactories large and small, each branch of industry being assigned to its own quarter or quarters of the city. We must visit in fancy the shops where "goodly Babylonish garments" and rich carpetings were offered for sale, where the finest work of the potter was displayed, where precious unguents and perfumes were to be had, where countless articles of bronze, of silver, of gold, and of all sorts of precious stones, were enticingly set forth. We must observe what a number and variety of clay cylinders and tablets were made and sold, and realize that we have before us the panorama of an Oriental Athens and Rome in one — a place of knowledge and inquiry; of universal reading and writing; of immense monetary and property interests; of system, law, and complex administration. We must have before our mind's eye the men of the city, with their long linen tunics reaching to the feet, their woollen mantles, and the short white cape over all; their thick-soled sandals, their long hair bound up into fillets, and their delicate perfumes; every one of them with a staff in his hand carved with an apple, a rose, a lily, an eagle, or some other fanciful device.[1] Finally, to understand what manner of men the Babylonians were we must resort to their temples, and see how much of their life was attached to and moulded by the worship of their gods.

---

famous tower of Genesis has been favoured by the preservation of its gigantic ruins. But, according to Herodotus (I, 181), the tower of Babylon was one stadium square at the base, that is, about six hundred feet.

[1] See Her. 1, 195.

CHAPTER II

SILENCES OF PROPHECY TILL THE CHALDÆAN EPOCH

§ 1065. Prophetic disciples were active during the reign of Manasseh and the Deuteronomic time (§ 942), but prophecy did not cry aloud. It may have been stifled in the attempt in the former period. But why did it not find a voice during the latter?[1] Was it because it was making itself felt in legislation? Not exactly; for in Deuteronomy it was resounding in echoes and vibrations rather than in its own fresh, spontaneous utterance (cf. § 943, 1012). *Inter leges silent prophetæ.* One figure, greater than Josiah or Hilkiah or any other contemporary, is missing from the picture drawn for us of the episode of Deuteronomy and the reformation (§ 846 ff.). Jeremiah, the most spiritual of the prophets, and personally the most interesting, had begun his prophetic career in 626 B.C. (Jer. i. 1), five years before the finding of the "book of direction." Why did neither he nor Zephaniah nor Habakkuk take part either in the promulgation[2] of the "law" or in the direction of religious affairs generally during the life of Josiah? The fact itself is startling. The great prophets of the Old Testament fill the whole stage

---

[1] Zephaniah (§ 830) probably delivered his brief prophecy before 621 B.C. Nahum (§ 831 ff.) confined himself almost entirely to Nineveh. Jeremiah's work under Josiah will be considered later (§ 922 ff.).

[2] It is usually supposed that in Jer. xi. 1–8 the prophet is charged "to make an itinerating mission in Judah for the purpose of setting forth the principles of Deuteronomy and exhorting men to live accordingly" (Driver, *Intr.*⁶ p. 255; cf. Cheyne, *Jeremiah, his Life and Times*, p. 56). Such a commission, however, was out of harmony with the vocation of Jeremiah (§ 1066 f.). The true explanation is given in § 1100.

of its action with their substance or their shadow, and we naturally associate them with all that was monumental in church or state. The subject has been glanced at already. We have said that they were not professionals (§ 851), and that they were idealists rather than practical men (§ 943). But the case demands somewhat fuller notice.

§ 1066. As to the more official character of the work of the prophets, we may observe : (1) They were licensed to preach and ordained to the ministry by Jehovah alone, and their divine investiture placed them not only above but outside of the prophets of the official or hereditary class. Moreover, just in proportion as the teaching of the prophets concerning Jehovah and his claims upon his people became purer, the prophetic office was more widely separated from officialdom of any sort, from association with any class or order of men. (2) Hence the true prophet was an immediate, original force, unfettered by personal entanglements. An official position of any kind would detract from the moral influence of the prophetic word. A professional prophet might be suspected of ulterior motives in delivering his message, especially in a community where divining and soothsaying were indigenous customs. An independent prophet of Jehovah might perhaps be thought fanatical or fallible, but he could never be fairly regarded as designing or mercenary, as an intriguer or a conspirator. (3) Similarly, the word of the true prophets, unlike that of the professionals, had no external validity or authority. It claimed simply to be the word of Jehovah. Its speakers were neither the slaves nor the agents of a king or a court or a hierarchy. The age of Deuteronomy and the succeeding time shows clearly the distinction, from this point of view, between them and the prophetic guilds. The prophets generally appear as closely connected with the priests, and, indeed, in some cases, subject to them (Jer. xx. 2 ; xxix. 26)[1];

---

[1] Cf. W. R. Smith, *Prophets*, pp. 85, 389.

and the subserviency of both alike to the ruling forces in the state is notorious.[1] The ministry of the independent prophets was as much a protest against professional servility as it was against the tyranny of tradition and custom. Compulsion was alien to them, and persuasion was their chief resource.

§ 1067. We see accordingly how such a man as Jeremiah stood aloof from the enforcement of the practical enactments of Deuteronomy. He could not identify himself with the violent measures of repression, for that would have prejudiced him with the people who were, as far as his agency was concerned, to be won over by the genial methods of moral inducement. His commission to proclaim far and wide the penalties of the violation of the moral law (§ 1100) makes him a typical prophetic figure, standing out in relief from the scenes of image-breaking and eviction and scourging and imprisonment that marked the practical operation of the law of Deuteronomy. What an interval separates Samuel (1 Sam. xv. 26 f.) or Elijah (1 K. xviii. 40) from Jeremiah! The one executes official punishment, the other does not even announce it.

§ 1068. Something similar may be said of his lack of interest in the other great feature of the Deuteronomic movement — the reformation of ceremonial worship. What distinguishes him here is his noble disdain of ritual or ceremony as a spiritual or even as a religious function. This is characteristic of the true prophet everywhere. But Jeremiah stands in the very midst of the idolatry (ch. vii. 16 ff., 31) which it is the aim of Deuteronomy to supplant by a centralized and more rigorous ceremonial, and tells the worshippers that God does not care for sacrifice at all (vii. 22 f.; cf. § 1094).

§ 1069. Something more startling still confronts us.

---

[1] A good instance is afforded in the history of Jeremiah himself. His fellow-townsmen of the priestly village of Anathoth, who doubtless had acted under Josiah in harmony with the Reformation, actually attempted to put him to death under Josiah's successor (Jer. xi. 21).

Not only did Jeremiah stand aloof from the enforcement of Josiah's reforms; he seems to have had no official dealings with him at all. Yet eighteen years of his prophetic career had passed before Josiah's death. It is true that he must have spent a part of his time, especially in the earlier years, in his native Anathoth, where he had received the call to the prophetic office, and with which he continued to have much to do throughout life (cf. xi. 21 ff.; xxxii. 7 ff.). But his mission was mainly to Jerusalem (ii. 2 al.), and his message was such as to challenge the attention of the highest and lowest alike. Moreover, Jeremiah, in spite of his diffident sense of youthfulness (i. 6), was little if at all younger than Josiah, and in view of his commanding gifts and aggressive ministry one would expect that he would hold a sort of tutelary relation toward the young king. What is perhaps the most striking of all is the fact that in the extant prophecies of Jeremiah there is not a single contemporary personal allusion to Josiah (see xxii. 15 ff.). Could Josiah dispense with him? Or, what is much the same thing, did he merely tolerate his preaching and mildly patronize him? Either the one or the other, it would seem.

§ 1070. Are we prepared for such a conclusion? Does it shake our faith in the theocratic character of Josiah's work of reform? Not necessarily. God fulfils himself in many ways, and for its immediate purpose, at least, the scourge of Josiah and his priests was as necessary as the pleadings and remonstrances of Jeremiah, and apparently as effective within its proper sphere. And if the king moved in a lower and narrower spiritual sphere than that of the prophet, we may assure ourselves that he could not do otherwise. We have no evidence that he was a man after Jeremiah's heart, or was deeply imbued with the most advanced prophetic spirit. Was any Hebrew ruler of a kindred mind with the truest prophet of his time? We have credited Hezekiah with deference to the prophetic word (§ 797), but he did not enter fully into the spirit of reform until his chastisement had brought him under the ascendency of Isaiah. The case of Josiah, who, would seem likely to be the most amenable of all kings to direct prophetic influence, shows that the independent prophets were always in advance of the best authorities of their time. The broad explanation is that precedent and custom, which determined the occupation of most of the citizens, ruled also in affairs of religion and worship by means of the professional priests and prophets, who had a powerful moral hold upon king and people alike through ceremonial and legal prescription. In short, the most enlightened and progressive officials of the nation were able to utilize the finest results of the prophetic teaching of an earlier era, but could not reach out beyond them. The reformers under Josiah were not discoverers like the independent prophets. They were inventors, and the king gave and secured them their patent rights.

§ 1071. What we learn definitely of the relations of the preaching prophets to the king and officials generally is this: That the two spheres lay quite apart; that the prophets interested themselves in all parties and classes in the state, but only in their moral and spiritual relations; that their function was critical; that they confined themselves to reproof and admonition and did not take part in theories or measures of practical reform. Hence while they did not inveigh directly against evil kings, they did not enter into formal relations with those of the better sort. They even exercised their oracular functions but little, and, to do the later kings justice, they troubled even the greatest of the prophets very seldom by asking their counsel, except in circumstances of extreme national peril. Even Josiah, therefore, had little public association with Jeremiah, and of private friendship between these two illustrious Israelites we have no information.

§ 1072. There was one apparent exception to the general fact that prophecy did not concern itself with specific public measures. Prophecy took for a special province the international relations of Israel. This, however, is just in accordance with its fundamental character as shown in its historical development (*e.g.* § 295 ff., 723 ff.). And the active interest of the prophets in international matters was promoted by the fact that as far as moral influence was concerned they here had the field to themselves. While reform in worship or ritual, or even in outward manners, was under the direction of the priests and the rulers of the people, with the king at their head, in the region of foreign adventure these national guides were all at sea, and especially incompetent to estimate its moral and religious dangers. This wider region of statesmanship accordingly fell to the prophets.

§ 1073. What the prophet Isaiah dared and achieved in this preëminent region forms one of the most inspiring, and at the same time one of the most fruitful, themes of Old Testament history. It might be supposed that there was also room and occasion for prophetic intervention and counsel in the difficult and tragic situation which arose toward the end of the reign of Josiah. Did the tolerance of the prophets extend to this critical point? Perhaps the most surprising of all the biblical silences of this time is the absence of allusion, direct or indirect, to the prophetic attitude toward the policy of the court party, and especially toward Josiah's ill-fated campaign against Pharaoh Necho. Did Josiah consult the prophets at all? What counsel did they give him? We can hardly conceive of Jeremiah encouraging such aggressive warfare. Where was he at this crisis? Where were Nahum and Zephaniah and Habakkuk? Or did Josiah resort to the priests for an oracle? We have perhaps a hint from a distant source. The beautiful Twentieth Psalm was possibly composed on this occasion. It certainly was not the product of a later time, for after Josiah no king reigned in Israel who had the divine approval. This hymn of sacrifice on the eve of a campaign may very well have been composed just before the battle of Megiddo. Celebrating as it does a sacerdotal function, it represents a time when the kingly authority and the priestly service were richly informed by the prophetical spirit. Such a time was that of Josiah.

§ 1074. We have now perhaps sufficiently defined the sphere of the genuine prophets of Jehovah, and explained their silence on what might seem to be matters of vital moment to religious morals. We have also found that no public acts come under their censure up to the death of Josiah. What concerns us at present is the views they have placed on record of the events which culminated in the first great captivity of Judah. There are four prophetic names which give distinction to the period from Josiah to Jehoiachin : these are, Zephaniah, Nahum, Habakkuk, and Jeremiah. We have already considered the message of the first two (§ 830–832) and have observed that their practical outlook does not extend beyond the consequences of the destruction of Nineveh (§ 1065 note). Habakkuk shares with Jeremiah the distinction of interpreting the career and heralding the fate of the Chaldæan monarchy, and of unfolding their significance for Israel and the kingdom of Jehovah. It will now be proper for us to give a rapid summary of the history up to the captivity, and then to try to understand it in the light of the prophetic commentary.

CHAPTER III

JUDAH'S VASSALAGE TO THE CHALDÆANS

§ 1075. Shortly after the battle of Carchemish (§ 1043) Nebuchadrezzar received the news of the death of his father, who had already named him as the successor to the throne. So strongly established in popular favour was the Chaldæan dynasty that when he arrived in Babylon to make good his claim he was acknowledged on all hands as the rightful heir. The task of relieving Syria and Palestine of the Egyptians and their influence was one which required the personal direction of the king, and it could not have been long ere he returned to the scene of conflict. The details of his progress southward and the retreat of the African intruders are not known to us. His advance, however, could not have been long delayed. Not to follow up the victory by driving the Egyptians out of Asia would have been to invite the enemy to divide the Westland with him, after the fashion of the old Hettite compact (§ 163). To delay would have given the Egyptians time to establish themselves more firmly than ever in Palestine. We accordingly conclude that the army continued to operate in Syria during the absence of the king, and that in the course of the next year (604 B.C.) Nebuchadrezzar himself appeared in Palestine, and received the submission of Jehoiakim.[1]

---

[1] This is not the usual construction, which is based upon the assumption of the correctness of the number "three" in the text of 2 K. xxiv. 1. There it is said that Jehoiakim was the willing subject of the Chaldæans for three years out of the eleven of his reign. He died in 598 while in

§ 1076. We have every reason to suppose that Jehoiakim offered no direct opposition to the Babylonian advance. In any case, if he had done so, he must have been promptly deposed. It is indeed an evidence of the clemency of the new dictator that he did not proceed at once to extreme measures, when he saw that the allegiance of the kingdom of Judah was withheld. In general he was desirous of disturbing as little as possible the already existing relations, the only condition he required anywhere being the acknowledgment of his sovereignty and the payment of the accustomed tribute. One perpetual source of suspicion and irritation there undoubtedly was: the proximity of Egypt and her habitual intrigues with the Palestinian communities. A projected or incipient insurrection, or the very whisper of a conspiracy aided and abetted there by Egypt, brought down the wrath of the Chaldaean overlord, and then it went hard indeed with the luckless offender.

§ 1077. It could, indeed, have been only the expectation of help from Egypt that encouraged the ruling class at Jerusalem to the act which we have next to record. It was toward the end of his reign that Jehoiakim refused to wear any longer the yoke of subjection. Of the feelings of the people toward the suzerain we are informed by Jeremiah (§ 1091 ff.). But we do not know all the circum-

---

rebellion, and Nebuchadrezzar would thus seem not to have become his suzerain till 602 or 601, three or four years after Carchemish. Josephus goes so far as to say that the king of Babylon took at once "all Syria as far as Pelusium, except Judah," and that four years later he sent a great army against Judah, which then submitted for three years (*Int.* x. 6, 1). All the historical conditions are suited if we may assume that "six" (שש) was originally written and not "three" (שלש). That is, Jehoiakim would have submitted from 601 till 598, when Jerusalem was actually besieged by the Chaldaeans. Little light is thrown on the question by Dan. i. 1, where the old interpreters have found ground for assuming a "first captivity" in "the third year of the reign of Jehoiakim." That was, however, one year before the battle of Carchemish!

stances that led to this fatal step. Most probably it was due to the disinclination of the landed proprietors and independent classes generally to pay their annual share of the tribute due to Nebuchadrezzar. In the event of their refusal to provide the stated indemnity, Jehoiakim had no resource but to deliver up the royal treasures, or to despoil the temple of its revenues or its adornments. Impoverishment, if such really threatened him and his people, was, however, to be preferred to the certain ruin which unaided rebellion would entail upon them. On the other hand, the expectation of help from Egypt was, to the people of Judah, not so unreasonable as it appears to us. The new Chaldæan empire, victorious though it had been, was still without the prestige of long-established renown. Nor could the ordinary observer realize that it had inherited the genius and power of old Assyria. Moreover, Egypt had all the advantage of being an aggressive neighbour, whose interest lay in keeping the Chaldæans at a distance from her border.

§ 1078. The mode of repression adopted by Nebuchadrezzar showed an advance in military methods beyond that employed by the Assyrian overlords. To harass and impoverish the open country he put in commission the irregular warriors of the half-nomadic peoples of the east of Judah,[1] — Aramæans, Ammonites, and Moabites (2 K. xxiv. 2). Though accustomed to forage and border raids, they had been restrained from such incursions during the good conduct of the people of Judah. Hence their employment against them as rebels to the central authority added a twofold terror to the unequal strife. Behind these came the troops of the regular army. How long the war lasted we cannot tell with exactness. We know that it came to an end in 597 B.C. But before its close, Jehoiakim,

---

[1] The enmity of border tribes contributed much to the disasters and humiliation of the closing days of the Judaic monarchy. See Ps. cxxxvii. 7; Jer. xii. 14; Obadiah; Micah vii. 8.

whose life and liberty were forfeit,[1] died in Jerusalem (2 K. xxiv. 6).

§ 1079. Jehoiachin, the son of Jehoiakim, was now placed upon the throne by the court party, who still dared to hold out against the Babylonian assault. He was but eighteen when his father died, and three short months sealed the fate of the hapless youth called thus early to this forlorn hope. Scarcely had he ascended his tottering throne when the Great King himself appeared with his army before the city. What injury he had wrought upon the surrounding country we cannot say. Probably it suffered less from the imperial troops than from the raiders of the border; for Nebuchadrezzar was no Sinacherib, and did not indulge in savage and wanton destruction. When further resistance was seen to be useless, the young king appeared outside the walls with his widowed mother and all the officers of his court and surrendered at discretion (2 K. xxiv. 8 ff. ; cf. Jer. xxii. 24 ff.; Ezek. xix. 8 f.).

§ 1080. The chastisement of the insurgent state was severe and effective, though the loss of population was numerically not very great. The purpose of punishment for rebellion under the Assyrian régime had usually been to intimidate from further revolt by remorseless severity. The Chaldæan policy aimed in this instance to discourage any further insurrection by making it physically difficult — by depriving any future seditious movement both of leaders and resources. The captives, who numbered in all about ten thousand, were divided into three classes, the nobles or the officials and courtiers of the capital, the princes or heads

---

[1] It is hardly necessary to point out that the apparent harshness of Nebuchadrezzar implied no departure from the regular procedure toward vassal states described in an earlier chapter (§ 285 ff.). The fact that Judah did not submit at once after the defeat of the Egyptians, he had already overlooked (§ 1076). That the punishment of rebellion upon second probation was so severe was apparently due to the presumptive intriguing with Egypt. It is needless to remind the reader that the subjects of Assyria were regarded by Nebuchadrezzar as legitimately his own, and that their submission was expected as a matter of course.

of the local communities (§ 536), and the skilled artisans (2 K. xxiv. 14).[1] The money indemnity was paid in due course, and was provided from the royal treasures and the utensils and ornaments of the temple, most of which had been spared since the days of Solomon. The sacred vessels, being of no particular use as such to the Great King, and being also mostly of inconvenient size, were broken up for the melting-pot (v. 13).

§ 1081. Jehoiachin was made a close prisoner for life; and thus, in less than a decade, there was afforded the spectacle of one Hebrew king led captive to Egypt and another carried away to Babylon. His final fate is recorded with unusual minuteness (2 K. xxv. 27 ff.). Of his intervening experience we know nothing except that several children were born to him in captivity (1 Chr. iii. 17 f.). Imprisonment, as a rule, did not mean the destruction of family and domestic life. After thirty-seven years, on the accession of Evil-Merodach (§ 1369) in 560, he was not only given his liberty, but in compensation for his long restraint was made a member of the king's household, enjoying his favour and bounty till death put an end to his checkered career (Jer. xxii. 26, 30). The bulk of the people were carried away to a thinly settled district by the Kebar, a canal near Nippur (§ 1272), in northern Babylonia. This unique settlement, of which the prophet Ezekiel was one of the most influential members, will soon require our attention again. Here we must pause for a little to hear the comment of the prophets upon these stirring events. The story itself has not yet been half told; for its leading incidents and characters can only be fairly understood in the light that falls upon them from the prophetic record.

---

[1] One might infer from the language of the record that "all" of the available spoil, animate and inanimate, was deported to Babylon. But the comprehensive phrase designates merely a large number, according to familiar Hebrew literary usage. The depletion was serious, but by no means general, as we learn from the subsequent history.

CHAPTER IV

JEREMIAH AND THE COMING OF THE CHALDÆANS

§ 1082. Jeremiah is almost wholly a prophet of the Chaldæan era. There is little or nothing in his extant works which can be directly connected with an earlier time. Jeremiah was as little an historian as might be, and what he reproduced of his earlier utterances in 604 B.C., twenty-two years after his call to the prophetic office (Jer. xxxvi. 32), was so intermingled and overlaid with thoughts and interests of the present as to be seldom distinguishable.[1] Even the greatest political event of his

---

[1] As is well known, the book of Jeremiah is in more disorder than any other prophetical work of the Old Testament. The two main recensions, that of the Massoretic text and that of the Septuagint, differ greatly both as regards the text itself and in the order of the several prophecies. The subject cannot even be touched upon here; the reader must turn to Driver's *Introduction* and to special treatises. Fortunately, the substance of the book is little affected by the variations, though, as far as mere bulk is concerned, the Septuagint is the shorter by about one-eighth.

As our business is mainly historical, we are not so much concerned with the order of the writing down or the publication of the several prophecies, as with the order of the events in connection with which they were respectively written, — two things which, in the book of Jeremiah, are by no means identical. As a guide to the reader, a preliminary explanation is necessary on but one point. According to Jer. xxxvi. 4, Baruch, at the dictation of Jeremiah, wrote down the prophecies which had been delivered up to that date, 605 B.C., or the fourth year of Jehoiakim (xxxvi. 1). And according to xxxvi. 32, after the burning of the roll by Jehoiakim in his fifth year (xxxvi. 9), or 604 B.C., Baruch took down in like fashion the contents of the original roll, and "there were added besides unto them very many words." When we come to inquire what things were said or done by Jeremiah up to December, 604, we find that in the book itself there are three distinct sources: (1) a con-

early ministry, the inroad of the Scythians, is not plainly alluded to (§ 813). He makes no direct allusion to the reformation of Josiah, the most important religious movement of the first half of his life (§ 1065), nor yet to the death of that monarch, the catastrophe which revolutionized Israel and his own career (§ 1069). The first event to which he makes unmistakable reference is the banishment of Jehoahaz (xxii. 10–12; § 1039); but his utterance was not written down till the reign of Zedekiah (cf. § 1143). We are forced to the conclusion that our prophet was an entirely subordinate figure in Israel until the Egyptian and Chaldæan epoch. That he should have ignored the events of his earlier and most impressionable years is unthinkable if these occurrences had coloured his thought or enlisted his interference. The same general conclusion has already been reached in our study of the specific function of the prophets (§ 1069 ff.).

§ 1083. Indeed, we may be reasonably sure of the time when Jeremiah made his first authoritative appeal to the conscience of his people. If chapters ii. and iii. represent in part his first extant discourse, as is generally supposed, we learn from it directly what we are seeking. They were given out at a time when Egypt was the ruling influence in Judah. One of the references is general: "And now, what hast thou to do with the way to Egypt to drink the waters of the Nile? or what hast thou to do with the way to Assyria, to drink the waters of the Euphrates?" (ii. 18). The other is specific: "Thou shalt be disappointed in Egypt, as thou wert disappointed in As-

---

nected series of discourses, substantially chs. i.–x., with no special notation of time or circumstance; (2) another set of discourses with the occasions or conditions stated or indicated, chs. xi., xii., xviii., xxv., xlvi.–xlix.; (3) a briefer group, mainly biographical, apparently written after the death of Jeremiah, chs. xix., xx., xxvi., xxxvi., xlv. From these three collections we shall have to make our citations as the order of events may demand. It is worth inquiring whether group (1) does not contain what Baruch rewrote in December, 604, and group (2) the substance, at least, of the "very many words" which "were added besides unto them."

syria" (ii. 36). The only occasion suitable for such utterances was the time after the battle of Megiddo in what might be called the Egyptian interregnum, when also he uttered the lament over Jehoahaz (§ 1039), who was dethroned and exiled by Pharaoh Necho. At no time during the latter half of Josiah's reign was there any need of negotiations with Egypt, nor can there have been any political occasion of seeking help in that quarter. During the latest years of Josiah the relations were actually hostile. A third passage would be absolutely conclusive, if it were not questionable whether it properly belongs to this discourse or not, since the section in which it occurs interrupts the course of the argument.[1] It runs thus: "The sons of Noph and Tahpanhes break the crown of thy head," following up the words: "His [Israel's] cities are burned up and are without inhabitant" (ii. 15 f.).

§ 1084. Why then was it not till 605 B.C. that Jeremiah committed any of his discourses to writing? Because in the days of Josiah he was only a preaching not a literary prophet, and if he had died with Josiah, we would have had no knowledge of him whatever, not even of his name. The conclusion just reached suggests some practical observations. We now have a satisfactory explanation not only of the silences of Jeremiah for the earlier years of his ministry, but also of his sudden and startling appearance in 605 B.C. It cannot be too clearly understood that none of the literary prophets made their record on merely domestic or local issues (cf. § 1072). In proportion to the magnitude of the international issue prophecy itself became of importance. This has been sufficiently illustrated by the various phases of the complications with Assyria. Now that the petty rôle of Egypt in Palestine is being abolished by Nebuchadrezzar (Jer. xlvi. 2), and

---

[1] See Cornill, *The Book of Jeremiah in Hebrew* (SBOT.), p. 67. It seems to be admitted that Jeremiah himself is the author of the interpolated passage. He must, then, have inserted it as an additional illustration of the state of things set forth in the main discourse.

the larger Chaldæan sovereignty comes before the prophet's mind, he is called to give a more memorable message. We can also now account for the vagueness of Jeremiah's allusions to the eventful time of Josiah. The usual supposition is that the earlier chapters of the book have these prior events as their substratum, and that their indefiniteness is due to the original discourses having been repeated from memory. It is more correct to say that his earlier sermons were in the very nature of the case of comparatively little importance and hence were not recorded at the time.

§ 1085. Having thus found the historical setting of Jeremiah's earliest literary productions, we may now follow more intelligently the most luminous points of his public career. In the opening series of his written prophecies there are three principal determining political conditions. The first is the Egyptian domination; the second is the situation created by the Chaldæan triumph at Carchemish; the third is the expected descent of the Babylonian forces upon Judah. The last named coincides with the occasion of the book of Habakkuk (§ 1130), and thus furnishes a fine opportunity of comparing the respective points of view and ruling motives of those master spirits of prophecy. As to Jeremiah himself, we cannot but observe how, from this epoch onward, his discourses become constantly clearer, deeper, and wider, and how, at the same time, the purpose and character of his life are more fully disclosed.

§ 1086. Jeremiah's first written discourse (ii. 1–iv. 4)[1] reveals eloquently the religious and political condition of Judah after the revolution brought on by the death of Josiah. It must have been delivered shortly after the accession of Jehoiakim, 608 B.C. In its literary form we find the substance of several distinct addresses, which the author, and Baruch his scribe (xxxvi. 4), made up

---

[1] That is, with the exception of iii. 6–18, which is now generally admitted to be out of place. Cornill (*The Book of Jeremiah in Hebrew*, 1895, p. 45) drops iv. 1, 2; iv. 10 he also rejects.

into one continuous composition. The whole discourse is a complaint on two main grounds: religiously Judah has been guilty of apostasy from Jehovah; politically it has committed folly in consorting with Egypt. The head and front of the offending in both cases is inconstancy and treachery. The moral and religious situation is naturally made most of. Doubtless the contrast with the days of Josiah,[1] when all forms of false worship were at least publicly and legally discountenanced and made a capital offence, gives point and emphasis to the charges; but perhaps nowhere in Prophecy is the degeneration of a people so realistically and powerfully set forth. Apostasy from Jehovah is declared to be in a sense treason to human nature (ii. 10–12). No island or continent,[2] the world itself, has ever seen the like. Every land, every people, has and keeps its own god. "See if there has been anything like this. Hath any nation made a change of gods which are yet not God? But my people have exchanged their glory for what is worthless. Be astonished at this, oh heavens! shudder and wither up."

§ 1087. This religious aspect of the popular infidelity looms so large before Jeremiah that we must read between the lines to find out the national situation. His people are clearly in some adversity from which their assiduous cultivation of the false deities can not and shall not deliver them: "Where are thy gods, which thou hast made for thyself? Let them rise up if they would save thee in the time of thy misfortune; for as the number

---

[1] These chapters cannot have as their historical basis the time of Josiah. It is conceivable and probable that reminiscences of the former period and its discourses are found here (e.g. iii. 19). Ch. iii. 6–18 is avowedly a reproduction of a discourse of that period. But there the complaint is general, and is couched in the somewhat stereotyped language of prophetic accusation. Here the charges are various, minute, and specific, and reveal a condition of things simply impossible under Josiah.

[2] Represented by Chittim (§ 42) and Kedar (§ 787). A striking instance of the synecdoche which is one of the most characteristic features of Hebrew rhetoric.

of thy cities have been thy gods, oh Judah!" (ii. 28). The trouble, we apprehend, is that which followed the death of Josiah: the deposition and captivity of Jehoahaz, the vassalage of Jehoiakim, and the uncertainty of the fate of the country in view of the aggressive and rising Chaldæan power. One thing, at least, was very clear to the prophet, as to his predecessors, that nothing was to be gained by relying upon Egyptian protection. "How dost thou change thy course so very lightly?[1] Thou shalt be disappointed in Egypt, as thou wast disappointed in Assyria" (ii. 36). And yet like Habakkuk (§ 1135), near the same date, Jeremiah here insists that, though Israel must be punished for its sin, the instruments of that chastisement shall be held to account for that same providential work which they are commissioned to perform. "Israel is sacred to me, and the first fruits of his increase. All that devour him shall be held guilty, evil shall come upon them, saith Jehovah" (ii. 3).

§ 1088. The second subject of prophetic comment in this series of discourses is the ensuing conflict between the Egyptian and Chaldæan forces at Carchemish (605 B.C.). Jeremiah's celebration of the downfall of the Asiatic empire of Egypt (Jer. xlvi. 3–12) is one of the most poetical of his compositions and assumes the form of a triumphal ode. It is easy to understand the feelings of the author. To every true prophet Egypt was an object of aversion often mixed with contempt. Jeremiah saw on the one side the hollowness of its pretensions, and the certainty of its demolition whenever the Chaldæan power, "the hammer of the whole earth" (Jer. l. 23) should strike it full and hard. On the other side, he beheld with indignation the spectacle of his people relying upon the friendship of Egypt, and, what was far worse, welcoming as counsellor and protector the ruler that had struck down the patriot Josiah.

---

[1] Read מַהּ (קלל) with Giesebrecht after the Sept. Literally: "How dost thou make so very light of changing thy course?"

§ 1089. The poem speaks for itself. It has all the energy but none of the obscurity of its prototypes, the old battle-songs of Israel. It has, however, much of their implacable and vengeful spirit, a spirit inseparable from the desperate struggles with foes equally remorseless and more powerful, which moulded both the history and the temper of the Hebrews. It begins with a derisive summons to the usurpers of the sovereignty of Asia to furbish up their weapons, don their armour, and rush into the fight (xlvi. 3, 4). But this is only a reminiscence of the vast array that went proudly into battle: for the conflict is already over: the field all bestrewn with fallen warriors is abandoned in terror (vs. 5, 6). Then follows a fine Homeric figure. "Who is this that rises high like the Nile, whose waters heave like the rivers? Egypt rises high like the Nile, and his waters heave like the rivers. He saith, I will rise high, I will overspread the land: I will destroy the cities and their inhabitants" (vs. 7, 8). This overweening boastfulness evokes another challenge from the prophet, who calls for the horses and chariots that were the ancient pride of the Egyptian army, and bids the mercenary troops take the field with them: the Ethiopians (Cush), the Abyssinians[1] (Put), and the Libyans[2] (Lubim). The expected march to victory will, however, turn out to be a going forth to defeat and death. It is Jehovah whom the Egyptians shall meet at Carchemish, and his sword shall be satiated with their blood, the only sacrifice that will appease his vengeance (v. 10). The blow thus falling upon Egypt will be fatal, the wound incurable beyond easing by the balm of Gilead, or healing

---

[1] This name is used here for Put for want of a better word. According to W. Max Müller, *Asien und Europa*, pp. 106-120, their country would seem to have lain north of Abyssinia along the Red Sea. Egyptian *Punt* is South Arabia, whence come the Abyssinians. It is seductive that the original Egyptian name of the people, *Chabet*, is so similar to *Chabesh*, "Abyssinia."

[2] Read here and Gen. x. 13 *Lubim* for *Ludim*. The Lydian mercenaries were not a permanent auxiliary of Egypt, like the Libyans (§ 345).

by any medicine (v. 11). The cry of Egypt is heard over all the earth, and with it goes everywhere her shame and reproach among the nations (v. 12).

§ 1090. Such were Jeremiah's sentiments as to the Egyptians and their fate. What was his forecast of their successful rivals? His words regarding the Chaldæans furnish a much better test of his prophetic insight and foresight. The fortune of the Egyptians was not beyond the outlook of a shrewd observer. In any case in dealing with the Egyptians he had to do with merely negative results. Their power was broken, and Palestine and Syria would soon see the last of them. But to cast the horoscope of the new and adventurous Chaldæan empire required a true vision of coming realities from a loftier standpoint. Jeremiah, however, shrinks back from no pinnacle or steep of the divine ascent, and from the height of prevision which he now attains he never after descends. One may say, indeed, that upon the all-important question of the relations of the Chaldæan monarchy to his own people he gained no essentially new light to the end of his days. From the beginning he accepted all the horror and shame of his country's probable ruin as a matter of divine and necessary right. The future had no great surprises for him, though many a bitter disappointment.[1]

§ 1091. The third subject which engaged the attention of Jeremiah at this eventful period (§ 1085) is accordingly the expected descent of the Babylonians upon Judah. It is alluded to in the second of those discourses contained in the summary destroyed by Jehoiakim and rewritten by Baruch (§ 1082 note), that is, in Jer. iv. 5—vi. 30. In chapter xxvi. it is thrust upon public attention as a practical question, though, as far as we know, the invaders or their leader are not mentioned by name till after the

---

[1] Like other large and sensitive souls, Jeremiah met the greater calamities and decisive strokes of fortune with calm serenity, while he was perpetually tortured by the wear and tear of the daily struggles and vexations incident to them.

battle of Carchemish. The former passage (iv. 5 ff.), while containing a summary of the offences charged against Israel during the whole preceding portion of the prophet's ministry, has for its more direct object to point out to the people the specific form in which their sin is to be punished. The agents were to be a people from the north (iv. 6, 15; vi. 1, 22; cf. xxv. 9). The Hebrews knew little about the exact relative position of distant nations. Babylon was almost due east from Jerusalem, but Jeremiah was thinking of the fact that the great invading armies of the past had come by way of the north, notably the destroying Assyrians; and he knew that the army which was predestined to put an end to the Egyptian sovereignty was soon to cross the Euphrates, and descend from the north upon Syria and Palestine. We may add to this what is recorded in chapter xxvi. 4–6, to the effect that Jerusalem was, for its sins, to be made desolate like Shiloh (§ 1093, cf. § 490).

§ 1092. We are now at the threshold of Jeremiah's memorable struggle with the ruling classes among his own people. Let us look at the parties and the issues in the light of the leading incidents. We turn to the narration in chapter xxvi. 7 ff. The story opens (xxvi. 7) with a scene assigned to "the beginning of the reign of Jehoiakim," a vague expression which apparently includes the regnal period up to 605 B.C. The narrator does not go behind the actual events, but lets the story speak for itself. The prophet appears at one of the great annual feasts, and gathering up his former complaints and appeals into one terrible warning, he declares that not only the holy city but the temple itself shall be destroyed and desolated, because the people had so persistently refused to listen to the prophetic word. Those of the ruling orders whose prerogative was most directly attacked, the priests and professional prophets (§ 1066 ff.), broke out in a frenzy of rage, demanding the death of that one of their own original circle who had ventured to oppose the orthodox traditional belief of the inviolability of the temple, and to ignore the representatives of religion generally in the state. The priests and prophets had the popular feeling with them, since it was easy to convince the people that such utterances against the sacred place were profane and blasphemous. The tumult that followed brought the matter to the attention of the princes of the king's household (§ 531, 536 ff.). To them the priests and prophets appealed as civil judges, demanding capital punishment for Jeremiah. The princes, hearing both sides impartially, declared that he had done nothing worthy of death, since he had simply spoken in the name of Jehovah. The fact was, that inasmuch as he had not gone into the details of the ruin of the city and no special national foe was named, his announcement did not so directly touch their dignity or prerogative, and hence they could afford to treat the case on its merits. Their decision was reinforced by the voice of the "elders" of the people (§ 486, 537), who had concurrent jurisdiction with the princes. One of these cited the case of Micah the Morasthite, who in the days of Hezekiah had made a similar denunciation with impunity, and was in fact deferred to by the king and people, so that the divine judgment was revoked (vs. 17–19). But the priestly faction was abetted by a stronger influence than any enlisted in his protection — the king himself and the most servile of his ministers. An illustration of the spirit of this whole repressive movement is afforded by the fate of a loyal colleague of Jeremiah, Uriah son of Shemaiah. This faithful follower, delivering the same message, was obliged to flee to Egypt in order to escape the vengeance of the king. Thence he was dragged back a prisoner to Jerusalem, where Jehoiakim put him to death, and cast his body into the burial-place of outlaws and criminals. The powerful friendship of Ahikam (§ 843) served for a time to shield Jeremiah.

§ 1093. Encouraged by the anti-prophetic spirit of the king, the rivals of Jeremiah left no means untried to accomplish his proscription and death. The next change in the situation shows them to have almost gained their end. They were not scant of material on which to base their attacks. Chapters vii. to x.[1] of his prophecy contain a reiteration and expansion of the sermon which had so deeply stirred all classes of the people. The discourse strikes right at the religious leaders. It also shows well how the specific message of the prophet was being shaped and moulded by the quickening forces of Providence into a thing of abiding life and power. We observe how he defines more sharply the true relation of the temple to the national existence : "Trust not in deceitful words, saying: these (holy places) are Jehovah's temple, Jehovah's temple, Jehovah's temple. For if ye thoroughly amend your ways and your doings, if ye do justice between man and man . . . and do not go after other gods to your own hurt, then I will cause you to dwell in this place, the land which I gave to your fathers from of old and forevermore. Behold ye trust in deceitful words that count for nothing. Will ye go on stealing, murdering, committing adultery, and swearing falsely, and offering incense to Baal, and going after other gods which you know nothing of, and then come and stand before me in this place which is called after my name, and say : we have been preserved in order that we do all these abominations?[2] Has this house, which is called by my name, become a robbers' cave in your eyes?"[3] (vii. 4–11). The fate of Shiloh (cf. xxvi. 6) is then more amply detailed as a warning, and also the rejection of the Northern Kingdom.

---

[1] Exclusive, as is now generally admitted, of x. 1–16, of uncertain date.

[2] This is one of the clarifying sentences in which the book of Jeremiah abounds. The meaning is that the opponents of the true prophetic party actually claimed that Jehovah had set the seal of his approval on their conduct and religious practices by having "delivered" them and the holy places (v. 4), during all the Egyptian imbroglio, from the sword and pestilence and famine.

[3] That is to say, "Do you approve of its being like a robbers' cave ?"

§ 1094. More specific also now is his reference to the modes of false worship (cf. § 1086) practised by his people: "Do not thou pray on behalf of this people; and do not utter for them a cry or prayer, and do not intercede for them, for I shall not hear them (cf. xi. 14). Dost thou not see what they are doing in the cities of Judah and in the streets of Jerusalem? The children are gathering sticks, and the fathers are kindling a fire, and the women are kneeding dough to make sacrificial cakes for the Queen of Heaven,[1] and to pour out libations to other gods, so as to provoke me to anger" (vs. 16–18). We next encounter another of the great sentiments of our prophet (cf. § 1068). "Thus saith Jehovah of Hosts, the God of Israel, add (if you will) your burnt offerings to your festal sacrifices, and eat the flesh.[2] For I did not speak to your fathers, nor did I command them, when I brought them out of the land of Egypt, concerning burnt offerings and festal sacrifices. But this thing I did command them, saying: Listen to my voice, and I will be your God and ye shall be my people; and ye shall walk in all the way that I shall enjoin upon you, so that it may be well with you" (vii. 21–23).

§ 1095. The prophet's mood now turns to fierce denunciation. Only the strongest and most lurid images can do justice to his feelings. Of Tophet we have already heard (§ 718) in connection with the judgment upon Sinacherib. Jeremiah knows of victims more worthy still of such a fate, those who have themselves made its burning piles the scene of their profane and cruel rites. As one reads the

---

[1] Usually explained as Venus, goddess of the evening-star. In Stade (ZATW. VI. 123–132, 289–339) the view that the phrase is a collective for the host of heaven, finds a strenuous but unsuccessful defender. The worship is Assyrio-Babylonian as well as Canaanitish.

[2] The implication is that the sacrifices of the temple were kept up by the worshippers largely on account of the social and festive gatherings; for in these sacrificial feasts the god, the offerer, and the priest were common participants. But however they might vary or multiply the types of sacrifice, their motive was always unworthy and ignoble, in the view of the prophet.

judgment of the prophet, one cannot but think of what constitutes the essence of that Gehenna of which the valley of Hinnom was both the original and the Old Testament symbol — sin bringing not simply suffering but its own proper punishment. This is indeed the only explanation, the only moral vindication, of the worm that dieth not and the fire that is not quenched. "Cut off thy head-tire,[1] and cast it away: and utter a lament upon the woodless heights: for Jehovah hath despised and cast off the generation of his wrath. For the children of Judah have done evil in my sight, saith Jehovah; they have set their abominable things in the house which is called after my name, to desecrate it. And they build the high places of Tophet which is in the valley of the son of Hinnom to burn their own sons and daughters in the fire — a thing which I have not prescribed and which has not entered into my mind.[2] Therefore, behold the days are coming, saith Jehovah, when it shall no more be called the Tophet or the Valley of the son of Hinnom, but the Vale of Slaughter: for they shall bury in Tophet till no place is left to bury. And the corpses of this people shall be food to the birds of heaven and the beasts of the earth, and there will be none to scare them away" (vii. 29–33).

§ 1096. Still another horror is announced, the most ghastly of all to an ancient Oriental and the most to be deprecated: "At that time, saith Jehovah, they shall bring out the bones of the kings of Judah, and the bones of its princes, and bones of the priests, and the bones of the prophets, and the bones of the inhabitants of Jerusalem, from their graves. And they shall scatter them to the sun and to the moon, and to all the host of heaven, whom they have loved and whom they have served,

---

[1] The city is, as usual, personified as a maiden.
[2] Equivalent to saying, "which I disavow and abhor." Litotes is a favourite usage of Hebrew rhetoric.

and after whom they have walked, and of whom they have inquired, and to whom they have bowed down. They shall not be gathered up, nor shall they be buried; they shall be garbage on the face of the earth. And death shall be chosen rather than life by all the remnant that shall survive of this evil race in all the places whither I have thrust them out, saith Jehovah of hosts" (viii. 1–3). Such was the fate reserved for recreant Israel: death without a grave, no resting-place for the disembodied ghosts, no union with the ancestral shades, no reunion under the family head, for souls fugitive and outlawed, exiled and homeless forever.

§ 1097. Next we have a glimpse, all too rare, into the inner workings of ecclesiastical parties in Jerusalem. The keynote of the complaint is found in ch. viii. 10: "From prophet to priest every one of them acteth deceitfully." The preacher wonders why there is no sign of change or turning in the course of the offending people, who rush into sin as the horse rushes headlong into battle (viii. 4–6). More insensate than the bird of passage, which unfailingly observes the times of its going and returning, they ignore the imperious law of life and conduct of loyalty and duty which is just as truly a law of nature under the ordering of Jehovah[1] (v. 7). In defence of their course in any special case, they appeal to their written teaching (law) of Jehovah. To this Jeremiah replies that their scribes have falsified Jehovah's revelation: "The pen of the scribes has wrought deceitfully"[2]

---

[1] Observe that to the ancient Semites the divine influence and control were operative just as truly in the life of animals as in the spirit of man, since superhuman action impelled all activity in all alike. Moreover, to them there was no well-defined distinction between nature and the supernatural such as we so confidently make.

[2] This reference is somewhat obscure. It cannot be meant that any portion of the writings already "canonical" was falsified by the scribes. This they did not dare, and probably did not desire, to do. Two explanations are possible. Either, like their New Testament antitypes, they "made void the commandments of God by their traditions" (Mark

(v. 8). Having thus added treachery toward their countrymen and unfaithfulness toward Jehovah to their shameless moral and religious abominations, nothing remained for them but the extremest modes of exemplary suffering (vs. 10–13). Again as before it is the foe coming from the north that is to execute the vengeance of Jehovah: " From Dan has been heard the snorting of his horses: at the sound of the neighing of his steeds all the earth hath trembled " (v. 16).

§ 1098. In Jeremiah grief perpetually struggles for the mastery with indignation. In the fierceness and fury of his wrath there is often heard an undertone of pity and remorse, like the far-off moaning of an indignant sea, or the wind's wailing interlude in the roaring of the tempest. Ever and anon we hear a half-stifled sob suddenly quenched by an outburst of anger. But at last the heart within the man insists on utterance; the revulsion throws him prostrate in an agony of distress; and then a torrent of tears follows upon the thunder of his passion. In such a passage of his discourse the hyperbole requires no explanation. Tears are at once an intellectual and a spiritual solvent, and clarify alike the deepest thought and feeling. Thus with tears of smitten grief he utters the incomparably pathetic words of his lamentation for his people seen in banishment without their king, still unsaved at the end of the season of grace, beyond the reach of healing by all the balm of Gilead (vs. 18–22). Equally moving and translucent are his tears of shame for the vices and crimes of his people, mingled with vexation at their incorrigible treachery and deceit. " Oh that my head were waters and my eyes a fountain of tears, that I might weep day and night for the

---

vii. 13, Matt. xv. 6). — that is, they nullified the received " teaching " by their comments and glosses, — or else, while divine revelation was admittedly still made in Israel, these prophets and their scribes, in contradistinction to Jeremiah and Baruch, misrepresented Jehovah and thus falsified his teaching. The latter solution is the more probable.

slain of the daughter of my people! Oh that I had in the wilderness a lodge for wayfaring men! . . ." (ix. 1-9).

§ 1099. We must make room for another passage without which any account of the spiritual and mental history of our prophet would be defective. It may not be in its right place in the current texts; but it is appropriate almost anywhere among these discourses. It sets on the broadest basis Jeremiah's own faith and devotion as a species of moral enthusiasm, inspired by the knowledge and contemplation of a God whose very nature expresses itself in righteousness and mercy. "Thus saith Jehovah: let not the wise man boast of his wisdom; and let not the mighty man boast of his might; let not the rich man boast of his riches; but if any one will boast, let him boast of this, that he understandeth and knoweth me, that I am Jehovah that doeth kindness and justice and righteousness in the earth, for I have pleasure in these things, saith Jehovah" (ix. 22 f.). This specimen of the grand prophetic style is the Old Testament confession of faith, to be set beside the victorious avowal of St. Paul, Gal. vi. 14 (cf. also 1 Cor. i. 31; 2 Cor. x. 17).

§ 1100. The next step — a brief one in Jeremiah's career — brought him from the position of an indignant accuser to that of a suspected traitor. The transition stage is described in chapter xi.-xii. 6. The rather fragmentary record is introduced by a reminiscence of an earlier time [1] (cf. § 961), when Jeremiah was directed to

---

[1] This section was, of course, not written down till 605 B.C. (§ 1082); but xi. 1-8 are introductory and explanatory. The formula, xi. 1, "The word which was to Jeremiah from Jehovah, saying," is the one usually employed when the time or occasion is indefinite. An attentive view of the whole section will show clearly the motive of the initial reminiscence. The charge brought against the people of conspiracy (xi. 9), which is naturally connected with the actual plot against Jeremiah (xi. 18 ff.), is directly based upon their infraction of the "covenant" (xi. 10), which covenant Jeremiah himself had been commissioned to preach to his fellow-countrymen (xi. 1 ff.).

address the people of Judah and Jerusalem, exhorting them to observe the commands of Jehovah, particularly the "covenant" (Ex. xxiv. 7; Deut. v. 3), that is, virtually the moral and spiritual requirements contained in JE and Deuteronomy. In contrast with the ideal community that was to be schooled and nurtured into obedience and purity of life and worship, the people of Jehovah are a band of recreant idolaters (xi. 9 f.) whose gods are as many as their cities, and in whose cities every street has an altar breathing incense to Baal (xi. 13). Therefore the threats of the book of the Covenant must be carried out (xi. 8), and when the doom is fulfilled there shall be no reprieve: their own gods shall be deaf to their cries; Jehovah shall be deaf and dumb (xi. 11 f.), nor shall any intercession be made for them (xi. 14). All this is a matter of moral cause and effect, and not of ceremony and ritual (§ 1065 note).

§ 1101. These denunciations, sweeping and general as they sound, have a specific and definite occasion, and this is none other than an attempt on the life of the prophet himself, made by his fellow-townsmen of Anathoth. The exact circumstances are not related. It is natural, however, to couple the plot with the threats uttered at the entry of the temple (§ 1092). Still more significant is the fact that in the appeals for capital punishment against Jeremiah, the official priests had taken the leading part, and that Anathoth, where the attempt was made, was a community of priestly families. The local priesthood were of course under the control of the central body at Jerusalem. Without the instigation or authority of the latter they would scarcely have undertaken such a serious enterprise, odious as Jeremiah was to the whole of the regular priesthood. In the present case a blow straight and strong had been aimed at the priesthood, and the resentment was uncontrollable. Jeremiah, however, had a powerful friend at court (§ 1092), and the time had not come for an open attack upon his life. Hence treachery was resorted to, and it would even seem that some of his own kindred were concerned in the nefarious scheme (xii. 6).

§ 1102. The guilty parties are connected with the plot by Jeremiah himself (ch. xviii.). The record runs parallel with the account of the scene before the temple (ch. xxvi.), and apparently relates what occurred soon thereafter. The prophet sees a potter at his wheel, rejecting work which had been spoiled, and making a new vessel according to his own design (xviii. 1–4). This transaction is applied to the case of Israel, which is a vessel spoiled for Jehovah's purposes, so that He has to reject it, according to the theory and practice of his government of the world. The vessel, however, is a living people, endowed with the power of choice, so that repentance may yet stay the hand stretched out to destroy (xviii. 5–10). When the crisis is presented to the rulers of the people, they stubbornly persist in their own destruction (xviii. 11 f.). When the sentence is pronounced against their land and nation (vs. 13–17), they enter into a formal conspiracy against Jeremiah, basing their action on the ground that he has usurped the function of the regular guides of the people, the priests, counsellors, prophets: "for direction shall not fail from the priest, nor counsel from the wise, nor the word from the prophet" (v. 18). Here again the immediate question was one of professional rivalry (cf. § 1093). But the grievance that brought upon Jeremiah the enmity of the whole official class was his supposed treason, in giving over his country to the new foreign power that should take the place of the routed Egyptians (§ 1091 f.).

§ 1103. This conflict was to Jeremiah the beginning of sorrows. He had ardently hoped that the prospect of subjugation by an irresistible foe would move king and people to some serious attempt at reformation. But they could not see things with his eyes. This false worship, imitative, exotic and sickly, and the dependence on foreigners which it had encouraged, had made them feeble, hesitating, and vacillating in all civic action, internal or external, so that a practical fatalism paralyzed both thought and enterprise throughout the body politic. Thus the threatened invasion, real and imminent as it was to Jeremiah, was to them only a remotely contingent peril, till it came thundering at their gates. In like manner, though habituated to the formulæ of prophetic teaching for generations, they could not interpret its language, which could only be "spiritually discerned." Above all, the range and scope of its practical application were wholly beyond their ken. Slaves as they were to ceremony and ritual, even when giving Jehovah the chief place in their formal services, they were without that "inspiration" which endowed Jeremiah and his little circle with a sense of the living power of Israel's God both in the political and in the moral realm. As the outward functions of religion filled out their idea of worship, so they could not conceive that the object of their devotions was active and potent beyond the visible sphere of their customary formalities. As religion with them took the place of morality, so sight took the place of faith, the present of the eternal, Jerusalem of the world. The vulgar belief reasoned thus: "Jehovah dwells in Zion: He must protect Jerusalem against all enemies, else how should He save himself? We, who are his people, dwelling in Jerusalem, are safe as long as Jerusalem and Jehovah himself are safe." Doubtless in many minds similar sentiments prevailed, grounded upon like arguments, with regard to the gods associated with Jehovah in the popular worship.

§ 1104. No intellectual and moral hostility can be stronger than that which arises between a prophet and a professional dogmatist. When the issue at stake is one of supreme practical importance the contest is virulent and deadly. Since neither party, in the strict sense, reasons, recourse is had to other modes of attack. In the present instance the official prophets and priests construed Jeremiah's judgment upon the city and temple as treason, while he assailed them in good set terms as the real enemies of Jehovah and of his government, as aiders and abetters of all those forms of impiety and immorality which were rife under their administration. In their view death was the only fate that he deserved; by fair and open means if possible, if not, then by assassination. On his part there is, at this crisis, just as little self-restraint. His mouth also is full of cursing and bitterness (xviii. 21 ff.; cf. xii. 3), and he invokes upon them, their wives, and children, the most terrible of divine visitations. Making all allowance for Oriental extravagance and rhetorical redundance, the imprecations are so appalling and, as we may say, so unchristian, that some comment upon them is necessary even in an historical summary like the present. An explanation may help to satisfy us, since justification is impossible, and since the process of explaining away has justly become discredited.

§ 1105. Observe firstly the form and mode of this attack upon Jeremiah. His opponents were guilty of the basest treachery. There was apparently nothing to extenuate the wrong, except perhaps Jeremiah's aggressiveness and iteration. Machinations against his life, the plan of assassination being frustrated only by special revelation (xi. 18), were bad enough; but his own kindred were actually employed as the instruments, and that while, as it would seem, he was on one of his accustomed visits to the home of his youth. Secondly, the sting of the cruel design was its ingratitude. Jeremiah knew that his message was the true one, and that its acceptance alone could save his city and country. If he claimed any superiority over his rivals, it was because he was the accredited messenger of Jehovah. Moreover, his moral and spiritual demands were in accord with earlier revelation, and therefore should have been at least respected by all parties in the state. But he was sentenced as an impostor by nearly all his fellow-citizens, with the king at their head, and persecuted as a traitor.

§ 1106. What most concerned Jeremiah was the vindication of the truth of God, the determination of the question whether in critical instances the faithfulness and righteousness of Jehovah would be demonstrated. To his rivals the main question at issue was whether Jehovah would approve of their present political measures (cf. Jer. xxviii. 1 ff.). His intense insistent temper made it a wearying business to abide the long-deferred decision. But it was not this that made the sharpness of his heartache. It was that he must endure the defaming and mocking of the majority for his belief and trust in Jehovah — in his own words, "because the word of Jehovah is made a reproach to me and a derision all the day" (xx. 8).

§ 1107. Another consideration presents itself. He was confounded and baffled by the mystery of his trouble. Old Testament prophets, pre-exilic and post-exilic alike, regarded suffering, no matter how inflicted, as the direct consequence of their own transgression. Indignation against his enemies, as his interviews with Jehovah reveal, was mingled with reflections as to his own shortcomings, of which the disappointments and apparent failure of his life seemed to be the result. The elements of human sorrow were never presented to any soul more bitter or undiluted. But neither he nor any other sufferer of the olden time could analyze the contents of the cup which the Father had given him to drink. And so, if we wonder at his self-despair, alternating with incoherent maledictions against his persecutors, our pity of him must be tempered with something like admiration, as we behold him in the very desperation of bewilderment, casting himself at the feet of the Master and taking to himself the blame for the wreck of his hopes, of his career, and of the cause of God and Israel.

§ 1108. Again, this spirit of revenge belonged to a special stage of Jeremiah's experience and of his prophetic career. Such a consideration is of biographical and literary value, since it enables us to group into one collection those scattered passages of his memoirs which exhibit an extreme of rancour and intolerance. But it is also instructive as showing that it was a transient phase of his development; in fact, a necessary stage in his spiritual and moral education. Finally, we may think more justly of these outbursts if we recollect that, while they would be sinful in us, they were not necessarily so improper in the ancient prophets of Jehovah. We have been taught by the incarnation and sacrifice of the Christ, that even the most evil of men are not entirely reprobate. On the other hand, Jeremiah and his fellows were in a real sense not acting or speaking for themselves alone, but for the faithful people of Jehovah, that nameless band who were despised and wronged, and could speak only through him for justice, righteousness, and mercy. To claim vengeance for oneself alone is always ignoble. But it is a species of "noble rage" to demand condign punishment for those who have contemned and crushed the suffering saints (cf. § 597 ff.).[1]

§ 1109. In every strenuous and victorious life there comes a time, soon or late, when the climax of effort and endurance is reached, and after this supreme ordeal has

---

[1] Reference may be made in general terms to the so-called vindictive or imprecatory psalms, some of which are supposed to have been composed by Jeremiah himself at this period of his life. The proof of such authorship is not very obvious. But it is not necessary to suppose that the canonical prophets, and the psalmists known or supposed to be known by name, were the only examples or "types" of vicarious suffering in the olden time. It is not out of place to observe that if the right historical method of interpreting the Old Testament did nothing more than further the explanation of such obnoxious passages, it would deserve well of the church and the world. The writer has known a lady, the wife of a clergyman and the mother of two clergymen, who refused to the end of her long life to read or sing the "cursing psalms." Why they are ever sung by modern Christians is one of the mysteries that can only be explained by the final philosophy of human nature. But it is to be hoped that the coming generation may be able to read them without either feeling shame for the Book of Books or uttering apologetic sophistries in behalf of its consistency and moral perfection. The Bible is only consistent with itself when viewed as an historical development.

O

been passed the soul is sure of itself and proof against all new disclosures and surprises. Such a time came to Jeremiah with this "sorrow's crown of sorrow"; and it is strange, divinely strange, that his strengthening and confidence came not with a promise of relief or comfort, but with the assurance that his present conflict was but a foretaste of sterner and more agonizing strife. "For thou hast run against footmen and they wearied thee; then how wilt thou compete with horses? In a peaceful land thou art secure: but how wilt thou do amid the jungles of Jordan?"[1] (ch. xii. 5). Yet it was well for him that he should now know the worst that could befall. Henceforth he knew that there were none upon whom he could rely (cf. xii. 6) save Jehovah alone. The rock which dashed his ship to pieces bore him up, wounded and bleeding, beyond the reach of the breakers. And so we soon find him still in the midst of bitter conflict, with no abatement of outward storm and stress, but maintaining against all appearances his confidence in Jehovah, by reason of the word of faith and promise within him (ch. xx. 9 ff.; § 1112).

§ 1110. Before this point is reached, however, events take place which intensify the outward conflict and bring Israel some steps nearer to its doom. Again the potter's vessel (§ 1102) and the valley of Tophet (§ 1095) come into view. A finished product of the skilled workman's labour is brought by Jeremiah before a company of "elders of the people and elders of the priests," outside the city gate that led to Gehenna. An irrevocable decree of destruction is pronounced upon Jerusalem, whose terrors are to be concentrated in that scene of horrible desecration. Then the vessel is broken before their eyes, to

---

[1] Literally, the "splendour of Jordan," that is, the thick foliage and rank vegetation with which the banks of the Jordan were arrayed, and which, according to ch. xlix. 19 (cf. li. 44) and Zech. xi. 3, were the haunt of wild beasts, represented by the lion, and therefore avoided as dangerous for travellers.

symbolize the catastrophe (Jer. xix. 1-13). Naturally the ire of the priesthood was excited by the harangue and the judgment. During their fiercest rage, Jeremiah, after the symbolic action, returned to the city, and, taking his stand in the court of the temple, reiterated the words of doom in the audience of the people (v. 14, 15).

§ 1111. At length it was felt that a warning, public and exemplary, must be given to such an incorrigible offender. Accordingly, a member of a leading priestly family, Pashhur, son of Immer, who was chief officer of the temple, had Jeremiah arrested for sacrilege, bastinadoed, and placed in the stocks over night near the "upper gate of Benjamin," at the northern side of the temple court. On the following morning he was released, the legal punishment having been fully inflicted. Jeremiah then, fully aroused and implacable, pronounced a judgment upon his persecutor personally, in addition to a detailed repetition of the sentence upon the land and its rulers (xx. 1-6; cf. Am. vii. 16).

§ 1112. After this strain upon a mind and soul to which all personal antagonism was a fiery trial, the harassed prophet, borne down for a moment with a sense of the terrible destiny which he had accepted, breaks out against himself and his own fate in terms almost as horrible as those which he had employed against his foes (xx. 14-18).[1] This utterance (cf. Job iii.) sounds to us like an arraignment of Providence. But "cursing one's day" was a practice in which Orientals, pious or impious, frequently indulged when in a despairing mood; and the language of Jeremiah is merely an expansion of familiar formulæ. It is accompanied, however, by a direct protest to Jehovah, which turns at last into words of adoration. This noble passage runs as follows: "Thou didst beguile me,

---

[1] These verses are placed by Cornill, following Ewald, before vs. 7-13. The whole passage (vs. 7-18) is assigned by Cornill to the time of Zedekiah, but its contents suit the present stage in Jeremiah's life admirably, following up as they do his complaints in chs. xi. and xii.

Jehovah, and I was beguiled. Thou hast overpowered me and overcome me. I have become a laughing-stock all the day; every one is mocking me. For whenever I speak I cry out, 'injustice and oppression,' because the word of God has become a reproach to me and a scorning continually. And I keep saying, 'I will mention it no more, and speak no longer in his name;' and then it becomes in my heart like a burning fire shut up in my bones, and I become weary of holding in, and I cannot do it. For I have heard the slanders of many people, and fears are all about me. 'Denounce him, and we will denounce him, too,' say all my sworn companions, who are watching for my fall; 'perhaps he will be entrapped and we shall prevail against him, and take vengeance upon him.' But Jehovah is on my side as a mighty champion; therefore my persecutors shall stumble and not prevail. They are grossly put to shame because of their folly, yea, with an everlasting reproach which shall not be forgotten. And, Jehovah of Hosts, that dost try the righteous, that seest into the reins and the heart, I shall see thy vengeance upon them, for to Thee I have confided my case. Sing ye to Jehovah; praise ye Jehovah, for He hath delivered the soul of the needy from the hand of evil doers" (xx. 7-13). Truly this hard-trained spiritual athlete ran better against the horses than against the footmen (cf. § 1109).

§ 1113. We are now in a position to measure more accurately the moral interval between Jeremiah and the ruling parties in the state. Except from one point of view Jeremiah's course was unpatriotic and wrong, and that point of view, though all-important to him, seemed to his opponents ridiculously irrelevant. He was to them an unpractical amateur in politics, and, as a matter of fact, he was anything but a politician. The Chaldæans were nothing to him, nor he to the Chaldæans, save for the kingdom of God. But that kingdom was bound up with the body-politic, which was its material mode of expression. He did not distinguish between its outward form and the inward spirit or motive, which employed king and princes and elders and priests and prophets as its instruments and servants. But with that clear singleness of view which is perhaps the surest note of Hebraic inspiration, he regarded every event that affected the fate of Israel as the direct action of Jehovah, while his professional rivals did not differentiate Jehovah from the other divinities except as the controller of Zion and the temple, his sacred seat. Another and more cardinal distinction was that according to his genuine prophetic conception Jehovah was not only immanent and active in Israel, but being the God of the whole world he controlled also the actions of outside nations upon Israel.

§ 1114. All this, however, is only theoretical and belongs to the sphere of Biblical theology. Jeremiah's discourses, his pleadings and threatenings, his reproaches and denunciations, his strong crying and tears, belong to history and literature, that is, to humanity. What was it that converted the belief of the universality and necessity of Jehovah's interference in human affairs [1] into the inward sense of his presence and his urgent concern for his earthly kingdom? More definitely still, what gave Jeremiah his assurance of the hostile advance of the Chaldæans, such as Amos, Hosea, and Isaiah entertained of the Assyrians, and of the divine necessity of their coming, while his compeers and colleagues entertained neither the one idea nor the other? The answer is the open secret of the Old Testament, of its history and its teaching. Jehovah has a moral not a mere mechanical relation to his people. He demands their worship not merely because he is the God of Israel, requiring rites and ceremonies as the badge and expression of servitude, but because true homage paid to him is a sub-

---

[1] A doctrine which, of course, was never formulated by Jeremiah or any other of the prophets, or abstracted by them from their consciousness of Jehovah's activity in the sphere of human history.

mission of the heart and life to his moral requirements — righteousness, justice, and mercy (ix. 24) — which supersedes all ritual and sacrifice (vii. 22 f.). On the other hand, all immorality — injustice, faithlessness, cruelty, deceit — is rebellion against Jehovah, or, in other words, violation of his moral law, which, in its very nature, demands punishment. National immorality demands national punishment. The scourge of the nation must be the strongest of the foreign powers, that is, once the Assyrian, now the Chaldæan. Because of the godlessness and unrighteousness of Jehovah's people, their chastisement by the Chaldæans is an inexorable necessity. Hence this was the great burden of Jeremiah's messages to the people and the king. And this purpose so dominated him, that he was emphatically a man of one idea, and therefore one who, beyond the circle of his few devoted followers, was feared and suspected.

§ 1115. One more public appearance was vouchsafed to the importunate, hard-beset prophet. Ch. xxv. 1–13 contains the abstract of a discourse delivered by Jeremiah "to all the people of Judah and all the inhabitants of Jerusalem" in the fourth year of Jehoiakim (xxv. 1, 2). This address marks an advance. The message gains in force and clearness. But, as we shall see, it has serious consequences to the preacher himself. What is essentially new in it reads as follows (xxv. 8, 9): "Thus saith Jehovah of hosts, because ye have not heard my words I will send and take all the families of the north — and to Nebuchadrezzar, king of Babylon, my servant — and will bring them against this land and against its inhabitants, and against all these nations round about, and I will devote them to destruction." That Jeremiah should now name directly the author of the impending disaster was appropriate and perhaps inevitable. For four years the young Chaldæan conqueror had been famous throughout western Asia. He had perhaps just been proclaimed viceroy by his father. Moreover, it was his triumph at Carchemish, achieved in this very year (xlvi. 2), which made it obvious to the prophet that the ultimate subjection of Syria and Palestine was inevitable.[1] But hitherto, in accordance with the habit of prophecy, he had spoken in general terms, since there is but one reference in the earlier discourses to Jehovah's personal agent in the humiliation of his people (iv. 7; cf. li. 44, Num. xxiii. 24).

§ 1116. The immediate effect of the message was, however, practically nothing more than this, that the ruling class, with the king at their head, had now a better case than ever against Jeremiah. To him it appeared more than ever necessary that the people should be collectively warned, and that the real character of the impending danger should be plainly stated. The national gatherings at the temple furnished the best opportunity, and in those days none were so numerously attended as the general fasts. These were not statutory, but were convoked by the priests, under the direction of the court. It was the anxiety and unrest of these troublous times that prompted the people to propitiate Jehovah at his shrine. They were prepared to listen. The prophet was eager to speak. But he was now "restrained" from appearing in the temple (Jer. xxxvi. 5), probably on account of temporary ceremonial impurity.[2] Hence

---

[1] It is fair to say that the words alluding to Nebuchadrezzar in xxv. 9 are regarded by Hitzig, Kuenen, Cornill, and others, as having been taken over from xxvii. 6. Their absence from the Sept. counts for little (cf. note to § 1082); but they are here introduced ungrammatically, and may be out of place. However, the same thing is virtually said in v. 11, which is retained by Cornill. The interesting question of the genuineness of other portions of ch. xxv. 1-13 cannot be discussed here. See Schwally, in ZATW. VIII. 177 ff., who is closely followed by Cornill in his *Text of Jeremiah*; and cf. Driver, *Intr.*[6] p. 270, 272 f. The suspected passages are not necessary to the development of the story, and are therefore not taken into account here. We have, of course, nothing to do at present with what follows v. 13, which is a summary of one or more discourses on foreign nations, and is therefore in the Sept. united with the series chs. xlvi.-li., being indeed separated from vs. 1-13 and placed after ch. xlviii.

[2] See W. R. Smith, RS.[2] p. 456.

he committed his discourses to writing, by the hand of Baruch, who was also to read them in the hearing of the people. His former addresses were to be also included in the volume, because they had now become of public importance (Jer. xxxvi. 1-7).

§ 1117. This change of form suggests one to two observations. In the first place, it was something new in the history of prophecy that the author was not the preacher. We have here the beginning of the public reading of the Scriptures. In this first instance something was both lost and gained by the delegation to another of what was once a function of the prophet. The message was bereft of the personal force of the seer and orator. On the other hand, when it came to the business of reading instead of speaking, it was appropriate that a practised writer should appear in a rôle to which Jeremiah was so little accustomed. One whose strength lay in appeal, invective, and warning, would be apt to lose his power over his audience when obliged to present his impassioned thoughts in a formal recital. Moreover, the occasion was notable in the literary history of revelation by reason of this change of the form of discourse. Observe that the discourses of Jeremiah, as we have them, are not unsuitable for public reading. They are copious, often diffuse, and, as a rule, expressed in the homely phrase that needs no analysis to bring it home to the understanding and the heart. Contrast with this style of prophetic oratory the discourses of the other great prophets from Amos onward. These are mere summaries of the spoken discourses which never appeared in such a form as that given by Baruch to the words of his master.

§ 1118. As we have seen, the command to write was given in 605 B.C. There is no record, however, of any public reading during that year, and we must assume that none took place till December of the next year, the fifth of Jehoiakim (Jer. xxxvi. 9). There is little doubt that the gathering during which the reading took place was the first national fast that was proclaimed after the command given to Baruch to write down the discourses.¹ The writing was therefore done carefully and deliberately. The place chosen for the lecture (xxxvi. 10) was one already distinguished by addresses to the throngs of temple visitors. Jeremiah himself had spoken there (§ 1092), and it was close thereby that he had suffered the punishment of the stocks at the hands of the overseer of the temple (§ 1111).² This noted resort was at the northern and most frequented gate of the inner temple court. Here the king's chancellor, Gemariah, son of Shaphan, had an office, whence he could, in the name of his master, exercise control as far as it might be needed over the public administration of religion. He and his brother Ahikam were protectors of Jeremiah; and Baruch doubtless felt a greater measure of security in the proximity of a friend at court.

§ 1119. The solemnity of the occasion, the novel mode of address, the reiterated challenge to the king and rulers in the announcement of Nebuchadrezzar's coming domination, created a deep impression among the hearers. A son of Gemariah, named Micaiah, was present to represent the highest official authority, while the magnates themselves, though well aware of what was going on,

---

¹ Our modern versions and many expositors fail to represent the original fairly. In RV. a new paragraph begins with xxxvi. 9, as though the fast in question were a different one from that referred to by Jeremiah in v. 6. But there is no break in the original at this point, and the natural understanding of the story must be that Jeremiah, at a time several months after the command to write (v. 4), instructed Baruch to read at the approaching fast. This injunction ends with v. 7. and v. 8 begins the description of the reading and the subsequent episode.

² Various designations are given to this gate of the temple forecourt. In xxvi. 10 and xxxvi. 10 it is named "the new gate of the house of Jehovah," in allusion to the fact that it was built, or perhaps rather rebuilt, by Jotham. In 2 K. xv. 35, where this fact is recorded, it is called "the upper gate," while in Jer. xx. 2 it is designated "the upper gate of Benjamin," as being on the north side of the temple area (cf. Ez. viii. 3; ix. 2). See Nowack, HA. II, 36 f.

ignored the proceedings by absenting themselves. The young man was so startled by the contents of the roll, that he deemed it his duty to report them to his father and the council, who were assembled, probably in anticipation of the disclosure, in the room of the under-secretary Elishama in the royal palace. The result of the communication was that Baruch was summoned to appear before them in person with his portentous volume. On his arrival they bade him read the document before them. A great consternation was the result (xxxvi. 11–16).

§ 1120. The king could be kept in ignorance no longer. The princes, now cognizant of the manifesto, would be held guilty of treason if they failed to report. They dreaded the consequences to Jeremiah, whom some of them regarded with superstitious fear and some with profound regard. Hence they bade Baruch see to it that he and Jeremiah hide themselves with all possible secrecy. Then they repaired to the northern side of the court quadrangle where lay the suite of rooms set apart for the winter residence of the king (cf. Am. iii. 15). Here Jehoiakim was found sitting before a fire of coals that was burning in the brazier in the middle of the room. They did not bring the roll with them, but laid it by in the secretary's office, hoping that the king would be content with an oral report. When this had been given he demanded that the roll be brought and read in his presence. The effect upon Jehoiakim of the reading was even worse than the courtiers had feared. Not more than three or four pages[1] had been read when he seized the manuscript, and taking the secretary's pen-knife, cut it into fragments and threw them on the fire till they were entirely consumed. Gemariah and two others had appealed to the king not to commit the sacrilege, but after the deed had been done all

---

[1] Literally "doors," that is, the rectangular columns into which the manuscript was divided, the successive lines of each page being written parallel to the length of the roll. The material in this instance was probably papyrus.

the by-standers, dreading the royal displeasure, refrained from any expression of horror or dismay (xxxvi. 17–24).

§ 1121. The reverence for the person and office of Jeremiah entertained by some of the principal nobles was thus offset by the reckless impiety and petulance of the king, who, we may be sure, was supported in his attitude by many, probably most, of his advisers.[1] But even in Jehoiakim we notice a change of policy toward Jeremiah. When the leader of the independent prophets had made his previous harangue beside the court of the temple (§ 1092) the protection of Ahikam sufficed to safeguard him. Now, however, the command went forth that Jeremiah must be put to death. He hid himself to save his life, and the secret of his hiding-place was faithfully kept.

§ 1122. Such an edict was in keeping with the harshness and moral insensibility that marked Jehoiakim. Jeremiah himself has recorded his reputation for injustice, greed, and selfish luxuriousness (xxii. 13 ff.). Like all covetous men he was essentially irreligious. He disliked extreme opinions, and as he had a lofty conception of his kingly rights, he was determined to put down all agitation that would make government troublesome. Though idolatry flourished under him, he was no innovator in matters of faith and worship like Ahaz or Manasseh.[2] Indeed all the successors of Josiah, young men and immature and anything but statesmanlike, were rather opportunists and time-servers than radical subverters of the time-honored theocratic institutions. Jehoiakim simply adapted himself to the ruling conditions. He found that the popular type of religion now established by prevailing usage,

---

[1] Not, however, in his burning of the roll. One of them, who was the king's instrument in the execution of Uriah (Jer. xxvi. 22 f., § 1092), namely, Elnathan, son of Achbor, joined with Gemariah in imploring the king not to do such a perilous thing.

[2] Notice that the invasion of Judah by Nebuchadrezzar and his irregular auxiliaries (§ 1078) is declared to have been a chastisement brought upon the land on account of the sins of Manasseh (2 K. xxiv. 3 f.), not of Jehoiakim, under whom the calamity was endured.

suited best the mass of his subjects, made the kingdom more congenial to the neighbouring states, and most easily satisfied the cliques of priests, prophets, diviners, and their parasites, who, with the decline of the kingdom and the curtailed jurisdiction of the civil authorities, tended more and more to become the dominant element in the state. Hence he favoured the concurrent exercise of all prescriptive modes of worship, and compromised Jehovah's prerogative all the more willingly because of the reaction that was in progress against Josiah's reformation. A similar temper seems to have governed his general public policy. He accepted the yoke of Egypt, and wore it after the sceptre of Syria had passed from that ambitious monarch. He exchanged it for the yoke of Babylon without making any useless resistance. And yet he was finally cajoled into a fatuous rebellion against his all-powerful suzerain.

§ 1123. Moreover, it was Jeremiah's persistence in proclaiming the approach of Nebuchadrezzar that made Jehoiakim his open and implacable foe. With the king went the majority of the nobles and princes, who now found themselves united with the priesthood in opposing the alleged betrayer of his country. One cannot entirely condemn the attitude of the politicians, who were doubtless animated by intense though mistaken patriotism. But they would have had more sympathy from the prophet himself as well as from the after-world if their course had been more open and independent; for the great question with them was how they should play their part as between the opposing forces of the Chaldaeans and Egyptians. They held that the power to be deferred to in the meanwhile was Egypt, which was still the nominal suzerain of Palestine. But the battle of Carchemish had shown that its control was precarious at best, and the time might soon come when the practical question would be how best to conciliate the victorious Chaldaeans. Meanwhile a waiting policy was maintained, with a leaning toward Egypt as the nearest power and the one in present possession. The attitude of Jeremiah, who, among men of leading, was almost alone in the contrary opinion, and who at the same time placed the stigma of impiety and wickedness upon all who did not agree with him, must have been exasperating in the extreme to the heads of the state. They were willing to tolerate his prophesying, as the prescriptive privilege and craft of his order; but it was quite a different matter to let his words steal away the hearts of the fighting men, weaken the hands of the leaders, and bring shame and confusion to Israel.

§ 1124. This irreconcilable antagonism remained to the end. At critical periods the errors and recklessness of the king and his counsellors provoked the indignation of the prophet, and denunciations and threatenings were poured upon the heads of the delinquents. But Jeremiah's career was not one of unbroken warfare with the chiefs of the people. During his interdiction from public speech (§ 1121) his disquieted soul found other means of expression. The stream was as strong and full as ever, but instead of wearing away or tearing down the banks it deepened its channel or broke tumultuously upon the hidden rocks. The section, chs. xiv.–xvii., gives a partial record of his utterances and reflections during this period which apparently extended nearly to the death of Jehoiakim. If our chronological data are correct, the dreaded Nebuchadrezzar did come upon the land within a few months of the public announcement (§ 1075). Then Jehoiakim submitted to the Chaldæan yoke.

§ 1125. Along with this humiliation came other troubles of national magnitude. Chief among these was a terrible drought (Jer. xiv. 1–6) which Jeremiah interpreted as a token of Jehovah's displeasure and for whose removal he intercedes in the most piteous terms (xiv. 7–9). Hear how this "Israelite indeed" (cf. Amos vii. 2, 5) pleads for his country with his God! "Oh, Thou, the hope of Israel, and its saviour in the time of distress! Why shouldst thou be like a sojourner in the land, or as a traveller who has turned aside for a night's lodging?"[1] (v. 8). The interview with Jehovah now becomes a dialogue — a passage peculiarly valuable for the psychological study of the mode and process of prophecy. It is the very centre and heart of the book of Jeremiah. In it the motives of his life and work appear in vivid contrast with the spirit and conduct of his professional rivals, while the interests at stake in the contest are brought out in exceptionally dramatic form. The outlook for himself and his mission was of the darkest, but no darker than the prospect which lay before his country. And here he was in hiding, helpless and mute, thrown back upon himself, or rather upon his God. The fire within him burns so that his words seem to be flashed upon the page in letters of flame. Jehovah renounces his people: their fastings and prayers and oblations are of no avail. He forbids his and their own true messenger to intercede for them; their portion is death by sword and famine and pestilence (xiv. 10–12). Jeremiah replies: "Alas, Lord Jehovah! the prophets are saying to them: ye shall not see the sword, and ye shall not suffer famine, for I will give you sure prosperity in this place" (xiv. 13). To this Jehovah rejoins that the prophets have given a lying message, that they shall perish by that very sword and famine which they have decried, and that the people whom they have deceived shall share their fate (xiv. 14–18).

§ 1126. Jeremiah, however, need not reproach himself with failure, though his people perish in disobedience and impiety; for Jehovah continues: "If Moses and Samuel were to stand before me (Ps. xcix. 6) my soul would

---

[1] There is a twofold meaning here. In the first place, this was Jehovah's own land, and he was inseparable from it (§ 581). Hence the very tie of nature seemed to be broken by his disregard. In the second place, it was the function of Jehovah to give rain (Ps. lxv. 9 ff., civ. 13 ff.), and not of the Baal, whom the people of Canaan looked upon as the fertilizer of the land and especially as the rain-giver (Smith, RS.[2] p. 100 ff.). Cf. xiv. 22, where this prerogative is denied to "the vanities of the nations" and the powers of the heavens.

not turn toward them: send them out of my presence and let them depart . . . those that are doomed to the pestilence, to the pestilence; those that are doomed to the sword, to the sword; those that are doomed to the famine, to famine; those that are doomed to captivity, to captivity . . . because of Manasseh, son of Hezekiah, king of Judah, for what he did in Jerusalem. For who will have compassion on thee, O Jerusalem? and who will bemoan thee? and who will turn aside to ask for thy welfare? . . . Thou hast rejected me, saith Jehovah, going away backwards, and I have stretched out my hand against thee, and have given thee to destruction. I am weary of repenting . . ." (xv. 1-9). The dialogue ends with strong words of comfort. And thus he fared in many a terrible struggle into which he fell after inactivity had been forced upon him, and his work seemed worse than vain,—when he was a shunned and hated man, haunted by the mystery of the fate that made him, against his will and his very nature, "a man of strife and contention with all the earth" (xv. 10); persecuted for the cause of Jehovah himself, whose words were the joy and gladness of his heart [1] (xv. 15 f.); a lonely man shut out from the cheerful ways of men (xv. 17); whose pain was perpetual and his wound incurable; deserted even by his God, who seemed to him like the vanishing waters of a summer brook sought in vain by the thirsty traveller (xv. 18). What he anchored his storm-driven soul to at last was the assurance that Jehovah had not really deserted him or disowned his work: "If thou wilt stand before me again, I will let thee stand before me,[2] and if

---

[1] Vs. 12-14 are quite foreign to this otherwise closely connected discourse and evidently belong elsewhere. Vs. 13, 14 are mutilated from xvii. 3, 4. V. 12 is in the manner of Jeremiah, but it is difficult to know where it should be placed. V. 11 anticipates vs. 19-21, but spoils the beauty of this unique discourse in the place where it stands. It is perhaps best with Cornill to exscind vs. 11-14 entirely.

[2] For the construction, see König, *Syntax der hebräischen Sprache*, § 361 *m.*, and his index of passages.

thou wilt bring out the precious from the worthless,[1] thou shalt be my mouth-piece, and thy enemies shall resort to thee (Gen. iii. 16; iv. 7) and not thou to them. And I shall make thee for this people an impassable wall of bronze, and when they fight against thee they shall not prevail against thee: for I am with thee to preserve and to deliver thee, saith Jehovah . . ." (xv. 19–21).

§ 1127. Still deeper must the prophet go into the valley of deep darkness in the fulfilment of his mediatorial ministry. He had served his people as teacher, monitor, accuser, and intercessor. Now he must in his own person and fate symbolize their ruin, their reprobation, and their abandonment by Jehovah. As fathers and mothers were everywhere to be made childless, and children made orphans, by the sword and famine and pestilence, so he in his personal experience must forego the hope of domestic joy, the love and solace of wife and child. Not for himself alone did he remain through life a singular solitary man: the bareness and isolation of his lot must recall to him the grief and desolation of unnumbered homes visited by the angel of death (xvi. 1–4). For any who should die — even for his own nearest and dearest — he should forbear to grieve, keeping far away from the stricken house and the circle of mourners. In the day of Israel's calamity, the dead should be so many that the wonted tokens of sorrow would be discarded; all kindly offices and all compassion would go out of use, because God's "peace" would be cancelled in the land (xvi. 5–7). Nor must he enter the house of feasting. How can he feast and make merry when the voice of mirth and of gladness, the voice of the bridegroom and of the

---

[1] The expression is a pregnant one: bring out the gold from the base metal so as to separate the two. Jeremiah is admonished that steadfast adherence to the rightful moral principle of God's government, and absolute reliance upon Him, are the conditions of his service. The "precious" is the will and the truth of God; the "worthless" is all that tends to obscure or belittle them, including the prophet's own repining and want of perfect faith. We thus learn Jeremiah's ideal of duty.

bride, are heard no more? (xvi. 8, 9; cf. xv. 17). Again, the evil is traced to its source (xvi. 10-12; xvii. 1, 2) and the doom of banishment pronounced (xvi. 13) with all the accompanying miseries" (xvi. 16-18; xvii. 3, 4)[1]. Then the prophet, more humble than ever toward God and sterner than ever toward his rivals and persecutors, prays that his wounded spirit may be healed and his safety made sure, while with proud humility he protests the singleness and purity of his purpose and desire: "As for me, I have not hasted away from following Thee as shepherd, nor have I desired the desperate day:[2] Thou knowest it; what my lips uttered came straight before thee" (xvii. 14-18).

---

[1] No attempt is made here to bring into consistency with the discourse ch. xvi. 14. 15; xvii. 5-13, which interrupt the connection, though they are the thought and expression of Jeremiah.

[2] Literally, "the incurably sick day"; like the Homeric $\ὀλέθριον\ ἦμαρ$, $νηλεὲς\ ἦμαρ$, etc. Cf., for the epithet, xv. 18, xxx. 12, 15; Isa. xvii. 11.

CHAPTER V

HABAKKUK AND THE CHALDÆANS

§ 1128. Habakkuk is reckoned a star of the second magnitude in the firmament of Hebrew literature, yet he shines with a splendid radiance all his own. Only the brevity of his work precludes him from a place in prophecy beside Isaiah and Jeremiah. His little book is unique among the prophetic writings in its perfection of form. It is at the same time all aglow with life and energy, and fascinates us with its various beauty. In its combination of grace and strength it is equally rare and admirable. In its harmonious union of passion and reflectiveness it is unrivalled in all Biblical literature. Moreover, it is the most suggestive of all prophetic poems. Few compositions of the Old Testament are so closely packed with educative thought. Amos and Isaiah are the only compeers of Habakkuk as interpreters of events, as masters of the Hebrew philosophy of history. Intellectually he is chiefly distinguished by largeness of view; morally by his impartial sense of right and justice, in which he has a close kinship with the writer of the book of Job and with Jeremiah. Perhaps no other poem of equal length has a range of vision so wide and so lofty. Jehovah's immortality, his purity, his supreme exaltation, his general and special providence, his control of the nations, his consistency and veracity among the paradoxes of history, his justice and zeal in the judgment of oppressors and in the vindication of his servants; the essential personal character of national and corporate sin; the function of the world-powers as moral scourges; the selfishness and wrong of oppression, its crime against struggling humanity, its futility when matched against the retributive justice of Jehovah, its self-destructiveness; the security afforded by steadfastness and rectitude; the serene confidence and joy that only trust in Jehovah can give — these are the themes that are suggested or elaborated in this incomparable poem.

§ 1129. With all the variety of subject-matter the prophecy of Habakkuk is a unit; the unifying interest being its great theme, the Chaldæan power. In this singleness of view there is a remarkable parallel with the prophecy of Nahum, whose exclusive attention to the fall of Nineveh we have already considered (§ 831). It is significant that these two brief compositions, which resemble one another so greatly in general literary type and in moral purpose, should deal with the character and career of those two nationalities which most decisively determined the fate of Israel. Their similarity in theme and plan and style, as well as in mental and moral attitude toward the problems before them, make it probable that one production influenced the other. Nahum wrote very shortly before the fall of Nineveh, and it will appear (§ 1137) that Habakkuk composed his prophecy within the next decade.

§ 1130. The theme of Habakkuk is the part and place of the Chaldæans in the order of Providence and in the discipline of Israel. The foundation of his argument is the eternal postulate that sin must be punished by suffering. He starts out by boldly inquiring why Jehovah shuts his eyes to the notorious and flagrant wrong-doing and oppression that are rife in the land. "The oracle is torpid, and justice never comes to light; for the wicked encompass the righteous, and therefore justice comes forth awry" (i. 2–4). The poet now brings Jehovah upon the arena with the reply: "Look ye among the nations, and consider, and wonder greatly, for I am to do a work

in your days which ye shall not credit when it is told.
For, behold, I am bringing up the Chaldæans, that fierce
and impetuous nation that marches over the breadth of
the earth to take possession of dwelling-places not its own.
They are fearsome and terrible. Their right and their
might[1] come from themselves alone. Their horses are
swifter than leopards and fiercer than wolves of the
desert: their war-steeds gallop as they come from afar,
flying like the vulture that hastens to devour. Every one
of them comes for outrage; their faces are set straight
forward, and they gather captives as the sand. They
have a contempt for kings, and princes are their sport.
They scorn every kind of fortress; they raise earthworks
and capture it" (vs. 5–10).

§ 1131. Thus far the Chaldæans appear as instruments
of Jehovah's punitive justice. But the prophet is too
clear-sighted as well as too patriotic to be satisfied with
judgment upon the transgressors in Israel. It is not
because his own people are worse than the Chaldæans
that they receive from Babylon this chastisement. Nay;
as compared with the true Israel, these foreigners are the
most flagrant of offenders. His sense of justice now
challenges Jehovah again with equal boldness, as the successful impiety of the conquering nation rises before his
imagination. "And then he rushes like the wind and
passes on; but he is guilty — he whose god is his own
strength. Art Thou not from of old, Jehovah my God,
Thou holy one of Israel? Thou[2] dost not die. Thou,
Jehovah, hast set him here for judgment, and as a stone
of chastening (cf. Isa. viii. 14) hast Thou founded him.
Too pure of eyes Thou to behold iniquity, and who canst
not look upon evil, why dost Thou look upon transgressors and keep silence, while the wicked are devouring
men more righteous than themselves?" (i. 11–13). The

---

[1] More exactly, "their prerogative and their exaltation."

[2] This and a few other needed emendations are here made without special comment.

poet here implies that Jehovah, whose everlastingness is but the proof and symbol of his righteousness and faithfulness has made it plain that the mission of the Chaldaeans is to test and sift Israel. But still the puzzle remains how their triumphant impiety can be tolerated by the God of innate purity. He then goes on to say that men, who have been created by Jehovah as numerous and yet as unprotected as the fish of the sea or the creeping things of the earth, have been wantonly snared by the Chaldaean. Elated by his success and impunity, the spoiler makes an idol of his own huge drag-net, and continues to seize and slay his defenceless victims (i. 14-17).

§ 1132. In search of a moral interpretation of these paradoxes the prophet resorts to his watch-tower. Only thence can he discern the far horizon where the earthly blends with the heavenly without a break in the line of vision. "At my post will I stand, and take my station on the watch-tower; and I will look out to see what he will speak to me and what reply he will make to my argument. And Jehovah answered me and said: 'Write down the vision and make it plain upon the tablets, so that one may run while reading it. For the vision is yet to come to pass in its time, it hastens toward the consummation, and shall not belie itself, if it lingers, wait patiently, for it shall surely come and shall not be deferred. As to the faint-hearted,[1] his soul is not right within him; but the righteous shall survive by his steadfastness'" (ii. 1-4).

§ 1133. It is, then, the revival of faith and confidence in the prophet's own soul that gives him the answer. It is his own steadfastness and fidelity[2] that carries him

---

[1] I follow Bredenkamp, הנה עֻפְּלָה for עֻפְּלָה הנה. It is want of steady trust in Jehovah that makes the "vision," or the expected solution of the Chaldaean puzzle, appear a delusion and disappointment. The steadfastness that bears a man up is the property of the "righteous."

[2] This is the Old Testament ὑπόστασις of things hoped for (Hebr. xi. 1), the basis and potency of the New Testament "faith." The quotation of the verse in Hebr. x. 38 is thus justified. Cf. § 962, 1008, note.

through the crisis of trial. This inward process of self-renewal, this readjustment of his relations to Jehovah, is part of the life of the true prophet. Such a solution of the problem is subjective, but it is none the less sure and real. Coming as it did on the verge of Israel's last great national struggle, it became the watchword of the faithful then, and forever thereafter. Just because it so reveals the impulse and motive of the religion of Israel, it is the vital centre of the Old Testament. Here we can place our finger upon the heart of Israel and feel it beat. This text must be the starting-point of our study of biblical theology; for the saving truth of olden time was a vision, born in the life and death struggle of individual souls.

§ 1134. When this has been said there is no need of further perplexing thought. In imagination the prophet has already overborne the crisis. He sees clearly now the essentially futile character of the Chaldæan régime, and the rest of his vision is devoted to characterizing it. It is so essentially and variously bad, that it will work out its own punishment in a series of terrible revenges. As Habakkuk always sees historic events and processes in mental images, the records of which are a sort of half-tone reproduction, we must not look for descriptions, but poetic pictures, in which sentiments, hints, suggestions, side-lights and flashes of truth take the place of accurate delineation. They are, for that very reason, all the more instructive, for what they lack in exactness they gain in depth and power, since the illustrations employed are not the naked facts of history, but essential principles of Jehovah's moral government. A mere summary of the remainder of the prophecy will suffice now that the main thesis has been established.

§ 1135. The poet having already (i. 6 ff.) set forth the irresistible force of the Chaldæans in the impending conquest of Israel, turns now to their general policy of aggression and spoliation which is to meet its well-deserved and inevitable doom. This is hit off in a pregnant sentence or two: "He is treacherous like wine,[1] a turbulent and restless wight, who has enlarged his appetite like Sheol; he is insatiable like death; he draws to himself all the nations and gathers to himself all the peoples." Having given the moral key to the situation, the poet now disregards, characteristically, the details of the Chaldæan decadence, and produces the climax of rhetorical effect by bringing upon the scene, like the assessors of a Roman court of justice, the nations themselves that now lie prostrate under the feet of the oppressor. Through their mouths he utters a series of epigrams containing the gist of the moral case against the Chaldæan power, and connecting with each of the charges the announcement of doom (ii. 6-20).

§ 1136. If the closing chapter of the book was written by Habakkuk himself,[2] the sublime theophany which takes up most of it is appropriate to the occasion of the prophecy as a whole. By such appearances of Jehovah in the glory of his power, bending all the powers of nature to his service, prophets and poets habitually represent (*e.g.* Ps. xviii.) his intervention in behalf of his suffering people. No crisis more worthy of divine interposition had ever occurred in the history of Israel; for the faithful few whose destruction was thus threatened were the forlorn hope of the kingdom of God upon earth. Even the closing passage, the serenest and most victorious in all prophetic poetry, is consistent with the main idea of the book. The absolute trust in Jehovah here exemplified is the best illustration of the central truth, which is, after all, a fact

---

[1] I have retained substantially this expression of the received text, but its connection is very doubtful, and, without a slight emendation of the introductory words, quite unintelligible.

[2] It is thought by many to be post-exilic. But the language is not of the distinctly later type, and the only arguments of weight are based upon the liturgical words which were used for the hymns of the second temple: the title, the musical terms, and the colophon. But as the chapter is a pure ode or psalm, it may very well have been adapted to a liturgical use from its original prophetic purpose.

of personal experience, that the righteous is saved by his steadfastness (§ 1132).¹

§ 1137. From what has been said there can be no doubt as to the approximate date of the prophecy of Habakkuk. It was written after the battle of Carchemish, and also after the Chaldæans had supplanted the Egyptians in Palestine. More definitely, it was composed just before the rebellion of Jehoiakim had brought the forces of Nebuchadrezzar against the land. This situation suits the conditions exactly. The prevailing impiety (cf. 2 K. xxiv. 3; Jer. xiv.–xvii.), all the more lamentable after the reformation of Josiah, was, in the prophet's view, to be

---

¹ The analysis and explanation of the book given in the preceding paragraphs are not accepted by all scholars. A number of influential critics, dissatisfied with the alleged strained and artificial interpretation resulting from the current arrangement, place i. 5–11, the rise and character of the Chaldæans, after ii. 4, the vision on the watch-tower. This transposition is adopted by G. A. Smith in his recent work, *The Book of the Twelve Prophets* (II, 116 ff.), to which the student is referred for a succinct account of the matters at issue. The two essential points of the change are that the evils complained of in i. 2–4 are viewed by these authorities not as having been wrought in Israel itself, but as having been inflicted by an outside nation, and that the Chaldæans are regarded as about to be raised up for the purpose of quelling the oppressor, the author of these evils. An appearance of consistency and simplicity is undoubtedly gained by the new arrangement; but I am constrained to stand by the received order chiefly on the following grounds: (1) The evils of i. 2–4 are such as more readily spring from internal disorder and maladministration than from foreign pressure. (2) It is impossible to determine who the outside oppressors are that are supposed to be described in i. 2–4, 12–17. They are certainly not the Assyrians, who had ceased to exercise direct influence upon Judah at any date to which Habakkuk can be reasonably assigned. To maintain the opposite is to misunderstand the Asiatic situation after the Scythian invasions. They cannot be the Egyptians, to whom the description of i. 14–17 is almost ludicrously inapplicable. (3) As has been pointed out by Davidson, it is most remarkable, on the theory of transposition, that the supposed foreign people of these verses is not mentioned by name. The difficulties raised by the hypothesis are greater than those which it seeks to remove. Some weight must be attached to the traditional order. Nor must we forget that a certain degree of obscurity as to the plan and purpose of the prophecy is to be expected from its condensation and the abrupt transitions which it exhibits throughout.

punished by the oncoming of the Chaldæan troops (Hab. i. 6 ff.). The Babylonian power had been felt by the nations generally, and was known by Habakkuk to be irresistible. But it had not yet been let loose upon Israel. As we have already seen (§ 1080), Nebuchadrezzar's treatment of Judah had been studiously forbearing; and it was only the conspiracy of Jehoiakim that brought down his wrath upon that luckless people.[1] The date of the prophecy is therefore about 600 B.C.

§ 1138. It was thus in the very midst of Jeremiah's prophetic work that Habakkuk gave his message. But the greater and more important part of Jeremiah's task was wrought after that event, and it is fitting that we adjust the one to the other just at this critical point. It is instructive to notice the progression of prophecy up to the date before us. Jeremiah was contemporary with all three: Zephaniah, Nahum, and Habakkuk, and doubtless learned from them all. Zephaniah (§ 830), with the twofold burden of the Scythian invasion and the apostasy that followed the reformation of Josiah, sees no clear way out of the trouble, and contents himself with objurgations upon the sinners in Jerusalem and the wicked nations round about, with Assyria in the forefront. Nahum is more specific. He made a special study of Nineveh as the long triumphant, but now moribund incarnation of violence, cruelty, pride, and ambition which are preparing for her unique and absolute ruin. Habakkuk, supreme seer and poet, confronted with the image of the new Chaldæan power rising upon the crumbling ruins of the

---

[1] Thus we may explain the use of the phrase in i. 6: "I am raising up the Chaldæans." Smith says (*Book of the Twelve Prophets*, ii, 123): "How can the Chaldæans be described in i. 5 as *just about to be raised up*, and in 14–17 as already for a long time the devastators of the earth?" The answer is that they are described as raised up for a special purpose, namely, to punish Israel, exactly in accord with 2 K. xxiv. 2. The instance is parallel to Am. vi. 14, where the Assyrians, who had been long noted as world-scourgers, are mentioned, about 760 B.C., as being "raised up" against northern Israel.

Assyrian, finds the old formula of national sin and punishment insufficient. He sees paradoxes in the divine providence where his predecessors were content to make every national trial a vindication of Jehovah's moral government. The Chaldæans are, indeed, the instrument chosen to punish the sins of Israel, but the Chaldæans themselves require explanation. Will that which the great Isaiah said of the Assyrian a hundred years ago (Isa. x. 5 ff.) hold true of the more brilliant and irresistible Babylonian? It will, if the punishment of the lesser offender can be brought under the same law as the triumph of the greater (ii. 13). This is the problem upon which the prophet wreaks his soul. Can it be that Jehovah is behind the remorseless tyrant that slays his creatures (i. 14) unceasingly as a sacrifice to his own power and pride? The answer comes to him who sees the end of the oppressor's career (cf. Ps. lxxiii. 17). But to discern the final issue is given only to patient, steadfast trustfulness, in other words, to the soul that has already found the source of its own salvation in trusting God and doing the right. This is the pearl of great price which the prophet has found in the deep dark waters of doubt and perplexity and set in the bosom of his discourse.

§ 1139. Habakkuk thus summarizes and appraises the career of the Chaldæans as the scourge of Israel, before that career has well begun. He not only supplements, but in a manner anticipates the work and word of Jeremiah, the martyr prophet of the Chaldæan era. But what a contrast in temper, genius, and style between these two greatest moral teachers of the time! The one was so brilliant, so serene, so self-poised; the other so humanly passionate, so self-distrustful, so minutely dutiful. The one was a man of thought; the other, with all his diffidence, a man of action. Habakkuk is like a searchlight, that travels far and near and reveals the danger points for many a league around. Jeremiah resembles a ship's headlight, which shows the rocks and shoals that lie directly in her course. The enthusiasm and serenity of Habakkuk must have sustained many a fainting soul in the days of Israel's humiliation. Jeremiah's active devotion and his priestly consecration made him a tower of strength to all faithful ones in every vicissitude. The book of Habakkuk forms the best general introduction to the inner history of the true Israel during the Chaldæan period, and from it we now return to the word and work of Jeremiah.

CHAPTER VI

JEREMIAH AND THE FIRST REBELLION

§ 1140. The agony of such a struggle could not last much longer, and it was well for the prophet that a change in the whole political situation relieved him of the strain of the irreconcilable strife. We may assume that with the coming of the Chaldæan he was relieved from surveillance and the public ban. Probably he did not feel called upon to prophesy till the rebellion of Jehoiakim brought turmoil and hopeless disaster to his country. When the "desperate day" (§ 1127) arrived, raiders and freebooters swept across the border, following the half-disciplined levies of Moab and Damascus and backed up by the imperial army itself (§ 1078). Israel had now still further reason to respect the prophetic word. But there is no chiding in his recorded utterances, only an outburst of grief, in the name of Jehovah, for the sufferings and desolation of his people, followed by a judgment upon the merciless invaders. "I have forsaken my household, I have rejected my inheritance. I have given the beloved of my soul into the hand of her enemies. . . . Many princes have destroyed my vineyard: they have trodden down my possessions, they have made my pleasant possessions a desolate wilderness. . . . For a sword, the sword of Jehovah, is devouring from one end of the land to the other: no mortal hath any peace. They have sown wheat and reaped thorns: they have made themselves sick without profit. . . . Thus saith Jehovah concerning all my evil neighbours who break in upon my inheritance which I have bestowed upon my people Israel, Behold I will tear them up from off their land, and the house of Judah I will tear up from their midst" (xii. 7–14).

§ 1141. An episode of the invasion and the blockade of Jerusalem, recorded in Jer. xxxv., furnished the prophet with a rare text for a new discourse. It is also worth noting because it suggests to us the condition of a great part of Israel during such times of peril and dread. A band of Rechabites, to save their lives from the Chaldæan and Aramæan soldiery, had given up their wonted life in tents and taken refuge within the walls of the capital. They were but one of many little communities whose pasture-lands and open fields were shorn by the razor that had been brought from over the River to make smooth and bare the land of Jehovah (Isa. vii. 20). Jeremiah had lived over in imagination the horrors and the sufferings of the invasion and devastation of his country. He now made a practical use of this case of the fugitive Rechabites. Permitted once more to go "in and out" among the people, he at the divine command invited the heads of this pastoral tribe into one of the rooms of the court of the temple, where the sacrificial feasts were wont to be held (xxxv. 3, 4). There he set bowls of wine before them and bade them drink (v. 5.). They refused to imbibe on principle, though, as the names of the leaders imply (v. 3), they, with their ancestor, Jonadab, were adherents of Jehovah, of whose service wine was the chief libation. The ancestral prohibition (§ 416), along with the custom of their tribe, was enough to keep them firm against all solicitation (vs. 6–11).

§ 1142. Jeremiah then came out to the open court, where the people were assembled for worship and sacrifice, and gave them a notable sermon (vs. 12–17). The Rechabites had obeyed their father in this matter, because they held his command to be sacred. The people of Judah and Jerusalem had disobeyed Jehovah's revealed will. This was an affair of outward observance; the other a concern of heart and soul and life. The one was an injunction delivered but once, and that long ago; the other a charge reiterated perpetually by Jehovah's messengers sent to them for that very purpose. Both parties were sincere in their professions of attachment to their respective patrons and lawgivers. To which must the praise of obedience be awarded? The lesson is an obvious one to us. But we must not think that his auditors were conscience-stricken and abashed. They most probably thought that what he said was clever and striking; but they also had abundant precedent for the way in which they honoured Jehovah, of whose worship this unfashionable prophet seemed to have such a narrow conception. The armies of Nebuchadrezzar marching to Jerusalem gave, for the time at least, a stronger support to the prophet's appeals than did the case of these eccentric and outlandish ascetics. Yet the men of the tent occupied a moral position far superior to that of the more privileged men of the city. They stood for a principle held consistently for hundreds of years (see § 416). And it had been their salvation morally as well as physically. This is the secret of the "first commandment with promise" (Ex. xx. 12; Eph. vi. 2 f.).

§ 1143. We pass now to Jehoiachin, the ill-fated son of an ill-fated father. For one whose reign was so short he furnished much matter for prophecy. But the brief term of this boy-king was the most fateful yet known to Judah and Jerusalem. His fate deeply impressed Jeremiah who witnessed his banishment, and Ezekiel who shared it. The retrospective lament of the latter (Ezek. xix. 5–9) is a poetical embellishment of the king's fierce defiance of the Chaldæan and of the manner of his surrender and deportation, and thereby he also typifies the fortunes of all the latest kings of Israel. To Jeremiah, already committed to the task of prophet and censor of an expiring monarchy, the events of these three months were of more direct and practical interest. Israel was rapidly nearing its doom. Striking figures (Jer. xiii. 1–14) set forth Jehovah's rejection of his people and their folly and pride, the prelude to their utter destruction. Then comes a passage of wondrous power and beauty (vs. 15–17): " Hear ye and give heed; be not haughty, for Jehovah hath spoken. Give honour to Jehovah your God, before He brings on the darkness and before your feet stumble upon the murky hills. And ye shall look for light, and He shall make it deep darkness and change it to thickest gloom. And if ye will not hear, my soul shall weep in secret for your pride; and my eyes shall weep bitterly and run down with tears because the flock of Jehovah is carried away captive." This last pathetic warning addressed to Jerusalem is the prelude to an elaborate elegy[1] (vs. 18–25). It first commemorates the hapless Jehoiachin and the queen-mother: —

> " Say to the king and the queen-mother
> Take a lowly seat,
> For there has fallen from your heads
> Your diadem of beauty."

Then it turns to the cities of Judah and especially the terror-stricken capital, bewailing their misery and tracing it to its cause.

§ 1144. What Jeremiah further says about Jehoiachin seems to be partly a reminiscence and partly an afterthought written down in the reign of Zedekiah (Jer. xxii. 20–30). In it, as in ch. xiii., the fate of Jerusalem with its cedar-built palaces — compared to an eagle whose nest is in Lebanon — is closely linked with that of the youthful king. The language employed is strangely harsh and pitiless. " As I live," saith Jehovah, " though Coniah,

---

[1] See Cornill, *Text of Jeremiah*, p. 16 f., for the arrangement in elegiac " metre." The unpoetical vs. 26 and 27 make a lame and impotent conclusion to this noble discourse. Much better would it be to regard them as a later addition by a writer ignorant of the elegiac measure. Verse 26 is merely a prosaic repetition of v. 22 *b*, and v. 27 is a brief cento of some of the harsher of Jeremiah's accusations.

the son of Jehoiakim, king of Judah, were the signet-ring upon my right hand, surely I would tear him away from it. And I will give thee into the hand of them that seek thy life and whom thou dost dread, into the hand of Nebuchadrezzar, king of Babylon, and into the hand of the Chaldæans. And I shall hurl thee away, and thy mother that bore thee, into another land, where ye were not born, and there shall ye die. . . . Is this man Coniah a despised broken thing, or a vessel for which no one cares? Why have they been hurled away and cast into a land which they know not?"

§ 1145. One would have expected some pity or sympathy for this luckless youth called at the age of eighteen to a post of terrible responsibility, danger, and difficulty. His case was altogether different from that of his father. The perilous insurrection against Babylon had been undertaken by Jehoiakim, who left it as a legacy to his son. That Jehoiachin failed to send his submission till the city was besieged was doubtless largely due to the same counsellors who had encouraged his father to hopeless rebellion. What could this boy have done to draw down upon him such an explosion of indignation and scorn? It is difficult to believe that this discourse was ever actually delivered to or at the distracted and helpless young king whose misfortunes were, for all that the record shows, as great as his offences. Apart from the hyberbole that marks Hebrew and especially prophetic rhetoric, we have to account for the phenomenon by assumptions which touch the very nature and inner process of prophecy. We have to remember that the Old Testament prophets almost exclusively regard suffering as the direct punishment of sin (§ 1107). Compassion was not always withheld from the sufferer (see *e.g.* xxii. 10), but he was held to be "stricken, smitten of God, and afflicted," and therefore "he was despised and rejected of men" (Isa. liii. 3 f.). There were many who went into captivity with Jehoiachin whose guilt was greater than his; but it is the head of the state that bears the brunt of the popular national calamity, as in a thunderstorm the lightning strikes the loftiest summit. Yet there is a law of compensation in the eternal reckoning of the good and ill of human fates; and if we knew all, we should doubtless see that besides the amelioration of his lot in exile (§ 1147) the thirty-seven years of Jehoiachin's imprisonment brought at least a vicarious blessing to his repentant fellow-exiles.

§ 1146. But there is, besides, another view of the apparently unfeeling language used of Jehoiachin. In the prophetic literature we must perpetually be on the watch for rhetorical colouring and figurative speech when the terms employed would scarcely suggest the peculiarity to a modern Occidental reader. We are familiar (§ 870) with the habit of the prophets of putting a part for the whole, so that a few leading traits of character are made to stand for the total personality. We are therefore not ready to make an exhaustive estimate of Jehoiachin on the basis of the selective and therefore one-sided rhetoric of the extant prophecies. But what is equally important though less obvious is the fact that the prophets in their interpretation of events represent as the immediate effects of the divine agency those ordinary events of human life and fortune which we are in the habit of ascribing to so-called second causes. As there was to the Semitic mind but one great and only cause, his action is set forth as involved in all human experience. Thus here the details of the fate of Jehoiachin are rendered, so to speak, into their equivalent of divine moral causation. A twofold literary phenomenon is thus presented. Evil brings the result of sin; the evils of Jehoiachin's lot appear in the guise of his sins. And Jehovah, as the cause of all things, is described as carrying out his own moral laws in the dethronement and banishment of the king.

§ 1147. But to prove that this outburst with regard to Jehoiachin was mainly subjective we have something better than deductive argument. The case of the exiled king was not in all respects so hard as is here prognosticated. The concluding verse runs (xxii. 30): "Write ye down this man childless; a man that shall not prosper in his days; for none of his seed shall sit in prosperity on the throne of David, or rule any more my people Israel." But, according to 1 Chr. iii. 17 ff., Jehoiachin had several sons in captivity (cf. § 1081), and Zerubbabel, the hero of the Return, was his grandson. Moreover, according to the genealogy of Matt. i. 12 ff., he thus became an ancestor of the Saviour of the world.

CHAPTER VII

JEREMIAH AND JUDAH'S LAST PROBATION

§ 1148. Our narrative of the later history of Israel, and our review of the story in the light of prophetical comment, have brought us to the first great captivity of Judah and Jerusalem. Upon the throne left vacant by the banishment of Jehoiachin, his uncle Mattaniah ("Gift of Jehovah"), the youngest son of Josiah, was placed by Nebuchadrezzar, his name being changed to Zedekiah ("My Righteousness is Jehovah") to indicate the change of relation (cf. § 1040). This new epithet possibly had reference to the solemn oath which he took before his own God (2 Chr. xxxvi. 13; Ez. xvii. 18 ff.) to be a faithful vassal to the Chaldæan king. His reign was one of the most unfortunate in the annals of royalty. His evil fate must be attributed in part to his unhappy circumstances, and in some degree also to his own folly and weakness. From the historical books of the Old Testament we get but little actual knowledge of the earlier and longer part of his reign. We are therefore the more indebted to the prophets Jeremiah and Ezekiel for information which to some extent supplies the want. Indeed, so large a part does prophecy play in the subsequent history till the close of the Exile, that it naturally weaves itself into our narrative as one of the elements of a single story.

§ 1149. The prominence of these two great prophets, the one in Jerusalem and the other among the exiles in Babylon (§ 1174 ff.), is suggestive of the changes that came with the collapse of the kingdom. Jeremiah was left behind by the Chaldæan authorities, probably because he might be depended upon to exercise a conservative influence upon the new and struggling administration. Hence he became relatively more important in a community depleted of its strongest personal elements. Again, the fulfilment of his predictions gave popular prestige for the moment not merely to himself, but also to the prophetical school or party of which he was the head. Accordingly, his oracular utterances were listened to for a time with deference, if not with approval, and, though finally opposed even with violence, he was henceforth more sure of himself and moved among the higher circles of his people with less apprehension. Moreover, Zedekiah and his immediate surrounding were quite different in character from the king and nobles who had silenced Jeremiah. Zedekiah, naturally self-distrustful, was little likely to be overbearing and intolerant with the burden upon him of a fallen cause and dilapidated kingdom. Thus we never find him personally resentful toward Jeremiah, though so often upbraided and condemned by the plain-spoken prophet.

§ 1150. These conditions provided Jeremiah with a motive to active work such as had hitherto been denied to him. The revolution thus marks an epoch in his public life, in his personal experience, and in his literary career. In a man of his brooding introspective disposition, and yet of ardent impulse, intense action is needed to bring out the highest possibilities of his nature, as the lark cannot sing until it flutters its wings and rises above the earth where it is wont to nestle. One remarkable result of his unimpeded energy is seen in the absence of querulousness and self-distrust in all the later prophecies of Jeremiah, as contrasted with those of the period of Jehoiakim.[1]

---

[1] The perception of this fact might perhaps have prevented Cornill from assigning Jer. xx. 7-18 to the period of Zedekiah; see his *Text of the Book of Jeremiah*, p. 28.

§ 1151. Of Zedekiah, the other outstanding figure in Jerusalem, one could wish to say something more favourable than that he was lenient and forbearing toward the stern and unbending prophet of Jehovah. But it is impossible for the impartial historian to set down much in his praise. He was but twenty-one when he came to the throne, and he had to rule a set of poverty-stricken, shiftless people, headed by turbulent, intriguing princes and nobles. Thus he had a task of almost insuperable difficulty to fulfil, and his failure does not of itself deserve condemnation. But he was no ruler of men. Perhaps he assumed the throne unwillingly. At any rate, he never played the king, and at critical times admitted to his own courtiers their superior power (Jer. xxxviii. 5). He was not petulant or headstrong, like Jehoiakim, but rather timid and vacillating. With good intentions, he yet failed signally in two capital affairs of state. Though accessible to the prophetic word he tolerated all sorts of abuses in the public services of religion, even to the grossest idolatry (§ 1155, 1183 ff.). Again, as a sworn vassal of Nebuchadrezzar, it was his plain interest, as well as his duty to his declining kingdom and war-cursed people, to remain the friend and confidant of the great Chaldaean. Yet he allowed himself to drift away from his allegiance and to make a league with foreign conspirators whose alliance had been for five generations the snare and bane of Israel.

§ 1152. And what of the people whom the unhappy young king was called to govern? To understand their condition we must look at the character and results of the Chaldaean invasion. Ordinarily, under the original Assyrian régime, deportation was accompanied by the total subversion of the state (§ 288 f.). In such a case the suzerain became the actual ruler, entered into possession of the forfeited territory, and administered it directly through his officers. Though Nebuchadrezzar did not deal with Judah in this fashion, he made no provision for the rehabilitation of the prostrate kingdom.

After the terrible chastisement it was left to shift for itself, and the luckless remnant of the population were an object of solicitude to the head of the empire only in connection with their payment of tribute. Hence, after the selection and deportation of the captives had been accomplished, the Chaldæan government ceased to have anything to do with the internal affairs of Judah and Jerusalem. Its duties to the rebel state ended with calling off the auxiliary bands of marauders (§ 1078) and withdrawing the imperial army of occupation. There was, apparently, even no resident agent to look after the revenue or to report to the court at Babylon matters that touched the welfare of the empire (cf. Ez. xvii. 13 f., § 1156).

§ 1153. The matters of most pressing concern to the remaining Judaites were the readjustment of private property and the raising of the tribute. The former process must have amounted to a complete social revolution, since, with the exception of some of the officials, only the poorest of the people were left behind. The details of the new allotment we do not know. It goes without saying that many bondmen and debtors would be freed, and that in the redistribution many fortunes would go to unworthy proprietors. In the scramble for wealth the deserving would often be thrust aside, and enmities created without number, which would continue to increase the social disturbance consequent upon the revolution. All this would happen in spite of the best attempts of the king's officers to do justice. There is one circumstance, however, which must have lessened the chances of a wholesale sequestration of property. Ezekiel, writing in the ninth year of this captivity (ch. xxiv. 21), speaks of the fate of sons and daughters left behind in the homeland. When such were found their claims to the ancestral property were doubtless respected. Besides, the nearest of kin to the exiles would often be appointed trustees for the absentees or agents for the sale of their estates.

§ 1154. The payment of the tribute was of most permanent practical concern to king and people. As it was to be sent yearly to Babylon, the question of ways and means became at once a matter of urgency. A more embarrassing situation can scarcely be imagined. The chief difficulty was created by the fact that those who were looked to as tax-payers were, for the most part, unused to the duties of freeholders and must have grudged every shekel which they were forced to give. At best, the raising of the first year's contribution was a terrible drain upon the impoverished and newly enfranchised classes of the community. If a strong man had been at the head of affairs, — to use the phrase of Ezekiel (xxii. 30; cf. xiii. 10 ff.), one who would repair the wall and stand in the breach on behalf of the people, — or if there had been patriotic counsellors in the cabinet, order, tranquillity, and a working fiscal system might have been established. But all that we can learn as to the conduct of the government goes to show that with the passing of the years of Zedekiah's reign the rulers became less able to cope with their difficulties. Thus, the dreadful alternative of rebellion, perhaps urged upon them at first against their will, became ever more welcome to them as the lesser of the two evils. The complications were added to by the condition and conduct of the surrounding peoples, Samaritans, Ammonites, Moabites, Edomites, Philistines of one city or another. All of these were communities of little wealth or responsibility, and of slight financial importance to the common suzerain. But we know that some of them greatly troubled the Judaites (Jer. xxvii. 3) by their seditious intrigues. It was natural that the citizens of Jerusalem, thinking of the lighter burdens of their neighbours, would find in the contrast to their own grievous imposts an additional motive to throw off the yoke of Babylon.

§ 1155. Besides the social troubles and the money question, the religious condition of the people was an additional element of disorder and discontent. The stereotyped phrase of 2 K. xxiv. 19 declares that Zedekiah "did evil in the sight of Jehovah according to all that Jehoiakim had done." Under his régime the popular religion was still of that merely conventional kind which tolerated any traditional mode of worship, any Canaanitish or Babylonian cult, as of equal ceremonial value with the direct and exclusive service of Jehovah. It, indeed, often combined the one with the other, or even sometimes gave the preference to foreign abominations. And yet to the opponents of the school of Jeremiah, whether of high or of low degree, Jehovah was still the supreme deity, and the ascertainment of his will was the great business of prophecy. Thus we have on the one hand the practice of the grossest and most grotesque usages of heathenism (Ezek. viii.; § 1182 ff.) on the part of representative men; and on the other the defiant assertion of a rival prophet, their oracle and champion, that he knew the mind of Jehovah better than did Jeremiah himself (Jer. xxviii. 1 ff.).

§ 1156. Such worship of Jehovah expressed itself somewhat in this fashion: "Jehovah is the God of the nation. He cannot abandon his people utterly or finally. It is true, he has permitted a calamity to fall upon us. But it is not so great as we thought it at first. We are still a people. Like other nations in our position we were not entirely subverted, and that meddlesome Jeremiah only guessed half of the truth after all. We are still the most important nation of the whole coast-land. Other peoples are coming to us for countenance and support (cf. Jer. xxvii. 3). Our brethren in exile are not dispersed among the nations, and they will soon return to our side (cf. Jer. xxviii. 4). Our preservation is a proof that Jehovah intends us to beat down our enemies. Babylon will come to an end like Nineveh, and the house of David shall be established for ever." Thus was the phantom of independence pursued till the very form and substance of national existence were lost. According to Ezekiel (xvii. 13 f.) "the king of Babylon took away the mighty of the land, that the kingdom might be made base, that it might not lift itself up, but that by keeping his covenant it might endure." He did not know the capacity of resistance and self-assertion left in the little kingdom — the fermenting spirit that lingered in the very dregs of the wine bottle which he had decanted.[1]

§ 1157. Already, early in the fourth year (594 B.C.), the people seemed ripe for revolt. At least, the discontented communities round about hoped to bring them to open insurrection (§ 1154). A combined embassy, with this end in view, was sent from the kings of Edom, Ammon, Moab, Tyre, and Sidon (Jer. xxvii. 3 f.). Their arrival brought into sharper antagonism the revolutionary and the conservative elements in the state. The professed prophets of Jehovah, looked up to by both parties (§ 1155), were now in greater vogue and estimation than they had been since the days of Josiah. They had the ear of king, court, and people. Jeremiah appears to have taken the initiative (xxvii. 5–22). He addressed a message to the intriguing kings through the ambassadors, to the effect that Jehovah, the creator and ruler of the earth, had given the whole known world into the hand of Nebuchadrezzar, king of Babylon, his "servant" (cf. Jer. xxv. 9 and § 1115); that the nation which would not submit to him should be punished with the sword and famine and pestilence; that the prophets, diviners, dreamers, soothsayers, and sorcerers, who had advised them to revolt, had merely uttered falsehoods. To Zedekiah also the word was sent, that he and his people should "bring their necks under the yoke of the king of Babylon and live," that they must turn a deaf

---

[1] I use the phrase of Jer. xlviii. 11 and of Charles Reade, *The Cloister and the Hearth*, ch. xxxiii, where the great dramatist suggests the horrors of deportation by making us see and feel how sad a thing it is even on the smallest scale and in the least distressing form.

ear to the prophets who were advising insurrection. An appeal was also made to the national pride in the temple and its appointments. The priests were addressed, perhaps for the first and only time (xxvii. 16), and were told that in case of a revolt the sacred vessels still remaining from the calamity of Jehoiachin would be carried away to Babylon, whereas the opposing prophets had actually declared that those already deported would soon be restored.

§ 1158. Provoked by these utterances, with their pungent rhetoric, the official rivals of Jeremiah at once took up the public challenge. A dramatic scene was enacted when a certain leader among them, from the priestly city of Gibeon (cf. Josh. xxi. 13, 17), Hananiah by name, himself also perhaps a priest, confronted Jeremiah in the temple in the presence of the priests and the worshippers. Jeremiah, to make his message more impressive, had illustrated his references to the yoke of Nebuchadrezzar by wearing in public a wooden yoke upon his own shoulders. His antagonist, full of the schemes for revolt to which he was a party, and pressing for speedy action, boldly declared, in the name of Jehovah of Hosts, the God of Israel, that the yoke of Babylon would be broken within two full years, that the vessels of the temple and Jehoiachin himself would be restored to Jerusalem along with all his fellow-captives (Jer. xxviii. 1–4). This was a much more satisfactory announcement than any which Jeremiah could make. It suited the popular mood and temper exactly, and must have made a hero of Hananiah on the instant. Besides, it had the merit of explicitness, and a reasonably brief time limit was set as a test of its verity. The main objection to it was that to have the test applied would involve the experiment of a rebellion against the most formidable power in the world, which had already brought Jerusalem and its beloved temple to the verge of destruction, and had only given them a partial respite by exceptional clemency.

§ 1159. To offset this seductive promise, Jeremiah could only express his sympathy with the patriotic desire for the return of the sacred vessels and the captives, but he added the warning to Hananiah that just as in the former days, the surest test of a prophet's divine commission is the fulfilment of his specific predictions (vs. 6–9). This was virtually an assertion by Jeremiah of his own superior credentials and authority, which could not be put down by a counterclaim on the part of his rival. Hananiah then resorted to something more spectacular and impressive. He took the bar of the yoke that was on the neck of Jeremiah and broke it before the people, saying, in the name of Jehovah, "Even so will I break the yoke of Nebuchadrezzar, king of Babylon, within two full years, from off the neck of all the nations." As there was nothing more that could be well said or done, Jeremiah went his way [1] (vs. 10, 11). This, however, was not to be the end of the matter. A revelation came to Jeremiah soon thereafter, that the yoke of wood should become a yoke of iron,[2] for Jehovah had put yokes of iron upon the necks of all the nations so that they might serve the king of Babylon. He addressed Hananiah as follows: "Hear now, Hananiah, Jehovah hath not sent thee, but thou makest this people trust in falsehoods. Therefore thus saith Jehovah, 'Behold I will send thee away from off the face of the earth; this year thou shalt die, for thou

---

[1] Cornill's usual sagacity fails him in rejecting the last sentence of v. 11, which stands in the Sept. and all the other versions. He says "it would be utter nonsense to suppose that the prophet, after this action, goes quietly home and does not speak what follows till several days have passed" (*Text of Jeremiah*, p. 71). But there is no indication that several days passed between the two encounters. On the contrary, the language of v. 12 implies, according to Hebrew usage, that the second interview followed very close upon the first. Most probably it occurred the very same day, while the people were still discussing the question of the hour; and Hananiah may have remained to make the most of the impression already excited.

[2] In xxviii. 13, for "thou shalt make," read, according to the Sept., "I will make."

has spoken sedition against Jehovah.'" And, as a matter of fact, Hananiah died two months after the public controversy. Thus the victory remained finally with Jeremiah, the prophet of the greater resource.

§ 1160. We can hardly regret the issue, though we may recoil from the violent measures that preceded it. We need not suppose that the death of Hananiah was accelerated by remorse for evil deeds. Professional prophet as he was (§ 1066), he was no conscious deceiver, though he was a mischievous fanatic. The folly of his policy did not wholly consist in its short-sighted ignoring of the logic of events. The fact that he had the evil elements in the state at his back should have made him hesitate about promoting their designs. Doubtless many plausible reasons suggested themselves to him in justification of his course (cf. § 1154). At bottom his error was the still very common one of imagining that true patriotism demands resistance to a foreign yoke, at any moral or material cost. He stood rather for Jehovah king of Zion than for Jehovah king of righteousness; and he became a victim of the stern exigencies of the conflict that was waged upon that issue.[1]

§ 1161. The advocates of rebellion now ceased their agitation for a time, partly, we may assume, on account of the signal triumph of Jeremiah. The death of Hananiah gave him a momentary ascendency in Jerusalem, and he used his advantage to the full. It is to this period that we have to assign the remarkable series of discourses contained in chs. xxii. and xxiii. of his book. The reminiscences of the earlier reigns (xxii. 10–30) we have already dealt with (§ 1039, 1122, 1144). They were intended to point a moral for Zedekiah, who is adjured (xxii. 1–9) to execute justice and righteousness, and deliver the wronged

---

[1] The case of Hananiah is well treated by Bennett, *The Book of Jeremiah*, xxi.-lii., p. 115 ff. His conflict with Jeremiah is discussed by Professor König, of Rostock (now of Bonn), in the *Sunday School Times*, Nov. 26, 1898, not quite impartially.

from the hand of the oppressor. If this saving counsel were heeded, even his own tottering throne would be made perpetual; but if not, the royal house should become a desolation. "For thus saith Jehovah: Thou art Gilead to me and the summit of Lebanon, yet I will make of thee a wilderness and cities uninhabited." Then the rulers of the people generally are addressed by Jehovah under the name of "the shepherds that destroy and scatter the sheep of my pasture" (xxiii. 1-4). In contrast to these recreants and the unworthy kings just characterized, the great declaration is made: "Behold the days are coming, saith Jehovah, when I will raise up to David a righteous scion, and he shall reign as king and deal wisely, and shall do justice and righteousness in the land . . . and this is the name wherewith he shall be called, 'Jehovah is our Righteousness' "[1] (xxiii. 5, 6). To this is appended the magnificent conception so characteristic of Jeremiah, that the time would come when even the deliverance from Egypt should be held as insignificant compared with the restoration of the exiles from all their places of captivity (xxiii. 7, 8; cf. xvi. 14 f.).

§ 1162. But it is to "the prophets" that Jeremiah mainly devoted himself during this crisis. This was the opportunity of his life to deal with his rivals on equal terms. He had before said many bitter words and made many complaints against them; now he arraigns them formally, on well-considered grounds. Some of the main points in the indictment are these: He declares that he is completely stunned and unmanned because of the awful consequences, past, present, and to come, of the wickedness of the people to which they have been instigated by priests and prophets, so that the land has been made like Sodom and Gomorrah (xxiii. 9-15). To distinguish between the true and false prophets he claims that the latter utter a vision out of their own mind, and not the word of Jehovah

---

[1] With evident reference to the name "Zedekiah" (§ 1148).

(v. 16; cf. xiv. 14). They also invariably promise good fortune to the wicked, an impossible event in the very nature of things (vs. 17–20). Moreover, if they had been in the counsel of Jehovah, they would have turned the people from their evil ways and deeds (vs. 21, 22). Jehovah, who fills heaven and earth, sees through even the most plausible delusion and exposes the pretence of impostors. They rely merely upon empty dreams. But the true prophet receives and declares the immediate word of Jehovah. The one is chaff; the other wheat. In contrast to the elusive and unsubstantial dream, the genuine word is " like a fire and like a hammer that breaks the rock in pieces" (vs. 23–29).

§ 1163. Intense as was Jeremiah's anxiety for the moral betterment and political safety of his fellow-citizens, he was not so preoccupied as to ignore the condition and the fate of his brethren in exile. Indeed, at this very moment, his mind was exercised about the final fate not only of Judah in bondage at home and far away, but also of the Babylonian oppressor whose fall was to bring about the liberation of his people (cf. Jer. xxv. 12 ff.; xxvii. 7, 22). Such is the motive of his utterance made "in the beginning of the reign of Zedekiah" (Jer. xlix. 34 ff.)[1] with regard to the downfall of Elam. In this passage, the impending subjugation of Elam is announced. The conquering people are not named; but it is not difficult to find out who they were. The time limit is fixed by the representation of Ezekiel (xxxii. 24 f.) regarding Elam in 586 B.C. (xxxii. 17), according to which that country had lately been crushed by a foreign power. On the other hand, Elam had a king of its own in 604 B.C. (Jer. xxv. 25). The prophecy was presumably uttered in connection with the military preparations that were being made by the

---

[1] The genuineness of this prophecy has been disputed by several critics, e.g. by Giesebrecht, *Das Buch Jeremia*, p. 245 f. His principal objection is that "a special oracle against Elam in the time of Jeremiah is very surprising in view of the great distance of the Elamites from Judæa."

aggressive power, and which were known to the Hebrews in exile as well as to other residents of Babylonia. Accordingly the fall of Elam took place about 595 B.C.,[1] when it became subject to the little kingdom of Persis. Thus Jeremiah, the prophet of exile, links himself with the earliest of those movements which finally led to the overthrow of the Chaldæan power and the liberation of his people from their captivity by Cyrus, "king of Anshan" (Elam), "king of Persia," and "king of Babylon" (§ 1382 ff.).

§ 1164. This was the most wide-reaching of the visions of Jeremiah. His thoughts, which so often crossed the Desert and the River, lingered among the canals, the pasture-grounds, and the templed cities of Babylonia. Many of the companions of his youth were there. There were those who had sheltered him from cruel wrong in his lifelong struggle, those by whom he had once hoped to save the state of Israel. There were his best pupils in the school of prophecy, above all, the idealistic, intrepid Ezekiel, to whom he had bequeathed the spiritual guidance of the colony. There was the better part of Israel awaiting its purification and deliverance. He was also supported in this sentimental regard for the remnant of Israel in captivity by the close political and civil relations maintained with them from the beginning by the people of Jerusalem.

§ 1165. Captivity could not sever the bond that united the exiles with the home-land, because their solidarity was not merely political or social. The blow dealt by Nebuchadrezzar to Judah was one almost to the death; but scarcely had it been given when the perpetual paradox of Israel's vitality asserted itself in a new and surprising form. The hope of the ultimate redemption of their people was a necessary part of the faith of the true prophets; and as the prospect of a regeneration in Jehovah's own land grew faint, the assurance was more and more borne in upon them that it would be accom-

---

[1] Cf. Meyer, G.A. I, § 466, who, from the same data, chooses 596 as the year of the Persian conquest of Elam.

plished by the discipline of exile. Thus what had been regarded and set forth as the climax of all national and personal woes (§ 801; cf. § 1039 and Deut. xxviii. 64 ff.) came to be viewed and dealt with as a saving and purifying process of education. Hence an interest in the absentees of Israel began to be cherished by the prophets proportionate to their despair of the remnant which sought to maintain the throne of David in Jerusalem.

§ 1166. This new attitude of prophecy is vividly shown in a "vision" of Jeremiah, vouchsafed to him apparently very soon after the departure of Jehoiachin and his fellow-exiles (Jer. xxiv. 1 ff.). Two baskets of figs placed as an offering before the temple, the one of them having very good and the other very bad fruit, set forth respectively the exiles and the people of Jerusalem.[1] The former were to be built up and restored to their homes, and should return to Jehovah with their whole heart. The latter were to be tossed hither and thither among the nations and be consumed by the sword and famine and pestilence. The central and essential truth of this prediction is a matter of history. With the hyperbole that marks the representation the readers of prophecy are familiar.

§ 1167. The first steps in the struggle against the revolutionists at home had ended with the death of Hananiah (§ 1159). The danger of rebellion had passed for the time. But a new danger had been aroused by the agitation. The embassy of the neighbours of Judah apparently excited the suspicions of Nebuchadrezzar. At any rate Zedekiah and the court found it advisable to send messengers to

---

[1] With them are associated "those that dwell in the land of Egypt" (xxiv. 8). This division of the dispersed of Israel included not only those who were carried away with Jehoahaz (§ 1039), but probably many fugitives also, who would attach themselves to the little colony as to a nucleus. The reference is instructive. (1) as it sets forth the disfavour with which Egypt was always regarded by the prophets; (2) as it illustrates the hopelessness of any sort of association with "Rahab" (Isa. xxx. 7) and its futile intrigues and alliances.

Babylonia to assure him of their loyalty.[1] The legates were friends of Jeremiah (Jer. xxix. 3), one of them, Elasah, being a brother of Ahikam, and the other, Gemariah, son of Hilkiah (§ 1118). The opportunity was therefore seized by the prophet to send a messenger to the leaders of the colony.

§ 1168. This letter with its appendix is Jeremiah's chief contribution to the history of Israel in Exile. Following up the motive of the vision of the figs (§ 1166) Jeremiah seeks to counteract the efforts of those prophets who were trying to persuade the exiles that they were soon to return to Jerusalem. He urges them to make themselves at home in Babylonia, to build houses, plant gardens, take wives and rear families; also to seek the welfare of the country of their banishment, if it were merely for their own sakes as its residents. For there would be no returning to Jerusalem till seventy years should pass. Yet Jehovah would watch over them with "thoughts of peace and not of evil," and they would be led to "seek Jehovah with their whole heart." As for the king that reigned in Jerusalem and his people, their doom was fixed; Jehovah himself would pursue them with sword and famine and pestilence and scatter them among the nations (xxix. 4–20).

§ 1169. The letter as it appears in our present texts[2] contains an instructive notice (xxix. 21–32) of the efforts

---

[1] This cannot have been the first rendering of homage by Zedekiah in connection with his accession, as might be inferred from xxix. 2, for the contents of Jeremiah's letter imply that the colony in Babylonia had been in existence for some little time; see especially vs. 8, 9, 15, 21, 24 ff.

[2] I agree with Cornill that vs. 22 b–31 a did not form part of the letter of Jeremiah, but were added by the author of the narrative portion of the book. The answer of Shemaiah to the letter (vs. 26–28) and the fulfilment of the prediction against Ahab and Zedekiah (vs. 22 b, 23) are on the face of them supplementary. Giesebrecht, *Das Buch Jeremiah*, p. xv, 154, looks upon the whole chapter as part of the memoirs of Baruch, of which vs. 3–23 contain his recollection of the contents of the letter. This is not in itself impossible; but the interpolations are not in accordance with Baruch's method.

made by certain of the exiles to break the force of Jeremiah's appeals and to undermine his influence generally at home and abroad. Foremost among them were three, named Ahab, Zedekiah, and Shemaiah. Fired with mistaken patriotism, and trusting that some political change might release them from captivity, they were enraged that Jeremiah should seem to shatter all hopes of restoration. It is not improbable that Ahab and Zedekiah committed some overt act of sedition in Babylonia. It is significant that these ultimately underwent the horrible fate of being burnt alive by Nebuchadrezzar — a punishment often enough inflicted by Assyrian kings upon rebels.[1] The magnanimous Nebuchadrezzar would scarcely ordain such a punishment for any other crime. The additional charge of adultery (v. 23) is an illustration of the moral plane upon which these degenerate prophets moved.

§ 1170. The other case, that of Shemaiah (xxix. 24 ff.) throws also a reflected light upon affairs at Jerusalem. He sent a letter to the "second priest" Zephaniah (see 2 K. xxv. 18), citing Jeremiah's message to the exiles and imploring him to use his authority to put the obnoxious fanatic "in the stocks and in shackles." Zephaniah contented himself with reading the letter to Jeremiah, and took no action. The position of Jeremiah had improved since the days of Jehoiakim. A priest as a state official is here called upon to suppress a prophet (cf. § 1066). Zephaniah is invoked as an officer of the temple, and the punishment, here cunningly suggested, was the same as that already inflicted upon Jeremiah by the first officer of the temple, Pashhur (§ 1111). It is also shrewdly insinuated in the description of Jeremiah as a crazy, self-intoxicated prophet (v. 26) that the public safety required his arrest. The reply of Jeremiah was in the form of a message to the whole colony, to the effect that as Shemaiah had usurped the function of a prophet

---

[1] Cf. KGF. p. 526 f., Tiele, BAG. 510 f., and Dan. iii. 6 ff.

of Jehovah he should be left childless among his people. What a vivid picture these incidents give us of the perpetual strife between the claimants to divine inspiration! And what a background do we see! A half-desperate people are looking continually for direction to their spiritual guides, and are only brought to a temporary acquiescence in right principles by the triumph of a true prophet through an appeal to the divine vengeance! Three times have we seen Jeremiah vanquish an opponent by cursing him in the name of Jehovah (cf. § 1159, 1169).

§ 1171. The embassy sent by the king of Judah seems not to have satisfied Nebuchadrezzar. The Great King was, however, appeased by the coming of Zedekiah in person in the course of the same year 594 (Jer. li. 59). To the poor suppliant the lesson should have been salutary. The long journey, the dread of sterner punishment, the humiliating ceremony of prostration and penitence, the oath of allegiance before Bel and Merodach, these were things which must have quenched in him any thought of future rebellion. Indeed, if he had been left to himself he would probably not have cherished the first seditious project, and certainly would not have countenanced the second. His tragic career is a tale of weakness rather than of deliberate folly or wickedness.

§ 1172. But the punishment came to Zedekiah and to his country all the same. Nor could his truest friend or counsellor say that it was undeserved or that the Chaldeans were the wrong-doers in the work of punishment. It was the fate of Jeremiah to defend this paradox all through his prophetic career, though as he was no speculative poet like Habakkuk, who made the paradox immortal (§ 1131 ff.), he left the solution to Jehovah, and made the grief his own. He had, however, this partial compensation, the assurance that the disturbed balance of justice would be rectified by the destruction of Babylon herself. Perhaps it was with some such feeling as this that he gave a special commission to Zedekiah's courier-attendant, Seraiah, the brother of Baruch (cf. Jer. xxxii. 12).[1] Seraiah was charged to read to the exiles all the words of doom that had been spoken concerning Babylon. Then, when he had finished the reading, he was to bind a stone to the roll and cast it into the Euphrates, saying, "Thus shall Babylon sink, and shall not rise again." In thinking of the discipline of the captivity we must not leave this lesson out of account. Here were the exiles bidden to make Babylonia their home, since their proper home was to be made desolate. But the time was coming when Jerusalem should be free and Babylon be the captive. Yet not at once, not till one generation and another should have passed away. The exiles were to live in hope, not for themselves but for their country and their religion. That is to say, they were summoned to lives of self-sacrifice. Without such a discipline of self-renunciation, with its ministry of faith and hope, the great restoration itself would have come in vain! It is thus from the most practical of the prophets that we learn best what a vitalizing and restorative force prophecy was to Israel. By this, rather than by the death of Hananiah, he showed that he was the messenger of Jehovah.

§ 1173. This message, so germinal and potential, was Jeremiah's last direct service to the exiles of 597.[2] With this his work for them was finished. Preaching must be specific, prompt, and pertinent, else it is unavailing. From distant Jerusalem he could not continue such a crusade as that which he had begun against the false prophets. But both his polemic and his teaching were at once taken up and developed by a prophet of their own who had long been in training for the work.

---

[1] The choice of one so close to Jeremiah for this responsible position during the journey is evidence that the prophet stood well with Zedekiah, at least at this juncture.

[2] Jer. xxx.–xxxiii., which deal mainly with the final restoration, include, of course, the exiles of the first deportation; but the outlook and treatment are throughout general and comprehensive.

CHAPTER VIII

EZEKIEL IN EXILE AND THE HOME-LAND

§ 1174. Jeremiah relinquished the rôle of prophet to the exiles in 593 B.C., and in 592 Ezekiel assumed it (Ez. i. 2). But Ezekiel though in exile was also a prophet of Jerusalem. He thus fulfilled a double function more completely than did his master Jeremiah. The same may be said of him as regards his profession and life-work. He was priest and prophet in one more fully than any other Israelite, or indeed than any Christian except, perhaps, Savonarola, though no mere man can combine the priestly and the prophetic character in completeness and harmony. Jeremiah was also of priestly birth, but he seems to have discarded the lessons of his youth, or perhaps rather to have outgrown them. To Ezekiel, who in exile was debarred from the sacerdotal functions which from the surroundings had perhaps never been congenial to him in Jerusalem, clung to the priestly habit of thought all through life. He became a theologian, while Jeremiah remained always merely a religious man, and therein was the greater prophet, replete with spontaneous power because full of human sympathy and passion.[1] Ezekiel was somewhat cloistral, always meditative and idealistic, yet withal intensely practical and statesmanlike in a large constructive fashion. In him the idea of the theocracy was matured. The kingdom of God was for him something built up out of the people of his choice according to

---

[1] In this and in some other respects, Jeremiah was to Ezekiel as Luther to Calvin.

principle and method. Yet this process was of the moral order throughout, and Ezekiel, as he developed his system in vision and reflection, did the work of a unique priestly prophet in laying a foundation of righteousness and holiness for a new kingdom of Jehovah.

§ 1175. The glory of Ezekiel has been obscured partly by his lack of mental and rhetorical tact and grace, but still more by the corruptions of his text, which have prevented his readers from getting readily at his meaning. His composition is laborious and massive, built up of many details. His style as well as his intellect itself has rightly been called architectonic,[1] and it therefore suffers all the more by apparent imperfection, as a carefully planned structure is marred by the dislocation of a stone or the fall of a column. But the few that have studied him profoundly have been most impressed with the depth and sublimity of his thought. His long-drawn-out visions are anything but visionary: in them his imagination bodies forth the profoundest convictions known to the ancient world of the divine holiness, majesty, and spirituality. In this he imitates and advances beyond Isaiah (§ 1176, note). The same largeness of view is shown in his conception of the providential guidance of Israel under the grace and omnipotence of a God supreme among the nations (ch. xx.). In the somewhat less congenial but more difficult sphere of human nature and its divine edu-

---

[1] Skinner, art. "Ezekiel," in DB. This and Cornill's sketch in *Israel. Prophetismus* (1896) are among the best estimates of the prophet that have been written. Good commentaries on Ezekiel are not abundant, but they are more numerous than those on Jeremiah. Davidson, in the *Cambridge Bible for Schools* (1896), and Skinner, in the *Expositor's Bible* series, are excellent within their practical limits. More critical, though less expository, are Smend (1880, second edition of Hitzig, 1847) and Bertholet (1897). Orelli (1888) is instructive, though too conservative. The text is treated in the work of Cornill. *Das Buch des Proph. Ezechiel* (1886) and that of Toy in SBOT. (1899). A reference to Driver, *Introd.*, or to Ewald's work in his *Propheten*, is almost superfluous. A study of the style and the logical and literary method of Ezekiel is indispensable for even a general understanding of his writings.

cation, he is less independent, following Jeremiah in his doctrine of the new heart and right spirit (xi. 19; xviii. 31; xxxvi; 26, cf. Jer. xxiv. 7; xxxii. 39) and setting forth more fully and inductively the great principle of individual responsibility (ch. xviii.; cf. Jer. xxxi. 29 f.). His influence on the history of his people is not easily estimated in a sentence or two, but will appear clearly in the course of our narrative.

§ 1176. We think first of his interest in the life and fate of Jerusalem during the four years that intervene until the final rebellion. He is all the more drawn to prophesy of Jerusalem because his fellow-exiles are unwilling to hear him (iii. 7 ff.).[1] The fortunes of the home-land, viewed in the light of its tragic and sinful past, furnished an ample field to his uncurbed imagination. It was mainly for this part of his work that he was prepared by those wonderful visions[2] which were vouchsafed to him by the

---

[1] It is after he ceases to be a public censor (iii. 22-27) that he sees the woes of Jerusalem (ch. iv. ff.). But the references to the opposition of his fellow-exiles must not be understood too literally, and the allusion to violence in iii. 25 is of course to be taken as a part of the general representation. In the first four years of exile he was naturally in sympathy with the efforts of Jeremiah to discourage the hopes of a speedy return (cf. § 1168), and doubtless he was looked upon with extreme disfavour by the opposing prophets and their party. But after the submission of king Zedekiah at Babylon, and the execution of the ringleaders Ahab and Zedekiah (§ 1169), there would not be so much open antagonism. On the contrary, we read of the elders of the people at this very period coming regularly to consult him (viii. 1; xiv. 1; xx. 1), and at a later time the people generally are represented as resorting to him to hear his discourses with great show of interest (xxxiii. 30 ff.). He was separated from them by a spiritual and moral chasm and repulsion rather than by personal enmity.

[2] These visions stand above rather than upon the arena of historical action, and do not enter into the main current of the life and thought that give character to Israel and form the normal basis of Revelation. It is highly probable that the original suggestion (Isa. vi.) furnished by the cherubim of the temple, was enlarged by familiarity with the imposing yet grotesque composite figures, symbolizing various superhuman attributes, which guarded the dwellings, palaces, and temples of the Babylonians. The subject of the cherubim is still somewhat obscure, though

Kebar (i. 4 — 28; viii. 1 — 4; x.). In these the holiness and majesty, the irresistible power as well as the omniscience of Jehovah, are expressed in images drawn from the symbolical figures of Hebrew and Chaldaean worship. These revelations brought to his mind what Jehovah was to his distracted people. The thought of these attributes of the God of Israel bore him up in view of the destruction of the holy city and the temple. For Jehovah is greater than his favourite dwelling-place; He may leave it and it falls defenceless; but He may appear in his glory on the alien soil of Babylonia.[1] The same thought sustained him in the presence of the overwhelming material greatness of Babylonia, as contrasted with the meanness and feebleness of the remnants of Judah. For they with Him on their side were yet to be stronger than all their oppressors.

§ 1177. Of actual occurrences in the history of Jerusalem before its final siege by Nebuchadrezzar, we learn nothing from Ezekiel His prophecy is made up of a series of judgments, and these are of an abstract character, evoked by general conditions rather than by special incidents. His predictions also do not relate to any intervening events of national importance, but to the all-absorbing catastrophe alone.

§ 1178. Very characteristic of Ezekiel are the means by which he represents the details of Jerusalem's distress and of the final calamity. The main process of destruction is the siege. This he beholds four years in advance by the

---

many have written upon it. For good short discussions one may consult Smend, *Alttest. Religionsgeschichte.* p. 21 f., 467 f., Nowack, H.A. ii. 38 f., and the article "Cherubim." in DB., by Professor J. E. Ryle. The biblical usage is well summarized in article כרוב in Brown's *Gesenius*.

[1] It has been pointed out (as by Cornill, *Der israelitische Prophetismus.* 117 f.) how closely Ezekiel resembles Isaiah in his view of the exaltation of Jehovah above his creatures. But notice the advance made by Ezekiel. The "seraphim" of Isaiah represent Jehovah only in his temple. But Ezekiel's cherubim appear even in an unclean and hostile land. Fresh revelations were associated with revolutionary events in the history of Israel, which implied an aspect of Jehovah's nature and providence hitherto unknown or unfelt (§ 1335 ff.).

inward eye. The vision is so clear that he can objectivize it in a picture. What he sees is engraved upon a tile, such as were found by the thousand in Babylonia bearing inscriptions or pictorial representations.[1] Thereon the main events and actions of the aggressive work of a formal siege are depicted in the order of their occurrence[2] (Ez. iv. 1–3; cf xxvi. 8 f.).

---

[1] The setting and the details of this representation are Babylonian. The very idea of a picture is foreign to Israelitish usage, which forbade the making of any image or likeness as promoting idolatry. Certain results of the singular absence of this form of art culture may be remarked. Inasmuch as even mechanical drawing was discouraged thereby, constructive skill in all directions, notably in architecture, was lacking all through the history of Israel. Again, the faculty of nice observation, which is so greatly promoted by the artistic habit, was very slightly developed. For example, there is no description of or even allusion to scenes or occurrences in the realm of nature in the Bible, except the most familiar and imposing objects and phenomena. Thirdly, the form and style of the literature are a constant testimony to the absence of this half-æsthetic, half-scientific education. On the other hand, Ezekiel, who lived so long in Babylonia, is the most methodical of writers (§ 1175) in the conception, plan, and style of his compositions. He, moreover, shows knowledge of designing and architecture (ch. xl. ff.; cf. Davidson, *Book of Ezekiel*, p. xxvii). The detailed working out of the siege is also Babylonish.

[2] No objection can well be taken to the above explanation of the command given to the prophet to "take a tile and engrave upon it a city." The other alternative is to understand the terms literally. In the present instance the carrying out of the command by actual mechanical process, while somewhat eccentric, would be neither impossible nor unexampled. In other cases (*e.g.* iv. 4–6) the absurdity of the literal interpretation becomes manifest. Here again we have a suggestion of the caution that is necessary when canons of Hebrew literary form and style are discussed. We should remember that just here the prophet forebore to teach the people in any way (iii. 26), so that the only conceivable motive of a spectacular performance could not have been present. The public silence imposed upon him must have lasted until the end of this series of visions and symbolical actions, that is, to the close of the siege of Jerusalem. Otherwise iii. 26 is meaningless. After this point was reached, he had free communication with the people, and then doubtless the command to explain the signs was fulfilled (cf. xxiv. 27). In the meantime, "shut up in his house" (iii. 24), he was visited by those who chose to come to him (cf. § 1176 note), and by them the visions and symbols were observed (viii. 1, etc.).

§ 1179. Another symbolical action, to be interpreted on similar principles, represents the sufferings and the fate of Israel and Judah. The prophet must lie on his left side one hundred and ninety[1] days to represent the number of years of the captivity of northern Israel, and for the years of the captivity of the kingdom of Judah to lie on his right side for forty days. In this way he was "to bear the iniquity of the house of Israel" (iv. 5) and of "the house of Judah" (iv. 6). "Lying on his side, held down as with cords (iv. 8) and unable to turn, he represents Israel pressed and held in the grasp of the punishment of its iniquity."[2] Simultaneously with this performance, that is, during the one hundred and ninety days, he is to live on a frugal and at the same time ceremonially unclean diet prepared by him in a peculiarly repulsive manner to set forth the scarcity of food during the siege, the sufferings of the beleaguered people, and the desperate means to which they would resort in the fight against famine.[3] The symbol also meant, in the spirit of Hos. ix. 3 f., that captivity would in a sense prolong such horrors, since all food partaken of in a foreign land was unclean, because it could not be offered to the absent Jehovah (iv. 9-17).

§ 1180. Still another symbolical action was enjoined. The prophet must disfigure himself by cutting off the hair of his head and his beard, and that with a sword. The hair must then be divided into three equal parts, one of

---

[1] The Hebrew text gives three hundred and ninety days, but the Sept., as given above, is undoubtedly correct. In this number the last forty years were common to the captivities of Israel and Judah. The reckoning is to be made from 722 B.C. (§ 360). We need not seek for exactness here. While Ezekiel gives forty years for the exile of Judah, Jeremiah had already announced seventy, and this was probably known to Ezekiel. Neither number is, nor was intended to be, accurate. The "left side" in Hebrew is a synonym for the north, and the "right side" for the south.

[2] Davidson, *The Book of Ezekiel*, p. 30.

[3] Compare the horrible sarcasm and hyperbole of the Assyrian legate addressed to the defenders of Jerusalem in 701 B.C. (2 K. xviii. 27).

which was to be burned, another to be struck with the sword, and the third to be scattered to the winds (Ez. v. 1–4). This procedure sets forth the fate of the people of Jerusalem (vs. 12 ff.), some of whom should be consumed by pestilence and famine during the siege, others fall a prey to the sword of the conqueror, and others flee far and wide to peril and death. Upon this there follows a discourse couched in the familiar prophetic language of threatening and denunciation but marked by more than usual severity and bitterness (chs. vi. and vii.).

§ 1181. The foregoing citations afford sufficient idea of the occupation of the prophet of the early exile during the first year of his official ministry. His work may seem to have had no great historical importance, inasmuch as he now held aloof from public life and did not seek directly to promote definite action either in Babylonia or in Jerusalem. Yet his peculiar methods of prophesying were not wholly without practical effect. The leaders of the people who had been hitherto hostile or indifferent now showed an interest which was more than curiosity. In the words of the promise made to Jeremiah (§ 1126), they resorted to him while he did not resort to them. Shut up in his house, he was visited by "the elders of Judah" in the sixth year of his captivity, just a year after the first of his previous visions. In this situation he fell into a trance, in the course of which he felt himself borne away to Jerusalem. Here he beheld various actions performed by leading citizens (Ez. viii.–xi.), which are the most instructive revelations made to us of the moral and spiritual condition of the people since the attempted reformation of Josiah.

§ 1182. This is what the prophet saw after his visionary journey through the upper air to the sacred haunts of his earlier days (viii. 3). First of all the glory of God was displayed as it had been in the plain of the Kebar (viii. 4). Then in startling contrast was seen an Ashera, such as that which King Manasseh had put in the temple

(2 K. xxi. 7) and Josiah had removed and burnt (§ 854), it having apparently been restored under Zedekiah. It is significantly called the "jealousy-image," as challenging most of all the indignation of the jealous God of Israel. This incitement to sensual iniquity, in the very precincts of Jehovah's dwelling-place, stood well within the outer court of the temple.

§ 1183. Passing this image he enters the gateway that leads from the outer to the inner court and the various adjoining side chambers and offices of the temple functionaries. In some of these cells, to which access was only gained secretly (cf. the symbolical action of vs. 7 and 8), many of the elders of the people were burning incense to various bestial objects[1] (viii. 6-12) in the desperate hope of moving all the supernatural powers in behalf of the declining monarchy. Those deities which were specially propitiated were native to the soil of Canaan, since the votaries were now dreading the forfeiture of home and country. Significant in this connection is the watchword of the obscure and clandestine mysteries: "Jehovah hath forsaken the land." It was as though the land, devastated and depopulated, and held in fee by a foreign tyrant, had been abandoned by its God, and given over to the demons

---

[1] Cf. W. R. Smith, *Prophets*, p. 202; RS.², pp. 290 ff., 357. The cult of these unclean animals was a survival and revival of primitive totemistic habits, and not an imitation of Egyptian beast-worship, which had to do only with living animals, and was, indeed, never naturalized in Israel or among any Semitic people. The representation of these objects of superstitious regard, as "carved on the wall round about" (viii. 10), — not "pourtrayed" (EV.) or "painted" (Smend), — is probably another touch of Babylonian influence (cf. xxiii. 14). These *bas-reliefs* were entirely foreign to Hebrew usage (§ 1178), and, however serious the innovations of the time may have been, the temple chambers would scarcely be decorated with such elaborate foreign devices to set forth the objects of a rude and simple cult. Ezekiel has in large measure transferred the associations of Babylonian temples and palaces to the temple of Jerusalem. The sacrifices made by Hebrews at a somewhat later period (Isa. lxvi. 3, 17), of various unclean creatures, were also in some way connected with demoniacal beliefs. Their motive, however, is as yet obscure.

that held their sway before even Baal and Ashtoreth had come in with the corn and the vine and the feasts of the blossoming year!

§ 1184. The prophet next sees in vision the part played by the women in the deterioration of faith and morals. He turns northward again to the most frequented entrance of the temple (cf. § 1118), "and behold! there were sitting the women weeping for Tammuz"[1] (Ez. viii. 13 f.). As in the previous exhibition, so we have here a specimen of a religious custom whose observance shows a radical departure from the pure worship of Jehovah. No symbol was more beautiful and more seductive than the great nature-myth which in one form or another enthralled the North-Semitic world from the Tigris to the Mediterranean. It was the everlasting mystery and process of the decay of nature, the ebbing away of the illumining, vitalizing, gladdening effluence of the spring and summer sun. The usage which is here commemorated, though it has its parallel in the Phœnician custom of the mourning for Adonis, and its foundation in immemorial Canaanitic tradition, is in the view of

---

[1] The myth of Tammuz has two main branches. In both he figures as a solar deity. In the primary and fundamental form, he is the principle of fertility, particularly in the vegetable world. Hence midsummer is the proper season of Tammuz. Indeed, "Tammuz" is the name of the fourth month of the Babylonian or Semitic year. Then the sun is in his strength, the powers of nature are most active, and it is then that in many parts of the world, if not indeed everywhere, the chief rites of sun-worship were celebrated. Even yet, among the Indians of the Northwest, the sun-dance perpetuates the universal cult. There, too, a (white) dog is sacrificed (cf. RS.,[2] p. 292 note). Tammuz is the analogue of Adonis, whose worship, naturalized in Greece, was originally Phœnician, and therefore Canaanitic. But the cult of Adonis corresponds rather to the second or special aspect of Tammuz worship, which is exemplified in this passage of Ezekiel and described further below. The name Tammuz is found only twice in the Bible, and nowhere else except as derived from the Babylonian. It is explained in cuneiform texts as equivalent to "child of life," on the assumption that the original form is *dumuz*. *Dumuz*, however, may be an artificial construction of priestly antiquarianism.

our prophet specifically Babylonian, else he would not have used the exclusively Babylonian name.[1]

§ 1185. Fortunately the treasures of the cuneiform literature afford an explanation worth giving of this much-debated passage. Notice in the first place that the vision is seen in the sixth month of the year (viii. 1). Turning to the native cuneiform table of months, we find that the sixth month *Ulul* (the "Elul" of Neh. vi. 15) is described as "the month of the mission of Ishtar."[2] What is the meaning of this portentous phrase? The main part of the answer is furnished by the famous "Descent of Ishtar,"[3] as it is usually called, a poem describing the journey of Ishtar to the underworld, the realm of Allatu, in search of her consort Tammuz. The poem in its present form embodies more than one variety of Ishtar-myth. An astronomical motive, based on the rising and setting of the planet Venus, is there combined with an eschatological motive having the practical purpose of setting forth to anxious inquirers

---

[1] The reader should bear in mind that Tammuz is not the same precisely as Adonis. The analogy of the respective rites does not constitute identity of the objects worshipped or celebrated. A community of origin between the Canaanitic mourning for Adonis and the Babylonian weeping for Tammuz is not yet proved, though it may be considered probable. We have to think similarly of the analogy of Venus and Ishtar.

[2] See V R. 29 nr. 1, line 6; cf. Haupt, *Keilschrifttexte*, p. 64, and Delitzsch, *Assyrische Lesestücke*, p. 92 f. In a list of months, with their presiding divinities (IV R. 33), Ulul is named as sacred to Ishtar. In the epic of Gilgamesh (formerly held to be "Nimrod"), the sixth tablet or book among the twelve (following the signs of the zodiac) describes the love of Ishtar for the hero and its results. The name "Virgo" for the sixth zodiacal constellation commemorates these associations.

[3] Published in TSBA. II. 179 ff., and IV R. 31; extracts in *Assyr. Lesestücke*, and Lyon, *Assyrian Manual*. The first translations with comments were made by Talbot, in TSBA., as above, and in RP. I. 141 ff.; by G. Smith, *Chaldean Genesis*; by Schrader, *Die Höllenfahrt der Istar*, these three having done most to break and clear the way. Recent essays are those of Sayce, *Hibbert Lectures*, 1887; of A. Jeremias, *Die babylonisch-assyrischen Vorstellungen vom Leben nach dem Tode* (1887); and Jastrow, RBA. (1898). Talbot, Schrader, and Jeremias have also given transcriptions of the text.

or mourners the condition of the departed in the underworld.[1] The fundamental idea is, however, evident in the main features of the story, and to this we shall have to confine ourselves here.

§ 1186. Tammuz, the impersonation of the fructifying, gladdening sun, is at the height of his glory in the heavens, shining "with all-triumphant splendour,"[2] in the month of July, and at the same time he has fully ripened the precious fruits of the earth. In September, when "the sun crosses the line," when the lengthening night begins to overcome the day, his supremacy is at an end; he has succumbed to the powers of darkness. This process of decline and decay, the harbinger of winter, was figured by the naïve fancy of primitive men as the banishment of Tammuz to the realm of the dead. But there is another factor in the fully developed myth. It was inevitable, in the very nature of things, that as the counterpart of Tammuz, regarded as the male principle of productiveness, a goddess should be thought of as expressing the female principle. And so it came to be popularly felt that the love and union of Tammuz and Ishtar were the source of all the beauty and fertility of the earth, of the perpetuation of the race of plants, animals, and men, of life itself, with its manifold activities and enjoyments. Hence, when Tammuz was exiled to the under-world, it was fancied that Ishtar descended thither to seek him and bring him back before his doom of banishment should become irrevocable. Thus with each returning year came the month of "Tammuz" and the month of the "mission of Ishtar."

§ 1187. But many of these old nature-myths were not merely symbols of the wonder-inspiring phenomena of the

---

[1] See Jastrow, RBA. p. 565, 571; Jensen, *Kosmologie*, p. 227 ff.

[2] So Shakespeare, Sonnet xxxiii. In these exquisite lines the supreme poet suggests to us how in such natural phenomena the whole ancient world could see an allegory of the gladness and sorrow, the hopes and disappointments, of humanity. A reading of the sonnet is a good preparation for the study of the nature-myth.

outer world — they became also parables of some of the most profound and mysterious processes and passions of human life. The imposing fact of life itself, with its varying sum of joys and sorrows, and the inevitable coming of death, with its silence, inaction, and gloom, exercised a potent influence on the imagination as well as on the sensibilities of early humanity. Behind it all lay the mystery of production and reproduction linked with that sexual passion which runs in all sensuous being. Moreover, primitive peoples were much more closely united by unconscious sympathy to lower forms of life and to the very earth itself, than the reflective and tutored men and women of our modern civilization. They did not philosophize or theorize. In types and symbols, made moving and memorable by poetic fancy, they "bodied forth the forms of things unknown." Yet such poems and stories, in which we philosophizing moderns have found the key that unlocks the antique mind and heart, were but the outward sign and expression of what was at once the inspiration and the habit of the deepest spiritual life which these poor children of the earth could know. They belonged to the potent realm of religion guarded by gratitude and fear. In the fond but real fictions of Tammuz, Ishtar, and their supernal and infernal colleagues, they generalized the countless influences and motives that were felt or suspected in the springing of the grass, the blooming of the flowers, the ripening of summer fruits, the pairing of birds and beasts and men, and the coming into the world of a new generation.

§ 1188. Thus appeared the two chief forms of the myth of Tammuz, the one being to the other as the winter is to the summer or as the autumn is to the spring. By them the miracle of the changing seasons was brought within the magic circle of the joys and sorrows and hopes and fears of human life, and transformed into a perpetual parable. It is with the second form of the myth that we are here particularly concerned. The "weeping for Tammuz" was, in the widest sense, the universal expression of sadness not merely for the departure of the beauty and richness of summer, but for all which this loss symbolized, the manifold evils which the course of nature brings to mankind. Among those peoples with whom thought and language, feeling and expression, were so closely allied as to be identical in common speech, among whom wailing and beating the breast were synonymous with mourning, the weeping for the dying lord of the day was simply the vicarious utterance of a widespread regret, a little noisy drama of cries and tears to image forth a world-wide tragedy, silent and perpetual as the process of the suns. What was most important of all, it became a religious rite and ceremony, simple, natural, and fascinating.

§ 1189. But here we are pointed to "the women weeping for Tammuz," and that within the precincts of the temple. An explanation of this obnoxious rite is furnished by the mission of Ishtar, or rather by the whole series of relations between the god and the goddess, of which Ishtar seeking her lost consort is the most significant episode. The suggestive feature of these associations is the desire for Tammuz. Here we strike upon the essential evil, the danger-point in the old nature religions. When the forces or phenomena of the outer world are viewed merely as natural emblems of the events and vicissitudes of human life, their contemplation has nothing injurious in it; it is as innocent as are the reflections upon it of a modern philosopher.[1] But when the emblem is made a symbol, and the resemblance becomes a representation, and the powers of nature are personified into the likeness of the gods, a new and mighty motive, the sanction of religion, is added to the human impulses which the supernal beings symbolize. Whatever passion or desire of

---

[1] It is almost needless to observe here that such a stage of the contemplation of nature never really existed among primitive men, with whom feeling took the place of reflection, and nature worship the place of objective observation.

s

men is either directly set forth or necessarily involved in this species of religious symbolism is thereby consecrated and legitimated, idealized, and intensified. In the present instance it is human love or lust that receives its apotheosis in the worship of Ishtar and Tammuz, and the inseparable common history of ancient religion and ancient morality testifies to the influence of such a deification.[1]

§ 1190. Herein lay the danger and the significance of "the women weeping for Tammuz" in the view of the prophets of Jehovah. This rite, as actually performed in Jerusalem in the sixth month of 591 B.C., may not have been directly associated with acts of sexual vice perpetrated under the license of religion. But at any rate, the moral evil was inevitably promoted by the religious ceremony. Indeed, at this stage in the history of Israel the introduction of the custom was tantamount to an authorization of those shameful practices which marked antique Semitic religion wherever a temple was reared and dedicated. Against them, as a concomitant of Baal-worship and a chief incentive to its cultivation, the true priests and prophets of Jehovah had inveighed and contended for centuries. The legislation of Deuteronomy (xxiii. 18) sought to suppress it entirely. Instances of its prevalence are recorded both of the northern (Am. ii. 7; Hos. iv. 13 ff.) and of the southern kingdom (1 K. xv. 12; xxii. 46; cf. xiv. 24). The very names (קָדֵשׁ and קְדֵשָׁה) of the votaries of this most pernicious of all social customs indicate this function as ministers of religion;[2] they were a common designation for profligate men and women (Gen. xxxviii. 21 al.). Repulsive as are some of the features of Tammuz worship, and ministering as it did to debasing and deteriorating passions, its history, taken as

---

[1] For the unethical character of the observance generally, see the remarks of W. R. Smith, RS.², p. 413 ff.

[2] Cf. Assyrian *ḳadištu*; and see Zimmern, *Babylonische Busspsalmen*, p. 40; Jastrow, RBA. p. 475 f.; Jeremias, *Izdubar*, p. 59 f.

a whole, is the most instructive of all subjects that engage the attention of the student of comparative religion. There is nothing which so plainly demonstrates the need of mankind for a divine purifying energy to withstand the most insidious and virulent of spiritual tempters. This was the monster that the religion of Jehovah slew in seemingly unequal fight. It was the veritable serpent of Eden,[1] and no miracle of the Old or New Testament was so great as the crushing of its head.

§ 1191. After this disclosure of the worship of a solar deity or special manifestation of the power of the god of day, the direct adoration of the sun himself by the elders of the priests (cf. ix. 6) is witnessed in vision by the prophet. In the Holy Place, in front of the altar, a score of men were seen, with faces averted from the glory of Jehovah in the Shechinah, doing homage to the sun-god (viii. 15 f.).[2] Like the other forms of idolatry, this was promoted by Babylonian influence. Already, at or near the same place in the temple, a representation of the horses and chariots of the sun in his journey through the heavens had been imported in deference to Assyria, presumably by Ahaz or Manasseh. It had been destroyed by Josiah

---

[1] Cf. Jastrow, RBA. p. 477.

[2] It is singular that most expositors (Davidson being an exception) have seen in viii. 17 a new and extreme form of false worship, mistranslated in the words of EV., "and lo! they put the branch to their nose." But the expression, which is quite obscure, must, whatever its exact meaning, be an amplification of the statement just preceding, "they have filled the land with wrong-doing." The other forms of idolatry are elaborately introduced with an indication of the places and modes of observance (vs. 2-16); and this would be so distinguished also if it were something so strange and specific. Some perceive a reference to "the Persian habit of holding before the mouth a bundle of twigs while invoking the god of light" (Orelli, *Das Buch Ezechiel ausgelegt*, 1888, p. 38). But how should the Hebrews, or, for that matter, the Babylonians, at this stage of their history, have been led to caricature, or adopt in any fashion, a religious custom of a people then so obscure and remote? A grotesque interpretation may be seen in the recent commentary of Bertholet, *Das Buch Hesekiel erklärt* (1897), p. 50.

(§ 856). But when Babylon became supreme the sun-god was again made an object of reverence. This was the climax of "abominations," since it was a more flagrant defiance of Jehovah than any other mode of false worship practised in Jerusalem.

§ 1192. The scene is now changed: after this vision of sin comes a vision of the oft-predicted punishment. Characteristically, the image takes its form from incidents of Assyrian and Babylonian warfare, such as have been brought in abundance before our own eyes in the cuneiform records. In the annals of the great conquerors it is often related[1] that the leaders in revolt and those of the people generally who had "committed sin" were put to a cruel death, while those who were guiltless of rebellion were spared. Sometimes the number of the slain or the deported is given with absolute exactness.[2] Such discrimination must have been the result of careful inquiry, after which the doom was relentlessly fulfilled. A similar process of selection, condemnation, and execution is seen by Ezekiel as enacted in Jerusalem (ch. ix.). Seven messengers from the throne of Jehovah are charged with "the impending punishment of the city."[3] To one of these legates, arrayed in white, the symbol of the divine righteousness (cf. Dan. x. 5; xii. 6; Rev. iii. 4 f.; xv. 6), and bearing writing materials, was committed the task of marking with a cross the foreheads of those who "were moaning and sighing for all the abominations" that were done in Jerusalem. The remaining six, with "weapons of destruction" in their hands, were charged to follow him and slay without mercy all who had not the badge of immunity (cf. Rev. vii. 3, ctr. xiv. 9).

---

[1] *E.g.* by Sinacherib, in his report of the capture of Ekron (I R. 41, 1 ff.); see § 675.

[2] As was actually done in fulfilment of this prediction by Nebuchadrezzar's general (2 K. xxv. 18 ff.).

[3] See Cornill, *Der Prophet Ezechiel*, p. 226 f., note on ch. ix. 1.

§ 1193. To set forth the utter destruction of the city itself a new image is resorted to, whose reality was only too well known in the Assyrian and Babylonian times throughout western Asia. Still in the guise of a vision the city is revealed as about to be enveloped in the flames of avenging fire. A corresponding revelation is made of the shining brightness of the cherubim, who are again displayed in the Holy of Holies. The terrible conception that the firing of Jerusalem by the Chaldæan conquerors after its capture was actually of divine ordination is vividly symbolized: A cherub takes of the coals of fire that burn within the wheels of the celestial figures and delivers them to the white-clad angel of destruction to be scattered over the city (ch. x.).

§ 1194. Transported again to the east side of the temple, the prophet sees before the gate a number of the princes (cf. § 1183), "devising iniquity and wicked counsel," which the context shows to refer to the suicidal policy of rebellion against Babylon (xi. 1–3). The attitude of the revolutionists is instructive. They said, "It is not just now that we must build houses:[1] this city is the cauldron and we are the flesh"; or, in modern language, "This is no time for the occupations of peace. We are stewing here in our own juice; let us strike for freedom." At this, the prophet is commanded to declare that they shall not in any case remain in the city, but shall be delivered up to strangers for captivity and violent death. While he is prophesying, one of the ringleaders suddenly falls dead (xi. 4–13).

§ 1195. Before the vision fades, however, there comes an enlargement of the prophet's outlook. Not all Israel was in Jerusalem. The exiles, present and to come, banished from the city and the temple, Jehovah himself

---

[1] The full expression is given in Ez. xxviii. 26; Isa. lxv. 21; Jer. xxix. 5, 28. The phrase is equivalent to settling down quietly. The antithesis is the saying, "to your tents, O Israel!" referring to the unsettlement and strife characteristic of the nomadic life (§ 465).

scarcely revealing his presence to them,[1] were yet to be restored to their own and Jehovah's land and city. "And they shall come thither, and they shall take away all its horrors and all its abominations. And I will give them another[2] heart, and a new spirit I will put within them,[3] and will remove the heart of stone from them and give them a heart of flesh, to the end that they may walk in my statutes and keep my judgments and do them, and may be to me a people and I to them may be a God. . . ." (xi. 14–21).

§ 1196. After the promise and the curse the glory of Jehovah removed from before the temple and rested upon the Mount of Olives (vs. 22, 23), no longer to protect and bless his city, but to stand aloof while it fulfilled its doom. Released from his trance the prophet finds himself once more among his companions in exile, to whom he relates all that it had been given him to see (vs. 24, 25).

§ 1197. Soon thereafter, at a date not indicated, Ezekiel, in an ecstatic mood, is impelled to another symbolic action, so as to make still more impressive the impending fall of Jerusalem and the end of the kingdom. He is to take his worldly possessions out of his house in the daytime, making ready for a flight under the cover of darkness. Then, when the night has come, he is to break through the wall of the city and seek to escape with his burden upon his shoulder (Ez. xii. 1–7). This proceeding is explained to mean that the "prince" Zedekiah is to attempt to save himself by flight at the taking of his city, but should be caught outside the wall in a net which Jehovah himself was to spread over him (cf. xvii. 20; xxxii. 3; Hos. vii. 12). Thence he was to be brought as a captive to Babylon. That city he was not to see with his eyes (cf. 2 K. xxv. 7), though he was to live there till his death. Of

---

[1] Notice xi. 16, "I have been a sanctuary to them but little."
[2] So the Sept.   [3] So the ancient Versions.

his subjects but a few should survive the destroying sword (xii. 8–16).[1]

§ 1198. A series of instructive utterances are now recorded, which show the inherent necessity and the moral justification of the fall of Jerusalem and the ruin of the state (Ez. xiii.–xix.). Prefaced to these are two striking declarations aimed at the popular delusion that effective prophecy was at an end in Israel and the kindred belief that any prediction that came from Jehovah must apply, not to the near, but to the distant future (xii. 21–28). The current sayings thus denounced ran thus: "The days keep stretching out and visions come to naught" (v. 22), and, "The vision that he is seeing is for many days hence, and for distant times he is prophesying." Against those who thus bring true prophecy into disrepute the genuine prophet of Jehovah brings a formal indictment (ch. xiii.). They accelerate the destruction of the house of Israel because they "prophesy out of their own minds," so that they never really "see" in the true sense of the word (xiii. 2–7). With want of practical as well as spiritual insight they announce peace when turmoil and calamity are inevitable (xiii. 8–10), like men who would stay up a decaying wall with a mere coat of plaster. With the first storm of the wrath of Jehovah it shall tumble to the ground (vs. 11–16).

§ 1199. A fitting companion rôle to that of the prophets was played by their female colleagues, the employment of whom, as a class of professionals, was as much an evidence of social disorganization as of religious degeneracy. It is noteworthy how in times of personal or national perplexity, when ordinary means of redress are exhausted, resort is had to occult superstitions that are usually ignored or derided. As intelligent people of the present day resort in sore sickness to a "Christian Scientist," or as Saul, sore pressed by the Philistines, sought counsel

---

[1] Another symbolical action (xii. 17–20), if it may be so called, is simply an amplification of iv. 10, 11, 16 (cf. § 1179).

from the divining women, whom, as a class, he had suppressed, so now the desperate people of Jerusalem turned from the prophet of Jehovah to necromancers and enchanters. The art of these "prophetesses"[1] apparently consisted in procuring tokens of the divine will or omens from responses given in connection with peculiar amulets consisting of fillets or kindred attachments worn by the suppliants. By means of these enchantments they "slew the souls that should not die and saved the souls that should not live . . . made the heart of the righteous sad, and strengthened the hands of the wicked that he should not return from his wicked way" (xiii. 17-23).

§ 1200. But the blame does not rest entirely upon false prophets or prophetesses, as Ezekiel tells certain of the elders of Israel who come to him to hear his word. The prophets are themselves borne away by the temptation to answer their clients according to their desires (cf. Mic. vii. 3). And when the people come to these seers fresh from idolatrous practices, or with idolatry in their hearts, an "answer of peace" is in any case impossible (cf. Ps. lxvi. 18). Nay, Jehovah himself may lead the prophet astray in his vision (cf. Isa. xxviii. 7), with the result that both deceiver and deceived have to bear their iniquity, and both alike perish from out of Israel (Ez. xiv. 1-11).

§ 1201. In a passage of more than usual power of expression Ezekiel next sets forth his favourite doctrine of individual responsibility. If his hearers doubt his assertion as to this wholesale destruction, they are assured that even the presence in Jerusalem (cf. v. 21) of renowned spiritual heroes of tradition, such as Noah, Daniel,[2] and Job, would not avail to save their people,

---

[1] W. R. Smith, *Journal of Philology*, xiii. 286 f. Cf. Peritz, *Woman in the Ancient Hebrew Cult*, p. 141 f., and above, § 851 note.

[2] Here and in ch. xxviii. 3 Daniel seems to be a national and even a world-wide celebrity. According to Dan. ii. 1, 48, he was, at a tender age, made chief ruler in Babylon in 603 B.C.

since, indeed, it was impossible in the very nature of things that they could save any but themselves by their own righteousness (ctr. Gen. xviii. 32). How much more when Israel is without the presence of such saints of Jehovah, and the four dark messengers, the sword, and famine, and noxious beasts, and pestilence, are already on their way to Jerusalem to smite and not spare. "And ye shall know that not without cause have I done all that I have done there, saith the Lord Jehovah" (Ez. xiv. 12–23).

§ 1202. In two parables the prophet further illustrates the character and fate of the remnant of Israel. They are compared (Ez. xv.) to a vine-stock that bears no fruit, and being useless for any sort of work is cast into the fire. The more familiar figure of an unfaithful spouse is elaborated with all possible detail. Jerusalem has abused all the kindness of Jehovah (xvi. 1–14), has been guilty of the vilest ingratitude by her idolatrous alliances with alien nations, following upon her own abominations, including even the sacrifice of children (vs. 15–34). The punishment shall be greater even than that of Samaria and Sodom, which she had surpassed in iniquity (vs. 35–51). But Samaria and Sodom and even Jerusalem shall at length be restored to favour (vs. 52–63).

§ 1203. Before the utterance of Ezekiel's next recorded prophecy, there is an interval of about three years (592–589 B.C.). It was apparently a time in which the political ferment of the home-land was allayed and the prophet of the Exile could minister with less reserve to his fellow-captives. Naturally, this brief period is devoid of stirring incident. Two passages remain as memorials.

§ 1204. One of these is the great discourse of the freedom and responsibility of the individual in the sight of God (Ez. xviii.). This conception, in which he follows his master, Jeremiah (cf. Jer. xxxi. 29 f.), was, as has been often pointed out, peculiarly suited to the needs and susceptibilities of the exiles. Their whole education in Palestine, personal and national, had tended to encourage in them the notion that the individual had no obligations, moral or religious, apart from the community to which he might belong — the state, the tribe, the clan, or the family group (cf. § 1000). Traditional prejudices and inveterate customs; intercommunal leagues and feuds; the centralizing tendencies of the national worship; the associations of ritual and sacrifice; the sacerdotal caste and functions, — all these stood in the way of independence in thought and endeavour in the moral and religious sphere. But these intellectual and spiritual bonds received a shock by the breaking up of that political and social system which had forged them and kept them fast. And the prophet, himself just emancipated, would fain strike a blow that should rid his clients of such fetters forever.

§ 1205. Providence threw at his feet the opportunity in the expatriation of the exiles. Their complaint was that they, though the most patriotic and devout of Israel, were now in captivity, while the less worthy were enjoying liberty and citizenship in Jerusalem; that in the very nature of the case they must now be suffering for the offences of their fathers, quite apart from any sin of their own (cf. Lam. v. 7). With bitter resentment against the obvious injustice of their lot they passed from lip to lip the popular satire, "The fathers have eaten sour grapes and the children's teeth are set on edge." "Not so," reasoned Ezekiel. "Every soul is in the hands of Jehovah, not in the grip of fate, and he allots to each the doom which it has earned for itself, by its own righteousness or by its own iniquity." Such is the inference to be drawn from the doctrine of Jeremiah. The personal application to those who have the care of these souls under Jehovah is peculiar to Ezekiel, and is taken up by him elsewhere (cf. § 1342).

§ 1206. The last discourse of this group (Ez. xx. 1–44) is given as a stern reply to those of the elders of the community who came to him for counsel in August, 591 B.C. It is a copious rehearsal of the shame and sin of

Israel's past history as a justification of the coming wrath, with a promise of final redemption in its captivity. The theological importance of the discourse is that the chastisement and salvation of Israel are represented as depending upon the sovereign will of Jehovah and the necessity of his being exalted among the nations of the earth.

CHAPTER IX

REBELLION, SIEGE, AND FALL OF JERUSALEM

§ 1207. The political agitation in Jerusalem which had not been wholly allayed by the failure of the half-formed conspiracy and the journey of Zedekiah to his master in Babylon (§ 1157, 1171), was again stirred up four years thereafter (589 B.C.) in a more active and dangerous form. Now it was not the petty communities of Palestine that urged revolt, but the turbulent empire of the Nile. Pharaoh Necho died in 594 B.C., having lived to witness the occupation of Syria and Palestine by his Babylonian rival, and the defeat of the efforts made in Palestine in 598, doubtless with encouragement from Egypt, to get rid of the yoke of Nebuchadrezzar. That he did not actively intervene on behalf of Jehoiakim and Jehoiachin was perhaps due to the need of action in Nubia. At any rate his son Psammetichus II. (594–589) found himself obliged at the beginning of his reign to march in that direction. Inscriptions in the Greek, Carian, and Phœnician languages at Abu Simbel, a little below the Second Cataract, are probably memorials of the encampment there of some of the mercenary troops to which the dynasty of Sais owed its security. The rôle of Necho in Asia was attempted by the next king Hophra ("Apries," 589–564) after the conclusion of this Nubian war.

§ 1208. The ambitious designs of this Pharaoh gave to the promoters of sedition in Jerusalem the pretext for action against the Chaldæan tyrant which they had so long desired. It became now a difficult task for Jeremiah or any of his colleagues to make head against the tumultuous passion for revenge and civic freedom, nor was it easy for the average patriot to perceive how romantic was the scheme of insurrection. The petty kingdoms of Palestine, which had been cowed by the threats of Nebuchadrezzar in 593, now banded together again. They gave little material help at the testing-time. But the alliance with Tyre seemed to guarantee the sinews of war; and Tyre held out bravely for many years (§ 1213). So now Jerusalem's heart went out toward Egypt, untaught by the sad two centuries of her cajolery and fickleness. The exact time of the agreement with Egypt and the beginning of the revolt we cannot determine, but the accession of Hophra in 589 suggests an approximate date, and we know that Nebuchadrezzar marched into Judah before the end of 588.

§ 1209. We have a graphic picture of the moral situation[1] from the pen of Ezekiel in a famous allegory or riddle. A great eagle, broad-winged and variegated, came to Lebanon, broke off the topmost bough of a cedar, and carried it to the land of the merchants, an image of the capture and deportation of Jehoiachin. Then he took of the seed of the land and planted it as a vine (cf. Ez. xix. 10 ff.) beside its native waters, trusting that its branches might turn toward himself — an image of Nebuchadrezzar installing Zedekiah as his vassal king. But the ungrateful vine spread its branches toward another great eagle, — Zedekiah turning toward Egypt, — rousing the just resentment of the one who had planted and watered it (Ez. xvii. 1-10). The application is then made in literal terms: It was a solemn covenant confirmed by a

---

[1] The chronological order of Ezekiel's prophecies is exceptionally disturbed by the position of ch. xvii., which would naturally come between chs. xx. and xxi. The occasion of the transposition is apparently the desire to place together the three illustrations of the unfaithfulness, ingratitude, and perfidy of Judah and its kings (chs. xv.-xvii.).

sacred oath to which Zedekiah had "given his hand."[1] This covenant he has broken by sending ambassadors to Egypt. But his perjury and treachery will avail him nothing. Even his allies the Egyptians will give him no help when his city is besieged by the Chaldæans. It is Jehovah himself whom he has offended, and it is his judgment which shall be executed upon Jerusalem by the king whom he has deceived (Ez. xvii. 11–21). Yet from the very topmost bow of the cedar — the house of David — a twig shall be taken and planted which shall become a goodly tree, making a home for birds of every wing — the restored kingdom of Israel (Ez. xvii. 22–24). The whole passage is a pendant to the great discourse of Jer. xxvii. delivered in 593, following up the earlier declaration of Jer. xxv., made in 604, at the very beginning of the reign of Nebuchadrezzar (§ 1115, 1157).

§ 1210. In default of an official report of the march of Nebuchadrezzar against Palestine (cf. § 1213) we have from Ezekiel an ideal picture of the Great King taking counsel with his gods as to the attack on Jerusalem. It is given in the course of a declamation almost lyrical in form and spirit, upon "the sword of Jehovah," which is described as sharpened and furbished for its terrible work among the doomed and guilty people of Jerusalem (Ez. xxi. 1–17). It is the sword of the king of Babylon which Jehovah uses as his own. Before it is drawn to strike, he who is wielding it stands "at the parting of the ways" at a place where the prophet sets up two fingerposts, one pointing to Rabbath Ammon, and the other to Jerusalem. In perplexity as to which road he should take, the Great King resorts to his oracles: "He shook the arrows to and fro: he consulted the teraphim, he inspected the liver. In his right hand comes the lot

---

[1] Presumably the oath was sworn both by the gods of Babylonia (cf. Ez. xvii. 16) and by Jehovah (Ez. xvii. 19), the God of the land whose favour the over-lord supposed he had acquired (2 K. xviii. 25), and in whose local existence and power he fully believed.

'Jerusalem,' that he may open his mouth with shrieking and raise the battle-cry, set battering-rams against the gates, throw up ramparts, and erect siege-towers" (xxi. 18–22).

§ 1211. The figure, though somewhat mixed, gives its own interpretation. One feels himself transported to the Babylonian environment of the prophet, the proper home of oracles and prognostications (cf. Isa. xlvii. 12 ff.), whose literature abounds with records of omens for kings preparing for warlike expeditions or setting out upon them.[1] The procedure here indicated was somewhat as follows.[2] The king of Babylon, or rather the priest as his mediator, comes before the image of his god, a prescribed formula of prayer is recited, and an animal sacrifice offered. The deity gives his answer through special forms of the lot. Here two are instanced. The liver of the animal might be inspected, to see whether its colour or texture indicated a propitious result. But in the present case, where a choice between two courses is aimed at, a more specific mode of decision must be adopted. Hence resort was had to belomancy or rhabdomancy,[3] as it is called, or divination by

---

[1] The omens noted for the expeditions of Sargon I and Narâm-Sîn (§ 90) were of this general character. The subject of such omens of national import is treated in Jastrow, RBA, p. 332 ff. Contrast the style and spirit of the beautiful prayer in Ps. xx., uttered under similar circumstances (§ 1073).

[2] The "teraphim" are named here as a general expression in deference to Hebrew usage. The fitness of the term as used for the special personal protecting deity of the king is obvious: (1) the teraphim were domestic tutelary divinities; (2) they were often consulted for oracles. Cf. Jud. xvii. 5; 2 K. xxiii. 24; Hos. iii. 4.

[3] It is to Jerome that we owe these terms, as well as the earliest account of the process of divining by arrows, which he gives in his commentary on the present passage. See Gesenius, *Thesaurus*, s.v. קסם, where authorities are also quoted as to the prevalence of the usage in Arabia. In connection with the same subject, Wellhausen, *Reste arabischen Heidentumes* (1887), p. 126 f., comments fully upon our text. Cf. W. R. Smith, *Journal of Philology*, xiii, p. 278. On Babylonian divination generally, see Lenormant, *La divination chez les Chaldéens* (largely superseded); King, *Babylonian Magic and Sorcery* (1896); Jastrow, RBA, chs. xvi.–xx.

means of arrows. A number of these were put in a quiver or case, after being inscribed with the name or some other distinguishing mark of the several objects represented by them. They were then shaken, and the arrow which was first drawn out indicated the choice — in this case Jerusalem.

§ 1212. Thus Ezekiel interpreted the preparations for war, the rumours of which were borne by busy tongues to his secluded dwelling. Pending the actual march he repeats his denunciations against Jerusalem, on account of her many gross and incorrigible vices (Ez. xxii.). He then concludes these intervening prophecies by an allegorical review of the relations between Samaria and Jerusalem, on the one hand, and the several foreign nations with which they have intrigued, on the other, showing the moral and religious infidelities against Jehovah of these two sister-kingdoms (Ez. xxiii.). In these as well as in his vaticinations during the siege of Jerusalem, we see a paradox somewhat similar to that presented by Jeremiah (§ 1107 f.). A prophet overflowing with love for his people uses against them the language of contempt and loathing, while he seems to gloat over their sufferings and their punishment. The explanation is (1) rhetorical extravagance of speech; (2) indignation against wrong and irreligion; (3) the racial habit of looking at people not as individuals but as a class, whose sensibilities are not so obvious to a censor.

§ 1213. The expedition of Nebuchadrezzar against Palestine started in 588 B.C. It was vast (Jer. xxxiv.) and formidable. He established his headquarters at the central strategic point, at Riblah on the upper Orontes (§ 1038). There he was midway between Carchemish, the fortress won from Egypt, and the border of that country which he intended to subdue.[1] Thence also he could strike speedily

---

[1] We have monumental reminders of the marches of Nebuchadrezzar through Syria and Palestine, though unfortunately they contain no reference to his military operations. In the Wady Brissa, not far

at the revolted cities of Phœnicia. Tyre, indeed, was with Jerusalem a chief point of attack. It had long been the only Phœnician state capable of resisting a strong foreign power.[1] Now, more prosperous than ever, it was as unwilling to yield its commercial franchise to Nebuchadrezzar as formerly to Esarhaddon (§ 754). It is probable that a force was sent at once to blockade the Tyrians — who, after their manner, retired to their "new Tyre" (cf. § 681) and long resisted the besiegers. We do not know that the Ammonites, after all (cf. § 1210), remained in revolt. At any rate, they were unfriendly towards Judah during this whole period (Ez. xxv. 1 ff.; Jer. xl. 14; cf. xlix. 1 ff.). The territory of Judah was certainly the chief field of the Chaldæan military operations. While a sufficient army advanced upon and invested Jerusalem, the other fortified cities were rapidly taken, till soon Lachish and Azekah alone offered resistance (Jer. xxxiv. 7), and these doubtless surrendered before the fall of the capital.

---

from Riblah, at the foot of Jebel-Akkar, on the eastern slope of the Lebanon range, two long inscriptions, accompanied by *bas-reliefs*, were found by H. Pognon, French vice-consul at Beyrut, who published them, with plates, in his work, *Les inscriptions babyloniennes du Wady Brissa*, Paris, 1887. They relate, like most of the other inscriptions of the Great King, to his buildings and fortifications in Babylon. Another is written in archaic characters on the right side of the Nahr el Kelb, or Dog River, eight miles north of Beyrut, and was discovered beneath an overgrowth of shrubs and ferns in 1881. The old high road from Damascus to the coast led along this river, and on the opposite side had already been found the names of Ramses II., Sinacherib, and Esarhaddon. The inscription is mostly undecipherable through weathering. What can be made out most surely is a list of wines of southern Syria, in which that of Helbon stands conspicuous (cf. Ez. xxvii. 18). The contents of the Wady Brissa inscriptions show that they could not have been written as early as Nebuchadrezzar's first campaign (§ 1078), as Renan seems to suppose (*Histoire du peuple d'Israel*, III, 288).

[1] We cannot infer from Ez. xxviii. 20-24 that Sidon had revolted from the Chaldæans. This brief prophecy is of a general character and merely indicates that Sidon shall be punished, because of old time it had been "a galling brier and a smarting thorn to the house of Israel," — an allusion apparently to the men-stealing raids of the Phœnicians (Am. i. 9).

T

§ 1214. It was on the tenth day of the tenth month of the ninth year of Zedekiah, that is, in January, 587 (2 K. xxv. 1; Jer. xxxix. 1; lii. 4; Ez. xxiv. 1 f.) that the Chaldaean army appeared before Jerusalem. Of the details and progress of the siege operations we are not informed. Presumably the north side of the city, as in all the ancient sieges, was the quarter chiefly assailed. Only there indeed could the storming towers and mantelets be brought into play. The resistance was stubborn and brave; for it was known that this final revolt if unsuccessful would meet with no mercy.

§ 1215. Of the feelings and temper of the besieged some indications are given by Jeremiah. Zedekiah fell into a panic as soon as the extent and energy of the besieging force were fully displayed. The words of Jeremiah were still ringing in his bewildered ears. Now that their fulfilment seemed possible the stern and faithful preacher gained an ascendency over the king which he never wholly lost. Zedekiah had always felt that Jeremiah had the ear of Jehovah as the rival prophets had not, and as an oracle was now in great request, he sent a deputation — Pashhur,[1] son of Malchiah, and Zephaniah the priest — with a message: "Inquire, I pray thee, of Jehovah for us; for Nebuchadrezzar, king of Babylon, is making war upon us: perhaps Jehovah will deal with us according to all his wondrous deeds, and he will go away from us" (Jer. xxi. 1, 2). The expectation was not so fatuous as it might appear. The nearest precedent for the present situation was the siege of Jerusalem by Sinacherib. If Jeremiah was the true successor of the great Isaiah, might not Zedekiah be equal in fate to his ancestor Hezekiah, and receive such an answer as that which presaged the destruction of the Assyrian host? Jeremiah's client was, however, soon undeceived. The answer was, if possible, a fiercer and more cruel threatening than any

---

[1] Not to be confounded with the son of Immer, who put Jeremiah in the stocks (§ 1111).

yet delivered. It told of the helplessness of the armed defenders of the city, because Jehovah himself was to fight against them. Jerusalem was to be taken and put to the flames. There was but one chance of safety for the inhabitants: if they were to go out and fall away to the Chaldaeans, they should live (Jer. xxi. 3–10).

§ 1216. For such a heart-breaking reply the king was scarcely prepared. He had become accustomed to these reiterated threats and had looked upon them as outworn generalities. But they took on a more serious aspect when the swords of the besiegers flashed before him in the level rays of the January sun. Moreover, the answer contained an element of danger. The very suggestion that safety might be gained by individuals if they were to go out and enter the camp of the besiegers must have weakened the defence (cf. xxxviii. 4), and indeed in ordinary cases would justify a charge of high treason. Yet this prophet of evil now added to his offence by again assuring Zedekiah that Jerusalem would fall and he himself be brought before the king of Babylon for judgment (Jer. xxxiv. 1–3). There was, however, a certain mitigation of this cruel fate: the life of the captive king was to be spared, and he was to be interred at last with a royal funeral (xxxiv. 4, 5).[1]

§ 1217. The prophet's softening mood towards Zedekiah was in some measure both cause and effect of a temporary change in the conduct of both king and people. The resentment of the army officers was smothered for a

---

[1] Indicated by the words, "With the burnings of thy fathers, the former kings which were before thee, so shall they make a burning for thee." This was the burning of aromatic spices performed at the burial of Asa (2 Chr. xvi. 14) and denied to Jehoram (2 Chr. xxi. 19). We must not take too literally the details of such personal predictions. It is useless to say that such an interment was possible in Babylonia to the exiled king of Judah, and equally unnecessary to explain the promise as conditional, like Jer. xxxviii. 20 (so Hitzig and Orelli). Rather must we put the declaration in the same category as the unfulfilled prediction concerning Jehoiachin (§ 1141 ff.).

while, and the terrors of the siege unnerved the courtiers lately so bellicose and confident. Jeremiah seized the opportunity to promote a practical work of grace among his intimidated fellow-citizens. We recall here the part played by the system of slavery in the social and national life of the Hebrews (§ 539 ff.). The condition and treatment of slaves at this period was of vital importance to the state, of more importance indeed to the masters than to the servants themselves. The habitual temper of the ruling classes (§ 587 ff.) and the sudden changes of fortune which had brought some of the poorest of the people suddenly to the front (§ 1153), combined with popular irreligion and frivolity to foster the selfishness and cruelty which seem almost inherent in Oriental social life. Against these evils such legislation as Israel had (§ 586) seemed to have but little effect. For example, it was an ancient prescription of the first Book of the Covenant that provided for the release of Israelitish slaves after six years' servitude (Ex. xxi. 2); and it was not long since the same enactment had been published in a more precise and elaborate form (Deut. xv. 12 ff.). This humane and wholesome statute had been disregarded. Now it was suddenly brought home to the masters that such a policy was suicidal. Every freeman counted as a warrior, fighting at his own expense (§ 520); a body of freemen counted for more in the defence of the city than a force largely made up of discontented slaves, and Jerusalem never had sorer need of defenders.

§ 1218. But now this year 587 witnessed such a jubilee as was never seen in Israel before or since. Partly moved by interest and partly pricked by an uneasy conscience, the masters released all their slaves, not merely those who had passed the legal term of servitude, but those also who had been lately acquired (Jer. xxxiv. 8 ff.). The manumission seemed to propitiate the offended Lawgiver, for it was followed by the withdrawal of the besieging army. And what appeared doubly auspicious, it was an army of relief from Egypt that led to the raising of the siege. "For Pharaoh's army was come out of Egypt, and when the Chaldæans that were besieging Jerusalem heard tidings of them they went away from Jerusalem" (Jer. xxxvii. 5). The grateful people now became elated with the prospect of the defeat of their enemies, and ere long they were as confident and careless as ever. Soon it occurred to them that perhaps their great sacrifice had been unnecessary. Their gratulations were mixed with the remorse of disappointed avarice as they saw themselves defrauded of their property by their own sentimental weakness. Such an act of romantic generosity should be undone if possible. The king and the nobles took the lead in showing that it was possible, and soon the poor freedmen found themselves again under their accustomed burdens. Nothing better illustrates the moral degeneracy of Jerusalem, or shows how good a case Jeremiah had against the leaders of his people.

§ 1219. The occasion demanded a strong word from the prophet. His fierce denunciation was perhaps more telling than any he had hitherto uttered. He did not now give an oracle whose authenticity might be questioned, or any assertion of his personal prerogative. Nor was the offence one of the conventional sins of the upper classes, whose reprobation had become a commonplace. His indignation had all the moral force and freshness of Elijah's denunciation of the crime against Naboth. Jeremiah's charge was irresistible because he could claim that the sufferers were defrauded of rights which had been granted to unfortunate Hebrews from the very beginning of the nation (xxxiv. 13 f., cf. § 543). Thus the sin was committed against Jehovah not merely as the God of righteousness and mercy but also as Israel's ruler and lawgiver. Finally, the guilt of perjury was brought home to the sacrilegious oppressors; for the emancipation had been confirmed by a solemn oath and covenant (xxxiv. 18 f.; cf. Gen. xv. 9 ff.).

§ 1220. The transaction furnished a fine opportunity for a renewed announcement of the coming doom of the city. Indeed, it was a sort of moral vindication of Jeremiah's next disclosure. For Zedekiah had in the meantime sought once more a favourable oracle. Thinking that the liberation of the slaves would procure the divine favour, and that the Chaldæans would be worsted by the Egyptians, he had sent another deputation to Jeremiah, saying, "Pray now to Jehovah our God for us." Thus Hezekiah had sent to Isaiah when Jerusalem was ready to fall before Sinacherib. The answer now was that the Chaldæans would return to fight against Jerusalem and would take it and burn it with fire (Jer. xxxvii. 3–10). The oracle seemed cruel and improbable, and reawakened the resentment of the rulers against Jeremiah. The Egyptian interlude lengthened itself out, and the Chaldæans did not soon return.

§ 1221. The hopes of the deluded Jerusalemites rose yet higher. With the lengthening reprieve of the city the popular wrath against the prophet of evil omen grew almost beyond control. It was apparently only the moral advantage given him by their selfish poltroonery that kept them from laying violent hands upon him. Such an outspoken rebel would be sure, however, to furnish occasion for a plausible charge of high treason. The opportunity soon came, and in a fashion that left his enemies nothing to be desired. He had business to attend to in his native Anathoth, connected with his personal share of the family estate (cf. § 1225). Making his way northward through the gate of Benjamin,[1] he was arrested by a sentinel named Irijah on the ground that he was "falling away to the

---

[1] It was near this gate that the Chaldæans had been encamped (§ 1214); and although it was also the chief avenue of communication with all the northern country, the worse of the two possible motives for his attempted exit was naturally attributed to him. Doubtless, also, many of the citizens had already passed through that same gate and "fallen away to the Chaldæans" (cf. xxxviii. 19).

Chaldæans" (Jer. xxxvii. 11-13). He denied the charge, but in vain. Irijah brought him before the "princes," who constituted the king's council. The charge was not so flimsy as at first sight it seems to us. The main body of the enemy was, to be sure, far from Jerusalem, but spies and bands of scouts were everywhere. It may even have been believed that he was seeking a meeting with one of their emissaries, in the neighbourhood of the city. As he was professedly expecting the surrender of the city within a very few days, was it not fair to suppose that he would help to make good his prediction? One or two influential well-wishers in the council might have cleared or at least shielded Jeremiah. But now there was no Ahikam at court to champion his cause (§ 1092). Zedekiah, though the greatest sufferer then and thereafter by the word of Jeremiah, was still well disposed to him. But he was powerless against his own courtiers (cf. xxxviii. 5).[1] So the judgment was passed: the prophet was denounced and beaten, and then cast into the prison reserved for state criminals. It was the house of Jonathan, the official secretary, beneath which vaulted cells had been constructed (xxxvii. 14 f.). Here he was left, to die of starvation and neglect, like many thousands of Oriental prisoners before and after him (cf. Isa. li. 14).

§ 1222. Meanwhile the decisive turn of affairs had taken place which settled the fate alike of accused and accusers, of masters and slaves, of true men and traitors. Not many days passed when, as any experienced observer might have foreseen, the Chaldæan army again appeared before Jerusalem. How it had disposed of the Egyptian army of relief we are not informed. The Egyptians may have occupied Gaza (Jer. xlvii. 1) and advanced no farther.

---

[1] Another passage (xxxii. 3-5), apparently written by a biographical compiler (cf. Cornill, p. 63), states that Zedekiah had put Jeremiah in prison because of his announcement of the impending capture of the city and of the king himself. This is also true in the sense that the royal authority had to be given to the sentence of imprisonment for treason.

Certainly no great battle was fought, and it is reasonable to suppose that after a slight skirmish the troops of Pharaoh Hophra beat a hasty retreat (Jer. xxxvii. 7). The Chaldæans met with no opposition from the fortified towns of Judah. The Chaldæans resumed the blockade of the capital, fearing now as little from the restless Egyptians as from the unwarlike Tyrians.

§ 1223. The leaders of the revolt had had control of civic affairs from the beginning of the siege, and they maintained it to the end. They were, indeed, the only ones in the city capable of leadership in any fashion, and to their credit be it said, they met the crushing reverse of fortune like truest patriots. They could hardly expect deliverance now, and prolonged resistance could only aggravate the final punishment. Yet there was no sign of flinching, no compromise with the enemy, or offer of surrender for easier terms. They strove to the last to keep up the spirit of the defenders; and however their own hearts may have failed them, they frowned sternly upon every symptom of despair and every suggestion of submission. Let us give our meed of admiration to this forlornest hope of a desperate yet not wholly ignoble cause. At this distance of time we can afford to be impartial. We are not dealing with modern South Africans but with ancient Hebrew patriots. Some of them had acted wickedly and all of them foolishly; but as to the mainspring of the rebellion for which they were now suffering the penalty, who can say that the motive was wholly wrong? That they believed they were right may be argued from their heroic demeanour in the presence of the cruel death which from the beginning they kept in view as the fate of unsuccessful rebels. To most interested contemporaries it always appears that of two opposing policies one is entirely right and the other entirely wrong, because the feverish demand for immediate action obscures the larger issues of the controversy. For us it should be possible to see that the higher and broader patriotism of Jeremiah might coexist in the same moral realm with the more impulsive and erratic self-devotion of his rivals, as the retrograde motion of the comet is made in obedience to the laws of the solar system as well as the direct motion of the planet.

§ 1224. Jeremiah lay helpless for a time in his dungeon. It was to Zedekiah himself that he owed his comparative freedom. With the return of the Chaldaeans, the king's trembling heart again turned towards the prophet, whose predictive word had once more been verified. He had him secretly to his house, and said: "Is there any word from Jehovah?" and Jeremiah said: "There is," and added: "Thou shalt be delivered into the hand of the king of Babylon." After reminding him of the failure and collapse of the rival prophets, he concluded by begging Zedekiah not to let him go back to the dungeon in the house of Jonathan. The king succeeded in having him placed in the "court of the guard," that is to say, in the court-yard adjoining the royal residence, where suspected persons and other less obnoxious civil prisoners were kept in a sort of "honourable confinement," though probably fettered by the foot-chain. Here he was not to be dependent, as in the dungeon, upon a casual visitor for a precarious supply of food, but was by the king's command to receive a griddle-cake daily from the baker's bazar. This was supplied to him regularly till all the bread in the city was exhausted at the end of the siege (xxxvii. 16–21).

§ 1225. To prisoners of his present class, friends and acquaintances were admitted under the surveillance of the guard. While in this court of the guard Jeremiah received a visit from Hanameel, his cousin-german of Anathoth. Between these two a transaction took place, singular for the place and time, but signally illustrative of Jeremiah's transcendent faith and foresight. It was in connection with the family estate that he had made the frustrated attempt to go to Anathoth (§ 1221), and now Hanameel comes to see him in his prison upon the same business.

Jeremiah was asked to fulfil the duty incumbent on him as the representative of the family (cf. Ruth iv. 4), to buy the property from Hanameel.[1] This settlement of the title to his property suggested the whole question of the gloomy and desolate future of the fatherland. The visit of Hanameel, thus fulfilling his own thwarted purpose, he greeted as a providential token of the final restoration of peace and order. Hence he made the purchase from Hanameel, according to all the legal requirements,[2] on the ground of Jehovah's promise: "Houses and fields and vineyards shall again be bought in this land" (xxxii. 6–15).

§ 1226. The inspiration to transact this business he had thus recognized at once as coming from Jehovah. But no

---

[1] There seems to be general misunderstanding of the nature of this transaction. It was only the legal title to the estate that was in question. Legally, Jeremiah, as the chief agnate, should own it, but he could only secure the right by paying the occupant the value of this right, not necessarily the full value of the property. This helps to explain why so trifling a sum was paid. The expositors attempt to show that the seventeen shekels (about eleven dollars) was not an unreasonable price.

[2] The legal process of the transfer of the title is fully described in Jer. xxxii. 9–14, a passage which is our only source of information on the matter. The minute account needs scarcely any commentary except to say that it is now generally agreed that the words rendered in EV., "according to the law and custom," which are wanting in the Sept., should be omitted. Stade (in ZATW. V, 176 f.) and Cornill (*Text of Jeremiah*, pp. 22, 64) follow Hitzig in maintaining that there was only one copy of the contract, a part of which was folded up and sealed and a part left open. This is unnecessary. It is not supported by v. 10 (cf. v. 44), which speaks not of one copy, but of one document or record. Moreover, the text, as left to us after the emendations of Stade (followed by Cornill), speaks just as plainly as ever of two copies, "the sealed and the open" (vs. 11, 14). The only difficulty in this natural view of the matter comes from v. 10, which seems to say that the deed was sealed before it was signed by the witnesses. Giesebrecht, who has well treated the question (*Das Buch Jeremia*, p. 176 ff.), suggests satisfactorily that the witnesses signed their names on the outside of the sealed copy to avouch the fact that it was sealed by both contracting parties. The open copy was to be used for ordinary reference, and the one that was sealed could be appealed to in cases of dispute. Such we know was the custom among the Babylonians, among whom the forms of business procedure in the East originated.

sooner was the deed handed over for safe keeping to his secretary Baruch than the audacity of the performance suddenly overwhelmed and disheartened him. It is such traits as these that bring this typically human prophet so near to us! Our deepest and truest intuitions are those which surprise and awe us most by their presumptuous rashness. Their worth is approved to our trembling faith when we have turned them over and over in the light that flows from the fountain of truth. So Jeremiah appeals to Jehovah in his embarrassment. "Alas, Lord Jehovah! the earth works have been brought close to the city [1] to take it; and the city is given into the hand of the Chaldæans, and what Thou hast spoken has come to pass, and, behold, Thou seest it! And Thou hast said unto me: Buy the field for money and call witnesses, whereas the city has been given into the hand of the Chaldæans" (xxxii. 16, 24, 25). To this appeal an answer came rehearsing fully the previous announcement of the city's doom and its justification (xxxii. 28–35), but assuring the prophet more strongly than ever of the final restoration of the old order of things in civic and business life (vs. 36–44).

§ 1227. As the impending fall of the city drew nearer and nearer, Jeremiah, eager to save the lives of the citizens, became more urgent in advising a general surrender. His plea was as far as possible from being a seditious harangue, and was indeed a common-sense appeal to the instinct of self-preservation. "He that abideth in the city shall die, and he that goeth out to the Chaldæans shall live" (xxxviii. 2). But as this sort of counsel would make an end of all discipline, it had to be checked and punished. Hence the civil and military leaders demanded that Jeremiah be put to death. "For he is weakening the hands of the fighting men who are left in this city, and the hands of all the people, in speaking such words to them" (xxxviii. 4). The poor king, broken in heart and hope,

---

[1] The point of this special consideration may be learned from § 1230.

and dreading a revolt against his own person, yielded to their request, with the deprecating remark: "Behold, he is in your hand, for the king cannot do anything against you." When, however, they had gained the coveted opportunity, they hesitated. The fatal deed was too great a crime. What seemed at first a military necessity began to look like murder, or at any rate like sacrilege against a prophet of Jehovah. A happy thought struck them. They would not slay him! they would merely let him die! In the courtyard, in the quarter assigned to the king's son Malchiah, was a foul empty cistern. Into this Black Hole they lowered him; then left him to sink and suffocate, or failing that, to starve to death (xxxviii, 5, 6).

§ 1228. From the fate thus prepared for him he was delivered through the good offices of an Ethiopian[1] court-officer, a trusty servant of the king, Ebed-melech by name. Taking pity on Jeremiah, he resolved, if possible, to secure relief. To make his case good, he appealed to the king on general principles of equity, and therefore approached him, not in his palace, but at the city gate of Benjamin, where, within sound of the siege operations, he still dispensed the royal justice. Here his bewildered mind, freed from official intimidation, could right itself for a moment. Perhaps with the hope that in some way the prophetic function might yet bring help to the state, he asserted his kingly authority, defied the princes, and gave orders for the release of Jeremiah. At his command Ebed-melech with a sufficient guard of thirty men rescued the prophet from his perilous durance. The prisoner was restored to the court of the guard. There he remained till the day when Jerusalem was taken (xxxviii. 7–13, 28). To Ebed-melech came the

---

[1] It is suggestive of the immemorial servitude of the non-Semitic Africans that Cushites were employed as body-servants in Israel through all the history of the kingdom. Compare 2 Sam. xviii. 21 f. and Jer. xxxvi. 14. The latter passage tells us that the great-grandson of a certain Cushite in Jerusalem was called "Jehudi" (Judaite), possibly that the prejudice of colour might be disarmed (cf. Jer. xiii. 23).

prophetic word that because of his faith in Jehovah his life would be spared in the ruin of the city (xxxix. 15-18).

§ 1229. The nobles respected the resolution of the king, and let Jeremiah alone. Perhaps they had not so much reason to fear him now. They had apparently secured some sort of a pledge from Zedekiah that he would not follow the counsel of Jeremiah and leave the city suddenly, to make terms with the enemy for himself and his retinue. This he could easily do, as the palace commanded the gate of the king's garden (§ 1231). We have a full report of the last recorded interview between Zedekiah and Jeremiah. By his private orders the king had Jeremiah brought to him in one of the chambers of the temple. Here he begged of him a final word from Jehovah. Jeremiah could do nothing but repeat his well-worn message that the only safety for himself, his family, and the city lay in his going out to the Chaldæans (xxxviii. 14-18). The king, afraid to venture against his council, protested that he dreaded the mocking of those who had already deserted to the besiegers. Jeremiah urged upon him the prospect of the far more bitter reproaches of his own household who would through him be delivered up to the king of Babylon, besides the sure fate of his wives and children, and the sack and burning of the city (xxxviii. 19-23). With this comfortless assurance the king's last hope was gone. He could only beg from Jeremiah that when the nobles should inquire of him what he had said to the king, he would reply that he had begged of him not to let him go back to the dungeon in the house of Jonathan the scribe. Zedekiah's fears were well grounded. The inquiry was made and the answer given as he had desired (xxxviii. 24-27).

§ 1230. Not long thereafter came the end. Famine within the city, with its heart-breaking horrors (Lam. ii. 20; iv. 10), pressed the defenders sorely. But surer and swifter than famine itself was the work of the Chaldæans. A year and a half had passed since the blockade began. But this was a short time for the successful siege of a great fortress; and the period of active hostilities had been shortened by the inroad of the Egyptians (§ 1218). In an important siege the greater portion of the time was occupied with the erection of the storming-wall and the other preparations for direct assault upon the fortifications [1] (cf. § 1178). When the city wall was high and strong, it was useless to attempt to undermine it. It must be attacked not far from the summit. It was from the earthworks erected for this purpose (Jer. xxxii. 24) that the battering-rams and storming-towers were brought to play upon the wall. Hence enormous labour was necessary before a suitable base of operations could be secured upon the sloping approaches to the city. When aggressive action was fairly begun, unless the besieged were numerous and skilful enough to disable the besiegers by arrows or other deadly weapons, only the very strongest walls could long endure the constant battering, followed by the pickaxes, crowbars, and wall-hooks by which the stones were dislocated and removed. Moreover, a force of defenders, weakened or diminished by famine, could not long withstand a constant shower of missiles from the siege-towers. So we are told of Jerusalem that on the ninth day of the fourth month of Zedekiah's eleventh year (July. 586 B.C.) a breach was made in the city wall (Jer. xxxix. 2; lii. 5 ff.; cf. 2 K. xxv. 3 f.).[2]

---

[1] It is from the sculptures of the Assyrian kings that we get our chief information as to the methods of sieges in the ancient East, and the explanation of such terms as are used in Ez. xxvi. 7 ff. (where "buckler," in EV., should be replaced by mantelet or *testudo*, and "axes" by wall-hooks or *falces*). The Assyrians first made of besieging an art and science which were not essentially changed till the general introduction of explosives. Illustrations are given in Nowack, HA. I. 367 ff., and in BA. III. 178 ff. Cf. the lifelike description of the siege and defence of a small fortress of the fifteenth century A.D. in Reade's *The Cloister and the Hearth*, chs. xlii. and xliii.

[2] The entrance was forced on the north of the city. We are not to understand that one of the great gates was broken in. The gates were virtually impregnable against ancient modes of attack, being made of the toughest wood, overlaid with copper or iron, and being shut and securely barred when the siege was closely pressed.

§ 1231. When an opening had been forced in the city wall, it was resolved to make the entrance by night, so that escape, might not be easy to any of the people. Among the Chaldæans were many Judaite fugitives who would act as guides. The city was not given over at once to pillage and devastation. This was rightly considered folly by the business like Assyrians and their successors. Important points were seized, and when all was securely held, a council of the leaders decided in detail the fate of the place and people. Accordingly the Chaldæan king's chief officers in Palestine, who had been summoned in view of the impending capture, were among the incoming troops (cf. Jer. xxxix. 3). The lower or newer section of the city in the north was abandoned by the besieged as soon as they saw that all was lost; and the Chaldæans advanced to the Middle Gate in the inner or older wall that separated the lower from the main city. Here no defence was in any case possible, but already, as soon as the enemy had been descried, Zedekiah and his party, taking advantage of the darkness, escaped by the way of the gate of the King's Garden, in the southeast of the city, at the entrance to the Fuller's Field, at the point where the eastern inner and outer walls came together. The Chaldæans were surprised; for it was thought that a sufficient guard had been set at all the possible places of exit. The discovery of the flight was not made till the king and his troops were missed by the searchers. By this time the fugitives of the royal party were well on their way up the Arabah. They were overtaken near Jericho, and brought before Nebuchadrezzar in Riblah for judgment (Jer. xxxix. 4, 5; lii. 7-9; cf. 2 K. xxv. 4-6).

§ 1232. The occupation of the city was conducted under strict discipline and without rapine.[1] The Chaldæan commis-

---

[1] A word or two upon this point are needed. It is impossible to determine exactly what was done or not done by the Chaldæan army of occupation, because there is no official report of the taking of the city. We can, however, infer a great deal from what we know of the procedure of

sion made up its report with customary thoroughness, and it was a full month before the chief executive officer, Nebuzaradan (*Nabūzēriddin*, " Nebo has given progeny ") entered to dispose finally of life and property in the name of the Great King (Jer. lii. 12; cf. 2 K. xxv. 8). Cases calling for capital punishment were remitted to Nebuchadrezzar (§ 1235). As to the city itself the principles were kept in view that had been followed by the sanest of the Assyrian kings in their treatment of Palestine: only so much destruction was wrought as would make the repetition of disorder impossible.

§ 1233. (1) For this end the effacement of the national worship was essential. The temple was therefore destroyed by fire — a catastrophe which subverted at a single blow the traditions, the symbols, and the appliances alike of the religion of Jehovah and of the usurping cults that had roused the wrath of reformers and prophets. (2) Before this or any other house in Jerusalem was set on fire, care was taken to remove all valuable property. The

---

conquerors under this régime, which was essentially a mitigated imitation of the Assyrian. We may observe: (1) The army was a great machine, operated with a single purpose, — the carrying out of the imperial policy. The officers were civil as well as military functionaries, and their troops obeyed orders with mechanical precision. (2) Under the Assyrian system as developed by Tiglathpileser III, the object of war was not the destruction of enemies, but the utilization of their country and resources for the service of the great gods and their vicegerent the Great King. Hence, as a rule, deportation, or the enslavement of prisoners, took the place of slaughter. (3) The minute details of the disposal of conquered cities, given by the later Assyrian kings, — the ringleaders slain, the rest of the people spared, so many men, women, and children carried away captive, so much spoil of various kinds confiscated, — imply a careful inventory of the contents of the city and their conservation under the eye of responsible officials. Hence the mention of these officers in connection with the entrance of the troops into Jerusalem in Jer. xxxix. 3, — a passage added to the original account, but not a mere idle interpolation. (4) Women and children had a value as merchandise or as servants, and they were carefully spared. But the infliction of the death penalty was an execution, and as such was a matter of formal record. 2 Chr. xxxvi. 17 is a rhetorical embellishment. "The king" did not enter the city at all.

smaller utensils of the temple could be transported intact. But the larger articles of copper or bronze were broken up and carried away to Babylonian foundries — a performance which must have impressed the vulgar mind as a signal triumph for Bel and Nebo, and which to the new administration served as a partial compensation for the loss of tribute and for the "sacrifices" made by Babylon during the war, if one may apply here the cant of modern imperialistic warfare. (3) The city wall was broken down. In this the lord of Nēmitti-Bēl and of Imgur-Bēl (§ 1058) would see the predominance of his gods. The temple and the wall were the two essentials of an ancient city, and both were of deep religious import. In the one the deity revealed his grace; the other, with its gates and fortresses and battlements, was the seat of his power and the symbol of his rule.[1] (4) Every dwelling in the city was not destroyed. But every "great house" was put to the flames. Thus were obliterated all the monuments of civic or personal pride, and all that gave value and desirableness to a residence in Jerusalem, whose future inhabitants might house themselves with fugitives and outlaws among men or beasts. Thus the Great King's officers [2]

---

[1] See *e.g.* Ps. xlviii. 12 ff.; Isa. xxvi. 1, xlix. 16, liv. 11 f.; 2 K. iii. 27; Neh. xii. 27, 30; Rev. xxi. 12 ff.; Matt. xvi. 18.

[2] A list of these commissioners is given in the additions to Jer. xxxix. (v. 3; cf. 13). It has been copied from some Babylonian record quite imperfectly, the compiler not understanding the titles nor distinguishing them from proper names. Hence we are not quite certain how many there really were. "Nergalsharezer" is here accidentally repeated. It was a common name among Babylonian nobles (*Nergal-šar-uṣur*, "Nergal, protect the king," cf. § 744). He was probably Neriglissar, the son-in-law of Nebuchadrezzar, who became his second successor (§ 1370). "Samgar-Nebo" (properly *Šumgir-Nabū*, "Nebo, show kindness") is the only other one of v. 3 who appears to be mentioned by his personal name, and possibly "Sarsechim," meaning "prince of the captains," is merely his title. "Rabsaris" is the designation of an office — "chief of the heads," *i.e.* of the heads of the army (cf. 2 K. xviii. 17). Perhaps "Neboshazban" (*Nabūšēzibanni*, "Nebo, save me!" v. 13) is the Rabsaris here meant. "Rab-mag" has usually been explained as "chief of the Magi." But the stem of μάγος is *magus* (Behistun Inscrip-

fulfilled their task (2 K. xxv. 9–10, 13–17, cf. Jer. lii. 13, 14. 17–24; xxxix. 8).

§ 1234. The chief sufferers in the city were the wealthy and influential, and those who had taken a leading part in the revolt. The prime movers in sedition were relegated to Nebuchadrezzar's judgment-seat (§ 1235). The poorest of the people, with a few leading men as overseers, were left in the country (§ 1240 ff.). But the people of any importance were taken away to Babylonia. As to the numbers of the latter we have remarkable statements in Jer. lii. 28–30, to which little credence has usually been given, because of the smallness of the sum of the captives. The writer makes out three distinct deportations. The first, in the seventh year of Nebuchadrezzar, consisted of 3023 persons. The second, in the eighteenth year of the king, comprised but 832; while in the third (§ 1268), in the twenty-third year, 745 were carried away. The total thus made up 4600. The writer draws from a Babylonian source distinct from those used in 2 Kings, and a sober view of the situation will show that his information is reliable and evidently refers only to people whose names were recorded. Of these there would be much fewer in 586 than in 597. To Zedekiah had been left but a remnant of the freeholders (§ 1152), and the kingdom never became what it was under his predecessor.[1]

tion), not *mag*. Moreover, the Babylonians had as yet nothing to do with the "Magi." For another explanation of the still obscure name *Rab-mag* see KAT. p. 420.

[1] The question of the relative numbers of the several deportations has been a subject of controversy, as well as the more fundamental question as to how many deportations there really were and when they severally took place. To settle the meaning of Jer. lii. 28–30, Ewald conjectures, followed by Graf, Keil, Orelli, and Giesebrecht, that "seventh" is a copyist's error for seventeenth, on the supposition that this was a deportation of people of the land during the first period of the siege (B.C. 587). This is improbable. (1) The year named coincides with the deportation of Jehoiachin. (2) The principal deportation occurring in this seventh year would not be made till after Jerusalem was taken. The obvious

§ 1235. Few words are needed to tell the fate of the leaders of the revolt. Besides the king's party taken near Jericho, those adjudged guilty by Nebuzaradan and his council were brought before Nebuchadrezzar at Riblah. Against them the rigorous code of the law of rebellion was strictly enforced. These were the chief priest and his deputy, three keepers of the temple, five (or seven) of the king's courtiers left in the city, the commander of the garrison and the secretary of the army, besides sixty men of undistinguished name (2 K. xxv. 18 f; cf. Jer. lii. 24 f.). These were put to death, probably by beheading, along with the sons of Zedekiah. The hapless king seems to have been the only subject of torture. After witnessing the death of his sons, his eyes were put out and he was carried to Babylon, not so much to adorn the victor's triumph as to be a warning to all who might be tempted to rebel against the king of kings (cf. § 1052).

§ 1236. Such was the fall of Jerusalem and such were its concomitants. Events like these could not pass without leav-

meaning of the statements in Jer. lii. has been discredited because it seems so improbable that the deportation of 597 could be larger than that of 586. Meyer (*Entstehung des Judenthums*, 1896, p. 112 f.) gives the weight of his great name to the hypothesis that in 586 the greater number went into exile. By him, as by the others, it is not perceived that only those would be numbered who were independent persons. Slaves, as well as women and children, would not be recorded. Of these, a much smaller proportion were carried away in 597 than in 586, since on the former occasion it was made a matter of policy to remove the most influential citizens, according to the express statement of 2 K. xxiv. 14 ff. When the writer in 2 Kings makes out "ten thousand" as the number of captives in 597, he is using a round number (the looser reckoning in v. 16 being from another source) and reckons in, besides, the women, children, and slaves. In the lists of Neh. vii. (cf. Ezra ii.) the slaves are bunched together separately and without mention of the households (§ 405) to which they belonged. As to Jer. lii., Stade (ZATW. IV. 271 ff.) and Meyer favour an improbable hypothesis, that "the first number given refers to a deportation made in 598 from the country towns before the taking of Jerusalem; the second enumerates the runaways during the siege and before the fall of the city, that is, in 587; and the third, perhaps a supplementary deportation, in 582" (Meyer, *l.c.*). For the third deportation see § 1250.

ing their mark on the Hebrew literature. In one sense, and a very important one, they were the cause of this literature. For the passions and sentiments that gave life and colour to what was strongest and most vital in Hebrew thought and speech centred in the fate of Jerusalem, even before the Chaldæan era (Micah iii. 12). But it was what this catastrophe involved that made the doom of Israel: the loss of the temple, the pains and disabilities of exile, the hiding of Jehovah's face from his outlawed people. The calamity itself has but a meagre and defective record. The Hebrew mind lent itself but little to description or exact narration. The event was greater than the fact, and the moral significance of the event greater than either. Even the imaginative narrative of the epic is wanting; while Troy has had its Iliad the greater woes of Jerusalem have been sung only in dirges.

§ 1237. Yet these dirges, or "Lamentations," are the best known of ancient elegiac poems; and, strangely enough, the popular estimate of their reputed author has been based upon them rather than upon his actual works. For Jeremiah did not write the Lamentations. The notion that he was their author is the offspring of an age which believed that any biblical writer could have composed any or all of the sacred books, and that only those men who are named in the Bible could have been concerned in its composition. Many reasons may be urged against the traditional view, which was started by the Septuagint translation, misled by an ambiguous suggestion of 2 Chr. xxxv. 25. Jeremiah, though he has been a great force in literature, was himself no literary artist. But the Lamentations reveal more conscious structural elaboration than any other book of the Bible. Again, these dirges do not indicate Jeremiah's essential temper or his prevailing mood; for though a man of sorrows, he was also a man of action. When once his outbursts of grief were over, he was forming plans for the future and cherishing hopes. The writer of Lamentations is absorbed in his despair.

He sees no lifting of the cloud. His thoughts dwell in the past. His words show nothing of the original foresight and insight of the great prophet. Moreover, Jeremiah had no time or opportunity after the capture of the city for laborious composition, which must have required the leisure of the student as well as the practised hand of the poet.[1] Such a series of poems would seem to have been produced some years after the calamity which they depict, as the result of reflection and amid a circle of meditative devotees. The place of composition was most probably Babylonia.[2]

§ 1238. The chief value of these unique elegies is that they give us a picture of the destruction and desolation of Jerusalem, not as foreseen or dreaded, but as accomplished facts. They are of course not descriptions. There is in them no single complete picture or representation. They are a stream of ejaculatory reflections, whose note is that of breaking waves rather than that of a running brook. Yet the total conception of the subject which we gain from them is fairly complete, because every one of the poems touches upon all the phases of the great catastrophe.

---

[1] Poetry may be composed rapidly, but not the poetry of the *De Contemptu Mundi* of Bernard of Clugny nor the poetry of the Lamentations. It was supposed that Bernard mastered his metre by special inspiration, so difficult was it with its triple rhymes, following the threefold division of the hexameter. Any careful student of the original of the Lamentations will acknowledge the skill and patience of their author, with his dexterous management of the so-called Kina metre, the symmetrical structure of his strophes, and the laborious adaptation of the letters of the alphabet to form a complete acrostic. Ingenious rhyming was a favourite occupation of the scribes of Clugny, and the writers that moulded the Lamentations were of a kindred school.

[2] For the treatment of special questions, the reader is referred to Cheyne, in the *Pulpit Commentary* (cf. *Jeremiah, his Life and Times*, 1888, p. 177 ff.); Driver, *Intr.*[6] p. 456 ff.; art. "Lamentations," in *Encycl. Brit.* (W. R. Smith); Löhr, *Die Klagelieder des Jeremia* (in Nowack's "Handkommentar"), 1893. It is not quite certain whether all of these poems come from the same author. Chap. iii., at least, which differs most from the others, is possibly later. This question is not of great practical importance, as the theme and contents of all are so uniform.

If we do not seek for the actual facts of history, but for historical situations, we shall be amply rewarded for our search. There are mainly three sets of circumstances exhibited, — the condition of the city, of the temple, and of the survivors of the siege. The sufferings of the besieged by famine are made especially prominent (i. 11, 19; ii. 11 f., 19 f.; iv. 3–9). Less is said of the horrors that accompanied the capture of the city (ii. 12, 20 f.; v. 11), which are to be judged of in the light of the restrictions set forth above (§ 1232). The desolation of the city, and above all the ruin and profanation of the sanctuary, with the abolition of the temple services (i. 4; ii. 6 f.; iv. 1; cf. ii. 9), are a burden of shame and humiliation to the followers of Jehovah. The poet is compelled to believe that Jehovah himself is the author of the calamity, owning with consternation (i. 12 ff.; iv. 11 ff.), or with submission and penitence (ch. iii.), that all this evil has come as a punishment for the sins of the prophets, priests, and people. Most instructive is it to note that the author himself takes the place of the suffering people and the ruined city (i. 11–22; ch. iii.). This representative conception, especially in ch. iii., is a development of Jeremiah's intercessory pleadings (§ 1127), and is a sure mark of the progress of prophetic teaching.[1]

§ 1239. The Book of Lamentations is really a group of psalms, and these elegies would probably have found a place in the Psalter, the repository of the anonymous lyrical poetry of Israel, were it not that one topic is so elaborately and variously treated in them, and that they became associated with the name of Jeremiah at a very early date. Are there any other literary memorials of the great calamity? Two of the psalms of our present collection have been by some

---

[1] Namely, as contrasted with the position assumed by the poets and prophets of the preëxilic times. They spoke as members of a suffering community, not as themselves bearing affliction on its behalf. Here we have again a criterion of the relative ages of important sections of the Hebrew literature, especially of the Psalms (cf. § 599, 605).

ascribed to this occasion, — Ps. lxxiv. and, with more confidence, Ps. lxxix. The latter, indeed, is almost a formal *résumé* of the contents of the Lamentations. This fact does not exclude a connection with the Maccabæan era, to which Ps. lxxiv. really belongs. It may still, however, be used for the illustration of the supreme calamity, and it shows how the language of these mourners for Zion has become forever the classical idiom of patriots and exiles, giving articulate expression to their deepest grief and yearning: "If I forget thee, O Jerusalem. . . . " "Behold and see if there is any sorrow like unto my sorrow!"

CHAPTER X

THE REMNANT IN PALESTINE AND EGYPT

§ 1240. The fate of the survivors in Palestine has now to be recounted. The story is one of the most melancholy in the records of Israel. For the few leaders who remained the situation was almost desperate. The chances were all against rehabilitation. Deprived of the walled city and the temple, and of political autonomy, even a multitude of Hebrews in Palestine would have counted for little. Shorn of such advantages an Oriental community quickly dissolves, loses its name, and is absorbed in other tribes or peoples. Such a fate befell most of those who were left behind by Nebuzaradan (§ 1234). It was of little avail that measures were taken by the Babylonian government to give them a chance of self-support, that the estates of the disinherited exiles not ruined by the fire were given to the landless survivors of the siege. The spiritless occupants of the soil, without a strong city of refuge or a protecting Babylonian force, made but a feeble resistance to the Philistines. Edomites,[1] Moabites, and Ammonites who witnessed with malicious satisfaction the destruction of Jerusalem, and

---

[1] That the Edomites especially exulted over the fall of Jerusalem (cf. Ps. cxxxvii. 7; Lam. iv. 22; Ez. xxxv. 5 ff.; Ob. 10 ff.) has its explanation in the long and bitter struggles between that people and Judah. The frequent seizure of the Edomitic territory by the Judaites now brought a terrible reprisal. Somewhat different was the gratification of Tyre at the downfall of Judah as that of a commercial rival (Ez. xxvi. 1 ff.).

thereafter prowled through the neighbourhood in quest of booty. Over this remnant a native governor was appointed, Gedaliah, son of that Ahikam who had been the patron of Jeremiah, and presumably an opponent of the ill-fated revolt. It was at Mizpah, not far to the north of Jerusalem, that his headquarters were fixed.

§ 1241. But why should not the Chaldæans have protected the remnant of Judah? Gedaliah was governor under the king of Babylon, and Judah was now a Babylonian province. There were several reasons why Nebuchadrezzar decided to take as little trouble as possible with Judah from this time forward. He had no sentimental interest in Judah any more than in Samaria, Damascus, or Tyre. Indeed, to him, as to the rest of the world (cf. § 40), Judah meant practically the city of Jerusalem, and that city he had just levelled to the ground. Even if he were to restore it so as to re-create the nation, it would probably be again a centre of intrigue and disaffection. Judah had acquired that reputation for independence and turbulence which was afterwards used to its disadvantage by envious rivals (Ezra iv. 12 ff.). Moreover, political and military conditions had changed in the Westland. There important states had once played their part; but now they were obliterated or prostrate, and what the Great King cared most for was the possession of Tyre for commerce, and the command of the Philistine coast-road for defence or offence against Egypt. Hence, while making the province responsible for order and obedience, a native Judaite was appointed governor, and not a Babylonian officer, and the army of occupation was withdrawn.

§ 1242. Gedaliah set to work loyally and bravely to fulfil his double trust to his country and to the Chaldæan. His first care was to gather about him the true men who were left. Prominent among these were Jeremiah and Baruch. It would appear that Jeremiah at first preferred to share the fate of the exiles; for according to the more probable of the two reports left to us[1] he was among the captives at Ramah, five miles to the north of Jerusalem, and on the way to Babylonia, when a proposal, which had the force of an appeal, was made to him that he attach himself to the settlement in the immediate neighbourhood at Mizpah (Jer. xl. 1–6). In this generous offer Nebuzaradan was doubtless influenced by Gedaliah himself, who had regretted the loss of Jeremiah from his counsels and who saw in him the right religious head of the struggling community. Here apparently a final opportunity to return was given to those who voluntarily accompanied their

[1] It is a matter of uncommon difficulty to ascertain exactly what became of Jeremiah between the fall of the city and his settlement in Mizpah. There is an absolute contradiction between the statements of Jer. xxxix. 11–14 and xl. 1 ff. The divergence is lessened if we drop xxxix. 11–13 with the Sept., which in fact leaves out the whole passage vs. 4–13. It then remains for us to combine and reconcile xxxix. 14 with xl. 1. If Jeremiah had been handed over to Gedaliah to be cared for, how could he have been found later among the captives at the halting-place Ramah? Among the solutions so far proposed, the best seems to be that of Giesebrecht (*Das Buch Jeremia*, p. 213), who remarks that Nebuzaradan, on his arrival, superseded the princes named in xxxix. 3, and that the same event led to the transfer of Gedaliah from Jerusalem to Mizpah. He supposes then that Jeremiah, who was unknown to Nebuzaradan, was by him assigned to the ranks of the deported, but that when the train of exiles halted at Ramah, Gedaliah put in a successful claim for his release. The main objection to this hypothesis is that it is inconceivable that Jeremiah's career should have remained unknown to Nebuzaradan, who acted on the report of the "princes," and who must also have conferred with Gedaliah. Jeremiah, as a virtual partisan of the Chaldæans and one of the most influential of the citizens, was, from the beginning of the judicial inquiry, *persona grata* to the conquerors. This and every kindred theory assumes that Jeremiah had no freedom of action till the decision was made at Ramah. Such a supposition is indeed favoured by the mention of his "chains" in xl. 1, 4, but this is perhaps a graphic embellishment of the narrative. On the same principle we must not take the language of xxxix. 14 too literally. It is a working up, with realistic touches, of the general fact that Jeremiah was released after the capture of Jerusalem and handed over to Gedaliah. Bennett (*The Book of Jeremiah*, ii, 174 f.; comp. Cheyne, *Jeremiah, his Life and Times*, p. 183) thinks that it was at Ramah that Nebuzaradan first "found leisure to inquire into the deserts of individual prisoners." Stade (GVI. I, 696) rejects the whole of ch. xxxix. as well as xl. 1.

exiled friends. To Jeremiah the main question was where he could best serve the cause and people of Jehovah.[1] Possibly the prospect of a revival of the national spirit under the lead of Gedaliah, and the desire to prepare the way for the restoration, after the fulfilment of the "seventy years," helped to turn the scale. So here at Ramah, a place already associated in his deepest prophetic musings with the grief and fate of Israel (xxxi. 15), he bade a tearful farewell to his lifelong companions. Knowing that they would come under the care of his pupil Ezekiel, he felt the more reconciled to the breaking of the bond. Then the lonely man, now doubly homeless, turned to the remnant of his people with some little hope, and with unconquered faith. With him was Baruch, who was learning the lesson of his life's disappointment and finding in the desolation of the kingdom and its cities the explanation of the master's startling message of eighteen years before (Jer. xlv.).

§ 1243. The first official duty of Gedaliah was to take measures to reconcile the scattered bands of Judaites to the new government. Hence he issued a formal appeal to the chiefs who came to him (Jer. xl. 8) and sent messengers with the same declaration to those who still stood aloof. The announcement was to this effect: "Fear not to serve the Chaldæans: make your abode in the land, and serve the king of Babylon, and it shall be well with you. As for me, I am going to abide at Mizpah as agent for the Chaldæans[2] who will come to us.[3] But do ye gather in wine and summer fruit and oil and put it into your vessels, and abide in the cities which ye have occupied" (Jer. xl. 9 f.). For a time the outlook was promising. Foremost among

---

[1] Very improbable is the conjecture of Grätz, partially approved by Cheyne, that Jer. xv. 10-21 reproduces the inward debate of Jeremiah on this occasion; see § 1126. Bennett (*Book of Jeremiah*, ii, 176-178) well describes the prophet's state of mind before his decision was reached.

[2] Literally, "to stand before the Chaldæans."

[3] That is, for tribute and to take account of the administration.

those who fell in with the administration, along with some of lesser note, were Ishmael, son of Nethaniah, and Johanan,[1] son of Kareah (xl. 8). Besides these there was an influx, smaller or greater, of Judaite refugees from Moab, Ammon, Edom, and other border lands, who were lured by the promise of a settled government and of an unmolested tenancy of the lands left unoccupied. No details are given of the progress of the settlement. It was said in Babylonia that those left in the old land were full of hope and ambition (Ez. xxxiii. 24). But we can read between the lines of the record a story of hard struggles on the part of the people, who had border raids to repel and domestic quarrels to settle, with little genius for coöperation and little disposed to submit to authority. We must also keep in mind that to the most of them the Chaldæan overlordship was scarcely apparent, being displayed only to Gedaliah and his officials during the stated visits of the governor-in-chief from Riblah.

§ 1244. A chief conservative element was the character of Gedaliah. He was ingenuous, patient, large-hearted, mediating admirably between the governor-general of Syria and his own turbulent fellow-countrymen. But there was another helpful influence, of which Jeremiah was the directing genius. They were still in Jehovah's land, though his ancient seat was overthrown. In the "Watch-tower" city,[2] within view of the ruins of Jerusalem, they could erect an altar to his worship. There is indeed a tradition (2 Macc. ii. 1 ff.) to the effect that at the command of Jeremiah his companions took with them the fire from the altar of the temple, and that he bore

---

[1] The Hebrew text adds here "Jonathan," but the name does not appear in 2 K. xxv. 23 nor in the Sept., nor is it again mentioned. It is a clerical error, due to the similarity of the two common names.

[2] Mizpah is the modern *Neby Samwil* (cf. 1 Sam. vii. 5), about four miles northwest of Jerusalem, commanding one of the most extensive views in Palestine. It was a fortress of the second class (cf. 1 K. xv. 22), and was probably rebuilt after its destruction by Sinacherib.

away with him to Mount Pisgah the tabernacle and the ark. The allusion to the sacred fire is especially significant, as it is apparently a distorted reminiscence of this reërection of Jehovah's altar on Mount Mizpah. Moreover, there is more direct evidence that Mizpah, an ancient shrine and gathering-place (Hos. v. 1), was now a religious centre for the remnant of Israel. The pilgrims who were slain by Ishmael (§ 1248) as they came to Mizpah are said to have been on their way to "the house of Jehovah" (Jer. xl. 5). Here then a new sanctuary was set up under meaner yet purer auspices; and there at last Jeremiah had his way in the conduct of the sacred services.

§ 1245. But the enterprise which loyalty and piety were carrying on against tremendous odds was frustrated in a moment by fanaticism and treachery. Ishmael, son of Nethaniah (§ 1243), the cleverest and most unscrupulous of the chiefs, was ill at ease from the beginning of the settlement. He wished to live in his native land, but he would not endure the yoke of the Chaldæans. He hated Gedaliah because of his noble character, because he had been set above himself who was of the royal race, and because he represented the detested foreigners. He dissimulated his feelings; but finding it intolerable to live in the same region with the governor, he resorted to an old ally and kindred spirit, Baalis, king of the Ammonites. The two worthies hatched a conspiracy. They could not hope to overthrow the Babylonian domination; but if the governmental experiment should end in disaster, the overlord might abandon the country in disgust, and then would come the chance for the predatory Ammonite and the caitiff Israelite. Seizing an opportune time, he came over the Jordan with a small band of raiders.

§ 1246. Taking ten leading men with him of his own kindred, enough to do sudden murder, but not enough to excite apprehension, he paid a visit to Mizpah. His coming was not unexpected by Gedaliah, for Johanan, son of Kareah, had got wind of the plot and warned the governor, even offering to go out and put Ishmael to death while his expedition was getting under way. Gedaliah, however, was too magnanimous to believe such treachery possible, and forbade Johanan to take any action whatever (Jer. xl. 13-16). On their arrival, he invited Ishmael and his party to his table, where some of his council and the resident Chaldaeans were present to meet them. At a concerted signal the guests fell upon the host and his friends and did them to death (Jer. xli. 1-3). So little had Gedaliah mistrusted the villains that he had, as it would seem, left himself without a sufficient guard, and Johanan also was absent at the very time when he was needed most. It was the season of the pilgrimage. The most popular of the ancient feasts (Jud. ix. 27 ; xxi. 19 ff.), the feast of Tabernacles, in the seventh month (§ 862), had survived the national temple; and Ishmael and his party may have made themselves welcome to the townsmen by coming in the guise of offerers.

§ 1247. Their real feelings towards Mizpah, its shrine, and the administration of which it was the centre, were shown on the following day. A company of eighty pilgrims from Samaria, Shechem, and Shiloh,[1] with the marks of penance upon them, and bringing offerings to the sacred place, were approaching the town. Ishmael went out to meet them, also in the guise of a mourner, and offered to bring them at once to the governor, so that their safety and comfort might be secured. No sooner were they well within the walls, than he and his band murdered the whole company except a few of them who saved their lives by revealing certain places where they had stores of wheat and barley, oil and honey. The dead bodies were thrown into an ancient reservoir, originally intended for a military

---

[1] The coming of these worshippers from the old territory of Ephraim is a striking evidence that the settlement at Mizpah was a religious success, and that its "house of Jehovah" had, as a resort of devotees, taken the place of the temple at Jerusalem.

water-supply¹ (Jer. xli. 4-9). The massacre would deter others from resorting to Mizpah, and thus weaken the governor's defence. He then decamped, fearing the vengeance of Johanan, carrying with him the daughters of king Zedekiah and other residents of Mizpah who had been committed to the care of Gedaliah (Jer. xli. 10).

§ 1248. Tidings of these atrocities came soon to the officers at their stations. Johanan with some of his colleagues and a sufficient force pursued after Ishmael and overtook his motley band, "by the great waters that are in Gibeon." At this spot, less than two miles to the north of Mizpah, already renowned for two historic tragedies (1 Sam. ii. 12-24; xx. 8-10), the pursuers fell upon the freebooters: Ishmael escaped to the Ammonites with eight of his men. The prisoners had made their escape from Ishmael before the attack. Among them were Jeremiah and Baruch (Jer. xli. 11-15).

§ 1249. Under a stable government this episode of Ishmael would have been merely a serious incident. But to the remnant of Judah it seemed to portend certain ruin. Gedaliah was the only leader in whom both the Chaldæans and their subjects had confidence. He was a rare and noble soul, the last scion of a worthy house, fitted to do great things in better times, but not to deal with hypocrites and cutthroats. The vengeance of the overlords for the assassination was now to be dreaded, and none of the chiefs had the address or the courage to propose a conference. Flight from the ill-fated country was the first and governing impulse of the panic-stricken company that thronged from all quarters about Johanan. Instinctively they moved southward. Passing Jerusalem, they halted near Bethlehem. It was already agreed among

---

¹ Translate xli. 9, after the Sept. (cf. Cornill and Giesebrecht): " And the cistern into which Ishmael cast all the corpses of the men whom he had slain was the great cistern which King Asa had made on account of Baasha, king of Israel. It did Ishmael, son of Nethaniah, fill with the slain." (See 1 K. xv. 17-22.)

the leaders that it would be best to migrate to Egypt (Jer. xli. 16–18).

§ 1250. Their fears turned out to be not entirely groundless. The punishment that fell upon the land was presumably aggravated by the desertion of the chiefs, which left the Babylonian province in a state of anarchy. It took the form of another and final deportation. Of this we learn quite incidentally from a merely statistical passage which gives the number of the exiles. "In the twenty-third year of Nebuchadrezzar, Nebuzaradan, captain of the guard, carried away captives of the Judaites seven hundred and forty-five persons" (Jer. lii. 30; cf. § 1234). None of these belonged to Johanan's following, for these by this time were well out of the country. In this final displanting, the Chaldaeans were not so discriminating as before. They took all the surviving males whom they could secure with their families. This was in 581 B.C. The ill-fated régime of Gedaliah had thus lasted over four years.

§ 1251. The province then reverted to utter desolation, being apparently even disregarded by the governor-general of the West-land save for general strategic purposes. The old kingdom of Judah and Benjamin became a waste, visited only by Bedawin shepherds, fugitives, and travellers under escort. The Edomites, Moabites, and Ammonites made less of the desire of their eyes than they had hoped. They haunted the borders, however, and among them a few Israelites found precarious protection. If we wonder that there are no sure signs of political or literary activity there during the next forty-five years, the reason is now manifest. And this was in a sense the end of ancient Israel. Henceforth we know only of Judaism. It was the end also of Semitism as a governing force in southern Palestine.

§ 1252. Among the fugitives encamped near Bethlehem (§ 1249) none had the reputation or the dignity of Jeremiah. He had proved his political sagacity beyond cavil; and if he had not been so true a prophet and so profound a statesman he would have been chosen the chief counsellor of the enterprise. But the nobles of Judah never lacked a policy of their own, and the present leaders, reasoning from precedent and surface indications, like mere politicians, thought that their course was marked out for them beyond possibility of mistake. To stay in Judah, so they argued, was out of the question; and where were the conditions of living so obviously easy as in the borderland of Egypt? Pharaoh Hophra was still king of that country, where trade and agriculture were flourishing, and he had shown the will at least to help the Judaites in their time of greatest need (§ 1218). True, Nebuchadrezzar might come down upon Egypt for this and other acts of defiance; but such an eventuality could be reckoned with when it should arrive. The minds of Johanan and his colleagues were made up. But they would not go forward without the divine sanction, and Jeremiah was asked to furnish the needed approval (Jer. xlii. 1-3). They begged him to declare to them the mind of Jehovah (xlii. 4-6; cf. v. 20); but they felt sure of a favourable oracle.

§ 1253. It was not till the tenth day after this interview that Jeremiah received the divine answer. It ran directly contrary to the wishes of the would-be emigrants. It was delivered by Jeremiah to the whole company with characteristic comments of his own. Jehovah's declared will was that they should abide in the land, where He would protect and prosper them, and would make the king of Babylon favourably disposed to them instead of their dreaded foe. If, however, they would go to Egypt, the sword and the famine from which they were fleeing would follow them thither (Jer. xlii. 7-22).

§ 1254. With the assured hope of Jehovah's approbation, Johanan and the other chiefs had been perfecting the organization and preparing for the southward march. The exasperating delay in the arrival of the oracle must only have strengthened their purpose. They would reason that if the divine will was so unmistakably unfavourable, it might have been communicated sooner, so as to relieve their anxiety and make some other course more possible. They therefore suspected that Jeremiah's message was not a genuine word of Jehovah, and his seclusion during the nine days with his trusty Baruch gave occasion to a surmise that Baruch was the prime mover in this discouraging business. Making this a direct charge against the prophet and his secretary, they repudiated the oracle as a forgery (Jer. xliii. 1–3). The march to Egypt was begun or rather resumed, and ere long the whole of the settlement of Mizpah with the addition of many fugitives from far and near, besides the men of the military posts appointed by Gedaliah, found themselves in the frontier district surrounding the town of Tahpanhes. In spite of his evil prognostications Jeremiah was carried along with them, still attended by Baruch (xliii. 4–7). Smaller Jewish colonies were already in the country, not only in Lower but also in Upper Egypt (xliv. 1).

§ 1255. The prophet's work was now almost done. At Tahpanhes (the Greek *Daphne*, the modern *el Defenneh*, between Pelusium and Zoan, on the Tanitic branch of the Nile), Pharaoh Hophra had a palace. There was the manifest beginning of the empire of the Nile — a sovereignty always odious to the prophets of Israel, and particularly so to Jeremiah. The remnant of Judah had just evaded the jurisdiction of Nebuchadrezzar, the "servant of Jehovah," and had chosen to take refuge under the shelter of the Pharaoh. How little the exchange of masters would profit them was shown by a symbolic action which Jeremiah was commanded to perform. He was told to take large stones and bury them in the brick-work at the entrance to the palace.[1] Upon these stones Nebu-

---

[1] At el Defenneh, Mr. W. Flinders Petrie found, in 1886, the ruins of a fortress now called the "palace of the Jew's daughter," having a great open-air platform of brick-work, a sort of *mastaba*. Naturally, the stones of the prophetic story were not found, and never will be, since they were

chadrezzar should pitch his tent and set up his throne. Then he should smite the land of Egypt with his invincible sword, burn the temples of its gods, and carry off as his spoil its most splendid monuments (Jer. xliii. 8–13).[1]

§ 1256. In Jeremiah's bitter cup the bitterest drop was the last. He had already seen more than enough of what his people could do in the way of impiety and idolatry as well as ingratitude and despite to Jehovah's messengers. It has already been remarked (§ 1183) that in the most desperate public situations the superstitious populace resort most eagerly to supernatural powers other than the proper national God. What Ezekiel saw in vision of their practices in Jerusalem just before the fall of the city (§ 1183 f.) is paralleled by the religious observances of the colony in Egypt. In each case the women, as at once most devout and most impressible, were most active in the ceremonies of the idolatrous cult. Their own goddess or goddesses were naturally the favourite objects of adoration; and in the present instance they had (xliv. 19) the support of the male part of the community. The particular deity here honoured was the "queen of heaven," whose worship in the streets of Jerusalem had been denounced by Jeremiah himself twenty-five years before (§ 1094). This cult of Ashtoreth or Ishtar was universal among northern Semites, and therefore much more easily transferred to a foreign

---

never really put in the place described. If an attempt had been made to fulfil the command literally, the prophet or any other outlander would have been severely punished, — probably put to death, without benefit of clergy. The Judaites, of course, occupied a quarter by themselves as remote as possible from the Egyptian magnates. The symbolic action was of a character similar to that of hiding a girdle by the Euphrates, and the like performances (§ 1178 f., Jer. xiii. 1–7). It is hard to see just what is illustrated by this much-talked-of discovery.

[1] By synecdoche for the obelisks of Heliopolis (On, the "Beth-Shemesh" of the text). The business of carrying off Egyptian obelisks was begun by the Assyrian kings (§ 767 note), and has been carried on at intervals ever since. The fulfilment of this prediction was of a very general character. The victorious campaign of Nebuchadrezzar in Egypt (§ 1365) was undertaken after the death of the present Pharaoh.

land than the worship of Jehovah himself. The plea of her votaries that they had abundance of good things in the old days before the worship of their goddess was interdicted, that is, before the Deuteronomic reform (xliv. 17 f.), is not to be taken too seriously (cf. Num. xi. 5).

§ 1257. Lesser souls have found satisfaction in contempt for idolatry and idolaters. To Jeremiah indignation was more natural and proper. And it actually seemed to increase in proportion to the danger which he incurred by expressing it. His final denunciation (xliv. 2-14, 20-30) was never surpassed in terrific wrath. His last spoken words sound like a veritable curse upon the miserable remnant of his people, scattered about in this alien land. But no words of his were more truly fulfilled. Egypt became their grave; and there has been no resurrection save of the indignant soul of the prophet himself. Perhaps it was the consciousness that Jeremiah was in the right, and the sting of his invective, that led the rabble to put him to death by stoning. This tradition as to the manner of his taking off is in itself very probable. It was not an unfitting conclusion to his life, which for nearly thirty years had been a continued martyrdom.

§ 1258. The career and character of Jeremiah are the most valuable personal gift which we have received from ancient Israel. In the whole history of his race he stands in independence and fortitude nearest to the Christ. He is typical of all who contend for righteousness against public opinion, who defer to the voice of God because it is the truest and in the end the strongest. This, it might be thought, is nothing rare in religious or civil history. Perhaps not, since Jeremiah and Jesus set the example. But this is not all; courage and fidelity, moral attributes alone, do not make the prophet, but, along with courage and fidelity, the more spiritual quality of insight. What, then, was Jeremiah's distinction? Not merely that he was brave and true against fearful odds. He has gained his immortality and his power mainly by taking his stand upon a single concrete practical issue; namely, whether he should, as a servant of Jehovah, acquiesce in or oppose the policy of his country when he felt it to be wrong. The great conflict of his life was waged upon this issue. By this more than anything else has his prophetic character been estimated, and upon this ground he challenges our judgment.

§ 1259. The only way to judge of his position is to put ourselves in his place. How many to-day of the servants of God in Church and State in Britain and the Colonies take the position of Jeremiah? How many reject the motto: "Our country right or wrong"? How many try to define true patriotism aright to themselves and others? How many have without prejudice, and in the light of God's truth and justice alone, tried to find out how and where the responsibility is to be fixed for the cruel and ignoble war waged between Great Britain and a handful of her kindred in South Africa? How many, in the spirit of Jeremiah, hold up to reprobation the doctrine that what is individually and personally wrong may be nationally or internationally or diplomatically right? How many seek to look at the moral issues and the alleged causes of the war in the right proportion and perspective? And how many, like Jeremiah, can appreciate the character and the divine mission of the national adversary? How many think it worth while to contradict the countless unretracted slanders against the Boers, heard or read, and for a time believed, by as many millions of people as the Boers number thousands? How many rebuke the popular jubilation and triumph over the defeats and retreats of a numerically insignificant enemy? Very few appear to have done any single one of those things. Yet multitudes of God's servants in the British empire have courage equal to that of Jeremiah. Can the explanation be that "her prophets find no vision from the Lord" (Lam. ii. 9)?

§ 1260. "Where no vision is the people are uncontrolled" (Prov. xxix. 18). How and why? Essentially because the professional moral leaders, such as Jeremiah had to contend with, do not know the truth and effect of things. In other words, they do not look into the motive of moral forces and their consequences in the national life. Insight is the gift of the prophet; but this induces and implies foresight. Rather they are one and the same endowment, two modes of action of the same faculty. Here again Jeremiah gives us an example and suggests a practical test of our latter-day prophesying. Jeremiah's public mission was to expose a popular or national fiction. That fiction was the belief held by his countrymen that God was necessarily on their side because they had been the people of his choice. Other prophets had already asserted the opposite. But it was reserved for Jeremiah to make clear the practical issue. We know how the memorable contest resulted. Jeremiah was right because he saw that the question was not a political one, not even mainly a religious one, but a moral one, — that God's providence itself followed the moral law, that good could not come to the nation from evil devised or cherished by rulers and people.

§ 1261. Our prophets have a corresponding fiction to expose. Instead of Zion and the temple we take our stand upon the Empire; and most of our preachers and editors as well as our politicians assert that the supremacy of our nation must be established at any cost in order that civilization and morals and Christianity may be advanced (cf. § 955). And when all hell is let loose in any part of God's fair earth (Britain's soil and her non-combatants being immune by the divine complacency), pretty sentiments are uttered from hundreds of presses and thousands of pulpits about the triumph of righteousness, the spread of freedom, and the regeneration of the race. A true modern prophet would say: "What have been the motives and the methods of those who abetted the war? Have conciliation and forbearance and the Christian virtues generally played their part in diplomacy? Has everything possible been done both to avoid and to avert bloodshed?

Have the wrongs or the sensibilities of the rival people been regarded as well as our own? If not, though we may triumph now, we shall lose in the end. The better part of Britain's strength is her moral prestige. Her bitterest woe and shame is the ebbing out of her moral force. Unrighteous or unnecessary wars insure and accelerate her national decadence." It is the glory of Jeremiah to have shown that practical politics are within the sphere of a divine moral law. The terrible fulfilment of his predictions indicates his foresight and his insight. Only results that might be felt could quell the practical politicians; and their successors to-day are slowly but surely receiving the same lesson.

§ 1262. The wider meaning of the life of Jeremiah is for mankind. He is the most human of the prophets, with some failings both of word and act, yet with the strength of a moral and spiritual hero. He is one of the few men of history who, even while we regard them, are enlarged and transfigured from individuals to types. He was the ideal patriot, of an order of patriots scarcely known as yet to our Christian communities; a typical preacher and teacher, who wielded a rod indeed, but used it oftenest upon himself; a burden-bearer for his people; a man of sorrows, who suffered for them in his own person, as he loved them with a devotion sacrificial and intercessory (§ 1127). Thus, too, he continued to minister to his people and to humanity after the tragedy of his life had been finished. "The prophet never dies." His life and teaching formed a transition stage to the conception of the "suffering servant of Jehovah," so infinitely profound and potential. And now, still more than of old, his spirit rules the true Israel from the tomb. For while law and ritual (§ 1068) are shrinking slowly but surely into the background, and are going the way of all that rests on form and force, love and faith take the abdicated seats and gain an ampler and more potent sway. And when we are tempted to be untrue to the highest interests of our country or of humanity, or to our life's divine commission whatever it may be (Jer. xvii. 16), the tear-stained face of Jeremiah appeals to us through the beclouded past like the look of a wronged and deserted friend; and we hear his great strong word sounding high above the babble of our time, a trumpet call to loyalty and duty.

CHAPTER XI

THE EXILE AS AN EPOCH

§ 1263. The Babylonian Exile of Israel must seem, even to the casual observer, the most extraordinary event in the world's history. The whole career of the chosen people was a series of marvels, but compared with this all the other events of that career were commonplace. Such must be the judgment of the modern scrutineer; and such was the judgment of the greatest of spiritual seers, who was not permitted to share in the Exile, but whose faith was nourished upon the foresight of its results. To Jeremiah even the deliverance from Egypt was made insignificant by the outcome of the captivity (Jer. xxiii. 7, 8). To him the preservation of his people through the Exile to the Return was the climax of the self-revelation of the "ever living God." At the beginning of our survey of the national development of Israel our attention was arrested by the vitality and persistence of the people of Jehovah (§ 434), as seen in its evolution out of a community of fugitive slaves. Through that stage of its history, however, we may follow, by flights of imagination, if not by measured steps of scientific research, the upward and onward progress of the race. But here it would seem that the laws of development must be set aside. It appears not like a process of evolution, but like a work of recreation. In the ancient East, even more than elsewhere, the loss of political autonomy meant the obliteration of a people. Judah and Jerusalem suffered absolute national extinction, and yet the Jews have survived. There, too, deportation brought to pass what it was designed to accomplish, the crushing out of the national spirit; and yet exile had the effect of intensifying the patriotism of the banished Judaites (Ps. cxxvi., cxxxvii.). In all ages and regions the genius of a community or a people is most active and fruitful upon the soil of the home-land and under its skies. But the genius of Israel, which had been almost extinguished in Palestine, flamed out in Babylonia with unequalled splendour. The spiritual endowments of Israel, the faith and insight and devotion that were the hope of the world, were stifled and quenched in the days of its freedom and opportunity. But the spirit of Israel in its captivity reclaimed its heritage: it "led captivity captive and received gifts among men, that Jehovah God might dwell among them."

§ 1264. But it is not the task of an historian to resolve paradoxes. The seeming contradictions and inconsistencies of Israel's career are not isolated or irrelevant incidents. They are facts in vital and essential interrelations. We must strive to find the conditions of that foreign soil and atmosphere into which Israel was transplanted and from which it drew the physical and intellectual nourishment that repaired its lost vitality so that it could be called "a scion of Jehovah's planting" (Isa. lx. 21). We must learn how the loss of external privileges and advantages became itself at last actually a means of grace, and how, besides, they were replaced by new moral and religious helps, that touched more nearly the life of the spirit. We must inquire what that real Israel was which remained intact during a social and political catastrophe, and what was the essential vital truth that made this saving remnant the salt of the earth. We must learn how hope came from the loss of hope, and a new and deathless ideal from the destroying of the real: how the visions of a restored Jerusalem, cherished by a nameless prophet, laid the unseen foundations of the City of God.

§ 1265. The necessity of a broad and comprehensive view and method is most obvious when we come to deal with Israel in Exile. It was a time of political revolution, or rather devolution. What sort of government was that which was then forfeited? How much of the past had it retained? What elements passed over permanently into the new society? How was this society outwardly moulded under the foreign régime? It was a time of social change. How were the exiles distributed in Babylonia? How were they grouped together? What were their employments? How did Babylonian ways and business methods affect them? It was a time of moral testing and sifting. How did they abide the trial? What moral characteristics did they bring with them? Were these improved in exile, or did they deteriorate? How were they influenced by what they did and saw and heard in Babylonia? It was a time of intellectual stimulus. What writings did they bring with them into exile? What region of their life in Palestine did it especially touch or move? What were the new literary productions? How were these evoked and moulded? What were the gains from contact with the cultured and book-learned Babylonians? How did these fit in with their previous knowledge and conceptions? It was a time of religious trial and revolution. What religious views and beliefs did they bring with them into captivity? How were these rooted in their life and experience in the old land? What new light came to them through their residence among the kindred and yet alien Babylonians? How were their preconceptions altered through the recent facts of their own history and their wider knowledge of the world? How were they led to regard Jehovah in the light of his dealings with them and of the fates of the nations? It was a time of change in worship. The old sacred places were theirs no more. The temple, the official priesthood, the feasts, were perforce discarded. How had they regarded these *sacra* when in Palestine? What if anything now took their place?

§ 1266. Israel was remade by the Exile: this is a patent fact of history. It did not simply outgrow and shuffle off its past: it was torn away from it. It was seized and hurled far away over the desert. It was wrenched away from its land, its home, its hearth, its vine and fig tree, its market-place, its burying-ground, and its sanctuary. It had to begin life over again. To understand the new life we must once more take account of elementary social, political, and moral forces. The questions of transference and a new environment are now of primary importance; and their significance is enhanced when we consider not merely the strangeness of Babylonia, but its culture, its wealth, its antiquity, its organization, its easy supremacy over mankind in what appealed to sense or reason or imagination; and all this in contrast with the forlornness and helplessness of the bewildered captives.

§ 1267. At the same time, no period of the history of Israel serves better than the Exile as a standpoint for review and perspective. Although but few well-ascertained events excite the attention, the situation and the historical conditions are exceptionally clear and distinct. Israel's world is being shaped anew. The sun and moon and stars are out of the sky, but in the primordial light that comes from the play of cosmic forces the old familiar objects are seen in clear relief, in separate, unshaded distinctness. Here we have Israel reduced to its essential elements. It is now a people more manageable, more plastic, more intelligible than in the past. There is a haziness about the outlines in all the images that we form of the political and religious movements of the ages preceding the Exile. This is partly due to the gaps in the record, but partly also to the intrinsic obscurity of the mixed social conditions and politics of the country and the people. In both directions the Exile brings light and clearness. Henceforth for centuries the political relations of the Hebrews are simple and constant. They fit themselves, directly or indirectly, into the service of the empires that control the new order of the world; and there they stay. The writings, also, that illustrate the new era are plainer and more practical. The new prophecy, even when grandiose and expansive, is more objective, being always relevant to known contemporary events, while the earlier discourses often produce general rather than definite impressions. But what is of most consequence is the fact that in the Exile the whole intellectual and spiritual heritage of Israel — its beliefs, it usages, and its laws — are brought to the test of new conditions, and revised and readapted to the needs of a new community. And the further acquisitions made in the time and place mark of themselves a new epoch, bearing unmistakably the stamp of Babylonia.

CHAPTER XII

THE DEPORTATIONS

§ 1268. But first of all we must see exactly what is meant by the Babylonian captivity. As already indicated (§ 1234 and note, 1250), there were three separate deportations. The total of forty-six hundred, supplemented by the wives, children, and slaves, might easily represent twenty thousand souls, and of these the first deportation contributed between nine and ten thousand. It accordingly equalled the other two combined. Not only was it the largest numerically, but with it, according to the express statement of the record (2 K. xxiv. 14), went the flower of the city and nation. Besides Jehoiachin and his circle of nobles it contained such men as Ezekiel, and men of influence like the prophets who opposed the policy of himself and Jeremiah (Jer. xxix. 21 ff.). On the other hand, most of the popular leaders of the final revolt were put to death at Riblah (§ 1235), and the others, including such commanding figures as Jeremiah and Gedaliah, did not go to Babylonia at all.

§ 1269. Certain preliminary inferences may be made from these facts. First, the people of the Exile, in the comprehensive sense of the term, had laid in Babylonia the foundations of their social and civil system before the fall of Jerusalem. Second, we are to find among Ezekiel and his companions the men who determined the religious character and tendencies of the first half of the Captivity. Third, while the fall of Jerusalem was still a decisive factor in the religious and political life of the Exile, it was so mainly because of its importance to the people already in exile, who comprised nearly all of Israel that were to tell upon the future.

§ 1270. Let us look into the proscription and banishment of the exiles as a whole. The second deportation differed from the others mainly in the exceptional severity shown to the leaders of the final revolt. During the actual journey eastward the same general plan was followed in all three. In pursuance of the system so carefully followed out, a classification of the prisoners was made at the very beginning (§ 1232, note). The distinguished rebels were kept by themselves with a special guard. Those who were to be subjected to punitive servitude were also marked out. How many there were of the last-named class we cannot say with certainty. To judge from the silence of the Hebrew records and the evidence that the Judaites prospered in Babylonia, it would seem probable that these were not very numerous. Those who were free of blame or "sin" among the captives, and who were not to be subjected to hardship, also formed a separate division. This class would include those who chose to go into exile either from patriotic motives or from a desire not to be separated from their families or friends. While the lives and services of all the population of revolted countries and cities were forfeit, those to whom clemency was extended became merely prisoners of the state. Thus the choice was offered to Jeremiah and Baruch to go whither they would (§ 1242).

§ 1271. Representations are found on Assyrian bas-reliefs of men, women, and children being driven away from conquered cities, marching with bowed heads and with hands fastened behind their backs, and beaten by staves in the hands of their guards. Such pictures, like the other decorative sculptures, are typical, and therefore extreme. The march on foot, the fetters, and the drivers, were, however, facts of the Assyrian régime, ameliorated doubtless by the Chaldæans, and yet retained by them in their essential features. We must not, however, base our conceptions of the march of the Hebrew exiles upon these exaggerated designs. We must keep in mind the methods of the Chaldæan administration. Its governing principle was utilization and conservation. In the process of classification just alluded to, lists of the captives were made out by the "man with the writer's inkhorn at his side" (Ez. ix. 2 ff.; § 1191). The numerations and descriptions were sent to the capital, to be there put on record, and the officers in charge of the expedition were held responsible for the safe arrival of the conscripts. Excessive cruelty or neglect were therefore precluded by the mere official routine of an advanced civilization. Nor are we to assume that the whole of the exiles of each deportation formed one great band or caravan by themselves. Their arrangement and distribution would be determined by convenience — by the availability of troops for a military guard, by the facilities for transportation, by the season of the year, by the character of the several classes of the travellers as above defined, to whom different sorts of treatment would be given according to their rank, their merit, or demerit, and their ultimate destination or condition of servitude. In fine, we can only get a clear conception of the character of these deportations as a whole if we remember that this form of banishment was less a personal than a national penalty, consisting in the loss of the home-land by a transfer of residence.

CHAPTER XIII

THE HEBREW SETTLEMENT IN BABYLONIA

§ 1272. But what of the exiles after their arrival in Babylonia? And, first of all, in what places exactly were they settled? Upon this point we have some definite information with regard to a large portion of the greatest, or first deportation. The allusions of Ezekiel make it clear that there was along the stream called Kebar a large colony of his countrymen. The Kebar was an important canal of central Babylonia. In two business documents of the reign of Artaxerxes I (464–424 B.C.) mention is made of the stream *Kabar*, which, as Hilprecht says,[1] was a large navigable canal near the city of Nippur. Though its exact location has not yet been fixed, we may assume as almost certain that it was a branch of the larger canal, the Shatt-en-Nil (§ 94). Inasmuch as the Hebrew colonists could not well have been placed in a thickly settled district, it is probable that the Kebar lay to the east of the great canal.

§ 1273. Where the other bands or groups of exiles were settled it is, at least for the present, vain to conjecture, except that some, besides the royal captives and their households, were doubtless taken to the city of Babylon. The Great King, while eager for the development of the country as a whole, was specially concerned about his capital (§ 1055 ff.); and for labour upon his vast public and private works a contingent would be taken

---

[1] PCT. IX, p. 28. The word itself significantly means "large."

from every considerable importation of prisoners of war. That many were placed in other great cities of the empire is not probable. Naturally, many of the Hebrews made their way ultimately to one centre of industry or another, above all, to Babylon. But at first their residences would be determined by the policy of the king; and that was not favourable to the upbuilding of any possible rival to his beloved city. From the conditions of half a century later it would seem that the exiles came at length to be pretty widely distributed. Among the lists of those returning from the Exile occurs a group of names of places [1] from which certain persons, 652 in number, came to join the main body of pilgrims: Tel-melach, Tel-harsha, Cherub, Addan, and Immer (Ezra. ii. 59 f.; Neh. vii. 61 f.). It is said of these people that they could not prove their genealogical connection with Israel, from which we infer that during these two generations they were separated from their brethren.[2] At any rate, the centralization of the exiles would be discouraged by the imperial authorities in order to preclude the possibility of a concerted uprising. We conclude, then, that in the gradual allocation several small groups of the exiles were formed in separate districts (cf. § 1306).

---

[1] The names are interesting and some of them may be explained, though so far none of them is certainly found in the Inscriptions. Hilprecht (PCT. IX. 47) thinks *Addon* was originally the name of a person which is of frequent occurrence in the time of Artaxerxes I. and regards the word as Hebrew (*ib.* p. 27). It is not clear, however, why it should not be native Babylonian, whether as place or person. *Cherub* is probably Babylonian, though familiar to us as a Bible word, not a place-name. *Tel-melach* may be "Mound of salt," if the word is Hebrew; if Babylonian, it would be correctly *Tel-malah*, and means "Mound of the boatmen." *Tel-harsha* is probably Babylonian, though the meaning is uncertain. The "tels" are interesting as showing conditions similar to those of Tel-Abub (§ 1107). Place-names, indubitably Hebrew, are not found as yet in Babylonia. Kasiphia (Ezra viii. 17) is an additional settlement, named over a century later, and Ahava (Ezra viii. 17, 21, 31), also on a canal, seems to have been more than a mere gathering-place.

[2] We may note that nevertheless they grew to be quite numerous, and, still bearing the Hebrew name, were not absorbed by other populations.

§ 1274. We are on somewhat surer ground when we come to deal with the employments of the captives and their companions. The determining factors were (1) the antecedent occupations of the Hebrews; (2) the industrial requirements of the country; (3) the demands of the royal policy and projected measures of internal administration; (4) the ruling social and legal conditions of the employment of labour. Each of these matters should have some brief consideration, because it is only when we can follow a people through their daily occupations that we can trace intelligently their history as a community.

§ 1275. Taking the exiles of the three deportations as a whole, the majority of them were better fitted for agricultural employments in Babylonia than for any other occupation. They represented fairly well the population of Judah, who could not immediately adapt themselves to the requirements of art and manufacture in a highly civilized community. Outside the cities most of the inhabitants were shepherds,[1] independent or tenant farmers, farm labourers, vine dressers, and olive growers. Within the large towns and in the capital itself were many employed in the service of the landed proprietors on their country estates. On the other hand, the members of the guilds of craftsmen, such as the "carvers and joiners"[2]

---

[1] The persistency of the shepherd class, even in a semi-nomadic form, is illustrated by the case of the Rechabites. This class is of interest here, because some, at least, of its members were carried to Babylonia among the people of Jerusalem, where they had taken refuge during the first blockade (§ 1141). That they survived the exile, in fulfilment of the prediction of Jeremiah (ch. xxxv. 19), we learn from 1 Chr. ii. 55 and iv. 12 (Sept.). Cf. Meyer, *Entstehung des Judenthums*, p. 147.

[2] EV., "craftsmen and smiths." The former word (חרש), however, denotes those who worked with cutting instruments; hence it is used more explicitly of workers in wood, stone, bronze or copper, iron, gold, and silver. The second word (מסגר) cannot mean simply "smith," nor "locksmith," as it is often rendered. Probably the former refers to the cutting and shaping of the material, the latter to the construction of the manufactured article (literally, "one who closes up").

(2 K. xxiv. 14, 16; Jer. xxiv. 1; xxix. 2), weavers, potters, dyers, tanners, and house-builders, were not inconsiderable.

§ 1276. What the Hebrews in Babylonia ultimately became depended mainly upon themselves. Their circumstances at the outset depended upon the imperial policy and the needs of the country. Looking at the latter first, we observe that there were certain permanent demands for labour which were never abated during times of national prosperity and vigour. The weal of Babylonia was bound up with the water supply and its utilization. Works of canalization and irrigation could be multiplied indefinitely; and whenever established they required unremitting and intelligent oversight. The cultivation of the soil and the various processes of agriculture, thus made easier and more general, called for a large force of workers. Partly independent of agriculture was the care of cattle by the shepherd class. To these must be added the various avocations that furnished the appliances of rural toil and increased its efficiency and comfort. Hence, nourished by this fundamental industry, the arts of life which in Palestine (§ 484) had been practised only as far as was possible to a small and secluded community, were in Babylonia developed to a degree of perfection elsewhere unknown in Western Asia. Such were the arts of weaving, tanning, metal-making, brickmaking, and the building and furnishing of dwellings. Within the realm of leisure and luxury was the making of ornaments, of statues and statuettes, of decorated pottery, instruments of music, and other pursuits that served the arts of pleasure. Highest of all was the art of the writer, with the stylus, the graving tool, or the reed. Again, upon the same agricultural basis was erected an extensive system of trade and commerce, as active as it was various, and regulated by every safeguard and restraint that the experience of the trader or the wit of the lawyer or clerk could devise (§ 1064).

§ 1277. These were what we may call permanent industries and means of employment. But Israel came to Babylonia at a time of exceptional opportunity. Nebuchadrezzar, the great restorer of Babylonia, treated his prisoners of war as vassals and wards rather than as lifelong criminals. His administration, moreover, was hospitable towards foreigners, since the improvement and development of his country made their services desirable. His domestic statesmanship had a twofold aim. On the one hand, the wealth and power of Babylonia, as a whole, were to be enhanced by works of internal improvement, especially by extending the area of productive soil and increasing its annual yield. On the other hand, the work of putting and keeping in order the irrigation works and other great enterprises demanded a strong administrative and financial centre, so that the capital was necessarily aggrandized at the expense of other important towns as local rivals. It was mainly in carrying out the former of these aims that the Hebrews played their part. If they had come to Babylonia and had spent their years of tutelage under a cruel or a declining régime, their life, as a people, might have been crushed out by tyranny or exhausted by hopeless and impotent effort.

§ 1278. Most important of all the elements that made up their new environment were the conditions under which they made their living and did their work. The first question that presses upon us is that of the tenure and status of slaves in Babylonia, since we must take for granted that most of the Hebrews were assigned at first to bond-service (§ 1281). What has been said (§ 539 ff.) of Hebrew slavery may serve as a general guide, for in civilized ancient society usage and legislation prescribed nearly the same rules everywhere for the treatment of slaves. The main difference between ancient and modern slavery does not concern the treatment of slaves so much as their social position and prospects. Among the Babylonians, as well as among the Egyptians and Hebrews, slaves, especially prisoners of war and victims of border raids, might be treated with the utmost cruelty. Of this we have abundant evidence from the sculptured representations of labourers urged on in their tasks under the lash of taskmasters.[1] On the other hand, slaves were often, in everything save civic privileges, the equals of freemen. Many of them were far better off as slaves than they could have been as their own masters; and this good fortune apparently befell the chief part of the Hebrew exiles.

§ 1279. The privileges and duties of the servile class in Babylonia may be set forth by facts gathered from the monuments. Slaves were of several classes. First, there were the slaves of the state. These were mostly prisoners of war, who had been taken in battle or at the capture of a fortress or the surrender of a city. Originally, in days of savagery, such captives formed the bulk of the servile population (§ 542, note). Their treatment was, upon the whole, ameliorated by advancing civilization; but even under the least rigorous administration barbarous severity was shown to actual instigators or leaders of strife or rebellion. In the later Assyrian and Chaldæan times a careful classification of prisoners was made, according to which harsher or milder measures were adopted toward them (§ 1270). They did not all necessarily remain the property of the crown, for those of them to whom special leniency was to be shown might at any time be handed over to corporations or private employers of labour. The

---

[1] As in the parallel instance referred to above (§ 1271), we must beware of taking this as typical of the general system. Prisoners of war and state criminals usually furnished the labourers employed in great public works, where the rudest and heaviest mechanical force was required. Thus the Hebrew slaves in Egypt had been enemies of the state. It is colossal works of this character that are represented in the sculptures, which are in fact an illustration throughout of the prowess and authority of the monarch. The fact that a driver is placed over very small groups of workmen shows that such slave labour was of value only as it was forced, differing thus from ordinary servitude, as set forth in the following paragraphs.

second class were the temple slaves. Their number and importance naturally depended upon the fortune of the temples themselves, and this was fluctuating and uncertain. In Babylonia, however, there never was a time when the temples were not numerous and enterprising; and as their business included the whole range of handiwork, trade, manufacture, and mercantile employment known to the age and country, the central government itself did not make a more various and extensive use of slave labour than did these seats of the gods. At the present epoch, however, on account of the favour shown to Babylon and Borsippa (§ 1060 ff.) the provincial temples were declining in importance, and business under sacred auspices was being concentrated in the precincts of the fortunate shrines. Again, there were the slaves of private citizens, who were of various classes and orders — the manufacturers, merchants, and landed proprietors taking a leading place as the owners. Slaves were normally acquired by purchase; but both temples and individual citizens might come into their possession by endowment from the state, in consideration of services rendered or of an ancient claim. During the frequent changes of dynasty in the later Babylonian times, each successive administration sought to propitiate the powerful priesthood by substantial gifts, of which confiscated lands and their occupants came readiest to hand; and to the families of loyal supporters similar benefactions were made. The possession of slaves, however, was far from being a monopoly of the wealthier classes, and, in the course of business and changes of fortune, most people who had a modicum of money or land had also their servile retainers. Almost entitled to be classed by themselves were the slaves of slaves[1] (cf. § 1280).

---

[1] See Peiser, "Skizze der babylonischen Gesellschaft," in *Mittheilungen der vorderasiatischen Gesellschaft*, 1896, — an essay to which I am here greatly indebted. Peiser makes a special class also of the *glebæ adscripti*, those assigned or attached to a particular domain, who, at

§ 1280. For our present purpose it is important to notice that in Babylonia slaves generally, even those who were originally state prisoners, had the chance of rising through the several grades of servitude, and bettering their condition by sale, by gift, by endowment, by legacy; that they could become free by their own purchase, or by redemption through another, or by the generosity or the necessities of their masters; that they could be adopted into the family of an owner and eventually succeed to the possession of great estates; that by a very common form of business contract they were, when hired out by their masters, entitled not only to compensation during sickness or for injuries, but also to a remuneration for their labour, so that it was possible for them to accumulate a small capital and acquire slaves of their own; moreover, that they could become skilled craftsmen by a course of legal apprenticeship. These essential differences from modern and western slavery set in relief a fact of vital significance in the history of the Exile, that social conditions were not unfavourable to the enfranchisement and advancement of the Hebrew captives. It will also be observed that while in the main the system of servitude prevalent in Babylonia was similar to that with which they had been familiar in Palestine, it was at the same time better regulated by law and custom. Moreover, the position of freedmen was more secure under the more stable legal and business conditions of the Chaldæan empire. In general we may conclude that for the majority of the exiles, even for many of those who in the home-land had servants of their own, slavery was, for the first few years, better than freedom, even apart from the fact that in the servile state they were provided for in sickness, want, and

---

stated times, had to perform certain services for their owners, somewhat in the fashion of the villeins of mediæval Europe (cf. Hallam's *Middle Ages*, New York, 1880, I, 196 f.). They seem to have been mostly subject to the temples. The subject is obscure, and it can hardly be made out that serfdom on a large scale prevailed in Babylonia.

old age — a matter of consequence to many who had to begin anew the struggle of life in a foreign land with nothing which they could call their own.

§ 1281. The supposition (§ 1278) that most of the exiles were slaves in Babylonia, whether they had been free in their own land or not, may seem to be inconsistent with the glimpses of their life in that country which we gain from the book of Ezekiel, and with the exhortation addressed to them by Jeremiah (ch. xxix. 4 ff.) to make homes for themselves and to take part in the life and work of the country (§ 1168). But such freedom of movement and action as is thus implied was quite possible to Babylonian slaves, the only restriction being that the labour of their hands was at the disposal of others, and that they were not endowed with civil rights. We cannot insist on this point too strongly for the correct conception of Hebrew life at the beginning of the Exile. At the same time it is quite possible that several people of means who had not favoured the rebellion, besides those who were invited or permitted to accompany their banished brethren, were granted lands for their support, and became house-masters and men of property at the very threshold of their "captivity." But the number cannot have been great even in the chief agricultural settlement. Political reasons alone would impose a restriction, and there was, besides, the broad, economic fact that in all departments of industry most of the actual work was done by slaves.

§ 1282. We may resume and sum up as follows: The exiles may from the point of view of their relation to the state and to society be divided into four classes. There were first those who were political prisoners, such as the royal captives and their following of seditious nobles. They were kept in prison on a life sentence. Yet their confinement was not necessarily perpetual. Nor did the imprisonment in all cases involve the seclusion and privations of a dungeon (§ 1147). Extreme cruelties in Oriental imprisonment speedily end the life of the prisoner.

But many descendants of royalty and of noble families are found to have survived the Exile. Secondly, there were those who having property of their own, and not having been attainted as rebels, were permitted or encouraged to join the ranks of the deported (§ 1270). These would probably be allowed to purchase estates for themselves and become guests of the country (cf. § 549) without acquiring civil rights. Thirdly, there were the rank and file of active rebels. They were doubtless employed, at least at the beginning, as state labourers at the most servile tasks under rigorous compulsion. Finally, there were the body of the deported people not specially obnoxious. These were set to work as slaves, in various occupations.

§ 1283. The paramount importance of agriculture (§ 1270) is abundantly shown in surviving business documents. It is also clearly illustrated by the incidental testimony of the monuments, in the sculptured sketches of irrigating machines, in school-book exercises on the task and operations of husbandry, and in temple lists of vegetable productions due as contributions and classified according to the implements used in tilling the producing soil. All inquiry into the industrial, commercial, and social features of Babylonian life must begin with a study of its agriculture and the antecedent conditions of climate, soil, and water supply. Moreover, the principal colony of the exiles was planted in a region which demanded this employment and no other. To learn under what conditions they plied their calling will enable us not merely to follow aright their outward fortunes, but to understand how their character was moulded in their new national training school.

§ 1284. We must picture to ourselves a vast level region, whose surface is varied only by the mounds of cities or villages ruined or inhabited, or by occasional fortresses or military stations, and by the beds of watercourses. It was the very heart of Babylonia geographically that the chief colony occupied, but the most populous area was to the west and north where lay Babylon and its suburbs, and cities more ancient still. Nippur, the great old city in the neighbourhood, was once the central resort of the Babylonian Semites. Recent investigations upon its site have revealed the turning-points in its history. Like the rest of the most ancient cities of the lower Euphrates region, and indeed like ancient cities generally, its importance depended upon the supremacy of its leading temple. Nippur was the seat of the most ancient worship of Bel. The predominance of a rival temple of Bel would mean the decline of Nippur, and perhaps its forcible demolition.

§ 1285. What prejudiced Nippur most seriously was the rise and prosperity of Babylon. The great Chammurabi (§ 117), who aimed to make Babylon the centre of the revived and extended native monarchy, united the worship of his local deity Merodach with that of the more ancient and widely revered Bēl.[1] The consequences to Nippur and its prestige and prosperity were disastrous. It is not certain but that violence was used to make more complete the degradation of the venerable cult of Bēl. According to a recent explorer of its site "its temple was sacked, its statuary and rich votive gifts wantonly destroyed."[2] The same policy of neglect and disfavour was continued for sev-

---

[1] The results of this combination of the titles and attributes of Bēl and Marduk are well shown by Jastrow, RBA. p. 117 f. The appreciation of Marduk leads to his appropriation of the rôle and his assumption of the great name of Bēl, while "Marduk-Bel and Marduk are blended into one personage, Marduk becoming known as Bel-Marduk, and, finally, the first part of the compound sinking to the level of a mere adjective, the god is addressed as 'lord Marduk.'" One of the monumental indications of this syncretism is found in the designations of the outer and inner walls of Babylon (§ 1058). Singularly enough, the outer and inner walls of Nippur were called respectively *Nēmitti-Marduk* and *Imgur-Marduk* (II R. 50. 28, 29 *a* and *b*). Dr. Peters simply refers to the outer wall as "Nimitti-Bel" (*Nippur*, II, 212, 372).

[2] Peters, in *Nippur*, II, 257. It is just possible that, according to Hilprecht's supposition (PCT. I, ii, 33), this desecration was the work of the invading Elamites shortly before (cf. § 106 ff.). At any rate, it is clear that Chammurabi did nothing to repair the ruin wrought in the temple.

eral centuries. The kings of the Kasshite dynasty, who as foreigners had no local prejudices, restored the ancient splendour of the temple of Bēl, and therewith the prosperity of the city and district returned.

§ 1286. But a new work of destruction was undertaken under Nebuchadrezzar I (§ 178), and the temple was razed to the ground. It was not until near the close of the Assyrian supremacy that it was again reinstated. Esarhaddon recognized no rivalry between Babylon and Nippur, and his equanimity towards the former (§ 748 f.) was matched by a generous interest in the latter. His son Asshurbanipal, with more leisure and a more active Babylonian policy, continued to favour Nippur, with the hope of dividing the religious and therefore the political interest of Babylonia, which caused him so much trouble and loss. Large monumental remains of these patrons of Nippur have been found by the latest explorers. They have also discovered proofs of the opposition displayed by the revived Chaldæan dynasty in the days of which we are now writing. If the conjecture of Peters[1] is correct, Nippur was destroyed by the great Nebuchadrezzar in his zeal for the aggrandizement of Bēl-Merodach in the capital city of Babylon.

§ 1287. The demolition of a temple and the subversion of its worship involved loss of prestige and of business, both of which depended mainly upon the appreciation of the local shrines. Allusion has already been made to the business functions of that remarkable institution, a great Babylonian temple (§ 740, note). We can partly account for them if we remember that religion was the centre of Babylonian life generally. In practice this meant that the priests and other ministers of the dominant cults gained riches for themselves and their shrines through the sacrificial and votive offerings, the fees for divination, the gifts of chiefs and princes. It meant, however, more than this. In most civilized countries the professional ministers of religion

---

[1] *Nippur*, II, 202.

have been sooner or later debarred from civil functions and from civil business on any extensive scale. Even when, as in ancient Egypt, circumstances favoured their usurpation of the functions of state,[1] their authority was not tolerated for long. Neither in Babylonia nor in Assyria do we read of priests indulging in state intrigues, though in the revolutionary periods of Babylonian history their powerful support was sometimes given to one side or the other, so that they virtually were in those troublesome times a political force. Their strength, however, always lay in their own essential merit and efficiency. And this accounts for what is so remarkable, that, though usually without civic ambition, they became a great power in the general life of the country and the people.

§ 1288. Peculiar to these priests of Babylonia were their culture and their science, so that their prestige was not a mere illusion based on the credulity of the superstitious masses. They had the power which special knowledge always gives. They were the teachers and educators of the people, and they were liberal enough to profess in their schools not merely the mysteries of their own special calling, but all the learning of the time. This was the secret of their unique enterprise and success as business men. They were able to acquire and maintain great estates, to make large loans, to own many slaves and employ many labourers, to cultivate much land, to establish farms and buildings and waterways, and rear vast flocks of sheep and cattle. Of course there was in their favour the popular notion that the whole land was the property of the god or gods of whom they were the ministers. Hence they or the temples received tithes and substantial offerings, and hence landed property in their parishes easily fell into their hands. But the idea of the divine ownership of the soil was a common belief among ancient peoples; and

---

[1] In the twenty-first dynasty (§ 207). Significantly, the priestly rulers are not recognized as legitimate by Manetho, who acknowledges the rebellious dynasty of Tanis.

nowhere else was the priesthood so cultured, so sagacious, so wealthy, so enterprising, and so enduring.

§ 1289. This survey may help us to understand the condition of the district in which the main body of the colonists found themselves. Notice that, on the one hand, Nippur was after the earliest times never a great political centre, and that, on the other hand, its excavated records show that when not neglected or injured by an unfriendly king, its business interests flourished greatly.[1] The surrounding country shared inevitably in the prosperity or the decline of Nippur. What is the inference as to the question before us? I think it is fair to assume that the great Nebuchadrezzar, whose policy was unfavourable to Nippur and its institutions, but who had at heart the internal development of his kingdom, was now taking charge of the natural domain of that city, and that the planting of this colony of Hebrews in the neighbourhood was an incident of his administration of the district. It is further fair to assume that this community of Hebrews, like many others, was under the special oversight of state officials, to whom the provincial or district authorities were responsible for the good conduct and efficiency of the settlers.

---

[1] See, for example, *Nippur*, II. 114 f., where mention is made of the business records of the great temple under the friendly Kasshite dynasty. The mass of business documents found by Mr. Haynes (of the Pennsylvania expedition), in May, 1893, of which the first instalment is published by Hilprecht and Clay (PCT. vol. IX), belong to the Persian period, but they illustrate the historic importance of Nippur as a business centre.

CHAPTER XIV

CHIEF EMPLOYMENTS OF THE EXILES

§ 1290. As to the immediate environment and occupation of this principal colony, it is to be observed that the whole of Babylonia is normally, and in a sense naturally, unproductive; that according to the season of the year or the vicissitudes of the River, its sandy or marshy lands are inundated by floods or parched by drought; that sometimes it is easy and best to travel over much of its surface by boats or rafts, while at other times there is no water in the Euphrates itself for many miles of its course, and very little in any of its countless affluents; that the canal Kebar lay at or near the eastern limit of a network of watercourses included between the two great streams, the Euphrates and the Shatt-en-Nil. The first and the last care of the typical Babylonian was to regulate, conserve, and utilize the water of the River. His life was spent in reclaiming the soil and extending its productive area, by drawing off the superfluous water of the canals and reservoirs, by conveying it in a constant stream to needy regions, or by occasional outlets to districts dried by the summer sun. It was this that made Babylonia; but more — it was this that made the Babylonians. The difficulties and problems of the case were greater than in Egypt, and the energy, watchfulness, and contrivance that were needful made the people of the Euphrates greater than those of the Nile. Naturally there was need of state or corporate aid.

§ 1291. We may refer here to the description of the Babylonian river system already given (§ 71 ff.).

It was pointed out that, as this lower country was a perfect plain, being little more than a deposit of the two great rivers,[1] the course of the Euphrates was slow, and at the flood season there were great overflows; that at various points reservoirs were made for use in the dry season; and that besides, an immense number of canals, large and small, were created for purposes of irrigation and navigation. We shall now further divide the canalization of the country east of the Euphrates into three sections, determined mainly by the water supply of the Euphrates and Tigris, and the varying distance from one another of these two sources, or "heads," as they are called in the book of Genesis. The first division would embrace a district extending from a little north of Baghdad to the neighbourhood of Babylon. This region is marked by the numerous canals running from the Euphrates right across the narrow strip of land which here separates the Rivers. The second comprises a large region irrigated by the Euphrates by means of canals, which, however, do not reach to the Tigris, but either return to the parent stream or are spent in the sands and marshes. Roughly speaking, it would extend southward to about the ancient Tello (§ 95). The third portion contains what may be strictly called Southern Babylonia, including such ancient sites as Tello, Erech, Ur, and Eridu (§ 100 f.). Here the waters of the Euphrates are nearly exhausted by subsidence and deflection, and new sources of supply are found in the great canals that were led off from the fuller and more rapid Tigris well up the stream, and brought southwestward towards the lower Euphrates.

§ 1292. It is in the middle division that we are particularly interested. At the era of the Exile the life of the world pulsed to and from Babylon unceasingly. The

---

[1] It would be more correct to refer to prehistoric conditions and to say that this territory is a deposit of the several streams that formerly ran into the sea, branching off from the Euphrates and Tigris at the end of their middle course. Cf. Gen. ii.

water of the Euphrates clothed with verdure and beauty the soil which it had brought down from the far-away mountains of the north. Wherever the waters flowed regularly or were judiciously distributed there was fertility and plenty. Wherever there was either prolonged inundation or continued dryness there was desolation and barrenness. The last-named conditions are those which prevail at the present day; the former were maintained in the old Semitic centuries or rather millenniums, the times of Babylonia's greatness. But the main practical question then was, how to make the life-giving water reach far enough; how to economize it in one place that it might be available in another. It was only in exceptional seasons that there was a superabundance of the supply. By careful management there was enough for the region of the Euphrates proper such as I have indicated above. That is to say, this territory was not only habitable but luxurious; not only good for pasturage, but the most productive part of the world for grain, for herbs, and the fruits of the earth generally. But to the eastward of the range of regular irrigation there was barrenness, at least there was merely pasturage for flocks great or small. Instead of cities there were villages or encampments of Aramæan shepherds, whose tents were most numerous near or along the Tigris. Naturally the extent of arable and productive land varied greatly with the political fortunes of the people, their industrial habits and training, and their control of the water supply.

§ 1293. But everywhere and at all seasons vigilance and energy were essential to prosperity or even to a subsistence, possible affluence and equally possible penury being separated by narrow chances. The principal conditions, natural and artificial, were the height or breadth of the river at its flood and the number and size of canals drawing off water above the region affected. What the possibilities were may be illustrated from modern experiences. When the members of the second American exploring expedition to Babylonia reached Hillah, the region of ancient Babylon, on Jan. 2, 1890, they found the bed of the Euphrates at that point nearly dry, after months of drought which had left the river, in its normal course farther up the stream, much lower than usual. I quote from the narrative of Dr. Peters: "The rains which had fallen in the last two weeks had not been sufficient to make good the drought of the summer. What was left of the Euphrates seemed to have deserted its original course almost entirely and poured itself through the Hindieh canal into the Abu Nejm and other marshes."[1] This canal, which finally merges itself in the Pallakopas of the Greeks (§ 100), runs southwestward from a point about halfway between Babylon and Sippar (§ 94). A later passage gives an instructive explanation.[2] "Since the time of Alexander the Great, if not before, the Hindieh canal has been a perpetual source of trouble to the rulers of the country. . . . The lay of the land, as already stated, is such that the Euphrates soon showed a tendency to abandon its proper course, and descending by the Hindieh to form great marshes to the west and south of Borsippa. Dam after dam has been erected, and broken. The last dam broke about ten years ago,[3] and by the summer of 1889 the Euphrates had entirely abandoned its proper course. For months, at Hillah and below, the river bed was entirely dry. At Babylon the ancient quay of Nebuchadrezzar was exposed in its full extent, and to get water to drink people dug wells at the foot of it. On the other hand, the country to the west of the Euphrates suffered almost as seriously from excessive inundation, a great part of the region being converted into swamps. At the time of my visit the work of restoring the Euphrates to its proper bed had been going on under the direction of French engineers for two years. At a favourable point, where the Euphrates and Hindieh are only a kilometre

---

[1] *Nippur*, II, 53. [2] *Ibid*, II, 335 f. [3] Written apparently in 1897.

apart, a canal was dug connecting the two. A dam was then erected in the Hindieh for the purpose of forcing one-half of the water back through this canal into the old bed. Contracts were made with the sheikhs of various villages to furnish bricks from the ruins of Babylon. Boats loaded with these bricks and with stones brought from Hit and other points higher up the Euphrates were sunk to make a foundation, and on this was erected a dam of brush, earth, and bricks. The work was finally completed after my departure from the country, and I am informed that one-half of the water now descends by the old bed of the river."

§ 1294. Another set of conditions to the east of the Euphrates may be illustrated from the same narrative. A few days later the party crossed the river at Diwanieh, a town west by south of Nippur, and now the most important official post in central Babylonia. Dr. Peters writes: "At Diwanieh, all was changed since our last visit. There was not a drop of water in the Euphrates, and had not been for six long months. The people drank water from wells dug in the dry bed of the stream. The same condition prevailed in the Affech marshes,[1] we were told. The wells ran dry every few days, so that new ones must be dug. The next day a little stream of water came trickling down the Euphrates, and the whole town turned out to welcome it. . . . It was clear to me that as the water had reached Diwanieh, it must also reach the Affech marshes through the Daghara canal."[2] Two days later Dr. Peters went to Nippur on horseback. Of this stage of his journey he says: "We found all the canals and marshes dried up, and were able to take a straight course to Nippur, making the distance between that and Diwanieh only five hours; something less than fifteen miles. What

---

[1] To the west and southwest of Nippur, named from the Arab tribe which holds the district; also written *Affej*, originally *Affek*.

[2] A canal which once ran to Nippur from the Euphrates, leaving the latter at a point twenty miles below Babylon.

water had come down the Daghara canal had been dammed first by the Daghara Arabs, and then by the Behahtha, and the marshes were as dry as a bone."[1] During the excavations which followed, the water appeared in its usual beds and canals, partly on account of exceptionally heavy rains. Finally, when the camp broke up in May, nearly all of the party and the workmen with the baggage were sent out in boats to Hillah. Peters with a small escort went southeastward by water to visit Ur, Erech, and other famous old sites in southern Babylonia. Of his departure he writes: "We floated down to Hamud-al-Berjud's camp in turadas,[2] through the reeds, in canals so covered with the white ranunculus that one might have fancied snow had fallen. Here we lunched with our three chiefs and took a siesta. In the cool, toward eventide, we started again, and as darkness was falling, landed in front of the magnificent new muthif[3] of Hajji Tarfa, . . . and as we journeyed thither we heard on all sides a chorus of men's voices, working at the dams in the rice fields, for the waters were rising mightily, and the dry and parched land of a few weeks before was like to be turned into one mighty lake."[4]

§ 1295. The following *résumé* of the condition of the whole region from the same source may fitly be appended here even at the risk of some repetition: "In ancient days this whole country teemed with a vast population, and was dotted with innumerable cities. . . . Another class of ruins, the ruins of the ancient canals, I have not noticed at all, although they are, if possible, more numerous, more striking, and more characteristic than the ruins of the cities. They run like great arteries through the country, lines of mounds, ten to thirty feet high, stretching in all directions as far as the eye can

---

[1] See *Nippur*, II, 60–63.

[2] Round boats used on Babylonian streams and marshes (§ 1305).

[3] The guest house, or, more frequently, hut, of an Arab chief.

[4] *Nippur*, II, 102. Cf. the vision of rising waters in Ez. xlvii. 1–12.

reach. Once they carried life-blood to every part of the land, for the life of this country is water. Give it canals and reservoirs and dams, to distribute and control the water supply, as Nebuchadrezzar and other great kings did, and it is capable of supporting, by its enormous productivity, an incredibly large population. Break its dams, choke its canals, and it lapses into poverty and barbarism. Such is its present condition. There is a very scanty population, largely in the bedouin state. There are few towns, and those without industry or commerce. There is no irrigation except of the rudest sort, close to the river banks; and the land is alternately inundated and parched. There is no government excepting heavy oppression and irregular bribes and taxes. There is a general state of insecurity. There is not a road in the whole country, and no means of locomotion, and the most primitive and obstructive ignorance prevails everywhere. The first parent of our civilization is in his decrepit second childhood, but in the Tigris and Euphrates exists for him a fountain of perpetual youth. Some day water from that fountain will be held to his shrivelled lips, the life-blood will course once more through his atrophied veins and arteries, and he will rise to a new life, strong and vigorous as when in days of yore he begat nations and knowledge together."[1]

§ 1296. It was in the most vigorous and productive age of all the long history of Babylonia that the exiles of Israel were planted within its borders. It was in the eighth year of Nebuchadrezzar that the settlement was made. He was then freed from the embarrassments in east and west which had kept him busy in the beginning of his reign. With all his energy he was devoting himself to the development and enrichment of his empire. Hence his various public works great and small. The captives of his necessary wars must be made to fit into his plan.

---

[1] *Nippur*, II. 306. Compare the fine but all too short article, "Euphrates," in the *Encyclopædia Britannica*, vol. viii, by the late Sir Henry Rawlinson.

Hence the Hebrews were placed in the region of the Kebar. The very name of their chief gathering-place, Tel-Abub,[1] is suggestive of the work which they were to undertake. It means the "ruin-mound of the deluge." It was perhaps "a desolation of many generations,"[2] and distinguished among the similar ruined settlements of the country from a supposed association with the great deluge, which was commemorated alike in the traditions of the captive people and in those of the lords of the land. How appropriate was the fate of the exiles, that their life work was to be the repairing of a ruined settlement while their own home was itself in ruins!

§ 1297. There is another indication that the exiles occupied an abandoned district. If the land had been already in a satisfactory state of cultivation, it would have had a population, bond and free, which it would have been folly to extrude for the sake of untrained foreigners. Again, as some of the exiles were apparently men of property, the freeholds which they could most readily acquire were the waste-lands of the country, just as in the present century homesteads have been granted on easy terms to settlers in the United States and Canada. The whole situation thus assumed fits in well with the policy of Nebuchadrezzar. All economical and political considerations would move him to employ the immigrants in such a way as to gradually accustom them to the life and business of the country, without interfering with the possessions of others.

---

[1] Ezek. iii. 15, usually written, after the slight error of the received Hebrew text, Tel-Abib, and explained as "mound of corn-ears," or "Cornhill." But the word is a very common one in the Assyrian literature, though not as the name of a city, just as the phenomenon itself was very usual. The Babylonians did not speak Hebrew!

[2] The business of restoring waste places, assigned to his fellow-countrymen, may have suggested the frequent references to such a task or achievement in the writings of the Second Isaiah; e.g. Isa. xlix. 19, lviii. 12, lxi. 4. Observe also his allusions to the rushing, destructive flood (lix. 19), to the overflowing stream with its enriching waters (xlviii. 18, lxvi. 12), and to the "well-watered garden," in connection with the building up of waste places (lviii. 11).

§ 1298. To resume: the chief community of the exiles was planted as a crown colony in the centre of Babylonia; in a temporarily abandoned district; close to the mound of a noted ruin, on the edge of a considerable canal not far from the famous old city of Nippur, naturally within its sphere of influence, yet not under its jurisdiction; and the most important condition of its prosperity was the possibility of a good water-supply.

§ 1299. The general distribution of the canal system has already been indicated (§ 1291). A more particular survey of the watercourses of this region will show that its chances were not unfavourable. The Euphrates was not directly the main feeder of its streams. The great source of supply was the Shatt-en-Nil, the most important canal, indeed, of all Babylonia, because the most central besides being one of the longest. It is sometimes described as having left the Euphrates just above the city, running eastward to the Tigris and sending down a branch as far as Nippur.[1] This, however, can hardly be correct. The canal which thus starts from near Babylon was at first an independent artificial stream, parallel to the system of interfluvial drainage of North Babylonia above described. Through its importance to the capital and its union with the Shatt-en-Nil proper, it came to be considered the primary source of this great canal, which was really at first an independent branch of the Euphrates, like the Pallakopas. It separated from the main stream near Sippar, running downward by Nippur, and thence far along beside Erech to the sea, in the days when no dry land lay farther south. We have to think also of other watercourses as supplying the settlement, having the Euphrates as their source, such as the Daghara canal (§ 1294), running east or south from the parent stream. Most probably not one of these, but one derived from the Shatt-en-Nil, and running eastward, was the Kebar.

---

[1] Sir Henry Rawlinson, article "Euphrates," in the *Encycl. Brit.*

§ 1300. The function of the Kebar probably was to extend the water-supply farther out into the barren region that stretched away towards the Tigris. How such streams larger or smaller came to be multiplied is suggested by an entry in the diary of Dr. Peters of March 17, 1889, with regard to this very neighbourhood, Nippur being then the centre of his survey. " Yesterday Harper and I rode out to two small mounds about an hour and a half away to the northeast, called Abu Jowan or Father of Millstones. . . . There are several large canal beds in the neighbourhood. One we followed westward, but it disappeared about half an hour from Nippur. I think it originally went on and joined the Shatt-en-Nil to the north of the mound.[1] We passed several cross canals on the way. The sand-hills lie to the north and northeast of us; they are of fine sea-sand,[2] and constantly change shape as blown about by the wind. The Euphrates seems to be rising, and the water is approaching the mound on the north and west."[3] In the period of reconstruction with which we are concerned, there were, doubtless, also, apart from the Kebar, many old canal beds to be reopened, and, what was of equal consequence, new watercourses had to be dug until the whole country became reticulated with them. Not until then could it be permeated with the " water of life."

§ 1301. When the colony had been quartered in this region, they began to build more permanent dwelling-places. Those of them who soon or later came to have houses of the better class had no need of elaborate brick-making. The chief materials were obtained from the mounds of ruined towns in the neighbourhood; or a

---

[1] The great mound, namely, that of Nippur.
[2] This " sea-sand " gives the explanation of the arenaceous character of much of the surface of the country. It is brought up in large quantities by the frequent winds from the seashore and the adjacent desert. These winds, by the way, occasion many of the cyclones, which, combined with inundations or rain storms, produce a " deluge " (cf. § 1296).
[3] *Nippur*, I, 258.

lot of sun-dried bricks was ordered from the nearest factory. Most of them as slaves of native planters had, however, to put up with the ordinary simple structure — a hut of reeds matted together with tough marsh-grass and overlaid with bitumen. While shelter was thus being provided, their essential work had already begun. Dams and dikes were created to prevent possible overflows. Old watercourses half choked up were cleaned out, and new ones were started. The soil had also to be prepared in many places, especially on the marshy lands, where the reeds and thick grasses had to be removed by burning. Contrivances for the raising and carrying of water to the fields were also set in place and order before the first growing season had been entered upon.

§ 1302. Such in the main was the early employment of this important section of the exiles. We must not think, however, of these essays as being, to any large extent, independent work. The few who secured estates for themselves hired or bought native labourers, skilled and unskilled. The majority found their places under native overseers. To follow them up further at their work would be to see an extension of the same operations. We should observe the cutting of new aqueducts for lands newly reclaimed from the sand or the marshes, with reservoirs for the needs of the growing population; and here and there larger streams for towns and villages, with smaller channels planted at the centres of irrigation, diverting the water to the separate estates or to fields of grain, or to groves of date-palms. With increasing wants and resources came the adoption and use of various mechanical devices for the conservation, distribution, and regulation of the waters, the sluices, gates, and locks of the canals, the wheels[1] and other contrivances for raising water in smaller quantities and for conveying it to needy places.

---

[1] These water-wheels deserve more than a mere mention. We can judge of them only from modern survivals, but we may be sure that they were employed by the ancients also, though in a far better fashion, since

§ 1303. Thus went on, under the eyes and by the growing skill of the toilers, the regeneration of the district for which they were made so largely responsible. Acres of rich vegetation were yearly added to the productive areas — wheat and sesame indigenous to the country, and abundance of vegetables, particularly of melons and cucumbers, radishes, leeks, and onions, for which the country was renowned.[1] Palm trees abounded, not like the isolated grove of Jericho, but in long and stately rows wherever the kindly moisture bade them grow and thrive. And not least important were the pasture-grounds, widening out with the expansion of the water-meadow and the tilth. Here were reared the sheep and cattle that now served for food or wealth alone, and not also for sacrifice, and oxen for labour at the plough or the wagon or the water-wheel.

§ 1304. Thus "the desert was rejoicing and blossoming like a meadow-flower" (Isa. xxxv. 1), and the exiles still half-enslaved were renewing their life and prosperity. They were now in a goodly land. To north and south, but especially to the west, one looked over smiling fields and meadows of the richest green, and among them here and there the glimmering waters. Only to the east the

---

the latter-day inhabitants of the region invent nothing. The great water-wheels (*naoura*) are used where there is a strong current. Dams are run far out from the bank to raise the level of the stream and so increase the water power. This is used to turn large wheels, often of thirty feet in diameter, made mostly of boughs, with paddles of palm leaves. The wheels are attached to the ends of the dams or piers, and raise the water to a trough, whence it is distributed to the fields of grain or melons, or to the gardens along the banks. These wheels impede navigation seriously. The ox water-wheels (*jird*) are far more common and are used more in canals of lower Babylonia than in the main Euphrates. On a declivity on the bank of the stream, ropes on block-wheels run up and down, having water-skins attached to them, and being raised and lowered by oxen on the shore. See the illustration in *Nippur*, I, 136, and cf. *ibid.*, p. 154 f. and 320, and the article "Euphrates" in the *Encycl. Brit.*

[1] Cf. the list of vegetables and plants — seventy in number — in the garden of Merodach-baladan; see Delitzsch, *Prolegomena*, p. 84.

view was of bare and uncultivated steppes. This outlook was an incentive as well as a disappointment. In that spreading waste was the hope of a larger conquest of nature. Yet it suggested to them the presence of enemies. It was not always a time of verdure and fertility. Floods and storms and drought came now and then with desolation in their train. During the long months of drought it was the cattle that suffered most severely. Unless driven off from the dried-up marshes and meadows to other pastures near or far, they must perish as they perish frequently in less-favoured modern days. Nor were drawbacks lacking in the best of times. The greed or the carelessness of neighbours or rivals higher up the streams might preëmpt the water of a whole settlement; and it was not impossible that dams might be built over night that would dry up the aqueducts for a score of miles below. Always and for all things in this rich and capricious land vigilance and alertness were the first essentials, not on the part of individuals so much as on the part of the whole community who here were committed to common action and mutual helpfulness which their general condition otherwise did not easily evoke.

§ 1305. Such or the like was the chief employment of the Hebrew exiles as rooted in the watercourses which they found or made. But the Babylonian canal was something more than a giver of fertility. It was also a navigable stream, an avenue of commerce and travel. Such was the Kebar, over whose surface boats and barges moved to and from and past Tel-Abub. To some extent, this may from the beginning have given some employment to the exiles; at any rate they were ultimately involved in it with the development of the district, and contributed their quota to the many hands required to man and propel the vessels. Thus an essential part of their environment was the river craft familiar to Babylonians, who, from the scarcity of timber, often constructed their vessels of lighter materials. Thus there were seen rafts kept afloat by inflated skins;[1] or oblong punts, half raft and half wherry, made of hides stretched over willow branches;[2] or round little coracles, the modern *turadas*; or canoe-shaped vessels, often attaining to the dignity of barges, either propelled by oars or towed along the shore.[3]

§ 1306. There is room for plausible conjecture as to what became of the "carvers and joiners" (§ 1275) and the artisans in general, who were carried away in the first captivity (2 K. xxiv. 16). Insomuch as the chief demand was for agricultural labourers, it is altogether likely that many of these working-people were drafted off to the canals and the marshes. For the remainder, places would be found in various factories, especially in Babylon (§ 1273). These were naturally kept in bondage, though not necessarily in perpetuity (§ 1280).[4] After a time they would be undistinguishable except by name from artisans of Babylonian descent. Their chief disability as Hebrews would be that

---

[1] Illustrated on the Assyrian monuments. They were used for many purposes and were of various sizes, from the simple structures required to ferry over one or two passengers, to the larger rafts put together for the transport, in sections, over large rivers, of armies on the march, as by Tiglathpileser I, Asshurnasirpal, and Shalmaneser II.

[2] As described minutely by Herodotus, I, 194.

[3] On the modern streams of Babylonia the most characteristic vessels, besides the tub-like coracles, are the large boats, averaging about thirty feet in length, and made of a wooden frame, over which a thick matting of closely plaited grass or reeds is placed, secured by cords of bulrush, the whole being thoroughly pitched with melted bitumen. At Hit, one hundred miles above Babylon, on the Euphrates, there is a ship or boat yard. The process of making is fully described in the diary of Dr. W. H. Ward, of the Wolfe expedition, published in *Nippur* as an appendix to Vol. I (see p. 357 f., and cf. Peters, *ib.* I, 161 f.). For modes of navigating the Euphrates and Tigris, cf. Kaulen, *Assyrien und Babylonien*, p. 7 ff., where illustrations are given. On the largest streams, but scarcely on the Kebar, were still more capacious vessels, of which the "ark" of the Bible and of the Babylonian Flood story is a projection.

[4] Artisans were usually slaves in all ancient countries where manufactures of any extent were carried on. Even the foremen might be slaves. We are familiar with the employment of slaves in Athens as armourers and upholsterers. Naturally, only the masters were members of the guilds.

they could not easily mingle with their brethren or take an active part in the affairs of the remnant of Israel. Yet we must not lay too much stress on these disadvantages. After all, the chief factor in the case was loyalty and devotion to the fatherland and its institutions; and the sequel shows that at length many from all classes of the exiles took part in the restoration of Israel.

CHAPTER XV

THE EXILES AS A COMMUNITY

§ 1307. The relations of the settlements to the central government are not definitely known. We can only infer from general allusions in the Bible that in the management of their affairs as a people they were left pretty much to themselves. The king's officers who directed the march to the banks of the Kebar were replaced there by others, who disposed of the persons of this principal detachment and secured their orderly settlement. Thereafter royal officers had to exercise a general supervision, make a periodical inspection, and report to the proper department at Babylon, while others collected as regularly the inevitable imposts from the landholders and tenants of the district. As the settlement was an outgrowth of the policy of Nebuchadrezzar, we may assume that he kept himself informed of its progress.

§ 1308. As everything that concerns the Great King is a matter of biblical interest, it touches us sympathetically to know that this business of canal-making and of reclaiming the soil of his country was one of the things that were nearest his heart. In this he was but following in the path of the most patriotic kings of Assyria and Babylonia, who counted it one of their chief titles to honour that they had, by the making and equipment of canals and aqueducts, enriched and blessed their subjects. We are perhaps too apt to regard these ancient kings as mere selfish conquerors, and to forget that much of their time was spent in devising means for the upbuilding of their country by the arts of peace. The very names[1] which they bestowed on the chief watercourses reveal their deep sense of the life-giving properties of the streams, and their gratitude to the gods for their bounty to the land which was held to be their peculiar care. Nor will their piety seem to us superstitious or ridiculous when we remember that these "givers of life" converted into a blessing to the land what else would have been, as it once was and now actually is, a bringer of desolation and death. A principal result of our inquiry accordingly is that we have gained a conception of the living bond of interest between the humble Hebrew husbandmen and the rulers of the land. This goes far to explain the anomaly given in the fact that these exiles survived and prospered in the country of their conquerors for two generations.

§ 1309. For the question of the internal organization of the Hebrews in Babylonia we must confine ourselves to the larger settlements, to which was left the possibility of self-government. And the first thing that strikes us is the fact that in some way from the very beginning the solidarity of the survivors of Israel was maintained. There was no obliteration of any large number at any time. There was communication between the several sections of them when there was need of conference, always of course by the leave of the government officials, who were intolerant only of sedition, and with the consent of the employers of their labour.

§ 1310. What, then, was the internal organization of the colony or colonies? Fortunately, we may give at

---

[1] It is significant of the honour in which these beneficent streams were held that each of them had a name and character of its own. This is shown, for example, by a business inscription published in PCT. IX., nr. 48 (cf. p. 36 f.), where a single property producing a very moderate rent is described minutely as lying between two canals, one of them bearing the lordly name of *Sin*, and the other called *Shilihtu*, or "outflow," a name kindred in form and meaning with the "Shiloah" of Isa. viii. 6 or the "Siloam" of John ix. 7. Compare the names of the greater aqueducts cited by Delitzsch in Par. p. 187 ff.

least a general answer. Our preliminary studies as to the development of Hebrew society have shown us how simple and elastic was its fundamental structure. The community that so long maintained itself as a nation in Palestine was now reduced to its essential elements; and this was effected directly, not by exile, but by the abolition of the kingdom. We have to eliminate the last two main stages of development. First, we are to conceive the Hebrews in Babylonia as being without king and nobles (536 f.), and next as having discarded the administrative divisions with their rulers or princes (§ 530 f.). The doing away with city government is not so cardinal a distinction as it might seem, since the cities were administered virtually on the same principles as the old tribal communities, that is, by the "elders" and the family chiefs (§ 486). And these are just the functionaries whom we find referred to in the meagre records of the time and people.

§ 1311. That a great deal of social confusion prevailed in the earlier days of the colony must be taken for granted. It was the reërection of a community, the formation of a new and unique social organism, that then went on. But here, again, we must not exaggerate the difficulties or suppose that the changes amounted to a social revolution. In the large first deportation very many, perhaps most, of the families were left intact — not so much in the interest of the people affected, as for the benefit of the land to be cultivated. And where the old heads of the family groups and clans did not survive, new ones were readily chosen, the very disorder of the settlement making a choice imperative. The elders also would take their places, as in the times of old, by obvious merit, some simply holding over from the Palestine days, and others being newly elected. Hence, we find that in 591 B.C. elders act in a full representative capacity (Ez. viii. 1; xiv. 1; xx. 1). So much autonomy, indeed, was granted to the community, and so great was the influence of the heads of the people, that we find some few of them early in the history of the colony planning sedition and able to carry their measures to the danger-point (cf. § 1169).

§ 1312. On the whole, then, the Hebrew society held well together in exile. The fidelity with which the family records and genealogies were kept was both cause and effect of this social survival. There is no doubt that there were leading men who exercised a strong moral influence, and perhaps direct supervision, not merely in their own several communities, but over the exiles as a whole. Naturally, these had a recognized civil position, and were not merely great prophets or priests, like Ezekiel. A singular evidence of persistent loyalty and patriotism is the figure of the king or "prince"[1] as head of the nation, which was kept before the minds of the people all through the captivity, until at length the dream was, in a measure, realized in the person of Sheshbazzar and Zerubbabel (Ezra i. ff.). It was out of the question, however, that there could be any sort of magisterial headship to the exiles as a whole, this office being purely theoretical and ideal.

---

[1] For the period of the Exile itself, notice the usage of Ez. xlv. 7 ff. and xlvi. 2 ff., and cf. vii. 27, xii. 10. The two passages last-named are interesting as showing how the language of Ezekiel was influenced by his surroundings. In Assyrian the word for "king" (*šarru*) is Hebrew for "prince," and the word for "prince" (*malku*) Hebrew for "king." Compare the play on the words in Isa. x. 8.

Book XI

HEBREWS, CHALDÆANS, AND PERSIANS

CHAPTER I

MORALS AND RELIGION OF ISRAEL IN EXILE

§ 1313. What next concerns us is the progress of the exiles in their new home. Here we must narrow somewhat the scope of our inquiry. What was formerly most important to Israel now becomes more vital and significant than ever. That for which Israel was born (Isa. xliv. 1 f., 21, 24; cf. xliii. 7), made into a nation, and honoured with the divine favour and love (Isa. xli. 8 f.; xliii. 3 f.), is now to be made alone conspicuous. All else that marked Israel as a people — everything that was political and secular, and even what was officially religious — was now stripped off. Only "Israel" itself was left, to test the voluntary principle pure and simple in religion and morals.

§ 1314. To the making of the new Israel the external conditions contributed mightily. We naturally think first of the influence exercised upon the exiles by their physical environment. How different from the old surroundings was all that now met the eye! In the land of Judah hills and valleys formed the constant outlook. Almost the only plains were the bottoms of mountain gorges. The only streams were mountain brooks, or the deep-running Jordan, whose overflow went to the profit of reeds and jungles, and which lost itself in a lake of salt. It was, after all, a poor country, in spite of its vine-clad slopes and its olive-crowned heights — a land best fitted for humble shepherd folk with small flocks of small cattle and a hand-to-mouth subsistence. Here they beheld an illimitable plain, almost a dead level. Yet it had not the dull uniformity of the great desert which in the old land they had seen from afar, and which they had just traversed for many a weary mile. A naked plain, unrelieved by nature's kindly green or the incidental gatherings of human kind would have been intolerable, and would have tended to the degeneration and not to the regeneration of Israel. Even as it was, the aspect of the new land must, by unconscious contrast, have brought many a tear to homesick exiles, as they looked westward over the river and the Arabian waste and fancied that they saw in some sunset mirage the mountains that were round about Jerusalem. But the land of their banishment, level as it was, proved to be the very reverse of monotonous. Wherever they looked, to north or west or south, they beheld the mounds of cities great and small, the homes or the monuments of multitudes of men. Nor was there lack of variety in physical features. What the mountains and valleys were to Palestine the rivers and canals were to Babylonia. Nay, they were ever so much more; for they were the source and the chosen symbols of such wealth and prosperity as the exiles had never seen or imagined.

§ 1315. The effect of such an environment upon the new inhabitants was unique and profound. Insensibly they adjusted themselves to their surroundings, and gained from them deep and lasting impressions. One sphere of observation was of special importance. In the home-land the Hebrews had no conception of imperialism except from the effects upon themselves or their neighbours of the power of a real empire. Nationality, in the larger sense, was impossible in Palestine because the country was physically so broken and diversified.

Here, on the far-stretching plain, tribes and cities were welded together, and from the unified kingdom as a centre a levelling and combinatory influence had gone forth over almost all the known world. The distinction between a people and a nation, hardly possible to them before, now became quite familiar, and there grew within them a sense of the ineffectiveness of the squabbling communities among which they had run their career as compared with the empire into whose centre they were flung.

§ 1316. Another and an analogous mental departure of vital moment was induced by the thought of their own political history as contrasted with the growth of the colossal world-kingdom. Always loyal to their country's destiny in the past, always ambitious and sanguine, the slightest revival of patriotic hope now brought to them visions of a dominion not like to the narrow domain of the kings of Israel and Judah, but like to that of the king of kings. At least the controlling minds among the people were influenced by such associations, which, to be sure, acted in any case but slowly and subtly.

§ 1317. We are more particularly concerned, in the meantime, with the causes which promoted obviously the advancement of the people as a whole. To get any intelligent notion of their progress we should have to consider these causes as operating during a series of years or during the lifetime of the first generation of the exiles. Recalling what was said of the purpose for which the exiles were planted beside the Kebar, we perceive that their very employment there contributed to make them a community such as they had not been in Palestine. There the chief unifying bonds had been governmental and ceremonial. Both of these were now seriously impaired by reason of the destruction of the kingdom and of the temple (§ 1313). It was only a new social era that could offer similarity of occupation to any large section of the people. And here most of the shepherds, the vine-dressers, and the olive-growers became tillers of the soil, like those to the manner born. The nearer view which we have gained of Babylonian agriculture (§ 1301 ff.) shows how it could become a factor of prime order in the development of character.[1]

§ 1318. In our studies of the inner development of Israel one conclusion stood out with special prominence. Apart from influences of belief and worship it was the habit of life, the social environment, and the daily avocations, that were the great determining moral factors. The good and evil of the common life of the Hebrews in Palestine before the Exile were educed very largely through the stress and strain of social antagonisms through the relations of the master and the slave, of the creditor and the debtor, of the landed proprietor and the labourer, of the judge and the suitor (§ 571 ff.). We are now in a position to illustrate these observations by comparison with the new conditions in Babylonia.

§ 1319. In considering the employments of the exiles in their adopted home (§ 1290 ff.) we have learned that their occupation brought them into contact with a system of business vast in itself and having many connections. Thus not only was a new direction given to their practical energies, but their work was uniform, involving coöperation and minimizing conflicting interests. Moreover, this occupation was the main source of the national wealth of Babylonia itself, and the permanent calling of most of the inhabitants, consolidating their industrial and social life, and limiting their internal movements. The contrast with the conditions of the old life in Palestine, and especially in Judah, is obvious and need not be exhibited at length. The moral consequences of the change were effected somewhat as follows.

§ 1320. According to the testimony of the prophets, Israel was being inwardly and outwardly ruined by three great causes connected with the moral life of the people.

---

[1] Cf. Peiser, *Keilschriftliche Actenstücke aus babylonischen Städten* (1889), p. viii f.

These were sins of sensual indulgence, of cruelty and oppression, of treachery and falsehood. Of these the last sort of evil was most pervasive and dangerous, because it was involved in and promoted by the other two classes. But it was, in a sense, encouraged by the habits and traditions of the business life characteristic of the age and country. Industrial and commercial morality is a necessary step in the moral evolution of any community, and no considerable state has ever been sound and enduring without it (§ 990). Lying and cheating in sale and barter are universal in small communities everywhere. They are checked, in some degree, where the number of participants in the various lines of business is large enough to make covenant-breaking expensive and dangerous, and where the defrauding of the poor or weak by the rich or powerful would throw the wheels of commerce out of gear. Lying is so natural, easy, and apparently profitable, that where the religious motive is wanting, it is abated only when and where it becomes unpleasant to the liar. In earlier society nearly all morality being social, the practice of honesty, slowly and preëminently gaining ground and becoming an understood necessity in public and business transactions, was recognized at first in the courts of the local judges, and was at length made the basis of statutory law. In Israel, which had the additional sanction of the religion of Jehovah, and of legislation, more or less practical, given in his name, honesty never became the general practice, either in private or public life, till after the prophetic era (§ 953, 970). Social integrity being alien to the community as a whole and to the ruling classes, the prophets, who never succeeded in any case in breaking the force of social custom, put their protest on record and left the case with Jehovah. Their vindication and the enforcement of their lessons came in the strangest fashion. Where precept upon precept and line upon line had failed, their people were taught by men of strange lips and of another tongue (Isa. xxviii. 10 f.).

§ 1321. Wherever there is landed property there is a potential germ of business morality, since security in the possession and transfer of such property is the foundation of settled life. Accordingly, we find that while oppression, treachery, and fraud were still rife in Judah, ample legal safeguards were thrown around the titles to real estate. Thus, immediately before the final captivity a contract was formally made in duplicate, signed and sealed, and subscribed by witnesses, which provides for the sale of a small portion of land near Jerusalem (Jer. xxxii.; cf. § 1225). The terms employed suggest that the usages in detail were borrowed from Babylonian procedure. But this indirect allusion to the judicial forms of the great commercial community gives but a faint suggestion of the minute and careful provision that was made in Babylonia for the guarding of the rights of the parties to any business transaction whatever.[1]

§ 1322. Among the cuneiform records, the so-called contract tablets are the most numerous. They represent a period of over two thousand years, and are numbered literally by thousands.[2] Those of them which have been

---

[1] We have the testimony of Nicolaus of Damascus (in Müller's *Fragmenta Historicorum Græcorum*, Fr. 131) that the Babylonians "practise straightforwardness" (ἀσκοῦσι εὐθύτητα): quoted by Rawlinson, FM. "Fourth Monarchy," ch. iii.

[2] What has been published of business documents is only a small part of those already excavated. To the publications mentioned in note to § 422 are to be added: Strassmaier's *Babyl. Texte* continued, containing inscriptions of the reigns of Nebuchadrezzar, Cyrus, Cambyses, and Darius I (1889–1893); PCT. IX (1898) by Hilprecht and Clay: business documents from Nippur of the time of Artaxerxes I. The last named is of great palæographic value. It also contains transliterated and translated specimens, and a concordance of proper names, with an introduction. For the general reader the most instructive discussions are those of Kohler and Peiser in *Babyl. Vorträge* and in a series of essays issued by them (1890 ff.) in which, among other things, an attempt is made to show that many of the ideas of Roman law proceed from Babylonia. Fragments of old Babylonian laws of the age of Chammurabi are published and translated with commentary by Meissner in BA. III, 493–523. KB. IV, *Texte juridischen und geschäftlichen Inhalts*, is a selection of documents

most studied and are best understood belong to the Chaldæan epoch, with which we are now occupied, and the early Persian immediately following. Taken altogether they bear telling testimony to the antiquity, permanence, and complexity of the Babylonian business and juridical systems. A few points may be instanced to show what the Hebrews had to learn in adapting themselves to the necessities of settled life in their eastern home. Notice, on the one side, the entire absence of any system of credit in ancient Israel. A debt was the sign of helpless poverty (cf. § 575). If interest was to be paid, it was apt to be ruinous usury, so that all taking of interest was forbidden by the lawgivers. The only kind of security for a loan was the giving of a pledge, either by the debtor or by a friend in his behalf. The non-payment of a debt involved, as a rule, the enslavement of the debtor or his children. These semi-barbarous conditions were naturally both effect and cause of social instability (§ 584 ff.).

§ 1323. Now let us turn to Babylonian rule and procedure. Among this people the primitive conception that the creditor had a claim upon the person of the debtor, while leaving traces in the current forms of stipulation,[1] was superseded by the view that the creditor was entitled simply to the money due, along with interest or a fine for persistent non-payment. The borrower or debtor might have a credit with an agent who could settle on his behalf. On these principles there was developed a system of financial concerns, which to a commercial agency added the essential functions of our modern banks. Extraordinary care was taken to secure from any subsequent claim the

---

of all periods transliterated and translated by the competent hand of Peiser. Along with them should be read the treatise of V. Marx, "Die Stellung der Frauen in Babylonien" in B.A. IV, 1–77 (1899) with remarks appended by Delitzsch. L. Demuth and E. Ziemer give transliterations and translations with notes of one hundred texts of the times of Cyrus and Cambyses in B.A. III, 393–492 (1898). See also Sayce, *Babylonians and Assyrians, Life and Customs* (1899), chs. vi and vii.

[1] See Kohler in Peiser's *Babylonische Vorträge*, p. xxxiv.

debtor once freed from legal obligation. The rate of interest, usually twenty per cent per annum, was fixed if not by law at least by usage. It was slightly greater than that of Athens in the time of Demosthenes. Withdrawal from bargains, and business agreements generally, was made a matter of peculiar hardship. Nothing speaks more clearly for the business seriousness of this great people than the formal deprecation of bad faith by the parties to any sort of contract. In earlier times the curse of the gods was denounced upon the covenant-breaker. Later, a binding statement was frequently added in the instrument to the effect that the agreement would not be reversed. When, however, the contract was for any reason annulled, the dissident party paid at a fixed rate of interest for his release. The strict observance of these principles contributed as much as anything else to the maintenance of Babylonian domestic institutions through all political and dynastic changes.

§ 1324. Babylonia being an agricultural country, a large proportion of these business documents are deeds of sale or notes of hand relative to products of the soil. Corn, dates, date-wine, and onions are mentioned with special frequency. Very often a tenant pays the rent of his land in kind, according to a minute specification of the amount made in advance of the harvest. Sometimes there is merely an obligation to furnish a certain quantity of food or drink at a stated time. Cattle also figure in the contracts. A plantation may be mortgaged as security for the payment of a certain amount of its yield during a given year. Cultivated and waste lands on the banks of a canal are leased for a long term of years [1] with the buildings erected thereupon. Trained oxen with their implements of irrigation are hired,[2] along with a quantity of barley-seed.

---

[1] Sixty years in PCT. IX, nr. 48 (§ 1308. note).
[2] By three brothers for three years in PCT. IX, nr. 49, transliterated and translated, p. 39.

§ 1325. Such was the school for business training afforded to the Hebrews in captivity, as they gradually adapted themselves to their new surroundings and their proper employments, as they became assimilated in outward conditions to the native population, and began to compete successfully with those rivals when their business standing was once established. Their submission to those exacting requirements which for ages had closed the way to every talent except energy and educated skill, and had made difficult the acquiring of sudden wealth or unlawful gain, was itself a priceless and essential moral discipline. We must think of them not as unwilling guests or as transient occupants of the land, but as having at length followed the saving counsel of their martyred friend, to seek homes for themselves in the country of their exile, and to aid in its development and prosperity (§ 1168).

§ 1326. A decisive change in the condition of most of the exiles was made when they passed from slavery into freedom. The system of Babylonian slavery was, as we have seen, favourable to such an attainment. Special features seem to have been particularly helpful: for instance, the custom of apprenticing slaves for a fixed term of years to masters of one trade or another (§ 1280). The conditions were specified with great exactness, with a heavy fine for either party who should break the agreement.[1] We learn from this usage how the owner was eager to increase the value to himself of his human property.

---

[1] An instructive Babylonian contract of the time of Cyrus — the continuation of the social régime now under consideration — is explained by Demuth in BA. iii, 418 f. A certain lady binds over her slave to a master-weaver for the term of five years, she to feed and clothe the apprentice during that period. If the master fails to teach him properly within this time, he is to make good the deficiency by paying what the slave would otherwise have earned by his toil. A half-mina (about $22) is the penalty on either side for breach of the contract. Similar documents are published (*ibid.* p. 420–422) relating to apprenticeship to other occupations, one of which is that of a stone-cutter, the term in this instance being four years.

But the advantages to the slave were equally evident. Among these were the chances of his bettering his estate after he should become master of the trade.

§ 1327. We may thus see in the business and juridical systems of the Babylonians a moral agent of great value, working gradually but surely among the exiles, promoting their self-respect and ambition, and their advancement generally. That we may better estimate its actual influence, certain observations should be made at this point. First, all classes of the colonists were not equally benefited by these Babylonian institutions. The sequel shows that while many Hebrews rose to influence and dignity very many also remained dependent or servile. It was apparently this class that furnished most of the population of Jerusalem under the Persians. Again, such a moral education must be conceived of as affecting the Hebrews not merely during the Babylonian but in the Persian period. Certainly the most substantial of the Hebrew people remained in Babylonia after the conquest by Cyrus, and it was they who gave to the restored Jewish community for the first two centuries its moral as well as material backing.

§ 1328. Further, while such moral improvement as was effected by Babylonian influence was indispensable to the progress of Israel, the influence thus extended was not of itself a thorough-going instrument of reform. Veracity and honesty in business are rather an essential stage or condition in the saving of a people than a means of its salvation. The followers of Confucius are, it is true, much more likely to be christianized than those of Mohammed, for the reason that moral teaching pure and simple is better than theological teaching pure and simple; but the morality of the Confucian theory and practice has not saved China morally. What Israel learned from Babylonia helped it towards larger and truer views of the practical duties of life, and a wider and juster conception of the world and of its own place in the world's future. Beyond this, as a moral environment, its educative influence was not directly beneficial.

§ 1329. How then were the exiles otherwise affected by what they saw and heard in Babylonia? There were certain Babylonian institutions noxious in themselves which yet afforded a wholesome discipline to the Hebrew aliens. These were vitally bound up with the religion of the country, and they told upon the religious as well as the moral sentiments of the colonists. This twofold relation was at once the danger and the safeguard of Israel. The chief sources of peril were sexual immorality and idolatry. Within the sphere of the latter, as being closely akin to false worship, we may include magical superstition for which Babylonia was notorious, and which had already played a part in Hebrew social and religious history (§ 858, 1199).

§ 1330. Israel's chief safeguard against licentiousness was the religion of Jehovah. It was so foreign to the community of Jehovah's people that unchaste men and women were called "strange" or illegitimate. This notion was intensified by the direct encouragement and patronage of sexual indulgence by the most influential of foreign religions. The true religious teachers in Israel also made it a social evil as being a sin against one's neighbour (Ex. xx. 17). Sexual vice is generally but little restrained except when it is held to be not merely wrong but irreligious. Neither regard for the interests of society, nor philosophical reasoning as to its essential hurtfulness, can greatly avail anywhere against the impetuosity of passion. There is in truth but one all-sufficient and universal reason why unchastity is wicked — that it is a form of selfishness, and always involves a disregard of the rights of our fellow-beings. Even the least frequent offender must fairly admit that one at least of the participants is degraded or depreciated. This of necessity involves a lack of chivalry on the part of the other, and finally his moral self-surrender. But it is only under the influence direct or indirect of religion that a saving regard for our fellow-mortals is awakened and maintained. We may ascribe such regard to a "religion of humanity" when we will. But in the history of human society the restraining power has been found at its strongest and purest in the religion of the Bible. Proof is furnished by the career of the Hebrew people themselves. That unchastity was very prevalent in Israel up to the Exile is shown partly by the testimony of protesting prophets (as far as Ez. xxxiii. 26) and partly by the prevalence of "strange" religious rites of which such a form of immorality was an essential and constant feature (cf. Deut. xxiii. 18). After the Exile, when the noxious cults had ceased to prevail, little complaint is heard.

§ 1331. At least one form of immorality was guarded against with special care by the Babylonians. Adultery on the part of the wife was, from the days of the earliest to those of the latest legislation, punished with death, yet desertion of the wife by the husband entailed merely the payment of a reasonable money compensation.[1] There was also a certain discrimination in old Hebrew law, according to which an adulterer was not punished for the offence against his own wife, but for that against the injured husband (see Deut. xxii. 22 ff.). Indeed, there was not much theoretical difference in this sphere of jurisprudence throughout the ancient East. All the more emphasis must accordingly be laid upon the moral and religious training of the chosen people.

§ 1332. Wifely fidelity was thus well conserved in Babylonia. But, on the other hand, prostitution was

---

[1] See V R. 25, 1-7 *ab* (AL[3], p. 131) for early Babylonian usage (cf. Delitzsch in BA. IV, 85 f.), and for the time of Nebuchadrezzar II, see the marriage contract published by Strassmaier, and explained by Marx, BA. IV, 7. In the former instance the unfaithful wife was to be thrown into a river or canal, and the husband to pay a half-mina of silver; in the latter the wife was to be slain with an iron dagger, and the husband to pay six silver minas.

extensive and fashionable. In the first place, it was indirectly but greatly promoted by the social system. One of the most numerous classes of the contract tablets are the marriage covenants,[1] in which the principal matter is the settlement of the amount of the dowry with strict engagements for its payment under carefully stipulated penalties in view of possible withdrawal. Marriage was thus seldom a matter of sentiment. The consequences in the depreciation of female virtue were what they have been everywhere else where marriage has been made a convenience. Again, in the cities of Babylonia prostitution was encouraged by a religious sanction, which also gave countenance and character to the usage, even when it was carried on professionally and publicly[2] apart from the associations of religion. But when such indulgences took the aspect of sacrifices to the goddess of Nature (cf. § 1188 f.). they were immensely promoted by official patronage. The fees received by the female votaries as servant-maids of their respective temples were handed over to the sacred treasury and augmented the priestly revenues. It has, indeed, been generally believed upon the statement of Herodotus that every Babylonian woman was obliged once in her life to appear in the temple of Ishtar and play the rôle of the professional votary of the goddess.[3] But a slight acquaintance with Babylonian life would show any one the absurdity of this belief. Such

---

[1] See especially Marx in BA. IV, 13–39.

[2] Those who pursued their vocation on the public streets (see V R. 25, 7, 8, cd) were still regarded as sacred prostitutes, just as in the instance recorded in Gen. xxxviii. 14 ff., where the fee of a kid indicates the association with the impure goddess (cf. Dillmann on v. 17). From the two following lines in V R. it would seem that such persons were eligible for marriage. The word used is the same as that in Gen. xxxviii. 21 (see § 1190). But all the names applied to prostitutes in Assyrian, unlike the Hebrew זונה, were given to them in their character of religious devotees.

[3] See Her. I, 199. It may seem strange that Herodotus, who had been in Babylon, could have been so grossly deceived. But he was not allowed (as an alien) to visit the interior of the shrines (I, 183), and indeed he has very little to say of the sacred mysteries generally.

compulsory degradation is inconsistent with what we know of the position accorded to woman in Babylonia. The assertion has not a particle of monumental evidence to support it.[1] But that it had credence in its time serves to show how far the custom of which it was a caricature had been carried in wealthy, luxurious, and devout Babylonia.

§ 1333. Of such abuses the Hebrews had known enough and more in the home-land (§ 1190). But their point of view was now different, and the system itself was not the same. For although the indulgence of lust in the name of religion was sometimes permitted at local shrines, or even in the central sanctuary, the practice was thought of by the people at large as either a phase or an abuse of the national worship. Here, however, it appeared to be the direct outgrowth of an alien religion, a religion, moreover, which flaunted itself everywhere as the badge and boast of their conquerors. The system came to be a direct demonstration of the baleful effect of the worship of alien gods, since in Babylonia immorality seemed to be made the special property of the state and of the state religion.

§ 1334. Such a wholesome revulsion of sentiment was in its measure both cause and effect of an inward revolt against the Babylonian religion, which led finally to a renunciation of non-Israelitish worship generally. For the Hebrews in Palestine were still followers of Jehovah, even while they joined in the political recognition of the supremacy of the gods of Assyria and Babylonia or had resort in times of extreme distress to Canaanitic superstition (§ 1183). Above all, their daily life in the home-land had been largely made up of religious usages whose dominant motive was the acknowledgment of Jehovah by prayer and sacrifice. Here not only the objects but the forms and modes of worship were entirely changed. They saw

---

[1] On the contrary, many extant contracts imply freedom from such reproach on the part of those offered in marriage.

the religion of their conquerors enthroned in its undisputed realm. They were unable either to understand or to participate in its complicated ritual; and were at the same time cut off from that observance of their own rites and ceremonies, which had been the habit, and, with all its abuses, the inspiration of their lives.

§ 1335. Strictly speaking, we must regard the conditions just spoken of as not causes but occasions. The main influence was still as ever the prophetic teaching. And even now, had prophetic direction been absent, those very impressions would have led not to an exclusive faith in Jehovah, but to a state of practical godlessness, which would ultimately have resulted in an absorption into the Chaldæan religion. But here everything favoured the cause of the nation's true God. The testimony of his advocates in the past was on record. The gathered literature of Israel, which now at length came to have a sacred character as the relic and symbol of a national hope and purpose, appealed to minds and consciences which were formerly closed to it through perversion or indifference. What struck most powerfully was that which was most relevant. The protests against idolatry, the denunciations and appeals of Amos. Hosea, Isaiah, and Micah, the commands and proclamations of Deuteronomy (vi. 4; vii. 9), now fell upon attentive ears; and along with the written went the living word proclaimed by the living voice.

§ 1336. The preachers were, in the first generation of the Exile, disciples of Jeremiah with Ezekiel himself and his followers. In the second period others came forward, of a new and larger school (§ 1401 ff.). And never did preachers have a better text. The labourers at the close of the day, wearied by servile toil, and sore with the galling sense of loss and a broken destiny, were in themselves a challenge to the prophets to take up their parable.[1] The whole situa-

---

[1] Notice that in Ezekiel the exiles are represented as being willing to listen to the words of the prophet, though at first they would give no heed (iii. 7) and complained that he spoke in figures (xx. 49). Significantly

tion compelled inquiry. The supreme calamity had fallen. The earlier captives were not restored as had been hoped, and the *coup de grâce* had been given to their country in the captivity of their brethren. They were given leave to live in a strange land; but nearly all that made life worth the living was gone, — home and the home-land, the scenes and associations of earlier life, temple, altars, the very means and motive of religion. It became a question whether indeed they had or had ever had a God worthy of their regard. The gods of Babylonia might be monstrous and strange, but they were at least gods that could help their followers. What had Jehovah done for his people in their hour of need?

§ 1337. This dilemma was the opportunity of the prophets, who had now become pastors and watchmen for souls (Ez. ii. 17 ff.; xxxiii. 2 ff.). The case of the common man was this. He had thought of his Jehovah as a god of Israel not merely in the national but in the local sense. Even the first band of exiles, in expecting restoration to Palestine (§ 1169), looked forward to coming again under his direct protection. After the second captivity the whole colony thought of Jehovah as still being in Palestine, where indeed an attempt was made to continue his worship (§ 1244). But this was a vague and disheartening belief. Their teachers must now make them know and feel that their own God was in Babylonia, indeed more really in Babylonia than in Judah. But could it be so? Could a deity dwell where he could not be worshipped, on an alien and hostile soil? Yes, he dwells wherever his presence is felt. And he could prove his presence first of all through the sense of his power. But if he had been as powerful as the gods of Babylon, would his people have been vanquished and exiled? This was the old inveterate enigma, and now was the time to resolve it. Yes, for

---

they are described just after the fall of Jerusalem as being stirred by his words and eager to hear more of them (xxxiii. 30 f.) while the prospect of impressing them finally is more favourable (v. 33).

what if he had chosen to let his people be conquered and even dragged away from their own and his own land into this very region of the earth? Did he not do so? This present captivity was foretold by a succession of his professed spokesmen, whose authority was now vindicated by the event. One decisive step further was taken, in some such fashion as this: "Might not such a God, who evidently has an interest in Babylonia, wield some power also in Babylonia, or possibly even over Babylonia? Surely. Did not Jeremiah, whom we thought a fanatic and a traitor, always say that Nebuchadrezzar was the servant of Jehovah, to do his work in our punishment and banishment? So far, at least, he spoke truth. Here we are, as he foretold, without our temple, our altars, our vine and fig trees. But Jeremiah said, and Ezekiel says, that this is only part of his work, that in the fulness of time, but not at once, he will restore us to our land and our city. We have been forced to believe the harder part of the prediction. Perhaps the easier part may also come to pass. But only so if our God is here with us."

§ 1338. By some such reasonable process the sense of the truth of things spread in ever widening circles. And thus was gradually popularized in this remnant of Israel the notion of God's spirituality and omnipresence, of his moral supremacy, of his singular providence and purpose. Practically the exiles became monotheists, like the line of prophets whom they could now trace from Moses downwards. There was much difficulty and delay and bitter disappointment. Some perhaps were beyond the reach of persuasion; others through perversity or under false leadership lapsed into the idol-worship of the environment. How the seductions of Babylonian worship became more powerful within the very centre of the colony we learn from a later prophet of the Exile (see Isa. xl. 20 f.; xliv. 12–20). The process of education was slow and gradual, but therefore all the surer and more thorough.

§ 1339. This popular enlightenment on the vital question of true and false deities and the activity and power of the God of Israel, was monumental in the history of religion as the first example of the influence of "Scripture" upon a whole community. Progress having thus begun, an advance was made in actual religious knowledge and in the religious life. Prophetic reflection and teaching tended now, as before, to two great ends of Revelation,— a knowledge of the true relation of the individual soul to God, and a right conception of the character of God himself and his relation to his people and to the world. The former, which concerns us most at this point, was prepared for mainly through personal trial, which brought the sufferers near to God for help. The earlier stages in this training in spiritual individualism have been already traced (§ 607 ff., 987 f.. 1009 ff., 1025, 1204). It now remains to indicate some of the ways in which the experiences of exile promoted the sense of a personal relation to Jehovah.

§ 1340. The old popular conception is familiar to us. The community, that is to say the nation as a whole, claimed Jehovah as its protector and gave Him homage and service. The ties that bound God and people together were the national modes of outward worship, tending to uniformity and finally unified in the reform of Josiah. Thus Deuteronomy, while promoting individualism by inculcating holiness towards God, actually prejudiced it by the concentration of worship and the wide extension of a single type of ritual. Moreover, the renewal of the covenant in Deuteronomy was for and with the nation as a whole. However we may deplore the abandonment of the "book of direction" by the successors of Josiah, we must find some compensation in the march of events that shattered its practical logic while they strengthened its spiritual lessons and appeals. For if Jehovah was the God of his people in Babylonia, their relation to him must be different from that assumed in all previous current conceptions. Here they were not a people at all except in precarious continuity with an eventful past. They were scattered in broken and helpless bands of captives, with none of the means or appliances of worship indispensable to the winning of God's favour and inseparable from his self-revelation. And yet He had shown that He was with them still (§ 1337). And having felt his presence among them even there, they could not but reflect upon the new situation. The thought of each serious man was perhaps such as this: "The nation is gone: then Jehovah must be something more than the God of the nation. The tribes, clans, families, are all broken up: then He is not merely a God of tribes and families. Then He must be my own God." Many a poor soul, in its baffled longings for the courts of Jehovah, doubtless at length was able to say in the spirit of the psalmist (Ps. xliii. 3 f.) what he could not have said before his banishment:—

> "Send forth thy light and thy truth;
> Let them lead me;
> Let them bring me to thy holy hill
> And to thy tabernacles;
> Then will I go to the altar of God,
> To God, the gladness of my joy."

§ 1341. This idea of God's direct relation to the individual soul, like that of his spirituality (§ 1338), was nothing new in Israel. Did not the prophets in ever increasing measure realize it and live by it? But the prophets were always singular. It was the work of the Exile out of their gold to make current coin. This coin, to be sure, had much alloy in it from the soil of Canaan and Babylonia. One cannot but think of Jeremiah, who first gave articulate utterance to the doctrine of individual responsibility (xxxi. 30). We have just spoken of the renewal of the national covenant (§ 1340). We remember how Jeremiah was summoned to proclaim it to his people (Jer. xi. 2). And we have seen how out of sympathy he was with form and ritual (§ 1068). It is, therefore, in keeping with his character and ideals that he should conceive of a new and profounder spiritual relation. "See, the days are coming, saith Jehovah, when I shall make a new covenant with the house of Israel and the house of Judah. . . . I will put my law in their inmost being, and in their heart will I write it[1] . . ." (xxxi. 31 ff.). Such a thought was not transcended by any successor until the days of the Christ, who also brought about its fulfilment.

§ 1342. Yet when Ezekiel elaborates the idea of individual responsibility (§ 1204 f.), his vivid and ample illustration makes a weightier impression than the brief declaration of his master.[2] The sense of God's nearness to the several members of his community ("all souls are mine," v. 4) and of their consequent responsibility, seems more sure and real in the concrete presentation of the later prophet. Practically Ezekiel did his best work for his own time and people in his much-needed application of this doctrine, in asserting and reiterating (ch. xxxiii.) that the children should not suffer for the sins of the fathers, that every man should "die" through his own sins, or "live" through his own righteousness. The notion was natural to men not yet half emerged from tribalism that the solidarity of the family from the first ancestor downward involved the inheritance of sin and its punishment. And now that the acme of suffering and chastisement had been reached, they could not but regard their lot as the consequence both of their own offences and of those of their fathers. However imperfectly Ezekiel may have conceived of the actual consequences to men of the sins of the past, he ranks high as a friend of humanity in helping to rid men of a belief in imputed guilt and predestined doom, — the awful bugbear of ancient tribalistic superstition and of modern scholastic theology. That he concerned himself so greatly

---

[1] Cf. Ps. xl. 8 (EV.). This psalm is largely a reflex of the experiences of Jeremiah.

[2] Cf. Skinner, *The Book of Ezekiel*, p. 144 f.

with this question of the moral life and fate of men betrays his intense sympathy with his people, intellectual and spiritual. He was, perhaps, the first prophet to whom was committed, in the ecclesiastical sense, "the cure of souls;"[1] and it was the Exile that gave him his parish.

§ 1343. Yet it was inevitable that Ezekiel should work more for the community than for the individual, not merely because he was the child of his time and environment, but also by virtue of native and professional bias. His sympathy with Jeremiah in moral teaching, and his unlikeness to him in intellectual tastes and habits, we have already indicated (§ 1174). No better suggestion can be given of the dominant purpose of his life and ministry than to say that it was the continuation and adaptation of Deuteronomy. What Josiah and his men did in their time and measure for the later kingdom of Judah, Ezekiel sought to effect for the exiled community. His aims were practical and definite. He knew that without rites and ceremonies at holy places his Israel could not permanently survive. But he had to labour in an ideal region, for the essential conditions of the historic ritual were now wholly wanting.

§ 1344. This spirit in Ezekiel is shown in a deference to legal prescriptions and ritual obligations, such as the earlier prophets had not displayed (iv. 14; v. 11; xviii. 6; xx. 12; xxiii. 38 *et al.*). His ritualistic proclivities come out most clearly in the latest section of his book (chs. xl.–xlviii.). There he describes the restored and purified theocracy; and he does not refer to its moral and spiritual basis, but dwells upon its constitution and its modes of worship. He describes the new temple (xl.–xliii.) with its courts and gates and chambers (ctr. Jer. iii. 16). This is the single sanctuary of Deuteronomy. But he goes beyond Deuteronomy in restricting the priesthood not to the Levites, but to the family of Zadok alone (ch. xliv.). He

---

[1] Renan, *Histoire du peuple d'Israel*, III, 395.

allots lands to the priests near the temple (ch. xlv.). The civil ruler is to make it his main business to look after the sacrifices (ch. xlvi.). He also prescribes for the observance of feasts, and for a lustration of the temple at the opening of the year (ch. xlv. 18 f.).[1] And he divides up the Holy Land into parallel sections from the Jordan to the sea (ch. xlvii. 13–xlviii. 29).[2]

§ 1345. This vision of the new Jerusalem was seen in the twenty-fifth year of the prophet's exile, and his only subsequent utterance (xxix. 17 ff.) was made two years later (570 B.C.). His ministry thus almost covers the earlier half of the Captivity. At its close the moral and religious bent and tendency of the exiles were pretty well determined. Temptations to idolatry had now done their worst, though they were ever present (§ 1338). The testing and fashioning of character was a long and complex process. What Ezekiel says of the condition of his people comes in the form of objurgations, and is to be understood as representing the most unfavourable view. As helpful influences, we must count not merely the slow-acting moral forces that entered into their discipline (§ 1314 ff.), but also the permanent elements of the old religion. These now became doubly valuable. The sabbath could not be made a sacred feast-day; but it could still be a day of convocation, with a more direct and heartfelt worship. The priest might not present the worshipper's offering to Jehovah; but a richer blessing came from an answer to direct personal prayer. While the priest, as a living personal influence, became less and less, the prophet became more and more, till the acme of prophecy was reached in the

---

[1] That is, on the first of Nisan, in conformity with Babylonian usage. The old Hebrew year began in autumn (Ex. xxiii. 16; xxxiv. 22). This usage continued to the end of the kingdom, as we learn from the fact that the feast of the Passover was celebrated in the same year as that in which "the book of direction" was found (§ 852). The post-exilic date of Ex. xii. 2 may be inferred from this fact alone.

[2] Comp. Marti, *Geschichte der israel. Religion* (1897), p. 204 ff.

Second Isaiah. While the living prophetic word was presumably also present in the middle years of the Exile, the written word was prized, and was read and expounded also in the sabbath assemblies.

§ 1346. Too much can scarcely be made of the sabbath of the Exile. Whatever we may think of its earlier observance,[1] it certainly became henceforth a more than theoretical or formal holy day. It was also a Babylonian institution. In this possibly lay a peril, but one not so great as we might imagine; for Israel was cut off from its celebration as an alien rite, while the moral force of its weekly recognition by the ruling people of the world remained unaffected. It is quite possible that it was recognized as having been a sacred season common to the two peoples in remotest antiquity. As the Hebrews necessarily conformed their calendar to that of the people of the land (cf. § 1344), they may also have adopted the same sabbath days, the seventh, fourteenth, twenty-first, and twenty-eighth of the month. The Assyrian and Babylonian sabbath seems to have been practically a fast-day,[2]

---

[1] In Hosea ii. 13 (EV. 11) the sabbath appears as a day of "enjoyment." This accords with its statutory recognition as a "breathing-spell" (שׁבת, Ex. xxiii. 12). The idea of rest and refreshing is, however, secondary, as the root שׁבת properly means to "cease" (cf. the Assyrian usage as synonym of *gamāru*). This original sense of "quitting," came naturally to be applied to cessation from normal activity. The proscription of regular work (Ex. xvi. 4 f. JE.) was extended to trading (Am. viii. 5). Like the new moon celebration, also a day of enjoyment (Hos. l.c.), it became a time of religious gathering where oracles might be consulted (2 K. iv. 23).

[2] The essential facts regarding this sabbath are the following: The word itself (*Šapattu*) occurs, so far, but once (in II R. 16, 32 *ab*) in the Assyrio-Babylonian monuments. It is explained there as "the day for quieting the heart," a common phrase for propitiating (the gods). But in IV R. 32 there is given a hemerology of the month Elul (September), in which it is said that on the days above mentioned (and also on the nineteenth) the "shepherd of many peoples" (that is, the king as representing the people, like the "prince" in Ez. xlv. 22 ff.) should eat no flesh roasted in the coals, and no food that had come in contact with fire, should not change his clothes nor wear a white garment, or yoke (?) a

whose observance was guarded with extraordinary strictness. This may help to explain the fact that during and after the Exile the Hebrew sabbath was also more rigorously observed as a day of rest and abstinence.

§ 1347. But the Babylonian sabbath was of importance to the Hebrews mainly because it afforded them the needed opportunities for the cultivation of the religious life. Their religion, being of a social character, was chiefly promoted by stated meetings. As slaves, the greater number of them had no opportunity of assembling either in large or small groups for any formal purpose, except when leisure was granted to them in consequence of general social and industrial usage. Now if the employing and employed classes both observed the same day of rest, the opportunity came of itself. The sabbath meetings would thus be the chief occasion of religious development.

§ 1348. The main determining factor was the felt needs of the community. In view of past failures and present distress, the ruin of Jerusalem and the banishment and shame, the former mirth of the sacred feasts would give place to sighing and weeping. The situation and the mood itself are set forth by one of the surviving worshippers in immortal verse (Ps. cxxxvii.):—

---

chariot, or speak with authority (that is, officially); that no seer should give an oracle in a secret place; that no physician should minister (bring his hand) to a sick person. Each of these days is described as "baleful" (*limnu*). But this apparently means that it is unlucky to do any ordinary work on that day. We have here a Pharisaic strictness of observance. Though the word "sabbath" is not used, it is plain that it is intended. This is shown by its hebdomadal recurrence as well as by the character of its prohibitions. So far only the ancient Hebrews and Assyrio-Babylonians are proved to have had the sabbath, though the new moon was celebrated by all the Semites. The current view that the Hebrews learned the custom from the Canaanites (*e.g.*, Smend, *Alttest. Religionsgeschichte*, p. 139) is a mere assumption. The week of seven days was based upon the four phases of the moon; but the religious use of the seventh day is quite distinct from this division. This institution of the sabbath is the strongest single evidence of a close connection between the earliest Hebrews and Babylonia.

> "By the stream of Babylonia there we sat down;
> We wept, too, as we thought of Zion.
> On the willows in the midst thereof
> We hung up our lyres.
> For there our captors asked of us words of song,
> And our spoilers[1] words of mirth:
> 'Sing to us of the songs of Zion.'
> How shall we sing Jehovah's songs on an alien soil?"

Such days of assembly were days of fasting, humiliation, and prayer. Every religion takes its complexion from the temper and circumstances of its first worshippers; and the Jewish, as distinct from the old Hebrew type of religion, owes much of its sombre aspect and plaintive tone to the habits and associations of the exiles in Babylonia. Such a tone and temper have been, perhaps, more of a gain than a loss to Judaism. Nothing binds men together like the remembrance of common suffering kept alive by a perpetual memorial. From the Exile came forth the Synagogue.

§ 1349. Thus were laid among the exiles the foundations of a new religious community. What threatened to destroy the kingdom of Jehovah proved the best possible means of its restoration. The sifting process was long, of which Amos had spoken (ix. 9); and after much chaff had fallen, to be absorbed by the "alien soil," not all of the grain that remained was found good and worthy. But the good was of the choicest known in all God's husbandry. Only the most strenuous and patient could endure the strain on faith and hope. Only the most ardent and loyal could hold to the promise of Jeremiah or be sustained by the visions of Ezekiel. But the work in heart and conscience was done as never before or after in Israel's history. Self-searching, reflection, intrepid devotion, reached forth after a God who was not very far off, and found him to be nearer at hand than he had ever been in the temple or by the altars of Jerusalem.

---

[1] A slight emendation (שׁ for ש) after the Targum.

Moral steadfastness, always the most authentic warrant of inner convictions, here made assurance doubly sure. As the resultant of the working of these forces of mind and soul, two great facts were projected clear and full before the spiritual gaze. There was an Israel left, a people of Jehovah; and Jehovah was here among his people. Thus the great word of Jeremiah was being fulfilled (§ 1341).

CHAPTER II

HEBREW LITERATURE OF THE EXILE

§ 1350. The Exile was perhaps the period of greatest literary activity in the history of Israel. It certainly made a literary epoch of unequalled importance. This intellectual movement was in part due to inner development, in part to the effect of the environment. In the first place, with the passing away of the kingdom, there arose a desire to collect and arrange the records of the past, as well as the scattered fragments of its literature. Then came the work of the reforming school, which reasserted itself in the Exile after its policy had been vindicated by events. In its interest, earlier documents were edited, remodelled, and supplemented, so as to bring them into accord with the teachings of history and providence. Of spontaneous literary work, that of projecting a new ritual for the future restored Israel, was of epoch-making significance. Nor did the living words of prophecy fail to find a permanent record.

§ 1351. Such inner impulses to written composition were promoted by exceptional outward circumstances. Men of the priestly class, who had shown so much literary activity in the preceding age (§ 1017), were now without official occupation. At the same time, the interest of the priests in the edification of their people was as great as ever, and the business of informing them by tongue or pen would flourish by the mere conversion of energy. Possibly the strongest external influence was that of the people and institutions of Babylonia. The gradual diffusion of technical education by means of the employments of Babylonian life (§ 1301 ff.) was of itself a general preparation. A special incentive was the habit of writing, almost universal among the people of the land, and necessarily made general among the Hebrews as they came to be engaged in varied business. Add to this the effect upon a gifted people of a literary atmosphere and of a great literature of immemorial antiquity. The Hebrew literature of the Exile shows many tokens of Babylonian influence direct and indirect. Such are a more copious and systematic form and style of composition, the use of Babylonian imagery, allusions to Babylonian scenery and national customs, the employment of characteristic Babylonian phrases, and a larger view of the world and of the scope of providence and history.

§ 1352. Special emphasis must be laid upon two of the ways in which Hebrew literature was affected by the Exile, and chiefly through Babylonian influence. In the first place, distinctness and regularity of form were given to Hebrew composition. No production of an earlier time, except the prophecy of Amos, is marked by symmetry of structure. The works of Hosea, Micah, Isaiah, Zephaniah, Nahum, Habakkuk, and, to a large extent, Jeremiah, have all come to us in a greater or less degree unshapen and in disorder.[1] Single passages may be and often are models of choice rhetoric. Sanity and energy of thought, and the constant pressure of the realities of the outer and inner life of men, ensured the coherence and reasonableness of each single discourse. But there is not the coördination and concurrence of several parts, the continuity of purpose, the cumulative effect, which mark a considerable work of art. We do not expect from any Hebrew writer the sustained logical argument or the elaborate design that

---

[1] The abruptness of the transitions thereby entailed creates as much difficulty in the critical analysis as does the absence of the names of the authors.

distinguish the Greek philosopher or tragedian. But largeness and comprehensiveness of conception, with due adaptation of auxiliary details, were not beyond the scope of the Hebrew orator and poet.

§ 1353. The distinction in style and method between the earlier and the later is felt immediately when we observe the plan and system of Ezekiel, who was after all only mechanically an artist; or a little later, when we are confronted with the majestic unity and triumphal progress of the Second Isaiah; or, later still, when we follow the profound moral reasoning and internal cogency of the book of Job. It was not the habit of earlier writers or speakers to arrange their works artistically.[1] They sometimes edited their own separate discourses by writing them down and condensing them, as Baruch edited what was committed to him of the utterances of Jeremiah; but the disposition of their complete works was left to other and later hands. That the book of Amos forms an exception shows either that he was a unique original artist, or that the matter of the book was rearranged after the Exile.[2]

§ 1354. Another literary effect of the Exile was the increased employment of artificial, or rather of indirect modes of description and instruction, especially of symbol, parable, and allegory. I need only instance the prevailing types of Ezekiel's discourses and of those of Zechariah, and that greatest personification in all literature, the Servant of Jehovah, in the Second Isaiah. Apart from the influences of environment (§ 1351), it is quite probable that banishment, national and personal, promoted in its measure this form of composition. Friedrich Schlegel has expressed

---

[1] Longer compositions with an historical framework (J and E) necessarily involved a plan suited to the general purpose, but this scarcely comes within the province of literary art. The original Deuteronomy certainly shows no definite progress in its arrangement of topics. Contrast its structure with the systematizing of P.

[2] H. J. Elhorst, *De profetie van Amos* (Leiden, 1900), claims for Amos an intermediate date, 638 to 621 B.C.

the opinion[1] that the prohibition of sensible images of the Deity fostered the employment of types and symbols in the Hebrew literature. We may go further and say that the same propensity was encouraged by the complete abstraction of the writers of the Exile from all the outward reminders of the faith and history of their people. How different were the visions of Ezekiel in Babylonia from the single vision of Isaiah in Jerusalem! Was it not through a similar subtle interaction of mind, spirit, and environment, that Dante the exile became the seer of the Middle Ages, and that Bunyan the prisoner composed the most realistic and effective of allegories?

§ 1355. The literary activity of the exiles resulted in (1) historical compilation; (2) ritual and legal prescription; (3) original or living prophecy; (4) sacred song. An intense occupation with the past history of Israel, was, like the changes in literary form above mentioned (§ 1352 ff.), in great measure the result of disassociation from the long-cherished life and scenes of Palestine. While there was, in a sense, no present for the nation, the past appeared all the more significant and imposing. Historical interest became more intelligently directed, as well as more intense, when the survival of Israel in its banishment was changed from longing to hope and from hope to certainty. The past must be viewed not merely as a great fact, but as a lesson; not merely as a discipline, but as a preparation. The humble dwelling of the scribe was changed from a study into a school. Thought and utterance shaped themselves by the ideals and obligations of a wider future.

§ 1356. The conception of Israel's history which had been formed during the evil reign of Manasseh, and which found expression in Deuteronomy, became crystallized into a religious dogma during the Exile. The code of Deuteronomy, now canonized by the fall of its despisers, was a

---

[1] *Geschichte der alten und neuen Litteratur* (1812), ch. ix. He remarks that a similar prohibition has produced a similar effect among the Mohammedans.

monumental proclamation that the one great offence of Israel had been the false worship of Jehovah and the combination of his service with that of alien gods. Already, before the Exile, this conception had apparently affected the treatment of the earlier literature. But now the whole previous history of Israel was revised and supplemented in accordance with this interpretation. So deep and strong was the impression of the evil wrought in the heart and life of the nation by idolatry and disloyalty to Jehovah that no room was left in the minds of the scribes for the consideration of any other cause. Hence chiefly the striking absence from the historical books of reference to the actual sins and crimes of the people or its leaders, apart from the worship of idols or of Jehovah Himself in an unlawful fashion.[1] We feel that the extreme but searching moral indictment of the prophets is truer to the life; and we turn to them with satisfaction from the stereotyped phrases in which the religious delinquencies of this and that period or ruler are catalogued in the historical books. Probably the mass of the Hebrew people could be moved in no other way. Being Hebrews, they were accustomed to hyperbole in all sorts and modes of discourse, and it was necessary to present what was obnoxious in such a way as would admit of no qualification or abatement. But the Deuteronomic editors went further in their definition of false worship. Since all religious rites were interdicted by Deuteronomy, except at Jerusalem, the test of the "rightness" of any reign was its conformity to the code.

§ 1357. It was upon these lines that the book (or, as we now have them, the books) of the Kings was revised and reconstructed. The obvious divisions of this work are: (1) the reign of Solomon, 1 K. i.–xi.;[2] (2) the concurrent reigns of the kings of Israel and Judah, 2 K. xii.–

---

[1] Cf. Montefiore, *Religion of the Ancient Hebrews* (Hibbert Lectures, 1892), p. 232 f.

[2] Chs. i. and ii. are a close continuation of Samuel.

xvii.; (3) the reigns of the surviving kingdom of Judah alone, 2 K. xviii.–xxv. As for Solomon, the chief distinction accorded to him is that of builder of the Temple, the act which fixed the central worship, while his own religious infidelity is not overlooked. In the second and third divisions a striking contrast of modes of treatment is to be noted. Since the Northern Kingdom was founded under the auspices of the symbolical worship of Jehovah, this is regarded as the primal apostasy. Hence it was made a standing phrase descriptive of every northern king without exception, that "he did evil in the sight of Jehovah," or "walked in the way of Jeroboam (son of Nebat) who made Israel to sin." Of many of the kings of Judah a similar condemnation is given. Eight of them are commended, yet of all of them except Hezekiah and Josiah it is said that they failed to remove the "high places."

§ 1358. The book of Kings brings a new feature into Hebrew historical writing, in that for the first time the sources of certain facts are regularly mentioned. These are for the first division "the book of the acts of Solomon" (1 K. xi. 41); for the Northern Kingdom "the book of the Chronicles of the kings of Israel"; and for the Southern, "the book of the Chronicles of the kings of Judah."[1] The natural supposition is that allusion is made to works already existing, which would thus seem to be a digest of the events of the reigns of the two sets of kings and of their principal actions.[2] It is possible, but not so probable, that the official annals of the kingdom are intended. However, it was from them that the information was ultimately obtained.

---

[1] I need scarcely remind any of my readers that these books are not to be confounded with the canonical books of Chronicles.

[2] How little there is in Kings of "history" in the modern sense is seen for example in the account of Azariah (Uzziah), the most influential king that ever reigned over Judah. Of his public life nothing whatever is said (2 Kings xv. 1–7), so that we get our knowledge of him from the much-decried Chronicles and the Assyrian inscriptions.

§ 1359. A second principal element in this work is a series of stories interrupting the skeleton-like record of the reigns of the kings. These recitals have mostly to do with the temple and its worship and the acts of the greatest of the prophets. They are not written in the compiler's own manner, nor, so far as we can judge, in the manner of his time. On all grounds we may assume that they formed part of compositions already existing. Thus we have in Kings abundant evidence of the continuance in both kingdoms of that narrative and biographical writing which characterized the early monarchy (§ 914 ff.).

§ 1360. The date of the composition of Kings cannot be fixed with absolute certainty.[1] That additions were made during the Exile is clear, and the prevailing opinion of critics now is that the work had two Deuteronomic redactors, the former doing his work about 600 B.C., and the other perhaps towards the end of the Exile. It is reasonable to suppose that the former completed his task with the account of the reformation of Josiah, and the latter concluded his with the story of Jehoiachin (2 K. xxv. 27–30). The authorship it is useless to conjecture. It is enough to say that the work was the product of a formal priestly-prophetic school, and that this was not (cf. § 1068) the school of Jeremiah.[2]

§ 1361. In the spirit of Deuteronomy a revision and readjustment were made of Deuteronomy itself, which was enlarged by the addition of chs. i.–iv., an historical, and v.–xi., a hortatory introduction; also of chs. xxvii., xxix., xxx.; chs. xxxi. to xxxiv. being added after the Exile (cf. § 847). Judges was made virtually as we have it,

---

[1] Passages such as 2 Kings viii. 22; xvi. 6 ("unto this day"), merely indicate that the compiler was not always careful about his method of quoting from his sources; for "this day" is there clearly not his day.

[2] Who was formerly held to have written the book! Even Driver (*Intr.*[6] p. 199) says that "the compiler was a man like-minded with Jeremiah." There was as much mental and moral kinship between them as there was between the priest Newman and the prophet Carlyle.

without the later addition of chs. xx., xxi. Something similar may be said of Samuel, whose Deuteronomic form is reached by taking away the Song of Hannah and ch. xxii. of the second book (§ 909), these being of later date.

§ 1362. For the ritual and ceremonial service of the future Israel (§ 1355) an important work was done by the composition of the so-called "Law of Holiness"[1] found in Lev. xvii.–xxvi. It consists mainly of ordinances relating to ceremonial cleanness, to the Sabbath, the great feasts, and the temple service. Its association with Deuteronomy is shown in its hortatory conclusion and its insistence upon a single central sanctuary. This is not quite so significant of its date as is its more striking resemblance to Ezek. xl.–xlviii. (§ 1344). Like Ezekiel's scheme, it goes beyond Deuteronomy by its minutiae of prescription, being thus intermediate between D and P in method and spirit. The chief interest is sacerdotal and ceremonial. We may assume that it was intended as a law-book for the new Jerusalem of Ezekiel, and written by a pupil of that priest-prophet in the latter half of the Exile.

§ 1363. Prophecy in the Exile has already been discussed for the first half of the period. Its continuation belongs to the closing years of the Babylonian monarchy, and the history of its literary treatment is in large part post-exilic. But a word must be said on the difficult yet pressing question of exilic Psalms. On the question of pre-exilic Psalms we have already spoken (§§ 605, 909). If we disabuse our minds of the notion that the Psalms in general were written for liturgical purposes, and acknowledge that the most original and vital of the sacred songs of Israel were, like the choicest hymns of every other country and time, the offspring of an intense and deep religious life, we shall see at once that no period of Israel's history was more likely to give rise to such

---

[1] A modern name, happily suggested by Klostermann, on the ground of the ruling idea of the work as given in Lev. xix. 2. As we have it, it is imbedded in the work of P. It is known mystically as H.

poems of the heart than was the Exile. Hence, to make as small a choice as possible, it may be conceded on internal grounds that at least Ps. xxii., li., lxix., lxxi., lxxxiv., cii. belong to this period of suffering and probation. Others, such as Ps. cxxvi. and cxxxvii., written in Palestine after the first Return, belong virtually to the same period.

CHAPTER III

THE CHALDÆAN DOMINION

§ 1364. The reign of Nebuchadrezzar was long and prosperous. His devotion to the material and spiritual development of his own proper country kept him from the ambition and the curse of Assyrian imperialism. Our interest in him as a ruler is, therefore, an interest in civilization and patriotism. His influence on the destiny and character of Israel, which was of more consequence to the world than all his other achievements combined, was an indirect consequence of this statesmanlike policy. Of his wars after the fall of Jerusalem in his eighteenth year (586 B.C.), we know but little, for reasons already given (§ 1053, note). There is no good reason to suppose that they were numerous. Those with Egypt and Tyre, which are of the greatest biblical interest, were certainly the most important of them.

§ 1365. The war with Egypt consisted of a series of intermittent campaigns. Its main motive was to make it impossible for Egypt to again seize upon Palestine and Syria. This war and also that with Tyre have a biblical importance in connection with the prophecies of Jeremiah and Ezekiel. This makes regrettable the absence of full information regarding them. The general situation, however, is clear enough. The twenty-sixth Egyptian dynasty, or that of Sais (§ 1030), as we have seen, had great commercial aims and enterprise, and sought to secure the trade of the Mediterranean. For the most part at least, a close alliance was maintained with Tyre, which placed its ships at the disposal of Egypt.¹ Tyre, being besides an ally of Judah in the revolt of Zedekiah, was besieged by Nebuchadrezzar in 585, just after the fall of Jerusalem. It sustained a blockade by land of thirteen years,² the besieging forces with all the ships they could muster (cf. § 681) not being able to cut off supplies by water. Egypt was also invaded while Pharaoh Hophra (Apries), the ally of Zedekiah, was still on the throne. An Egyptian inscription mentions that the Babylonian army overran Egypt as far as its southerly border at Syene (Assouan). Egypt, therefore, for a time was subject or, at least, tributary to Babylonia. The next ruler, Amasis, a general under Hophra, was made king by the native Egyptian troops in an uprising against the Greek and Carian mercenaries who were favoured by Hophra.³ At his ascension he would seem to have thrown off the Babylonian suzerainty, for the thirty-seventh year of Nebuchadrezzar, in which an expedition was made against Egypt (§ 1053, note), falls in 567, soon after the Egyptian revolution. This, however, was near the close of the Great King's reign, and there is no evidence from any source that the subjugation of Egypt was effected anew. Perhaps it was found that in the divided and weakened condition of that country there was little danger of another invasion of Asia.

§ 1366. The biblical prophecies regarding these events are lengthy and specific. Jeremiah's predictions, given in chs. xlvi. 13 ff., were uttered in view of the impending retreat of Pharaoh Necho[4] from Syria and Palestine before

---

[1] Herodotus (II, 161) asserts that Hophra marched against Sidon and fought a naval battle with Tyre. This must have taken place at the beginning of his reign, and hostile relations were only temporary.

[2] Josephus against Apion, i, 21.

[3] Herod. II, 163, 169.

[4] Noteworthy is the imitation of Isa. xxx. 7, gained by a slight change in the pointing of v. 17: Call the name of Pharaoh king of Egypt, "A noise, that lets the occasion pass" — in English phrase, "a blusterer that misses his chance" (see Giesebrecht on the passage).

the army of Nebuchadrezzar (cf. § 1089). Among other calamities, the destruction of Memphis (v. 19) and the capture of Thebes (v. 25 f.) are foretold. Briefer, but equally explicit, is the prediction at Tahpanhes in xliii. 10 ff. (cf. § 1255). Ezekiel discourses of Egypt and its fate in four chapters (xxix.–xxxii.), delivered just before and after the fall of Jerusalem, except the later brief prophecy (xxix. 17–21). The oracles are modelled upon the same general plan, the overthrow of Egypt and its king being set forth in all, but with a variety of detail. Striking figures are employed and elaborated: the crocodile of the Nile (xxix. 3 ff.; xxxii. 2 ff.), the lofty, cedar-like Assyria (xxxi. 2 ff.). The king of Babylon is the agent of destruction, but he is a mere passive instrument in Jehovah's hands (xxx. 10 ff., 24 ff.).[1] Very singular is the later prophecy above alluded to, which was delivered fifteen years after the latest of the others (cf. xxix. 17 with xxxii. 17). In it Egypt is promised to Nebuchadrezzar as a recompense for his failure to gain anything by his campaign against Tyre. Here the Great King is described plainly as a servant of Jehovah, to whom he was to look for his wages. It is the image of a mercenary soldier, whose pay depends upon his success.

§ 1367. In view of this latest oracle another series of prophecies is more remarkable still. These are directed against Tyre (chs. xxvi.–xxviii.) and Sidon (xxviii. 20–24). The first discourse was given toward the end of 586, the year of the fall of Jerusalem (xxvi. 1, 2); the other two are not dated, but belong to the same period. In ch. xxvi. a detailed description is given of the impending siege of the city by Nebuchadrezzar, of the capture of the suburbs, of the taking of the metropolis and the slaughter of its people, its utter destruction and perpetual desolation. In ch. xxvii. Tyre is represented as a splendid merchant

---

[1] For other points see the summary in Davidson's *Ezekiel* ("Cambridge Bible"), p. 210 ff. Note especially the concluding dirge (xxxii. 17–32), which Davidson calls "one of the most weird passages in literature."

vessel laden with the produce of all lands, and at last wrecked amid the lamentations of all the merchants and mariners of the world. In ch. xxviii. a lament is uttered over the fall of the ruler of Tyre, in spite of his sagacity, skill, wealth, and magnificence. Yet at the close of the thirteen years' siege [1] the prophet states plainly that Nebuchadrezzar gained nothing by his operations. This is perhaps the plainest instance in Scripture of the conditional character of prophetic prediction.[2] The prophet's secular learning was not displayed in vain; for ch. xxvii. gives us the fullest description of Phœnician vessels and commerce that has come to us from antiquity.

§ 1368. In 562 the greatest kingly career that Western Asia had known was ended by the death of Nebuchadrezzar. He passed away full of years and honours, leaving an empire which to all outward appearance might last for centuries. In less than a quarter of a century it went the way of the Assyrian. The tale, brief as it is, is well worth the telling. The motives of the catastrophe lie without as well as within Babylonia and its people. External assaults from the rising Aryan power might in any case have brought it about eventually, but it was accelerated by its own lack of inner cohesiveness and by misgovernment.

§ 1369. The successor of Nebuchadrezzar was his son Evil-Merodach (*Amel-Marduk*, "the man or servant of Merodach"). His reign lasted but two years. As we have no inscription from him as yet, we learn of him only from a brief biblical notice (2 K. xxv. 27), and from a sentence in Josephus which says, on the authority of Berossus, that he governed lawlessly and wantonly.[3] This does not well

---

[1] The siege ended in 572, and this final prophecy was given in 570.

[2] Not of "prophecy," as is usually said. "Conditional prophecy" is an unmeaning phrase. Observe, by the way, that even this latest expedition against Egypt, of whose preparation Ezekiel was aware in 570, did not bring great success to Nebuchadrezzar (§ 1365).

[3] ἀνόμως καὶ ἀσελγῶς (Against Apion, i. 20). Another allusion in *Ant.* x. 11. 2. merely repeats the biblical statement.

agree with the magnanimous deed ascribed to him in Kings. The liberation and honouring of Jehoiachin was of course only one of a number of similar actions. Perhaps, as has been suggested,[1] he was not very deferential to the dominant priestly party, to whom the harsh judgment is to be traced. At any rate his reign was very short, and had a tragic end. He was slain in a revolt headed by his sister's husband Neriglissar (*Nergal-šar-uṣur*, "Nergal protect the king!"), who naturally took his place upon the throne (560–556).

§ 1370. Neriglissar vied with his father-in-law[2] in building up Babylon, regulating the Euphrates, repairing the palaces and especially the temples. This, in fact, is the sum of what is known of his reign. He appears, however, as an important personage in several contract-tablets of the reign of Nebuchadrezzar. He was probably the "Nergalsharezer" of Jer. xxxix. 3, 13, who was one of the officers entrusted with the care of the captured city of Jerusalem (§ 1233, note).[3] If this is so, he was a contemporary of Nebuchadrezzar himself, and his brief reign of four years may have been terminated by old age. He was succeeded by his son, Labasi-Marduk, the "Labarosoarchod" of Berossus-Josephus, who reigned, however, but nine months (556), when he was slain by a conspiracy of nobles.

§ 1371. One of the participants of the plot was a magnate named Nabonidus (*Nabū-naʾid*, "Nebo is exalted"), who was elected king and reigned till the downfall of the empire (556–539). From him we have several important

---

[1] Winckler, GBA. p. 314.

[2] This relationship seems indubitable, but strangely enough Neriglissar, in the longer of his two known inscriptions (the Cambridge cylinder, 1 R. 67, col. i. 14), calls his father Bêl-šum-iškun, "king of Babylon." This puzzle has given rise to much conjecture. See Tiele, BAG. p. 465 f. There is no evidence that Nabopalassar made any one joint-king with him. Yet this is, after all, the most probable hypothesis, especially as the name of Neriglissar would seem to indicate royal paternity.

[3] Cf. Winckler, GBA. p. 338 (note 81).

personal inscriptions;[1] and very many business-tablets of his time have also been found. He is famous as an explorer of ancient ruins and their buried records, and also as a builder and renewer of temples. His chief distinction, however, is that he paid more attention to the temples of the gods outside of the district of Babylon[2] than he did to those of the capital itself. Add to this the fact that he preferred not to reside in the capital, but lived in a suburban town named Tema. The command of the army fell to his son Belshazzar (*Bêl-šar-uṣur*, " Bel, protect the king!"), whose name is familiar to us from the book of Daniel, and who played his part well to the end. Early in his reign trouble came in Mesopotamia, but it was removed by outside interference (§ 1383). On the whole, his empire held well together by inertia.

§ 1372. Was his policy more popular with his people than that pursued by his predecessors? It would seem to have been so for a time at least. Certainly centralization had been carried too far. The temples being the centres of business, as well as the boast of the several cities of the country, the aggrandizement of the capital actually at length impoverished the provincial towns and threatened them with ruin (cf. § 1285 ff.). At any rate, this course of conduct which the present king's religiousness led him to pursue was welcome to the outside cities. But the time came when something more than piety and indiscriminate temple-building was demanded of the ruler of Babylonia, and the people of the capital at last grew indifferent to a king of antiquarian tastes and subterranean habits.

---

[1] Published in I R. 68 and 69, and in V R. 63–65. All of the inscriptions of his reign available up to date, 1134 in number, are given in Strassmaier, *Inschriften von Nabonidus. König von Babylon* (1889). Of the transcriptions and translations should be mentioned V R. 64 by Latrille (with commentary) in ZK. II. and ZA. I, and all of the inscriptions in I R. and V R. (with the addition of Br. M. 85–4, 30. 2) by Peiser in KB. III. ii, p. 80–120 (1890). For his annals, or the "chronicle of Nabonidus and Cyrus," see note to § 1382.

[2] For his work at Sippar, in the temple of the Sun-god, see § 87.

CHAPTER IV

CYRUS AND THE PERSIANS

§ 1373. We have arrived at the point of time when the old Semitic régime in Western Asia gives way to the Medo-Persian, or in a wider sense to the Aryan. Of the Medes we have had to speak repeatedly as a chief agent in the destruction of Nineveh. Now we shall have to regard them and their Persian congeners as partners in a still greater enterprise. Both of them were offshoots of the Iranian race. The Iranians were one of the many branches of the Indo-European family. This people, whatever may have been their starting-place, had long made northern and central Europe and west central Asia their home, and for many centuries had been seeking to secure a permanent residence in more southern lands. The Iranians along with their kindred, the Sanskrit-speaking people of Hindustan, constitute what is termed, in the strict sense, "Aryans." They were also closely allied to the Scythians, eastern and western, and the Armenians. What the condition of the Iranians was in prehistorical ages we can only vaguely guess. In historical times we know simply that along with the more or less civilized members of the race settled in Iran itself, there were great numbers of kindred nomads ranging along the northern steppes. From the settled tribes and clans was derived the name "Iran" (Ariana).

§ 1374. The country is a mountain plateau of about fifteen hundred miles in breadth stretching from the Tigris to the Indus and from the Persian Gulf to the present frontiers of Russia in Asia. It is divided into Western and Eastern Iran by the Great Salt Desert. The whole was about conterminous with the modern Persia, Afghanistan, and southern Turkestan. The principal seat of the early Iranian civilization was Baktria on the northern slopes of the Parapamisus or Hindu-kush. This also seems to have been the distributing centre of immigration, which moved in two main streams. One passed southward, occupying the whole of the eastern side of the plateau as far as the modern Beluchistan. Thence its advance guard marched westward below the salt desert and took up the southwest corner of the highlands, which was to become the kernel of the Persian empire, and was known to the ancients as Persis. The other migrators moved westward and made their home to the south and southwest of the Caspian, where they laid the foundations of the Median empire. It is noteworthy that while East Iran was settled long before West Iran, which was not occupied by Aryans till the eighth and seventh centuries B.C., it was the latter which gave the Iranians their place in history. The cause of this phenomenon is not difficult to discover. Eastern Iran was not fertile enough to form large centres of population, and it took no share in the culture of India, where the other great branch of the Aryans had early developed its own literature, philosophy, and art. The art of writing was unknown to the Iranians till they learned it from their western neighbours, to whom, indeed, they owed their advance in civilization.

§ 1375. The ancient people of Iran were a vigorous race, of simple temperate habits, and in their new home in the highlands they long maintained the traditions and customs of their primitive life on the northern plains. The social conditions of the old patriarchal system were transferred to the new state of things when agriculture became the basis of the community. The great landholders formed an aristocracy by themselves, to whom the peasants, mechanics, and traders were alike subordinated. As larger settlements were formed, the same type of social and civic organization was continued by the promotion of the more influential members of the ruling class. But no very extensive communities were developed in East Iran; and when in West Iran the Median monarchy arose, it was founded in emulation of the Assyrian empire.

§ 1376. What chiefly distinguished the Iranians as a people and gave them their predominance in Asia was their religion. The Iranians had the purest form of faith and worship known to any of the Indo-European peoples. The position and functions assigned to the chief deity are significant. With the other Indo-European nations they inherited the old belief in the supremacy of the sky-god, the lord of the shining heavens, invested him with an active personality, and ascribed to him the care of the lower world. The Aryans of India dethroned him from his ancient seat, and exalted in his place a series of grotesque and impalpable abstractions; while the Greeks and Romans and other Europeans degraded him by endowing him with the baser passions of the men whom he governed. In both cases the moral ideal was unrealized. The Iranian religion conserved the old simple childlike trust in the supreme dispenser of blessing, and it added to him other ennobling attributes. The god of light became here the god of truth and purity, the lord of wisdom (*Ahuramazda*, "Ormazd"), the spirit of holiness, through whom the blessings of which creation is full are conveyed to the creatures. To him was opposed the spirit of evil, of impurity, of falsehood, of death and destruction (*Angramanyu*, "Ahriman"), at the head of an army of demons, who continually fight against the good and righteous spirit, and fight in vain. Fire, the perpetuator of light, was primarily reverenced as its finest symbol, and the great purifying element. Thus truth and falsehood, order and disorder, life and death, were arrayed against one another in unchanging antithesis; and all men were incited to become allies of the powers of good in their war upon the powers of evil. To every man life must be an unbroken campaign against malignant foes within and without, who, even though perpetually vanquished, were never slain. This conflict must be real. Every subject of Ahuramazda was thus called to a holy war without reprieve or discharge. Every good action would advance the kingdom of the just, and every bad deed retard the final overthrow of the realm of evil. Nor was the motive confined to this world alone. After life was ended, the spirit (*Fravashi*) of the faithful warrior was transported to the realm of Ahuramazda, where he continued to be the helper of his descendants still on the earth. Hence arose the highest type of ancestor-worship known to men. Where deification was impossible, veneration, pure and intense, was kept within the bounds of reason.

§ 1377. Such are some of the principles of the Iranian religion. In spite of its necessary dualism, it was thus a noble spiritual and ethical system. When we consider that such principles as these were cherished by the rulers of the race in its conflict with Semitism, we are at once struck with the contrast to that system of thought and action which had held sway so long over the peoples of Western Asia. This contrast has not escaped the notice of broad-minded historians. " The monarchy of Persia," observes Ranke, " fulfils a lofty mission. It has other aims in view than conquest and plunder. It rises far above the cruel Assyrian monarchy. For the divinities of Iran, pure and shining like the hosts of heaven, demand neither hecatombs nor licentious rites. They are not to be imitated by destroying life, but by increasing and developing it. If they make war, it is not from motives of ambition, but to triumph over the powers of evil, to assure the final victory of the god of life. Asshur and the goddess who for the most part is named with him are warrior deities. Ahuramazda is a god of righteousness and truth. Subjection means, with the Assyrians, subjugation by violence; with the Persians, the fulfilment of a supreme will."[1]

§ 1378. Few words are needed to tell all that is known of the early history of that branch of the race which has given historical importance to the Iranians. Exactly when the little district of Persia (§ 1374) was settled by the peoples who gave it the name is not certain. It was at all events some time after the rise of the Medes (§ 823 f.). All the kings of old Persia trace their descent from Achæmenes (*Hakhāmanish*). He was the fourth ancestor of Cyrus the Great,[2] and may possibly have been the founder of Persis; that is to say, the first of the Persian chiefs who maintained a permanent settlement in that district. His son Teispes is the first who is named as king,[3] and that not king of Persis, but king of Anshan, a title by which all his successors are also named as far as Cyrus the Great. This Anshan (also written *Anzan*) is a very ancient region of southern Elam, which, probably about 595 B.C. (§ 1263), after the Assyrians had relaxed their hold upon that country, was occupied by a Persian colony[4] and made into a kingdom, after the pattern of the northern and western na-

---

[1] Quoted by Pressensé, *The Ancient World and Christianity*, p. 138.

[2] For convenience the ancestry of the two earliest lines of Persian kings may be appended. The names are given in the forms employed by the classical writers.

    1. Achemenes
    2. Teispes

3. Cyrus I	3. Ariaramnes
4. Cambyses I	4. Arsames
5. Cyrus II	5. Hystaspes
6. Cambyses II	6. Darius I

Cf. Tiele, BAG. p. 469; and on the possible ways of reconciling the lists of Herodotus, Darius, and Cyrus, Winckler, UAG. p. 126 ff.; Rost, in MVG. (1897), p. 208 f. The genealogy of Cyrus is given in his Cylinder inscription (VR. 35) l. 20-22; that of Darius in his Behistun inscription, and in Herod. VII, 11.

[3] By Cyrus, VR. 35, 21.

[4] Rost, in MVG. (1897), p. 205 f., points out the importance of Susa, the old Elamitic capital, in the early history of the Persian empire.

tions. But the name of Persian was always borne by all the race, and it is therefore probable that Persis itself remained the chief centre of population. Anshan, however, became tributary to Media, as this empire extended itself over the old Assyrian provinces east of the Tigris.

§ 1379. Under the policy of mutual tolerance and friendship pursued by the Medes and Chaldaeans, the former at length extended their dominion westward over all the uplands as far as the river Halys. This was done in the lifetime of Cyaxares, the conqueror of Nineveh, who reigned till 584 B.C. The Halys, indeed, was fixed as the boundary by a remarkable international agreement. We have had occasion to mention the early kings of Lydia (§ 773 ff.) down to Alyattes III (617–560), who finally expelled from his borders the Kimmerian raiders that had long disturbed the peace of his kingdom. Alyattes was the real founder of Lydian greatness. With the expulsion of the Kimmerians, Phrygia and Bithynia fell under his power. Many of the Greek cities of the coast submitted to him. In his eastward progress he met the advancing forces of Cyaxares, king of the Medes; and for several years war was fiercely waged between them. On May 28, 585, occurred that famous battle which was interrupted by an eclipse of the sun, said to have been foretold by Thales of Miletus. Nebuchadrezzar of Babylon and the king of Cilicia offered to mediate, since it was to their interest that the balance of power should be maintained. It was by the ensuing treaty that the boundary was settled.

§ 1380. After the compromise, Lydia continued to thrive apace. With the acquisition of Greek colonies on the coast it gained much culture and greater wealth. Through its trade with east and west it became a great commercial nation, whose monument is the coinage of money, first devised in Lydia. In 560, Alyattes was succeeded by his more famous son Croesus, under whom prosperity was more than maintained. In 584, Cyaxares died: his successor was Astyages. Nebuchadrezzar died in 562.

The sole heir of the empires of Crœsus, Astyages, and Nebuchadrezzar was neither a Lydian, nor a Median, nor a Babylonian, but Cyrus the Persian, the conqueror of Asia, the liberator of the Jews, "the friend and the anointed of Jehovah."

§ 1381. The fame of Cyrus was so great among the Greeks that they retailed fictions without end about his birth, his life, and his death. His influence upon the world was such that an extensive supernatural machinery was required to explain the catastrophes which he wrought. I shall have to pass over the entertaining stories which have been related about his infancy and childhood. They are not idle tales, because they had a serious motive. But they are not history. They are partly traditions, partly legends, and in the Greek handling at least very largely myths. Most of them describe him as having been of lowly origin but accompanied from his birth by dreams, portents, and marvellous auspices in general, till his great merits attested the fitness of the supernatural omens.

§ 1382. Cyrus (*Kurash*) was born about 590 B.C., one hundred years before the battle of Marathon. He was a son of Cambyses I, and the second of the name. Of his childhood and youth we really know nothing. It is not possible that he was the grandson of Astyages the Mede, as Herodotus and Xenophon assert. The first authentic notice reveals him already as an antagonist of Astyages, and at the same time throws a new and unexpected light upon the history of the time. It occurs in the annals or state chronicle of Nabonidus,[1] in the record made, as it

---

[1] Col. II, 1 ff. The entry of the year, as well as the beginning of the statement itself, is broken off, but the next entry is "year seventh." This document, sometimes called the "Nabonidus-Cyrus Chronicle," has been published last by O. E. Hagen in his treatise "*Keilschrifturkunden zur Geschichte des Königs Cyrus*," in BA. II. p. 205-257. It was first edited by Pinches in 1880 (TSBA. VII, 139-176). Winckler also gives the original text in UAG. p. 154 f. Pinches and Hagen have a transcription, translation, and commentary; and Schrader in KB. III, ii, p. 128-136, gives a transcription and translation. I cite it as Nab. *Annals*.

seems, for the sixth year (550), and runs as follows: "[Astyages his army] assembled and marched against Cyrus, king of Anshan to take [him prisoner]. Astyages his army revolted against him, seized him and gave [him] up to Cyrus. Cyrus (marched) to Agamtānu (Ecbatana). Silver, gold, goods and chattels of all sorts he carried as spoil to Anshan."

§ 1383. Shortly after this record was made Nabonidus, in a famous inscription already referred to (§ 87), gives important additional facts. He was eager to rebuild the decayed temple of Sin in Charran. He relates how Merodach, his chief deity, acting on behalf of the neglected Sin, told him in a vision that he must perform this pious work. He then continues: "Reverently I say to the lord of the gods Merodach: 'That temple which thou hast commanded me to make, the Scythian is round about it, and his forces are mighty.' But Merodach says to me: 'The Scythian of whom you speak, he, his lord, and the kings his auxiliaries will be no more.' When the third year came round, they (the gods) set Cyrus his petty vassal on the march. With his little band he dispersed the wide-extended Scythians. Astyages, king of the Scythians, he seized and carried away prisoner to his country."[1] Nabonidus then goes on to say that when Charran had thus been cleared of the barbarians he proceeded to rebuild the temple.

§ 1384. Our first remark concerns the word loosely translated "Scythian." As a collective, it means literally "wide-spreading hordes," and is a general term for the nomads, such as Kimmerians and Mannæans (§ 758, 773 ff.), and Scythians (§ 810 ff.), who since the days of Esarhaddon had invaded from time to time the uplands of Western Asia, and here and there had broken into the lowlands.[2] It is passing strange that Astyages the Mede should be

---

[1] V R. 64. col. I, 18–33.

[2] See Delitzsch, HWB., on the word in question, *Ummān-manda* (which apparently means "a large horde"). and Hagen in BA. II, 231. I translate "Scythian" so as to give the nearest name of a distinct people.

called by this foreign name. The explanation must be either that he was a "Scythian" who superseded the Median Cyaxares,[1] or that so many of these roving people had settled in Media, that they had given character and name to the people and country. I think that until fuller light is given we should decide for the former alternative. That the nomads under a strong leader were able to extrude the Medes from the ruling place is quite credible. So great was their influence that through them the Median policy (§ 1051) was changed, and before 552 they occupied Mesopotamia. The association of Charran with the successes of Cyrus gives colour to this hypothesis. Evidently Nabonidus was given a free hand in Mesopotamia after the northern hordes had retired. But why did they retire unless the victory over Astyages was a blow at the "Scythian" leadership? For the submission of Astyages, as we shall see, was not followed by a contraction of the Median dominion. The solution, therefore, seems to be that these turbulent foreigners were too strong for the legitimate government, and that the conquest of the Medes by Cyrus involved in the first instance the repression and perhaps a partial expulsion of the northerners. If this is so, the motive of Cyrus in opposing Astyages was not merely to overthrow the Median suzerainty, but to intervene in behalf of his Iranian kindred against these outlanders. It is further reasonable to suppose that a native Median party was discontented with the foreign régime [2] and that this gave encouragement to Cyrus to throw off the Median yoke.

§ 1385. How finely this conclusion harmonizes with the surprising fact reported by Herodotus [3] and signally con-

---

[1] So Winckler, UAG. p. 124 ff.

[2] Possibly a vague reminiscence of this state of things glimmers through the account given by Herodotus (I, 107-124) of the hostility of Harpagus, the trusted minister of Astyages, towards his master, which finally led him to invite Cyrus to dethrone that monarch.

[3] I, 127 ; cf. 125.

firmed by the contemporary scribes of Babylon, that when the Medes and the Persian revolters met, many of the former went over to the banner of Cyrus! Only discontent with the home government can account for an immense army making terms with a small one. And only the knowledge of such a feeling can account for the revolt by a petty underling with a handful of followers against the most powerful empire of the world. Cyrus, therefore, did not begin his matchless career either as a foolhardy adventurer or as a wanton aggressor. The story goes that Astyages was spared and well treated after his overthrow.

§ 1386. Henceforth the world-empire was Medo-Persian. Its moral force was mainly Persian, but its population was overwhelmingly Median or of former Median allegiance. Yet for purposes of administration it was soon made an absolute unit. Of the "Scythians" as a separate force we hear nothing thereafter. The adjutants of Cyrus were drawn from all portions of the empire. Mazares, Harpagus, and Gobryas, his chief generals, were Medes. Hyroeades, who took the lead in mounting the citadel of Sardis (§ 1388), was an Elamite. The speedy completion of the organization is to be explained by assuming that Cyrus visited the provinces in person, conciliating the local chiefs by his affability, and choosing with unerring instinct the most capable men as his governors. Thus first in the world's history was exemplified on a large scale the principle of delegated power (cf. § 56). He seems also to have established an efficient intelligence department.

§ 1387. During the two years thus occupied the career of the young conqueror and statesman was being anxiously watched by three nations — Babylonia, Egypt, and Lydia. Aggressive action was first taken by Lydia. A memorable campaign was undertaken by Croesus. He had expectation of help from Egypt, and a definite promise from Sparta in Greece. Seeking an omen from the oracle at Delphi, he received the famous answer, "By crossing the Halys thou wilt destroy a great empire." Thus encouraged, he advanced against the Medo-Persians in the spring of 547 without waiting for his allies. Cyrus, when informed of the movement of Crœsus, gathered his army, crossed the Tigris below Arbela,[1] and took the Mesopotamian route to Cappadocia by forced marches. Before he came up with the troops of Crœsus they had occupied the strong fortress of Pteria,[2] in the north of Cappadocia, and laid waste the surrounding country. In that neighbourhood a desperate but indecisive battle was fought. Crœsus, finding the army of Cyrus unexpectedly strong, retired to Sardis, his capital, to wait for his allies, thinking that Cyrus would not follow him, in view of the difficult terrain.

§ 1388. In this Crœsus was deceived. In less than two months after he had crossed the Tigris,[3] Cyrus marched

---

[1] Some details of the movements of Cyrus possibly form part of the record for the "ninth year" in Nab. *Annals* (II, 15-18). I give a translation of the somewhat mutilated passage. "(15) In the month Nisan, Cyrus, king of Persia, mustered his troops (16) and made a forced passage over the river Tigris below Arbela. In the month Iyyar, to the land ... (he went). (17) Its king he vanquished and seized his possessions. He made his garrisons occupy it, and (18) thenceforth his garrisons and a (?) were kept there." As to the translation of the disputed word *i-rab* (l. 16), cf. Delitzsch, HWB. at אנה II, and observe that the rapid Tigris was at this season fast rising. Various conjectures have been made as to line 16. Winckler (UAG. p. 131) says that some little kingdom between the Tigris and Euphrates is meant. Hagen (BA. II, 240) says that "the country in question lay not far from the Tigris below Arbela." Conjecturing from traces in the text as published by Hagen that the end of the line might have been *mât Lu-ud-di*, I inquired of Mr. Pinches his latest opinion. The eminent decipherer replied that after an examination in February, 1898, he then thought that the passage might easily read *mât Lu* and a part of *ud*, the rest of the line being worn off. That "the land of Lydia" is meant is therefore possible. On other grounds it had already been concluded that Cyrus just at this time was engaged with Crœsus (Meyer, GA. I, § 502 f.). Moreover, Nabonidus reported only the most important actions of Cyrus before his attack on Babylonia. He had already noted the conquest of Media (§ 1383), and he would naturally mention the fall of Lydia.

[2] Near Pteria is the modern town of Boghaz-keui, where are the remains of a great fortress, with Hettite sculptures on the walls of rock.

[3] Assuming, meanwhile, that Nab. *Annals*, II, 16 (see note above), is to be referred hither.

direct upon Sardis, and before the autumn was over, the capital and the kingdom were in his hands. The Lydian troops having been defeated before the city, it was invested by Cyrus, and in fourteen days it was taken by a stratagem similar to that employed in the capture of Quebec. A story is told[1] to the effect that Cyrus had prepared to burn Crœsus alive, that the pyre was raised, the fire kindled, and then extinguished by a miraculous shower. The cruelty of the tale has gained credence in recent times from no less an authority than Nöldeke.[2] But Cyrus was, at all events, neither superstitious nor whimsical, and the credible tradition[3] that Crœsus was spared and honoured by him during the rest of his life is inconsistent with the underlying motive of the story.

§ 1389. Sardis became the permanent centre of Persian power in the West. But of greater ultimate consequence was the annexation of the Greek cities and colonies dependent upon Lydia, for thereby came about the Græco-Persian wars that shook the world. Cyrus himself did not remain longer than was necessary to direct the plans for organizing the new realm. The Median Harpagus made the Greek settlements secure. To him the Ionians, the Carians, and finally the Lycians, submitted. The king of Cilicia became voluntarily a Persian vassal, and the same thing is related of the princes of Paphlagonia.[4]

---

[1] By Herodotus (I, 87), whose narrative, as that of a resident of the coastland, may be relied upon for the leading historical events, but not for stories in which religious credulity may be suspected.

[2] Art. "Persia" in the *Encyl. Br.* (Vol. XVIII, p. 566) by Nöldeke and Gutschmid, who can find no better term to describe Cyrus than "a savage conqueror." Much more just is the eulogium of the greatest of Oriental historians (Meyer, GA. I, § 506). Cf. the judgment of Duncker, *History of Antiquity* (tr. by Abbot), VI, 128 ff. The attempted cremation, Duncker (VI, 42 f.), followed by Meyer (GA. I, § 503), interprets as self-immolation on the part of Crœsus.

[3] In which Herodotus from Lydian, and Ctesias from Persian, sources agree. The latter says that Cyrus allotted to Crœsus a manor near the Median capital Ecbatana.

[4] Cf. the summary in Meyer, GA. I, § 503.

Cyrus meanwhile returned to the East, and soon all of east Iran (§ 1374) was attached to his rule. With the subjection of Baktria he became the recognized head of the Iranian peoples. Among them little coercion was needed. Yet their organization and protection from border tribes of the north required time, patience, and skill. To these eastern provinces, the proper home of his own race, Cyrus devoted some of the best years of his life; though his deeds which moved the civilized world were performed in other regions.

CHAPTER V

CYRUS KING OF BABYLON

§ 1390. The empire of Cyrus now extended from the river Indus to the Ægean Sea, the whole of the settled part of it having fallen to him in three years (550–547). Still more marvellous than the rapidity of acquisition was the manner of it. By the happiest fortune he had been spared the need of fighting many battles, and had never appeared in them as an oppressor. Even the subjection of the Greek cities was a part of the reduction of Lydia. That he burned no captured cities and villages and that he sought to protect their inhabitants instead of making slaves of them,[1] was also something new and welcome. It seems to have been appreciated by the subject peoples, for we hear of but few insurrections during his lifetime. Thus he played the rôle of a deliverer, such as that assigned to him in the Hebrew prophecy of his time.

§ 1391. It is not quite certain how the war with Babylon was directly occasioned. According to the most probable data it was not undertaken till eight years after the conquest of Lydia. By all precedent, it ought to have begun immediately, since Babylon had been in alliance with Crœsus, and the seizure of the whole empire of Nabonidus, except a few fortified cities, could have been possible at any time. It is clear that the generals

---

[1] We have no authentic details except with regard to Babylon. We have, however, results. Besides, what he did in Babylon (§ 1395) he naturally did elsewhere.

of Cyrus were held back, during these years, from descending upon the fertile and wealthy provinces that had been the spoil of invaders from time immemorial.

§ 1392. Of the internal condition of Babylonia during the closing years of the reign of Nabonidus, we gain some hints from the king's own records.[1] In his ninth year (547) the death of his mother is recorded. Belshazzar, in command of the army, and his men bewailed her three days, and an official mourning was also proclaimed in Akkad, or the district of north Babylonia. In the same year, as also in the seventh, tenth, and eleventh, the entry is made: "King Nabonidus was in Tema; the king's son, the magnates, and the army were in Akkad. The king did not come to Babylon for Nisan. Nebo did not go to Babylon, the New Year's feast was not held." The significance of these statements is obvious (cf. § 1371 f.). The king did not show any interest either in the affairs of the capital or in the defence of the country. Of that religion which was the strength and pride of Babylon, the New Year's feast was the crown. On this day Nebo was brought from his temple in Borsippa to Babylon, and there led along the streets by a prescribed route, in solemn procession. That Nabonidus should habitually ignore this ceremony, and thereby occasion its discontinuance, was a direct affront to the state religion, and an act of folly on his part which foreboded destruction.[2] The popularity which he had at first gained in the provincial cities (§ 1372) at length changed to indifference; while in the capital a feeling of resentment was aroused which was the forerunner of rebellion. There is abundant evidence that the priesthood of Babylon were more loyal to their profession and their

---

[1] Nab. *Annals*, col. II and III. The entries for only a few years have been well preserved. For the eighth year (548) no record was made. The eventful seventeenth (539) is recorded with great minuteness, the work having been completed after the king's deposition.

[2] The records themselves, primarily minuted by officials of Nabonidus, indicate the discontent. For the grand ceremony see RBA. p. 678 f.

craft than to any existing government (cf. § 660). It would have been easy to get the king out of the way, and Belshazzar was a man of character who would make a strong ruler in his place. Deeper designs, however, were cherished by these leaders in Babylon and Borsippa. The existing régime must be subverted, and who so worthy a successor as the tolerant and genial Cyrus? Of such a feeling Cyrus was perhaps made aware.

§ 1293. On this subject we may hear the scribes of Cyrus himself. In an inscription written[1] after his occupation of Babylon, they say of Nabonidus that he neglected the sacrifices of the gods, did despite to Merodach himself, and oppressed his subjects, so that the gods abandoned their seats in anger. They then continue: "Merodach took compassion on the people of Shumer and Akkad, who had become like unto dead men. In all the nations he looked over his friends, seeking a righteous prince after his own heart, to take by his hand. 'Cyrus, king of Anshan,' he called his name, nominating him to universal sovereignty. The land of Gutium, the whole of the wide-spreading hordes, he subdued to his feet. The people of mankind, whom he gave into his hands, he cared for in justice and equity. Merodach, the great lord, the protector of his people, beheld with joy his generous deeds and his righteous heart, and bade him take the

---

[1] Upon a cylinder now in the British Museum which was published in 1880, in JRAS., by Sir Henry Rawlinson, and by Pinches in V R. 35. It has also been given in Abel and Winckler's *Keilschrifttexte* (1890), and finally in the most exact form by Hagen in BA. II (1894) as an appendix to his treatise. "Cyrus-Texte." Translations and transcriptions are given by Hagen and also in KB. III. ii (1890), p. 120–127 by Schrader. Cf. Delitzsch in BA. II. 248 ff. and the art. "Cyrus" by King in EB., § 69. I cite it for convenience as V R. 35. A brief inscription found in 1850 by Loftus at Warka (Erech) is published by Hagen, BA. II, 257. It runs: "Cyrus, rebuilder of Esagila and Ezida, son of Cambyses, the mighty king, I am." Very many contract tablets have been found of the reign of Cyrus. Those in the British Museum are published by Strassmaier, *Inschriften von Cyrus* (1890). For others see Peiser, *Keilschriftliche Aktenstücke* (1889) and *Babyl. Vorträge* (1890).

road to Babylon, going by his side as a friend and companion."[1]

§ 1394. Turning now to the annals of Nabonidus, we see that in 539, the year of the march of Cyrus upon Babylon, a great change came over the spirit of the *roi fainéant*. Nebo came from Borsippa to Babylon (§ 1392). Bēl went out to join him in procession. The New Year's feast was celebrated "as was proper." But this was not enough. Whereas formerly Merodach and Nebo had been slighted, and the provincial deities honoured with rebuilt and rededicated shrines, now the images of those favoured gods were dragged from their seats to Babylon, and implored to protect the threatened capital.

§ 1395. But the presence of all the gods and their propitiation were a vain reliance (cf. Isa. xlvi. 1 ff.). Hear the next statement of the chronicle:[2] "In the month Tammuz (July), when Cyrus gave battle to the troops of Akkad in Opis by the stream Zalzallat,[3] he overcame the men of Akkad. Wherever they gathered he vanquished them. On the 14th day Sippar was taken without a battle. Nabonidus took to flight. On the 16th day Gobryas (*Ugbaru*), the prefect of Gutium, and the troops of Cyrus, without a battle, entered Babylon. Nabonidus, while looking behind him,[4] was taken prisoner. Till the end of the month the shields of Gutium surrounded the gates of Esagila; no one's weapon came into Esagila or into the sanctuaries; nor was any ensign advanced. In Marchesvan, on the third day, Cyrus entered Babylon." A few words from Cyrus himself describe the conclusion of the cam-

---

[1] V R. 35, 7-15. For parallels with Isaiah II see § 1411 and note.

[2] Nab. *Annals*, 1. 12-18.

[3] Hagen understands *u* ("and") before the word for "stream," and thinks of two localities and two distinct engagements (BA. II, 222 f., 243 f.). He is probably in error. It is not necessary to limit *Upê* to the mere city of Opis. The district of Opis is meant; notice the determinative *ki* "place," not *al* "city." A single locality only is therefore to be assumed. Hagen is right in thinking that Zalzallat is a canal.

[4] Compared by Hagen with Gen. xix. 17, 26.

paign: "His wide-spreading host, whose numbers like the waters of a river were not known, girt with their weapons, march by his side. Without conflict or battle he (Merodach) made him enter Babylon, his city. Babylon he spared from harsh treatment. Nabonidus, the king, who did not fear him, he delivered into his hand. The people of Babylon, all of them, and the whole of Shumer and Akkad, magnates and magistrates, bent low before him, and kissed his feet. They rejoiced in his sovereignty; their faces beamed delight. The Lord, who through his might gives life to the dead, who spares all from destruction and (?), they blessed with rejoicing; they honoured his name."[1]

§ 1396. A few words of comment will make the whole situation clear. This campaign of Cyrus is one of the marvels of history. As was its wont, his army marched suddenly, swiftly, and in perfect discipline. There was thus the less opposition, the less fighting, the less destruction of life, and the greater chance of an early peace and conciliation. Every movement was carefully planned beforehand. The force was mobilized in Gutium, which had become thoroughly Persian. Thence it moved south-westward till it reached the Tigris near Opis, or the north-east border of the Babylonia of that day. There the troops of Belshazzar, mainly drawn from Akkad — for the people of Shumer (§ 110), that is, the country around the capital, had no mind to resist — ventured to oppose the invaders at a point where a canal leaves the Tigris. They were defeated and scattered. This was the only battle of the campaign. Sippar, about forty-five miles southwestward, was entered without opposition. The capital was over fifty miles distant. In two days[2] it also surrendered without a blow being struck. Belshazzar was probably captured at the battle of Opis. Nabonidus, who had roused himself and gone northward

---

[1] V R. 35, 16–19.

[2] An instance of the mobility of the armies of Cyrus. The campaign seems to have lasted less than a week.

to be with or near the army of defence, fled to Babylon at the surrender of Sippar; but while hesitating about further flight was captured, presumably in his own palace grounds.[1] The fortifications of Nebuchadrezzar (§ 1058), which could have held out long against any army of the time, were as if they had not been. The mighty gates were thrown open and a welcome given to the army of Cyrus. The army had been in part, at least, loyal to the king; but after its defeat, a popular uprising confirmed the wiser choice of the priesthood (§ 1392).

§ 1397. It is not certain that Cyrus was with the army at any time during the actual campaign. But his ruling purpose was shown at its close as well as through its course. At once his policy was announced. "Peace was secured for the city. Cyrus proclaimed peace to all Babylonia."[2] But he himself did not appear in Babylon till three months and a half after the surrender. Meanwhile things took their course in the city as before. Neither sacred nor secular business was interrupted. The general Gobryas was entrusted with the appointment of royal prefects.[3] How much further the civil administration was changed we are not informed. Babylonia, however, was not treated as a province. Cyrus was really an emperor with at least two distinct kingdoms, and he ruled Babylonia immediately as its king. The contract tablets, while indicating this principal fact, give no hint of the rule of petty Persian officials during his reign. There was, of necessity, a court. Cyrus himself sometimes resided here

---

[1] So far as made out the contemporary documents throw no further light upon the final fate of Nabonidus and his son. According to Berossus, Cyrus granted a handsome residence in Carmania to Nabonidus for the rest of his days. A slightly mutilated passage in Nab. *Annals* (l. 22 f.) appears to say that "the son of the king died." This, however, is not quite certain. If Belshazzar's death is really there recorded, it took place during the same year. The Belshazzar, son of Nebuchadrezzar, of the book of Daniel, is doubtless the son of Nabonidus of the cuneiform texts. But the story of ch. v. finds no confirmation in the records of the time.

[2] Nab. *Annals*, III, 19 f. [3] Nab. *Annals*, III, 20.

and sometimes in Ecbatana, when his movements permitted him to live quietly anywhere.[1] He made Babylon at once a permanent seat of empire by having Cambyses, his son, consecrated as his heir by the priests of Merodach.[2]

§ 1398. We know more about the religious than the political life of Babylon after the surrender. Cyrus ordained not merely that the native religion should be tolerated and respected, but that it should be encouraged by his officers. It was, in fact, formally made the state religion of the kingdom. He himself appears as a worshipper, not merely of Merodach, but of the gods of Babylonia generally. He was indignant at the sacrilege committed by Nabonidus in dragging them from their seats and deporting them to the capital, and ordered them to be restored to their proper shrines.[3] The propitiation of the gods of Babylonia and his acknowledgment of their sovereignty he thus made his prime duty and privilege as king of the country (cf. § 1416).

§ 1399. Finally, we note his treatment of foreign slaves and exiles, of whom there were many in Babylonia. His proclamation giving permission to the Hebrews to return to their homes and their God we learn of from the book of Ezra (ch. i.). It is pleasing to know that this boon was not conferred upon them alone. He himself tells us of cities as far as the border of Gutium whose gods and people alike had been deported to Babylon. Now both the one and the other were restored: "The gods who inhabit them I restored to their seats, and made for them a dwelling-place there forever. All of their people I gathered and restored to their homes"[4] (cf. § 1415).

---

[1] Traditions seem to agree that Cyrus was busily occupied in the eastern provinces towards the close of his life. But even the place and manner of his death cannot be confidently stated.

[2] Cf. V R. 35, 27. 35. and Nab. *Annals*, III, 24 ff.

[3] V R. 35, 6. 32 f. Cf. Nab. *Annals*, III, 21 f.

[4] V R. 35, 31 f.

CHAPTER VI

PROPHETIC IDEALS

§ 1400. In a very real sense Israel in Babylonia began anew its spiritual life. There in servitude it was taught elementary lessons which it could never have learned in freedom. Its prison-house was from the very beginning its nursery, and was soon made its school. There its teachers, too, were trained: there they were broadened, deepened, and lifted above themselves, their people, their times, and the world itself. The moral influences of the Exile (§ 1313 ff.) had been acting long before the imagination of even the seers was fully awakened. It was the death of Nebuchadrezzar and the succeeding commotions which stirred the smouldering prophetic fire; and then it flamed forth brighter than ever. New thoughts were given forth in the noblest forms of poetic oratory: new conceptions of Jehovah, of his might and providence and purpose, of the destiny of Israel and the world.

§ 1401. The reign of Nebuchadrezzar had been so long and imperious that the Hebrew exiles thought of deliverance as an event in the indefinite future. But when he died, there was, after the manner of the ancient East, unrest and anxiety everywhere. Evidences of the inherent weakness of Chaldæism soon appeared and multiplied. The ensuing conspiracies and revolutions (§ 1369 f.) could not but confirm distrust, and the character and habits of Nabonidus (§ 1371 f.) added thereto. It was probably early in his reign that Isa. xiii.–xiv. 23 was written and circulated privately among the exiles. It has for its theme the destruction of Babylon by the Medes, and was apparently suggested by the aggressive spirit manifested by that people when under "Scythian" control (§ 1384). We know from Nabonidus that the northern frontier of Babylonia was harassed by subjects of Astyages (§ 1382 f.), and that it was not till Cyrus intervened that relief was given. The popular dread of them was reflected in that felt by Nabonidus himself. That this and no later date is that of the prophecy is probable (1) because the Medes[1] and not the Persians are referred to as the enemies of Babylon, and (2) because the mode of warfare ascribed to the aggressors (xiii. 15 ff.) was not that of the armies of Cyrus, but rather that which would be naturally expected from Scythian hordes; (3) because the invaders are said (xiii. 5) to "come from a far country, from the remotest horizon," an expression inapplicable to the Medo-Persian forces (see § 1396).

§ 1402. The predictive portions of this majestic discourse show strong assurance of the ruin and desolation of Babylon (xiii. 19–22) and of the restoration of Israel to its own land (xiv. 1, 2, 22, 23). But more significant is the characterization of the Babylonian world-power, which is given with such lyrical splendour in the ode inserted in the prophecy proper. It was not merely the Chaldæan régime of the time that was in the mind of the poet. When, in the most dramatic passage of the Old Testament, he pictures the oppressor of the nations quelled at last by death, and his former vassals in all the pacified earth rejoicing in their deliverance, and all the dead tyrants starting up with incredulous surprise as the king of kings comes to join his peers in Sheol, he is thinking of the historic tyranny of Assyria and Babylonia meeting its long-delayed, divinely predestined doom: "How is the oppressor ceased, the raging stilled! Jehovah hath broken the rod of the wicked, the sceptre of the rulers, that smote the peoples in fury

---

[1] No contemporary writer, as far as we know, refers to the Persians as Medes. In Isa. xxi. 2 the Medes are mentioned, but as forming part of the forces of Cyrus (see § 1404). It is inconceivable that both the towering personality of Cyrus and the race to which he belonged could be omitted in a prophecy of deliverance written after 547 B.C.

with unceasing blows, that played the tyrant over the nations, treading them down without restraint. The whole earth is now at rest and quiet; it breaks forth into singing. . . . Thy pomp is brought down to the shades and the sounding of thy viols. . . . How art thou fallen from heaven, O Day-star, son of the morning! How art thou hewn down to the ground, who didst lay low the nations! And thou saidst in thy heart, 'I will ascend into heaven; I will exalt my throne above the stars of God; I will sit upon the mountain of assembly in the recesses of the north.[1] I will ascend above the heights of the clouds; I shall be like the Most High.' . . . They that see thee shall look narrowly at thee, and stare at thee: 'Is this the man that made the earth to tremble, that did shake kingdoms, that made the world a desert and overthrew the cities thereof, that let not loose his prisoners to their homes?'" (xiv. 4 ff.).

§ 1403. Of an entirely different literary type is a long discourse (Jer. l. 1–li. 58), indicating clearly the same historical situation. Apparently on account of some resemblance in style, it has been annexed to the genuine prophecies of Jeremiah. Here again the Medes are named as more specifically "the kings of the Medes" (li. 11, 28; cf. l. 41), a phrase which points to the semi-independent nomad chiefs of the later Median times. More definitely still the aggressors are said to be coming from the north country,[2] and to be a gathering of great nations (l. 9, 41), for instance, "the kingdoms of Ararat, of Van, and of Ashkenaz"[3] (li. 27), such as belonged to the half-organized

---

[1] That is, in the north pole of the heavens, the seat of the chief of the gods, Anu (Jensen, *Kosmologie*, p. 22 f.). Cf. Ez. i. 4, also written in Babylonia, but not Ps. xlviii. 3.

[2] Contrast Cyrus and the Persians, who are said to come from "the east" (Isa. xli. 2; xlvi. 11).

[3] For Van (*Mannai* EV. "Minni") see § 758, where its association with the Medes is pointed out. Ashkenaz is the *Ashguz* of II R. 45, col. II, 29 (Esarhaddon). See Delitzsch in Baer's text of Daniel. p. IX, and KAT.² p. 610.

empire of Media before the day of Cyrus. The general tone of the prophecy is bitter and vengeful like Isa. xiii., and thus differs from the impartial temper of Isa. xl.–lv.. and the more genial Persian era. Nebuchadrezzar himself (Jeremiah's "servant of Jehovah") is here represented as a lion that crunched the bones of the hunted sheep, Israel, after another lion, Assyria, had devoured his flesh (l. 17). Hence vengeance is to be taken upon "the king of Babylon" (l. 18). That the author wrote in Babylonia is shown by his intimate knowledge of the country.[1]

§ 1404. Another prophecy (Isa. xxi. 1–10) intervenes between the Median period and the fulness of the time of Cyrus. The standpoint of the author clearly appears in v. 2: "Go up, Elam! lay siege, Media!" Here "Elam" is used by synecdoche for Anshan (§ 1378), before the title "king of Persia" had been assumed by Cyrus.[2] The discourse is intensely dramatic. The prophet sees in vision the siege of Babylon by the Persians and Medes (vs. 1, 2). The approaching catastrophe stuns him with its magnitude (vs. 3, 4). The anxiety as to the result is pictured in the successive reports of a watchman, who finally answers: "Babylon is fallen, is fallen" (vs. 5–9). The issue is then declared to the prophet's interested people. One cannot but feel that as the fall of Babylon approaches, the word of prophecy, in whatever form it may be uttered, becomes more sober and dignified.[3]

---

[1] Thus he not only refers to Pekod (§ 335). but to the "salt sea land" *Marratim* (l. 21), that portion of Babylonia washed by the Persian Gulf. *Par.* p. 182. Remarkable are the cases of the so-called Athbash, in which the last letter of the alphabet is put for the first, the second-last for the second, and so on. Thus in li. 1 קמי לב is put for כשדים "Chaldæa," and in li. 41 ששך is put for בבל "Babylon" as in xxv. 26. The use of cryptic writing was learned from the practice of the Babylonian schools.

[2] That is, 547 B.C.; see Nab. *Annals.* II, 15 (§ 1387, note).

[3] Isa. xxxiv. should be mentioned here, though its subject is not Babylonia, but Edom. It is very rancorous in tone, a feature which is no good indication of the time of composition, since the enmity between Judah

§ 1405. The destruction of Babylon is the prevailing theme in the compositions which have just been considered. But in the last and greatest work of the Exile this event is less prominent and is overshadowed by its consequences with the new perspective of divine revelation which it opened up. The author, whose writings for this period include at least Isa. xl.–lv., composed these discourses shortly before 539 B.C. To him the consummation is close at hand. It is so near and sure that he sees through and beyond it. It is to him no longer an object, but a medium of vision. Such indeed are all the events of his fateful time that touched the fortunes of his people. He is thus above all else a seer, the seer of a new and larger Israel. But he is more than this, he is the crown and flower of Hebrew prophecy. His supremacy was due in part to what he was in himself, and in part to his age and environment. He lived in the time of the greatest prophetic opportunity. He had the wider vision, not merely because he stood on the shoulders of Isaiah and Jeremiah, but also because he had seen more of God's world than they. Intellectually he is a product of two kindred but divergent civilizations. A pupil of the school that cherished the past of their country as only exiles can, he throws himself into line with the great motives of Israel's divinely ordained career (ch. xliii. 3 ff.; xlix. 5 ff.). But he can also follow the great world-forces, and sees as no native Palestinian could, how these apparently diverging tendencies meet at last in the harmony of universal subjection to Jehovah's reign. To use an astronomical figure, his visions were truer because their parallax was less, since they were made from the centre of the earth. Thus Babylonia prepared him to become the herald of a universal

---

and Edom was ineradicable and perpetual. Ps. cxxxvii. and Ez. xxxv. might suggest the time of the Exile; but the composite Obadiah and Mal. i. 2 ff. warn us to be cautious here. Isa. xxxv. has nothing to do with xxxiv. It is a hymn appended to the works of Isaiah; but its tone and resemblance to Isa. xl. ff. suggest the end of the Exile as its date.

providence. But this was not all. He had a rare education. His easy mastery of all his themes, his imperious command of the forms of speech, his happy geniality, his tolerance and breadth of sympathy, were not merely the result of long study and reflection, but of wide and close observation added to native endowment. He was especially familiar with Babylonian life and customs (ch. xli. 7; xliii. 14; xlvi. 1 ff; xlvii. 2, 12 f.). He knew the contents of historical inscriptions (§ 1411). But most of all is his Babylonian home revealed in his style and in his literary allusions. His discourse, serene, affluent, and glowing, is an image of a Babylonian landscape. As it unrolls itself, we think of fields and gardens and stately palms and bending willows and gently flowing streams, stretching away over an ample plain, and all standing out clear in the light of a cloudless sky.

§ 1406. What impresses one most in the writings of Isaiah II is the consummate beauty and power of his mere language. Words with him seem not an instrument of expression, but an actual organ of thought and still more of feeling. They are not so much voices that charm or thrill us as hands that hold us, caress us, and move us as they will. What Macaulay said of Milton, that his poetry acts like an incantation, is much more true of our author; for Milton had little of his pathos, his feeling of the *lachrymæ rerum*, the tearfulness at the heart of things, his sense of the yearning needs of all sentient beings,[1] such as brings together the divine Shepherd and his tired lambs (xl. 11),

---

[1] Very marked in Isaiah II is the absence of harshness and rancour. He does not abuse the idol-worshippers (xliv. 9–20; xlv. 20; xlvi. 6 f.). One feels that he is sorry for their stupidity. He is contemptuous of the insensate idols; but he does not describe them as thrown down (1 Sam. v. 3 f.) or hurled from their seats. They "stoop" and "bow down," and one can even trace the pity of the prophet as he depicts the vain efforts of the gods once carried in festal procession (§ 1392) to save themselves from deportation (xlvi. 1 f.). On the other hand, how he enters into the lot of the really suffering: the captive, the prisoner, and the oppressed (xlii. 7; li. 13 f.), the faint and weary (xl. 29 f.), the poor and needy (xli. 17 ff.)!

and even makes the Creator call his heavenly host by name, that they may not straggle from their ranks (xl. 26).[1] The peer of Isaiah II is not Milton but Vergil; and these two are alone in their combination of subtle, all-pervasive tenderness and sympathy, sustained and not overstrained fervour, splendour and simplicity of diction, the enchantment of perfect speech set to the music of the universal human heart. They stand, therefore, together among the chief of poets, though neither was a great creative genius, nor the first in power of thought in the literature of his own nation. Nor does the parallel end here; for Vergil, too, was a prophet of the fulness of the times. As Isaiah II gathered in himself the best hopes and promises of the earlier prophets, so Vergil was swayed by the purest moral ideas and aspirations of Greek thinkers and sages. Lastly and most remarkably, each of them stood at the close of a long period of international strife and bitterness, and expected the speedy coming of an age of peace and blessedness. How different the two conceptions were! And yet the coincidence is more significant than the difference. Of each of them it may be said, as Victor Hugo wrote of Vergil:[2]—

> "Il est un des cœurs que déjà, sous les cieux,
> Dorait le jour naissant du Christ mystérieux."

§ 1407. Such writing as that of Isa. xl.–lxvi. is not spontaneous. The eloquence that moves one's contemporaries may be improvised, but that which sways the world forever is the long travail of mind and soul. These gems of thought and feeling with their incessant play of many-coloured lights were polished to perfection. Moreover, if we confine our attention to those chapters which primarily belong to the end of the Exile, we must see that their permanent form was not given at once, so that, as was said

---

[1] Cf. the imitation in Ps. cxlvii. 4, and note the parallelism with vs. 2 and 3.

[2] Les voix intérieures, XVIII (1837).

already (§ 1363), their literary history extends beyond the period under present review.[1] But the most important fact is that, as we have them now, they are not wholly the production of the individual prophet whose genius moulded and elaborated them. The thoughts, so comprehensive, far-reaching, and final, are the ripe conclusions of a school led by the unnamed author. In the finished product the earlier writings of the period (§ 1401 ff.) found their correction and completion.

§ 1408. Hence the great political catastrophe was scarcely a problem to our author. Nor was it now hard to convince his hearers or readers that the day of Babylon was near to come. Cyrus and his omnipotence were in the mouths of all men. To an Israelite the overthrow of the oppressor was not the goal of desire; it was instrumental and secondary. The more difficult question was whether such an event would help or save the Hebrew exiles. To give the answer was the great practical achievement of the prophet. He had two classes among his own people to deal with. Among the new generation now grown up there were many who had lost interest in the hope and destiny of Israel. Those he sought to instruct and energize. Then among even the faithful leaders were many, perhaps the majority, who reasoned that the approaching change of dynasty, national and even racial as it was, meant only a change of masters. To show that it meant deliverance was now his great prophetic task. The personality of Cyrus was necessarily the main human factor. He studied Cyrus, followed his career of conquest, and especially his policy of conciliation. The truth was flashed on his mind that Cyrus was Jehovah's vicegerent or Messiah

[1] We have to conceive of several stages: the converse of the disciples and the master over the critical times; the communication to the little circle of the mind of Jehovah in broad suggestions as to the duty and the hope of Israel; the preparation by the master of separate discourses free and copious for wider circles; the condensing and coördinating and arrangement of such discourses for the permanent uses of the community.

("anointed one"). It was God's work that he had been doing. When Babylon's time should come to be subjected to him, he would still be doing God's work. And how so truly and well as in freeing God's own people, who were predestined to a new and more glorious national life? Hence Cyrus became an important factor in his theodicy, which was, of course, not metaphysical but concrete, and to be verified by the accomplished fact.

§ 1409. Hence, while the Restoration was the end in view, it was not the mode but the certainty of its accomplishment that forms the prophet's argument. Characteristic of him is his serene outlook upon the action of the gigantic forces that were to bring about the result, and his estimate of their relative competency. The world was filled not merely with the fame but with the deeds of Cyrus. There was and had been nothing seen or temporal to match him. As far as tangible power was concerned the prophet's own client, Israel, was, even as compared with moribund Babylonia, a mere worm of the dust (xli. 14). This genuinely prophetic and patriotic sense of the limitations of its own national power — something so hard to be acquired by any people, Hebrews or Romans, Boers or Britons — had been literally pounded into Israel through its centuries of tribulation. It was now indeed an ever-present thought in the mind of the bewildered exiles. Israel, therefore, was not a factor in the movement, except as it was itself to be moved. Cyrus had the field to himself. Even to the common man in Israel, no one else was in sight. But marching beside him, and holding his right hand, though he knew it not, and knew Him not (xlv. 4), was One who was subduing the nations before him, throwing open the gates of cities, endowing him with his eagle-like swiftness and easy success (xli. 2 ff.; xlv. 1 f.; xlvi. 11). And all this was being done not for Cyrus himself, not for the Persians or the Medes, the Lydians or the Greeks, but for the puny remnant of Israel, exiled for two generations from their home across the desert!

§ 1410. How the career of Cyrus was to affect Israel was not the concern of the prophet. He did not, strictly speaking, foresee events; he saw conditions. Prediction is essentially a view of details, while the spiritual element in prophecy has primarily not to do with results, but with factors and principles and their divinely constituted inner relations. Thus while the dazed secretaries of Nabonidus were noting the crossing of the Tigris, and the surrender of Sippar and of Babylon itself, and while the word came swiftly down the Shatt-en-Nil and along the Kebar that Babylonia had become Persian, the prophet was not greatly surprised. He had had a vision already which had seemed to involve these or some such incidental affairs. He has given us his theophany, compared with which the finest lyric representations of Jehovah's interventions (Ps. xviii.; Mic. i.; Hab. iii.) are as the Jordan is to the Euphrates, or as Sharon is to Eden: "Hark! there is a voice crying: Clear away in the wilderness the path of Jehovah; level up in the desert a highway for our God. Every valley shall be raised, and every mountain and hillock shall be lowered; and the rugged ground shall be made level and the ridges a plain; and the glory of Jehovah shall be revealed; and all flesh shall see it together, for the mouth of Jehovah hath spoken it" (xl. 3–5).

§ 1411. Yet our prophet did also make great account of Cyrus and of the world outside of Israel. Herein lies the sanity and trueness of his vision. To Cyrus, a non-Israelite, even a non-Semite, is given a unique distinction. He is called the anointed and the friend[1] of Jehovah. He is the one whom Jehovah calls in righteousness.[2] Jehovah

---

[1] Isa. xliv. 28; read רֵעִי "my friend" for רֹעִי "my shepherd" (as also in Zech. xiii. 7). Two parallels have been quoted in § 1393: "In all the nations he surveyed his friends," and, more striking still, "going by his side as a friend and companion."

[2] xlii. 6, so also xli. 2, cf. xlv. 13. See again § 1393: "a righteous prince after his own heart." The contention of G. A. Smith (*The Book of Isaiah* II, 165) that the expressions about "righteousness" on the

calls him by name, and surnames him as well.¹ What makes the tribute more impressive is that the language is imitated from that of Cyrus himself, with reference to the patron god of Babylon.² Our prophet gives him a nobler calling. Specifically as a co-worker with Jehovah, he is to rebuild Jerusalem, lay the foundations of the Temple (xliv. 28), and (xlv. 13) restore the exiles to their homes. His larger commission was, to be the instrument of letting the world know that Jehovah was God alone (xlv. 6). How is all this to be understood and justified? As already said, we are not in this, or in any other forecast of the sort, to look for a fulfilment in detail.³ There are two things only which touch the character of the inspired prophecy. One is the character of Cyrus, and the other is his religion. Unless these were approved by the prophet to whom both

---

cylinder and in Isaiah II, are not parallel is only technically correct. They run rather on converging lines. The righteous Cyrus was the agent whom Jehovah sought and called in and for righteousness.

¹ xlv. 4. The exact parallel is in the words of Cyrus (§ 1393): "'Cyrus, king of Anshan,' he called his name." To "name" is here to choose beforehand, to predestinate. The phrase is used very frequently in the inscriptions of the choice of a king (sometimes ages beforehand) by his patron god to rule as his vicegerent. To bear a name means also in Babylonian (and Hebrew) to have an existence; in connection with the divine election the underlying notion is therefore that of calling into being. The "surname" (כנה) is an honorific title, like the cognate Arabic *kunya* and the Latin *cognomen*. Comparing with xliv. 5 we learn that "Cyrus, king of Anshan," is analogous to "Jacob Israel."

² Our prophet was doubtless familiar with the language of Babylonian royal annals and proclamations, and a general reference to the phraseology would not be surprising. But such close analogies with several expressions occurring in one brief section of an inscription of Cyrus himself can scarcely be accidental. Is it not probable that in the literary working up of the discourses after the fall of Babylon the author adapted the phrases in question from the cylinder of Cyrus then just published? I have not by any means exhausted the parallels. In the quotation § 1393 every expression of the passage beginning, "In all the lands," seems to be imitated and specially applied by the prophet.

³ Yet, after all, the only fulfilment required by the terms of the prediction is that which has been already noted in § 1399.

were fully known, he could not have either honestly or intelligently written of him as he did.[1]

§ 1412. The material for a judgment of the character of Cyrus is scanty; but it is in a general way conclusive. The first thing to be noted is the largeness of his fame. In his own land his name is still a household word, surviving all political and social revolutions. No man outside the Greek and Roman world has been so much the theme of the classical writers, historians, poets, and philosophers. No one outside of Israel has such a place in the Hebrew literature. This singular preëminence of sacred and secular renown can have but one explanation. We may take for granted what may be called his Napoleonic qualities, force of will, energy, enterprise, versatility. But these are not the substance of his traditional reputation, which was that of a good rather than of a great man.[2]

§ 1413. His military genius may be taken for granted. But we have already had reason to note the absence of a merely aggressive spirit in his wars (§ 1390). Of his states-

---

[1] That is to say, Cyrus appears here as the agent, not as the mere instrument of Jehovah. If he were only the latter, his character might be, at least according to the ruling doctrine, a matter of indifference, as is that, for example, of Cecil Rhodes to those present day prophets who see the cause of righteousness prevailing in South Africa.

[2] As far as they go, his own records already cited confirm the impression produced by Isaiah II. The popular estimate of him is still based upon the accounts of the Greek writers, above all Herodotus and Xenophon. The former mentions his repeated acts of generosity to his rivals and otherwise gives a favourable picture. His story of the death of Cyrus at the hands of the queen of the Massagetæ is told to illustrate an underlying assumption of his history that acts of violence and presumption are followed by divine punishment (cf. Duncker, *History of Antiquity*, Eng. tr., VI, 121). The *Cyropædia* of Xenophon was written to show to the individualizing Greeks that several distinct peoples could form a single nation and be governed successfully by one man. Hence the idealizing of the life and work of Cyrus (cf. Duncker, *ib.* V, 358). But Xenophon had good opportunities of learning from the Persians the essential traits in the character of their hero. The men of the fifth century B.C., moreover, were able to trace the enduring results of the career of Cyrus: they could measure the shadow which was still cast by his personality upon the face of western Asia and eastern Europe.

manship and his habit of command we can speak more positively. He swayed men and nations with equal facility and by the same sort of faculty, winning their allegiance by winning their hearts. He was magnanimous, considerate, tolerant, as well as wise and daring. His spirit was cosmopolitan, and his happy genius fitted him to deal with all the races of the world. It was a new thing in history to find conquered peoples quietly acquiescing in a dominion wielded from a centre a thousand miles away. The marvel increases when we think how diverse his subjects were, of whom the most prominent only were Persians, Medes, Armenians, Scythians, Lydians, Greeks, Babylonians, Aramæans, Palestinians, not to mention the subdivisions of each, or the unclassified eastern communities. And this array of peoples, never before united under one or two or three sovereignties, were for a time fused into one by the magic of his genius. His faculty of organization alone, supreme as it was, could not have sustained his power during a month of his lifetime.

§ 1414. We see a moral trait also in his new art of governing, which gave freedom of action to each section of his empire, and thereby attached all to the central power. It had not occurred to his Semitic predecessors that any subject could serve the state voluntarily. Tiglathpileser III, Nebuchadrezzar, and Cyrus stand for three Oriental types of government. The first aimed to rule by denationalizing and disintegrating, the second by denationalizing and conserving, the third by local protection and personal oversight. This was as far as it was possible to go in the direction of local self-government without representation of the provinces in the councils of the empire. And it was an unspeakable blessing to the people of western Asia, harassed as they had been for ages by tax-gatherers and slave-drivers.

§ 1415. As far as the Semitic realm was concerned the most signal boon of the new system was that outgrowth of the sympathetic spirit of Cyrus, the revocation of the old

Assyrian system of the deportation and exile of offending subjects. To have put an end to this custom was of itself a unique distinction. But it was the rarest kingly sympathy which led him to decree that those already captive should be restored to home and country. One can feel that this is the mainspring of the personal gratitude and admiration felt for Cyrus by our prophet, as he sets before us in rapid strokes the pathetic picture of an Oriental prison and the joy of deliverance: "The cramped-up captive hastens to be freed, and he shall not die and descend to the pit, nor shall his bread run short" (li. 14).[1]

§ 1416. The question of the religion of Cyrus is one of historical interest as well as of Biblical importance. The first thing that strikes us is his tolerance. Under him and his successors religious wars of the Assyrian or Semitic type (§ 169) were impossible and unknown (cf. § 1377). But here again he was not content with relieving his world of an unspeakable curse. He became an actual patron of the local religions — endeavoured, in fact, to have as many established churches as there were separate peoples under his dominion. His proclamation regarding the returning Hebrews and their worship in Jerusalem is matched by his own report of what he did for the gods of Babylonia (§ 1398). It is thought by some that being a Zoroastrian (§ 1376), he had some sympathy with the spiritual religion of the Hebrews. This is not altogether impossible; but it does not explain his patronage of other forms of worship. Another opinion is that his whole procedure was a piece of good politics, and that he showed himself a religious indifferentist. There is no doubt about the excellence of the politics, but indifferentism is not to be inferred from his policy. This notion that Cyrus was

---

[1] We should not forget that this is Hebrew prophetic poetry. Our author does not mean to describe here the lot of the average exile. But his artistic sense is justified. It is the extreme instance which shows the effect of the system or the principle. In Oriental dungeons men starve to death, unless ministered to (Matt. xxv. 44) by friends; cf. § 1227.

a man of no religion is only less ill-considered than the view formerly held[1] that he learned the superiority of Jehovah from these very prophecies. What, however, is reasonably certain is that he was neither an agnostic nor a bigot, but a serious Zoroastrian; that, as a follower of Ahuramazda, he believed in the principles and practice of righteousness and in the possibility of its advancement; that as a good man he abhorred the idea of using force to spread his religious views, and as a sagacious ruler he was aware of the futility of that time-honoured practice; that while the religious motive actuated his career, it acted within as an impelling and directing force, and not without as an occasion of wrong and misery; that he saw sufficient good in all the greater religions to justify him in both tolerating and encouraging them; and that he promoted the happiness and welfare of his subjects by giving them the opportunity of serving God according to the dictates of conscience.

§ 1417. Cyrus, Alexander, Cæsar, these three changed the face of the ancient world. Men of the after time, even more than men of their own day, have been awe-struck by the almost superhuman genius and force of these rulers of the race. The historian, as he looks before and after, is moved more to thought and wonder by the effects of their deeds than by their deeds themselves, by what they left for others to do rather than by their own achievements. Such men can have no successors; and when they pass away, the world after them has to be made over again. After Cyrus came Cambyses, and then the collapse, inevitable when the force of the one strong hand had been fully spent. Under the great Darius the structure was recomposed, in part at least, after the mind of the founder; and the Persian dominion was better for the harassed races of

---

[1] Based in part on Ezra i. 2 ff. and in part on the statement of Josephus (*Ant.* xi. 2) that the predictions of "Isaiah" relating to him were shown to him after the capture of Babylon, and that he was seized with a desire to fulfil them by restoring the Hebrew exiles.

Asia than the outworn yoke of Semitism. Yet the geniality, the tact, and the humanity of Cyrus were wanting. These, however, were rather the attributes of an ideal ruler, such as the world has seldom seen, but such as, through and since Cyrus, it has desired and expected. Hence the better part of the Cyrus of history and prophecy is not that which he wrought for the Hebrews or the Babylonians or the Persians, but that which he was and is for humanity.

§ 1418. As with this hero of prophecy so was it with prophecy itself. The beauty and glory of the Second Isaiah were not reflected in the state or church of those exiles that returned to Palestine by the leave and encouragement of the great deliverer. No contrast could be greater than that between the prophetic picture of Israel's restoration and its actual process. Instead of "songs and everlasting joy" (Isa. li. 3, 11) there was continual bitterness of soul. Instead of imperial patronage and aid (xlix. 23) there was mere official tolerance or neglect. Instead of a host of eager patriots triumphantly reclaiming Jehovah's land and thronging thither from the ends of the earth (Isa. xlix. 19 ff.), a feeble band of settlers were huddled between the mounds of Jerusalem, which long remained without the bare essentials of walls and temple. Nor were the spiritual visions and hopes of the great prophet of the Exile more fully realized. The new Jerusalem, which was to be a light to the Gentiles (xlix. 6) and the hospitable shrine of votaries from the north and west, and even from the far land of China (xlix. 12), became the seat of a formal and exclusive worship, with a minute and rigorous ritual as the handbook of the most spiritual of religions.

§ 1419. But all this was inevitable, and in the order of providence if not according to the letter of prophecy. Is there a contradiction here? No, only a paradox. If the God of providence is also the God of prophecy, the paradox is solved as soon as we understand history, which is only the human side of providence. History is the fulfilment of prophecy as the finished statue or painting is the fulfilment of the artist's dream, with the superadded details of toil and circumstance. If God rules the world, then the actual must be the slow but sure fulfilment of his ideal. And his ideal, if any of his votaries have caught it at all, has been caught by the Hebrew prophets. It is their visions and none other that are being fulfilled in the moral progress of our race. The visions of the prophets are truer for us than the half-learned incidents of history, because they herald the fixed and necessary issues to which human events and actions tend in their zigzag and uncertain course. Moreover, the prophetic ideal is a living force which assures its own fulfilment (§ 13). Prophecy is thus not merely the interpreter and the forerunner of history, but also its guide and its goal. If there is anything fortuitous, it is the fate of men and nations. If there is anything certain, it is the progress of the prophetic ideal: justice, kindness, humility (Mic. vi. 8).

§ 1420. As we close our present survey, two ideas of infinite regenerative potency appear on the spiritual horizon, projected by our last great prophet — a universal brotherhood of men redeemed by Jehovah's grace, and the redemptive ministry of Jehovah's suffering Servant. These ideas are the forces that heal and uplift our hurt and stricken humanity. The last enemies to be destroyed in human society are tribalism surviving in militarism, and injustice materialized in cruel greed. They involve or induce all forms of impiety, crime, and misery; and in some of the most illusive and noxious of their disguises they deceive the very elect. Against them the Hebrew prophets, with their Goël the Christ and their true successors, have declared and waged eternal war. With weapons that are not carnal, but yet are mighty before God to the casting down of strongholds, they shall win the day. Men shall study war no more; the meek shall inherit the earth.

CHRONOLOGICAL OUTLINES

B.C.	
Before 7000.	First agricultural settlements in the Delta of the Euphrates in north Babylonia, the sites of the later south Babylonian settlements being still under the slowly receding waters of the Persian Gulf.
Before 6000.	Semitic emigration to Egypt, probably by way of South Arabia; agricultural settlements in Middle Egypt. Founding of cities, as Nippur and Kish, in central and northern Babylonia. Nippur, a central Semitic sanctuary sacred to Bêl.
Before 5000.	Rise of south Babylonian cities, as Erech and Ur. Kingdom of Shumer (Shinar) in central Babylonia. Development of petty kingdoms in the lower Nile valley.
5000–4000.	Successive rise of kingdoms throughout Babylonia. Akkad in north Babylonia takes the place of Shumer. Lagash (Shirpurla), then close to the Persian Gulf, rises to prominence in south Babylonia. Upper and Lower Egypt develop rival kingdoms.
c. 4000.	Union of Upper and Lower Egypt — First dynasty.
c. 3800.	Empire of Akkad extends to the Mediterranean under Sargon I, and Naram-Sin.
c. 3700.	Age of the great pyramids in Egypt.
c. 3600.	South Babylonia dominant in west Asia.
c. 3000.	City of Ur dominant in Babylonia.
c. 2280.	Babylonia subdued by the Elamites.
c. 2240.	Rise of city of Babylon. Chammurabi (Amraphel of Gen. xiv.) its king expels the Elamites and unites all Babylonia.
c. 2000.	Shepherd chiefs (Hyksos) found Asiatic dynasty in Egypt.
c. 1900.	Babylonians completely occupy and civilize Syria and Palestine. A large part of Israel goes down to Egypt.
c. 1600.	Babylonians retire from Syria and Palestine.
c. 1580.	Hyksos expelled from Egypt. Asiatics oppressed. Hardships of Israel in Egypt begin.
c. 1500.	Egyptian empire founded in Syria and Palestine.

B.C.
- c. 1400. Rise of the Hettite league in Syria. Egyptians give way to them in Syria.
- c. 1326. Treaty between Rameses II of Egypt and the Hettite king; Egyptians retain Palestine, and Hettites Syria.
- c. 1260. Merneptah of Egypt subdues Palestinian Israelites.
- c. 1200. Exodus of Hebrews from Egypt.
- c. 1190. Egyptians retire wholly from Palestine.
- c. 1170. Entrance of Egyptian Israelites into Canaan.
- c. 1130. Deborah and Barak judge.
- c. 1100. Assyria becomes more powerful than Babylonia, but does not occupy the latter country. Gideon judges.
- c. 1080. Decline of Egypt, Assyria, and Babylonia gives opportunity for development to Aramæans in Syria (Damascus, Zobah, etc.) and to Israel, with other peoples, in Palestine. Jepthah judges.
- c. 1050. Samuel judges.
- c. 1030. Saul is made king.
- c. 1000. David begins to reign.
- c. 965. Solomon begins to reign.
- c. 950. Temple in Jerusalem completed.
- 945. Libyan dynasty begins in Egypt under Shishak. Rise of Damascus.
- 934. Division of the kingdom. Jeroboam I in northern Israel, Rehoboam in Judah. Wars between Israel and Judah.
- 929. Shishak invades Israel and Judah.
- 918. Abijah king of Judah.
- 915. Asa king of Judah.
- 913. Nadab king of Israel.
- 911. Baasha king of Israel.
- 890. Baasha loses territory in the north to Ben-hadad I of Damascus. Revival of Assyrian power.
- 888. Elah king of Israel.
- 887. Zimri king of Israel.
- 886. Omri king of Israel. Founding of Samaria. Long peace with Judah.
- 875. Assyrians begin systematic conquest in Syria. Ahab king of Israel.
- 872. Jehoshaphat king of Judah. Alliance with Judah against Damascus.
- 855. Peace with Damascus under Benhadad II.
- 854. Shalmaneser II wages battle at Karkar with a western confederacy, including Israel and Damascus.
- 853. Truce broken; Ahab killed at Ramoth-Gilead. Ahaziah and Joram kings of Israel.
- 850. Jehoram king of Judah.

CHRONOLOGICAL OUTLINES 435

B.C.
- 843. Ahaziah king of Judah.
- 842. Jehu king of Israel; Athaliah queen of Judah. Shalmaneser receives tribute from Jehu.
- 836. Israel saved from destruction through the attacks of Hazael of Damascus by the Assyrian assaults upon the latter. Jehoash king of Judah.
- 815. Jehoahaz king of Israel.
- 799. Ethiopian inroad on Upper Egypt. Joash king of Israel.
- 797. Damascus taken by Ramman-nirari III of Assyria. Amaziah king of Israel.
- 783. Revival of north Israel. Assyrians retire. Jeroboam II king of Israel. Azariah (Uzziah) king of Judah.
- 769. Expansion of Judah. Azariah (sole reign).
- 763. Prophet Amos.
- 761. Jotham king of Judah.
- 743. Prophet Hosea.
- 742. Zachariah and Shallum kings of Israel.
- 741. Menahem king of Israel.
- 738. Israel terrorized and made tributary by Tiglathpileser III (Pul) of Assyria (745-727). Jotham (sole reign). Prophet Isaiah.
- 736. Pekahiah king of Israel.
- 735. League of Damascus and north Israel against Judah. Pekah king of Israel. Ahaz king of Judah.
- 734. Tiglathpileser III invades Palestine. Judah tributary to Assyria.
- 733. Damascus and Samaria taken by Assyrians; part of Israel deported; Hoshea Assyrian vassal in Samaria.
- 728. Ethiopian dynasty in Egypt (728-645).
- 724. Revolt of Hoshea. Prophet Micah.
- 722. Sargon II, king of Assyria (722-705), deports 27,290 people of Samaria. Annexation to Assyria.
- 719. Hezekiah king of Judah.
- 704. He joins in revolt against Assyria.
- 701. Sinacherib (705-681) invades Palestine; deports many people of Judah; retires from Jerusalem because of plague in his army.
- 690. Manasseh king.
- 689. Sinacherib destroys Babylon.
- 681. Esar-haddon (681-668) restores Babylon.
- 672. Esar-haddon conquers Egypt.
- 667. Asshurbanipal (668-626) reconquers Egypt.
- 648. Asshurbanipal ends great revolt by capture of Babylon.
- 645. Assyrians withdraw from Egypt.
- 641. Amon king.
- 639. Josiah king.
- 626. Swift decline of Assyria. Prophet Jeremiah.
- 621. Finding of the Book of Direction; reform in religion and worship.

B.C.
620. Prophet Zephaniah.
608. Pharaoh-necho invades Palestine and Syria. Josiah killed in battle with Necho. Jehoahaz and Jehoiakim kings. Judah a vassal of Egypt.
607. Nineveh destroyed by Medes. Prophet Nahum.
604. Necho defeated at Carchemish by Nebuchadnezzar (604-562). Judah submits to Nebuchadnezzar.
600. Prophet Habakkuk.
598. Jehoiakim revolts. Chaldæans invade Judah.
597. Jehoiachin king. First captivity.
597. Zedekiah king.
592. Prophet Ezekiel.
588. Zedekiah rebels. Jerusalem invested.
586. Jerusalem taken. Second captivity.
581. Murder of the governor Gedaliah. Many remaining Hebrews migrate to Egypt. Others deported — a third captivity.
567. Nebuchadnezzar conquers Egypt, but does not retain it.
562. Evil-Merodach, king of Babylon.
556. Nabonidus, last king of Babylon.
550. Cyrus, prince of Persia and Elam, becomes king of the Medes.
547. Cyrus conquers Lydia.
539. Cyrus conquers Babylon and becomes its king.
538. Proclamation of Cyrus freeing the exiles of Judah.

INDEX I

SUBJECTS

The numbers refer to the paragraphs of the work.

The tables of Contents should be used in connection with this Index when several references are set down for the same topic.

app. = appendix	L = land, region, or district
b. = son of (*ben*)	M = mountain or mountain
bat = daughter of	range
C = city or city state	n. = note
Ch = chief	O = officer or official
Cr = commander	P = people or race
D = divinity or demon	Q = queen
G = governor or viceroy	R = river
I = island	S = settlement or site
J = judge	T = tribe or clan
K = king or kinglet	W = watercourse

Aahmes I (K), 144, 346.
Abdashirti (Cr), 152.
Abdiḥaba (G), 152.
Abdili'ti (K), 675.
Abel-beth-maacah (C), 331, I. app. 13.
Abijah (K), 210.
Abimelech (K), 49, 189; (G), 152.
Abiyate (Ch), 788.
Abner (Cr), 203.
Abraham (Abram, Ch), 109, 406, 412, 445, 417 n., 732 n., 955, 959.
Absalom b. David, 205, 515, 526, 971.
Abu-Habba (S), 87.
Abu Nejm (S), 1293.
Abu Simbel (C), 1207.
Abyssinians ("Ethiopians"), 18, 23.

Accho (Akko, C), 152, 226, 675, 789.
Achaemenes (Ch), 1378.
Achāru ("West"), 133 n.
Achbor (O), 850.
Achimiti (K), 632, II. app. 4.
Achish (K), 197.
Achuni (K), 227.
Adar (Nineb, D), 57, 220, 818.
Adarmalik b. Sinacherib, 744.
Adbeel (P), 334.
Addan (S), 1273.
Addar (C), 152.
Adinnu (C), 228.
Adonijah b. David, 205.
Adonis (D, cf. Tammuz), 330, 1184 n.
Adoption, family, 404; tribal and national, 548 ff, 568; see Strangers.
Adoniba'al (K), 228.

INDEX I

Adrammelech, see Adarmalik.
Agriculture, Hebrew, 475, 484, 540, 567; Babylonian, 1276, 1283, 1317.
Agum-kak-rime (K), 123.
Ahab (K), 213 ff., 221, 228, 231 ff., 239, 519, 981 f., 1005; (exile). 1160.
Ahava (C), 1273 n.
Ahaz (K), 270, 308, 317 ff., 325 ff., 336; I. app. 12.
Ahaziah (K). of Judah, 221, 236, 254; of "Israel." 235, 635, 638 ff.
Ahijah (prophet), 979.
Ahikam b. Shaphan, 843, 850, 1092.
Ahriman (D), 1376.
Ahúramazda (D), 1376, 1416.
Ai (C), 185.
Akaba, gulf of, 755.
Akaba (C), 780.
Akkad (Agade, C), 80, 87 ff., 93 f, 98 f, 102, 105, 752; (L), 782, 1302, 1305 f.
Akkadian, see Sumerians.
Akki (O), 89.
Akzibi (Ekdippa, C), 675.
Aleppo (Chalman, C), 141, 202, 226, 228, 241.
Alexander of Macedon, 42, 737 n., 1417.
Allatu (D), 1185.
Alliances, see Federations.
Altruism in the Old Testament. 611 ff.; among the Hebrews, 958 f., 966, 972.
Alusharshid (K), 91 f.
Alyattes III (K), 775.
Amalekites, 183, 197, 204, 975.
Amanus (M), 96, 125, 201, 219, 257, 307.
Amarna (Tell el Amarna, S), and its inscriptions, 146 ff.
Amasis (K), 1365.
Amaziah (K), 254, 260 f.
Amedi (C. Diarbekr), 247.
Amen (D), 144 f., 207, 346, 770 n.
Amenophis (K), III, 145 ff., 162; IV, 147 ff., 162, 175.
Ammonites, 26 (18), 48, 50, 183, 190 f., 196, 204, 209, 215, 228, 263, 268 f., 273, 302, 337, 550 n., 675,
677, 761, 787, 972, 1078, 1157, 1213, 1240, 1243, 1251.
Amon (K), 806, 845.
Amorites, 26, 41, 48, 117, 131, 132 f., 160, 163, 183 ff., 201, I. app. 3.
Amos, the prophet, 244, 261, 302 ff., 320, 354, I. app. 4, 604, 637 ff., 1363.
Amraphel, see Chammurabi.
Amu (P), 132, 135.
Anat (D), 856 n.
Anathoth (C), 1101, 1221, 1225.
Animal worship, 1183.
Anshan (L), 98, 106, 1378, 1404.
Anthropomorphisms, 927.
Anti-Lebanon, 125.
Anu (D), 172, 856 n.
Anunit (D), 94.
Aphek (C), 194, 231, 234, 756.
Arabah (L), 262, 273.
Arabia and Arabs (collectively), 18, 23, 47 f., 125 f., 132, 134 f., 141, 228, 230, 675, 705 f.; North A., 97, 132, 134 f., 163, 228, 334, 630, 708 f., 741, 754 f., 786 ff., 802; South A., 145, 878; Arabs in Babylonia, 114, 117, 438; in Jerusalem, 675.
Aramæans, distribution. 25 (17), 75; I. app. 5; achievements, 64, 202, 368; political conditions, 47, 284, 286; trade, 64, 141, 202, 212; language, 701; settlements and history, 160 f., 179, 188, 201 f., 211, 223, 228, 247, 293, 351, 438, 660 f., 672, 780, 1078; see especially Damascus and Mesopotamia.
Arami (K), 228.
Aram-Naharaim (L), 75, 132.
Ararat (L), see Armenia.
Architecture, 341, 667, 737, 742, 762, 830.
Ardys II (K), 775.
Argana (C), 228.
Argistis (K), 256.
Argo (I), 346.
Ariel (Jerusalem), 772.
Arioch (K), 108 ff., 113 f., 117.
Ark of the Covenant, 194, 919.
Armageddon (C), 145.

Armenia (L), 154, 179, 222, 247, 256, 258, 284, 294, 311, 626, 735, 747, 1403.
Army (cf. Warfare and Weapons): Hebrew, 199, 205, 210, 245, 264, 266, 268 f., 458, 512 ff., 531, 700, 879; Egyptian, 144; Assyrian, 697 n., 813; Medo-Persian, 1396.
Arnon (R), 183, 243.
Arpad (C), 141, 226, 294, 624.
Arsu (K), 166.
Art in Israel, 269, 1178 n.
Arvad (C), 125, 145, 152, 180, 675.
Aryans, contrasted with Semites, 5 f., 28 f., 56; in Asiatic history, 823, 1373 ff.; cf. Kimmerians, Scythians, Greeks, Medes, Persians.
Asa (K), 211, 215, 1247 n.
Asdudimmu (C), 632.
Ashdod (C), 192, 632, 634 (653 f., 658 f.), 675, 684, 689, II. app. 4, 1032.
Asher (T), 186, 272.
Ashera (D), 152 n., 321, 330, 854.
Asherites (P), 530.
Ashkenaz (P), 1403.
Ashtoreth (Astarte, cf. Ishtar, D), 137, 200 n., 213, 321, 855, 856 n., 971, 1256.
Asi (Cyprus, I), 133.
Askalon (C), 152, 192, 332, 675, 689 ff.
Asshur (C), 74, 171 f., 179 f., 247, 258 f., 283; (D), 57, 59 f.
Asshurbanipal (Asshurbânapil, K), 90, 107, 763 ff., 802, 816 ff., II. app. 17, 1286.
Asshur-bêl-nishêsu (K), 175.
Asshur-dân (K), I, 178; II, 216; III, 258.
Asshur-etil-ilâni (K), 820, 824.
Asshur-nâdin-shum (K), 739.
Asshur-nirâri (K), 258, 281.
Asshurnâsirpal (Asshurnâṣrapil, K), 180, 216 ff., 282.
Asshur-rêsh-ishî (K), 178.
Asshur-uballit (K), 175.
Asshur-zâkir-shum (K), 671.
Assiah (O), 850.
Assouan (Syene, C), 346, 1365.

Assyria (L). 74.
Assyrians (P): classification, 18; character, 168 f., 268; extension, 39 f., 808 f.; culture, 816 ff.; colonies, 41, 175; trade, 141; political tendencies and government, 41, 52, 168, 172, 217, 221 ff., 282 ff., 361, 363, 382 ff., 723, 743, 1050, 1402; religion and deities, 57, 59, 168 f., 172, 220, 228, 259, 640; achievements, 65, 365 f., 368, 836; language, 80 ff., 115, 153 f.; monuments, 217, 220 n., 221 n., 237, 242, 248, 268, 281 n., I. app. 6, 15, 16, 666 f., 675, 690, 757, 817, II. app. 9, 16, 17; general history, 76, 78, 145, 150, 155, 170 ff., and see Contents; relations with Syria and Palestine, 161, 174, 212, 250 ff., 294, 305 ff., 326, 331 ff., 343 f., 349 ff., 512, 556, 624 f.; relations with Egypt, 150, 332, 625, 630, 632, 675, 678 f., 705, 708 ff., 756, 761, 764 ff., II. app. 14.
Astarte, see Ashtoreth.
Astrology in Israel. 856.
Astyages (K), 1380, 1382 ff.
Ataroth (C), 285.
Aten (D), 147.
Athaliah (Q), 235, 254, 320.
Athbash (cypher), 1403 n.
Atlantic navigated, 42, 66, 1031.
Azariah, see Uzziah.
Azekah (C), 1213.
Azupiranu (C), 89.
Azuri (K), 632, II. app. 4.
Azûru (C), 675.

Ba'al, lord and husband, 418, 426 n.; (K), 757, 761 n.
Baal (ba'alim, D), worship, 59 f., 137, 213, 321, 855, 856 n.
Baalis (K), 1245.
Baasha (K), of Israel, 211, 1247 n.; of Ammon, 228.
Bâb-salimêti (C), 780.
Babylon (Babel, C), 34, 39 f., 111 f., 117, 180, 247, 623, 660 f., 663, 673, 740, 748 ff., 783, 1056 ff., 1273, 1292 f., 1371 f., 1392 ff.

Babylonia: extent, 73; physical aspect. 1314.
Babylonians: classification, 18; age, 70; character, 122; language, see Assyrians; civilization, 79 ff.; achievements, 65, 93, 116, 153 f., 365 ff., 836 f.; religion and deities, 57, 87, 94 f., 99 ff., 107 f., 112, 117, 122, 799, 1053 f., 1060 ff., 1185, 1332, 1346; industry, 1064, 1276 f., trade, 90 f., 96 f., 103, 1059; general history, 86 ff., 149, 153, 174 ff., 223 f., 247, 293, 339 f., 670, 733 ff., 748 ff., 778 ff., 822, 1025 f., 1045 ff., 1364 ff.; relations with Syria and Palestine, 90 ff., 96, 100, 116, 123, 137, 141, 153 ff., 174, 679, 1043 f., 1171, 1210 ff., 1241, 1250; relations with Egypt, 96, 149, 1222, 1365 f.; relations with Medo-Persians, 1391 ff.; monuments, 87 ff., 95 ff., 117 n., 146 ff., 1051 n., 1053 n., 1371 n., 1382 n., 1393 n. See also Agriculture, Business, Watercourses.
Baghdad (C), 71.
Baktria (L), 1374, 1389.
Balaam's prophecies, 895.
Balich (R), 75, 218, 228, 343, 362.
Ban, the sacred, 550.
Banai-Barka (C), 675, 695.
Barak (J), 188, 479.
Barkal (M), 347.
Baruch b. Neriah, 1082 n., 1116 ff., 1242, 1248, 1254, 1353.
Bashan (L), 186, 243, 272, 315.
Bâzu (P), 755 n.
Bedawin, 127.
Beenah marriage, 412 f.
Bekenrenf (Bocchoris, K), 347.
Bêl (D), 57, 94, 112, 341, 1284 f.
Bêl (and Nebo), 341, 663.
Bêl-êpush (K), see Bêl-ibnê.
Bêl-ibnê (K), I, 172; II, 673, 735.
Bêl-kapkapu (K), 172.
Bêl-Merodach (D), 1056, 1285.
Bêl-nirâri (K), 175.
Belshazzar (Ch), II. app. 3; (prince), 1371, 1392.
Bêl-shum-ishkun (K), 1370 n.

Bene-berak, see Banai-Barka.
Benhadad (K), I, 211; II, 221, 228 ("Dadda-idri"), 231 ff., 236 f., 241; III, 245.
Benjamin (T), 188, 194, 196, 200, 204, 208, 275.
Bera (K), 109.
Bernard of Clugny, an illustration, 1237 n.
Beth-Ammon, see Ammonites.
Beth-arbel (C), 314.
Beth-Dagon (C), 675, 695.
Beth-Eden (L), 227.
Bethel (C), 185 f., 477, 687, 840, 928.
Bethlehem (C), 197.
Beth-shean (C), 812 n.
Bethshemesh (C), 260; (Heliopolis), 1255 n.
Beth-ziti (C), 675.
Beyrut (C), 152.
Bingâni (K), 92.
Bit-Chumrî (N. Israel), 133–212, 243, 248, 331.
Bit-Dakkûri (C), 662.
Bit-elû, see Esagila.
Bit-kênu, see Ezida.
Bit-Yâkin (L), 223, 340, 664, 666, 733 f., 751.
Blood-revenge, 398, 465, 486, 950, 972.
Boats and rafts, 1305 and n.
Boer question, illustrated, 955, 1223, 1258 ff.
Borsippa (Barzip, C), 112, 663, 783, 1061 n., 1063, 1392.
Bribery, see Venality, Gifts.
Bronze, I. app. 3.
Bubastis (C), 345.
Bunyan as a seer, 1354.
Burial of a Hebrew king, 1216 n.
Burraburiash (K), 149, 175.
Business, society, and morals, 990, 1318 ff.
Business documents, 422 n., 899, 1225, 1321 ff.
Bûz (P and L), 755 n.
Byblus (Gebal, Gubal, C), 145, 152, 675.

Cæsar, Julius, 766 n., 1417.
Cain the outlaw, 398 n.

INDEX I

Caleb the Kenizzite, 493, 550, 563.
Calendar, 748 n. (cf. 746 f.), 1344 n.
Caliphate, 47.
Cambyses (K), I, 1382; II, 1397, 1417.
Camels, 475.
Canaanites: classification, 24 (18); how far distant from Amorites, 131, I. app. 3; settlements, 126 ff.; political tendencies, 37, 47, 49 f., 52 ff., 127, 144. 184; culture, 141. 164, 166, 184; religion, 184, 495; relations with Israel, 185 ff., 200, 369 f., 472 f., 477 ff., 493 ff., 506 f.; relations with Egypt, 135 ff., 164.
Canals, see Watercourses.
Caphtor (L). 192.
Cappadocia (L. Kummuch, etc.), 154, 157, 179, 281, 294, 311.
Captivity, see Deportation, Exile.
Caravan traffic, 135, 202, 334.
Carchemish (C), 126, 141, 145, 162. 179, 201 f., 219, 227 f., 237, 628, 827, 1043, 1088 f., 1115.
Carians (P), 768, 1380.
Carthage (C), 42. 43, 45, 683.
Caspian Sea, 247 f.
Cattle among the Hebrews, 475.
Cavalry, see Army and Horses.
Census (cf. Imposts), 523.
Centralism, Hebrew, 52; Semitic, 56; Assyrian. 743.
Centralization of worship (cf. Temple). 992.
Ceremonialism in Israel (cf. Ethics and ritual), 1000 f., 1011 f., 1017, 1021, 1023, 1026, 1068, 1094, 1114, 1344.
Chabet (P), 1089 n.
Chabiri (P), 152.
Chabor (Habor, Chaboras, R), 71. 75, 218, 343, 362 f.
"Chaldæan Genesis." 886 n.
Chaldæans (P), 18, 112, 223 f.. 237. 247 f.. 293. 339 f., 438, 621 ff.. 660 ff., 671 ff., 733 ff.. 751, 780 f., 784 f., 822. 1046 ff., 1090 ff., 1129 ff.
Chalule (C), 739.
Chammurabi (Amraphel, K), 109, 111, 113 f., 117, 1056 n., 1285.

Chanirabbat (L, cf. Chānu), 746 f.
Chānu (L, N. Syria), 123, 161 n.
Chanun (K), 332, 625.
Chariots (cf. Army), 144, 519 f.
Charrān (Haran, C), 26, 47, 75, 141, 874, 1383 f.
Charu (S. W. Palestine), 132.
Chastity among the Hebrews, 616 f.; cf. Sexual Morality.
Chattin (L, Patin ?), 226 ff., I. app. 9.
Chayāpa (Ephah, P), 630.
Chedorlaomer (K), 109, 114, 117.
Chemosh (D), 59, 235, 855.
Chemosh-nadab (K), 675.
Cherub (C), 1273.
Cherubim, 1176 n.
Chetta-sira (K). 163.
Chiefs, 36, I. app. 2, 396 n., 444 f., 452, 560.
Chinnereth (Lake), 211.
Chittim (C), 42, I. app. 3, 681.
Choaspes, see Uknu.
Choser (R), 341, 827 n.
Christian Science illustrated, 1199.
"Christianity's Millstone," 615 n.
Chronicles, see Kings.
Chronology, 87 f., 107, 118 f.. 167, 180, 190, 234, I. app. 6, 634 ff., II. app. 6.
Chubushkia (L). 759 n.
Chu-en-Aten, see Amenophis IV.
Chumbaba (K), 107.
Chumbanigash (K), 623.
Cilicia (L), 132, 201, 206, 226, 243, 294, 311, 735, 773, 1379.
Circumcision, as an adoptive rite, 540, 551.
Cities and city life, Semitic, 31 ff., 47; Hebrew (Canaanitic), 477, 482 ff., 493, 496, 498, 501 f., 505.
Clans. 396 ff., 444 f., 448. 451. 500.
Clientage in Israel, 548 ff., 567.
Clothing, of the poor, 584.
Cœle-Syria (L), 125, 141.
Colonies, Semitic, 41 ff.; and see Phœnicians, Aramæans, Assyrians.
Communism. Hebrew, 50, 565.
Confucianism, 431, 1328.

Conquered enemies, how treated (cf. Deportation, Warfare), 1192, 1232 ff., 1270 f.
Copper in commerce, I. app. 3; cf. 630.
Corporate (tribal, national) religion, 1000, 1022, 1024.
Court officials, 205, 521 f., 590, 592, 697, 1154.
Covenant, Book of the, 474, 487, 502, 586, 847 f., 891 f., 1100.
Creation literature, 885 ff.
Cretans (P), 192, 520.
Crœsus (K), 1380, 1387 f.
Cuneiform, see Writing.
Cush, and Cushites, 145, 346, 655, 1207, 1228 n.
Cushanrishathaim (K), 188.
Cutha (Kūtū, C), 94, 102, 783.
Cyaxares (K), 1379.
Cyprus (I), 90, 93 n., 125, 133, 145, I. app. 3, 666, 681 f., 738, II. app. 4.
Cyrus (K), I, 1378 n.; II, 359, 1378, 1381 ff., 1408 ff.

D, see Deuteronomist.
Daban (W), 247.
Daghara (W), 1294.
Damascus (C L), 34 and n., 40, 47, 55, 126, 128, 141, 201 f., 209, 211 f., 215, 226, 228 ff., 235 ff., 248, 250 ff., 257, 262 f., 270, 273, 302, 310, 315 f., 333, 335 f., 376, 380, 516, 556, 624, 788, II. app. 7.
Dan (Laish, C), 109; (T), 50, 62, 186, 193.
Daniel the prophet, 1201.
Dante, as seer, 1354.
Darius Hystaspes (K), 359, 1378 n., 1417.
" Dark-haired " race, 89.
David (K), 197 ff., 415, 476, 478, 515, 518, 522 f., 529, 967 ff.; his poems, 898, 902, 908 f.; his biographies, 919.
Dayan-Asshur (K), 228.
Dead Sea, 273.
Deborah (prophetess), 188, 479; Song of, 187 f., 476, 479, 879, 897, 913, 918.

Debts and debtors in Israel, 575 f., 584 f., 1322; in Babylonia, 1323.
Decalogue, 463 n., 891 f.
Deceit and fraud in Israel (cf. Honesty), 296, 592 ff., 644, 955 ff., 970, 1320.
Deiokes (Dayakka, K), 824; (G), II, app. 3.
Deities, national, 50, I. app. 2, 854; and morality, 951, 985.
Delegated power, 56, 1386.
Delilah, see Samson.
Delphic oracle, 1387.
Delta of the Nile, 347.
Deluge literature, 885 ff.
Deluges, 1296, 1300 n.
Dependencies: Semitic, 39 f., 53, 55, 61, 683; Hebrew, 53, 204 ff., 112, 215, 262, 268, 474, 540, 645; Babylonian, 92 f., 97 ff., 109, 116, 123, 178, 1044, 1076 ff., 1152; Egyptian (and Ethiopian), 134 f., 143 ff., 346 f., 678, 1240 f., 1250 f.; Assyrian, 175, 179 ff., 218 ff., 242 ff., 282–316, 326, 331 ff., 339, 343 f., 348 ff., 357 ff., 382 ff., 630 ff., 650 ff., 675, 688, 733, 741, 749 f., 756, 762, 765, 768, 771, 776, 793 ff., 806 n., 821 f., 839 ff., 1036.
Deportation, 61, 283, 288 ff., 362, 666, 673, 675, 1156 n., 1232 n., 1234, 1250, 1268 ff.
Desert literature, 891 ff.
Deuteronomic editing, 925 n., 1356 ff.
Deuteronomy, I. app. 4, 502, 586, 846 ff., 865 ff., 943 ff., 1018, 1020 ff., 1343 f., 1361.
Diarbekr (Amedi, C), 247.
Dilmun (I), 89, 96, 666.
Diplomacy, Oriental, 148 ff., 163, 175, 207, 213, 231, 249, 316, 655, 679, 825 f., 1051, 1379.
Direction (teaching, the Law), 457, 488, 610; Book of Direction (cf. Deuteronomy), 846 f.
Disciples of the prophets, 995 f., 998, 1065.
Districts, administrative, 206, 530.
Divination, see Oracles.
Divine influence, 1097, 1113 f.

Doctrines (cf. Faith), 1008 f.
Drunkenness in Israel. 596, 641 ff.
Dungi (Ba'ukin, K), 102.
Dûr-il (C), 89.
Dûr-Sharrukin (C), 667 ff.
Dûr-Yâkin (C), 664.
Dushratta (K), 150.

E, see Elohist.
Ea (D), 85, 112, 738.
Earthquakes, 264 f.
Ebal (M), 186.
Ebedmelech (O), 1228.
Eclipses of the sun, 259, 265, I. app. 6, 1379.
Eden (L), 73, 112.
Edessa (C), 75.
Edom and Edomites, 18, 26, 48, 55, 132, 152, 204, 209, 215, 235 f., 248, 250, 254, 269, 273, 302, 325, 337, 379, 512, 633, 675, 761, 787, 1157, 1240 n., 1243, 1251, 1404 n.
Egypt and Egyptians, language, 80; writing, 872 f.; trade, 97, 334; place-names, 132 f.; relations with western Asia generally, 134 ff., 151 ff., 161 ff., 210, 215, 313, 348 ff., 367, 440, 653, 750; relations with Hebrews, see Hebrews, Judah, and N. Israel; references to Dynasty IV, 134; VI, 134; IX and X, 135; XII, 135, 346; XIII–XVII, 136 ff.; XVIII, 143 ff., 161 ff.; XIX, 163 ff.; XX, 166 f.; XXI, 207; XXII, 207, 210, 215, 345; XXIII, XXIV, 313, 347; XXV, 313, 348, 675, 678; 693 f., 756, 764 ff.; XXVI, 1029 ff., 1222, 1365.
Ehud (J), 188, 964.
Ekallâti (C), 180.
Ekbatana (C), 824, 1382, 1397.
Ekron (C), 55, 192, 675, 689 ff., 695.
Elah (K), 212.
Elam and Elamites, 54 f., 79, 90, 92, 98, 106 ff., 113 f., 120, 178, 247, 621 ff., 660 ff., 672, 736 ff., 751 f., 779 ff., 1163, 1285 n., 1404.
Elasah b. Shaphan, 1167.
Elath (C), 269, 325.

Elders, 36, 443, 486, 560, 1092, 1310 f.
Elegies, 898, 902, 1237 ff.
Eli (J), 195, 414, 490.
Eliakim (O), 697, 699; b. Josiah, see Jehoiakim.
Eliezer (slave), 406.
Elijah, the prophet, 239, 982 f.; biography, 935.
Elisha, the prophet, 239–244, 612; biography, 935.
Elishama (O), 1119.
Ellip (L), 674.
Elnathan b. Achbor, 1121 n.
Elohist, I. app. 4, 890 f., 894, 922 f.
Elohistic school, 930.
Elteke (C), 675, 695, II. app. 14.
Elukæus, see Lulē.
Employments of Hebrews: in Palestine, 483 f., 507 ff., 1275; in Babylonia, 1274 ff., 1301 ff.
Ephod, 506.
Ephraim, 186 (185), 188 f., 191, 196, 200, 212, 275, 935; (L), 275 n.; see Israel, Northern.
Ephron (Ch), 158.
Epical poetry, 883, 912.
Eponym canon, 216, 294, I. app. 6.
Erech (C), 88, 101 f., 104, 107 f., 1291.
Eridu (C), 101, 104, 112, 1291.
Esagila (Bit-elû, temple), 112, 117, 123, 749, 1060 f., 1395.
Esarhaddon (K), 341, 745 ff., II. app. 16, 1286.
Esau (Ch), 412.
Ethbaal, see Ithobal.
Ethics and ritual, 1017, 1023 ff., 1094, 1114.
Ethiopia, see Cush.
Eukæus, see Ulai.
Euphrates (R), 22, 71 f., 141, 145, 219, 222, 225, 228, 237, 329, 730 n., 1058 f., 1290 ff.
"European Morals," 616 n.
Evil-Merodach (K), 1081, 1369.
Exile (cf. Hebrews Exiled, Deportation), 290, 301 ff.; Babylonian, its character and influence, 1263 ff.
Exiles in Babylonia, 1399.

Exodus, of Hebrews from Egypt, 667. 879 ; the book, 925 f.
Explorations in Babylonia, 87, 91, 95 ; in Assyria, 667.
Ezekiel (the prophet), I. app. 3, 814, 833, 1081, 1143, 1174 ff., 1268 f., 1336, 1342 ff., 1353 f., 1362, 1366 f.
Ezida (Bît-kēnu, temple), 112, 117, 1063.
Ezion-geber (C), 209.

Faith, Old Testament, 667, 1008. 1132 f., 1138.
Families, 396 ff., 448, 1310 f.
Fasts, 1116, 1118, 1346 n.
Fatherhood, 427 ff. ; figuratively, 431 ff.
Fayum, the (L), 347.
Feasts and social gatherings, 499 f., 504, 576, 862, 871, 940, 994, 1092, 1246, 1314 ff.
Federations, of tribes, 47 ff., 53 f., 468 ; of states, 54, I. app. 5.
Fen countries, 734 n.
Fenchu (P), 132.
Finno-tartaric language, see Sumerians.
Foresight, prophetic, 1260, 1410.
Fortresses (cf. Sieges), 204, 212, 268, 311, 357, 664, 827, 1058, 1306.
Fuller's Field, 698, 1231.

Gad (T), 183, 191, 235 ; (prophet), 978.
Gâgu (Gog, Ch.), 777 n., 814.
Galilee (L), 272, 274, 331, I. app. 13.
Gambulu (P), 339, 661, 779.
Gamgum (L), 228, 629.
Gate of Benjamin, 1221, 1228.
Gath (C), 152, 192, 197, 243 n., 632, 689, II. app. 4.
Gaza (C), 152, 163, 192, 332, 625, 675, 689.
Geba (C), 194, 196.
Gebal, see Byblos.
Gedaliah (G), 1240 ff., 1249.
Gemariah b. Shaphan, 1119 f. ; b. Hilkiah, 1167.

Genesis (book), 925 f., 952.
Gēr, see Strangers.
Gerizim (M), 186.
Gezer (C), 152, 207.
Ghōr (L), 139.
Giammu (K), 228.
Gibeah (C), 196, 477, 965.
Gibeon (C), 185, 1218.
Gideon (J), 49, 51, 189, 415, 732 n., 965, 972.
Gifts (cf. Venality), 149 f., 594 f.
Gihon (W), 697.
Gilboa (M), 198, 515.
Gilead (L), 129, 138, 141, 186, 190 f., 196, 212, 233, 243, 262, 272, 274 f., 337 (331), I. app. 13, 530 n.
Gileadites, 316.
Gilgal (C), 185, 188, 477.
Gilgamesh epic, 912 n.
Gilza (C), 228.
Gimirrē, see Kimmerians.
Gindibu'u (Ch), 228 and n., 230.
Girgashites (P), 130.
Gobryas (Cr), 1386, 1395 f.
Gods, see Deities, Polytheism.
Goël (vindicator), 426, 486, 601 n., 966, 1420.
Gog, see Gāgu.
Gomer, see Kimmerians.
Government, see especially Hebrews, Assyrians.
Gozan (L), 343, 362.
Greece and Phoenicia, I. app. 3.
Greeks in Palestine, 632, II. app. 4 ; in Cilicia, 735 ; in Egypt, 768, 1030 ; in Asia Minor, 1389.
Gubi (L), 96.
Gudea (Nabû, K), 96, 98, 171.
Guilds and professions, 484, 569 f., 851 and n., 871, 934, 1066, 1306 n.
Gutium (L), 92, 109, 171, 780, 1393, 1395 f.
Gyges (Gūgu, K), 768, 773 ff.

Habakkuk and his prophecy, 1128 ff., 1172.
Hadad (D), 59 ; (Ch), 209.
Hadadezer (Dadda-idri, K), 204, 228.
Hadad-Rimmon (C), I. app. 5.

Hadrach (Chatarika, C), 258, 307 n., 315.
Hagar, the Egyptian, 430, 437 n.
Halys (R), 1379.
Hamath (C), 125, 141, 201 f., 226, 228. 230 f., 237, 241, 247, 262, 305 ff., 315, 331, I. app. 9, 624.
Hanameel of Anathoth, 1225.
Hananiah (prophet), 1158 f.
Hannah, mother of Samuel, 430; her Song, 908 f.
Haran, see Charrān.
Harpagus (Cr), 1384 n., 1386.
Hauran (L), 242 f., 787.
Hazael (K of Damascus), 236, 241 ff.; (Arabian), 741, 755.
Hazo (P), 755 n.
Hazor (C), 152, 331.
Heber (Ch), 550.
Hebraic peoples, 26, 284; and see Ammon, Edom, Moab.
Hebrews: origin, 26 (18); racial endurance, 434 ff., 963, 1263; character and spirit (cf. Semites), 434 f., 526, 546 f., 558; relation to outsiders, 548 ff., 556; colonies, 41; general political conditions, 47 ff., 266, 296, 372 ff., 470 f., 521 ff., 557; government, see Rulers, Chiefs, Elders, Judges, Princes, King, Court, Imposts, Law; achievements and mission, 67 ff., 385 ff., 1028; chronological place, 70; language, 153, 392 f.; writing, 877 ff.; trade, 206, 212, 231, 236, 524; culture, 1178 n., morals and religion, 61, 183, 195, 206, 210, 239 f., 271, 296 ff., 314, 317 ff., 354 ff., 373, 377 f., 381 f., 442, 451, 480 ff., 489 f., 493 ff., 504 ff., 533, 574 ff., 607 ff., 613, 640 ff., 795 f., 799, 805, II. app. 7, 840 ff., 927 f., 946 ff., 962, 1155 f., 1182 ff., 1320 ff.; tribal history, 165 ff., 436 ff., 182 ff., 369 ff., 472 ff., 879; the single monarchy, 195 ff.; the divided kingdom, see Israel and Judah; Hebrews exiled: in Assyrian lands, 362 f.; in Egypt, 1039 (1254 ff.); in Babylonia (cf. Agriculture, Employments, Slaves, Watercourses), 289, 1081, 1165 ff., 1176 n., 1272 ff.
Hebron (C), 137, 139, 152, 205.
Hereditary office, 560, 569 f.
Hermon (M), 125, 242.
Herodotus, 1332 n., 1412 n.
Heroic poetry, see Epical.
Heroic prose, 918 f.
Heroic virtues, 954, 963, 969.
Heshbon (C), 183.
Hettites (Chettā, Chattē, P), 41, 130, 132, 152, 156 ff., 179, 201, 206, 219, 226, 284, 294, I. app. 5, 367 f., II. app. 4.
Hezekiah (K), 55, 287, I. app. 12, 635, 637 f., 675, 688, 692 f., 695 ff., 791 ff., II. app. 11, 860 n., 1002; his Song, 909.
Hiel (Bethelite), 498 n.
High places, see Shrines.
Hilkiah (priest), 843, 846 f., 850 f.
Hillah (C), 1293.
Hindieh (canal), 1293.
Hinnom (valley), 855, 1095.
Hirelings, 541.
Hirom (Hiram, K), I. 45, 206; II. 310.
History, its scope and treatment, 4 ff.; of the Semites, 5 ff.; of the Hebrews, 9 ff., 385 ff.; Hebrew conception of, 434 f., 955, 1356.
History and prophecy, 13 f., 382 (386), 723, 1419 f.
Hivites (P), 127, 130.
Honesty, 1320 ff., 1328.
Hophni (J), 490, 589.
Hophra (Apries, K), 1207 f., 1252, 1255, 1365.
Horses (cf. Army), 144, 475, 419 f., 716.
Hosea, the prophet, 304, 312 ff., 320, 354, I. app. 10, 606, 994.
Hoshea (K), 287, 332, 343 f., 348 ff.
Hospitality, see Strangers.
Host of heaven, 856.
House-father, 405, 408 ff.
Household, 396, 400, 404 ff.
Huldah (prophetess), 851.
Hunting, 180, 819.
Hyksos (P), 135 ff., 346, 436, 437 n.
Hyrœades (Cr), 1386.

INDEX I

Ibadid (P), 630.
Ibleam (C), 267.
Ideals and practice in religion, 1012, 1021.
Idolatry (cf. Deities, Polytheism, Religion), 320 f., 639 f., 799, 854, 860, 986, 1087, 1333 f.
Ijon (C), 331.
Ilâbi'id (K), see Ya'ubi'id.
Imgur-Bêl (wall), 749, 1058, 1061.
Immanuel, 327 ff., 1. app. 12.
Immer (S), 1273.
Imperialism, 1261, 1315 f., 1364.
Imposts (taxes, fines, tribute, assessment), Hebrew, 205 f., 310, 474, 523, 1040; Assyrian and Babylonian, 286 f., 310, 675, 688, 1080; Egyptian, 1040.
Imprisonment, 108 f., 1221, 1224, 1227, 1415.
Indabigash (K), 782.
Individualism, spiritual (cf. Religion, personal), 1000, 1010, 1014 f., 1201, 1204 f., 1340 ff.
Individuals as sufferers, 606.
Industry in Israel (cf. Employments), 268, 483 f., 651.
Interest (usury) in Israel, 552, 576, 1322; in Babylonia, 1323.
Ionians, see Greeks.
Iran and Iranians (P), 823, 1374 ff.
Irḫulini (K), 228.
Irijah (O), 1221.
Irkanati (K), 228.
Iroquois compared with Semites, 29.
Irrigation, see Watercourses.
Isaac (Ch), 412, 444, 955, 959.
Isaiah, the prophet, 309, 318 ff., 326 ff., 354 f., 606, 641 ff., 649, 652, 654 ff., 702, 704, 710 ff., 728, 995, 998, 1354.
Isaiah the Second, 1345, 1353 f., 1405 ff.
Ischupri (C), 756.
Ishbosheth (Ishba'al, K), 203.
Ishmael b. Hagar, 430; b. Nethaniah, 1243, 1245 ff.
Ishmê-Dagân (K), Babyl., 104; Assyr., 172.
Ishtar (D), 94, 101, 1185 ff.

Isin (C), 104, 110.
Israel (see Hebrews), names, 133, 228, 232.
Israel (northern), 208 ff., and see Contents; national conditions, 212, 264, 271 ff., 374 ff., 527 ff.; changes of dynasty, 211 f., 236 ff., 267, 278, 316, 332; extent, 211 f., 230, 235 ff., 243, 262, 272, 352; relations with Judah, see Judah; relations with Phœnicia, 213, 233, 239, 264, 377; relations with "Syria" (Damascus), 231 ff., 243 ff., 252, 262 f., 270, 316, 376, 380; relations with Assyria, 228, 231, 240 f., 250, 253, 267, 314, 331 f., 380, 382 ff.; relations with Egypt, 210, 313 f., 344, 348 ff.; outcome of its history, 386 ff.
Issachar (T), 212.
Ithamar (K), 630.
Ithobal (Ethbaal, K), of Tyre, 92, 213; of Sidon, 675.
Ittai of Gath, 550.
Itti-Bêl (K), 92.

J, see Jehovist.
Jabbok (R), 183.
Jabesh (C in Gilead), 191, 196, 575.
Jacob (Ch), 412 ff., 444, 447 n., 955, 959.
Jacob's "Blessing," 905, 913.
Jacob-el (C), 369 n.
Jael (heroine), 964.
Jahaz (C), 183.
Jair (J), 191.
Janoah (C), 331.
Jashar (book), 896, 906, 913.
Jebusites (P), 130, 204.
Jehoahaz (K), of Israel, 245 f., 252, 1039; of Judah, 1039.
Jehoash (Joash, K), of Judah, 221, 243, 254, 317.
Jehoiachin (K), 1079 ff., 1143 ff.
Jehoiada (priest), 254.
Jehoiakim (K), 1039, 1075 ff., 1120 ff.
Jehoram (Joram, K), of Judah, 221, 235 f.
Jehoshaphat (K), 221, 231, 235.

Jehovah (Yahwè), in proper names, I. app. 9; his character, 1009 f., 1099, 1131, 1176; his relation to Israel, 378, 407, 426, 429, 444, 454, 457, 462, 488 f., 526, 535, 581 ff., 602, 700, 726 f., 894, 906, 911, 922, 999 f., 1024, 1099, 1114, 1334 ff.; his false worship, 320 f., 854, 1005 f., 1015; his omnipresence, 1337 f.

Jehovist, I. app. 4, 885, 923 ff.

Jehovist and Elohist (J E), 923, 935, 943 f.

Jephthah (J), 191, 965; his lament, 968.

Jeremiah, the prophet, 813, 1065, 1067 ff., 1082 ff., 1139 ff., 1215 ff., 1242, 1252 ff., 1341, 1349, 1366; his disciples, 1336; the book, 1082 n.

Jericho (C), 185, 498 n.

Jeroboam (K), I, 206 ff., 1357; II. 262 ff., 306, 519.

Jerusalem (C), 40, 57, 126, 128, 139, 152, 204 ff., 210, 243, 254, 260, 276 f., 318 ff., 325, 478, 675, 677, 687 f., 696 ff., 730, 861, 998, 1039, 1079, 1178, 1180, 1214 ff., 1230 ff., 1238 f., 1241.

Jesus and the Old Testament, 615 ff.

Jezebel (Q), 213.

Jezreel (Esdraelon, L), 139, 141, 198, 203, 243, 250, 272, 331, 364, 479, 530 n., 685, 1034; (C), 236.

Joab (Cr), 57, 203, 205, 523.

Joah (O), 699.

Joash (Jehoash, K), of Israel, 252 f., 262.

Job (the book), 599 f., 1353.

Johanan (G), 1243, 1246, 1248 f.

Jonadab (Ch), 416.

Jonathan, b. Saul, 196 ff., 415, 515, 732 n., 969, 972; (scribe), 1221.

Joppa (C), 152, 675, 695.

Joram (Jehoram), king of Israel, 221, 231, 235 ff.

Jordan (R), 125, 129, 141, 1109.

Joseph b. Jacob, as a moral type, 900 f.; tribally, 935.

Joseph-el (C), 369 n.

Joshua (Ch), 183 ff.; (book), I. app. 4.

Josiah (K), 807, 838 ff., 1027, 1033 ff., 1069 ff.

Jotham (K), 269, 308 f.

Jotham b. Gideon; his parable, 908, 910.

Judah (T), 186, 188 f., 196, 200, 905.

Judah (L and P): national conditions, 210, 272 ff., 296, 379, 527, 686, 791 ff., 1027, 1314; relations with N. Israel, 210 ff., 215, 239, 260 f., 268, 315 f., 378; relations with Edom, 215, 235 f., 254, 325; relations with Syria, 215, 231, 238, 243, 254, 270; relations with Assyria, 254, 306 ff., 383 f., 633, 648, 650 ff., 675 ff., 685 ff., 793 ff., II. app. 5.; relations with Babylonia, 679, 837 f., 1044, 1076 ff., 1090 ff., 1113 ff., 1130 ff., 1148 ff., 1208 ff.; relations with Egypt, 210, 215, 273, 652, 654 ff., 697, 711, 715 f., 719 f., 1076 f., 1087 f., 1123, 1165 n., 1208 f.; after the kingdom: in Palestine, 1240 ff.; in Egypt, 1254 ff.; in Babylonia, see Exiles.

Judaism, 1251, 1348.

Judges (rulers), 43, 50 f., 455, 457, 468, 487, 510, 590 f., 598.

Judges, the, 187 ff., 564, 920, 963 ff.

Judges, book of, 468 f., 917 f., 920, 1361.

Justice in Israel (cf. Law), 457, 461, 475, 486 ff., 502, 510, 578 f., 588 ff., 859, 1228; in Babylonia, 1322 ff.

Kadesh (C), on the Orontes, 145, 162 f., 202, I. app. 5; Kadesh-Barnea, 183.

Kaftu (L), 132.

Kalach (Calah, C), 175, 220, 249, 283, 311, 667, 820.

Kallima-Sin (K), 149.

Kalparuda (K), 228.

Kana'na (Canaan, L), 132.

Karaindash (K), 175.

Karbanit (C), 704.

Karduniash (L. Babylonia), 121.
Karkar (C), 228 ff., 624.
Karnak, see Thebes.
Karun, see Ulai.
Kasiphia (S), 1273 n.
Kassbites (P), 79, 120 ff., 141, 174 ff., 219 n., 223, 674, 1285.
Kaūshmalak (K), 337.
Kebar (Kabar. Chebar, W), 1081, 1272. 1290, 1299 f., 1305.
Kedar (LP), 787 f.
Kedesh (C), 331.
Keileh (C), 152.
Kenites (P), 186, 416, 493, 550.
Kenizzites (P), 186.
Khorsabad, see Dūr-Sharrukēn.
Kidron (valley), 697.
Kimmerians (P, Gomer, Gimirrē), 758 f., 774 f., 814, 1384.
King and kingdom: Semitic, 36 f., 50 ff., 396 n.; Hebrew, 50 ff., 195, 199, 205 f., 277 f., 371 ff., 468, 521 ff., 528 f.. 534 ff., 587, II. app. 1, 844 n., 989, 1070 f.; idealized, 603 f.; Assyrian, 171 f., 182 ff.; Babylonian, 98, 108, 120 f.
Kings (book), 1357 ff.
King's Garden, 1231.
Kinnereth (lake), 331.
Kinship, 396 ff.; its symbolism, 426, 429, 432 f.
Kipkip (C), 767.
Kir (L), 336.
Kirtē (Kirche?), 179, 217 f., 220.
Kish (C), 672.
Kishon (R), 479.
Kissia (L), 106, 120.
Kitlala (C), 228.
Kommagene, see Kummuch.
Kudur-mabug (K), 108, 114.
Kudurnanchundi (K), 107.
Kudurlagamar, see Chedorlaomer.
Kuē (L, E. Cilicia), 228, 230, I. app. 5, 629, 666.
Kummuch (L, Kommagene), 179, 218, 226, 228, 284, 294, 666.
Kundashpi (K), 228.
Kurigalzu (K), I, 149; II, 175.
Kushites (Cushites), see Ethiopians.
Kyaxares (K), 824 f.

Laban (Ch), 412 f.
Labasi-Marduk (K), 1370.
Lachish (C), 152, 688, 690, 693, II. app. 12, 14, 1213.
Lagash (C). 95 ff.
Laish (Dan, C), 41.
Lalli (K), 228.
Lamech's Song. 889.
Lamentations (book), 1237 ff.
Land, its acquisition and partition, 563 ff., 1344; private tenure (cf. Property), 580 ff., 610 n.
Landmarks, 583.
Language and social institutions, 391 ff.
Larissa (S). 827 n.
Larsa (Elasar, C), 101, 104, 108, 111.
Law, the, see Direction.
Law and legislation, 450, 474, 486 ff., 541 ff., 552, 576 f., 584 n., 847 f., 882. 891 f., 920 ff.
Law of Holiness, 1362.
Lebanon (M). 90, 125, 141, 219, 315.
Leontes. see Litany.
Levi (T), 935.
Levirate custom, 417.
Levites, as priests. 504, 863, 1019.
Leviticus (book), 924 n.
Libnah (C), 703, 709.
Libyans (P), 207, 345.
Litany (R), 125, 144.
Literature, defined, 883, 899; and writing, 882, 901.
Literature, Hebrew: conditions and occasions, 866 ff., 891 ff., 898 ff., 914 ff., 939 ff., 1350 ff., 1405; its spirit and style, 11 ff., 253, 435, 446, 449 n., 459, 697, 728 f., 744 n., 868, 890, 893, 904, 913, 927 f., 934, 1080 n., 1086 n., 1134, 1145 f., 1175, 1178 n., 1212, 1238, 1351, 1356, 1402, 1405 ff., 1415 n.; contents, 442 ff., 883 ff., 1335 ff., 1401 ff.; form, 887 f., 918, 938, 1117, 1237, 1352 f.; non-Hebraic elements, 886 f., 932; periods and epochs, 883, 899 ff., 907, 912, 937 f., 1350, 1400 f.
Local government, Hebrew, 52.
"Lost Tribes," 363.

Lulī (Elulæus, K), 675, 681 f.
Lybians (P), 210, 343, 770, 1089.
Lycians (P), 1389.
Lydia (L), 157, 773 ff., 1379 f., 1387 ff.

Maacha (L), 204.
Machalliba (C), 675.
Madai, see Medes.
Magdiel (C), 152.
Magic (cf. Oracles), 644.
Magog (LP), 814.
Makan (Magan, L), 91, 96.
Mākarā (Q), 145.
Maledictions, 1104 ff., 1112, 1159, 1169 f., 1257.
Mālik and *malk* ("counsellor" and "king"), 36, I. app. 2.
Manasseh (T), 183, 189, 196, 212, 275 ; (K), 761, 780, 790, 798 ff., 1003 ff., 1122 n.
Manda (Scythian), 758 n.
Mannāi (PL), 628, 758, 777, 1384, 1403.
Manṣuati (C), 250.
Mar(u)duk, see Merodach.
Marduk-nādin-achē (K), 180.
Marduk-zākir-shum (K), 671.
Mari (K, Benhadad III), 251 f.
Marratim (L), 1403 n.
Marriage, 417 ff., 426 f., 949, 1332.
Marsimanu (P), 630.
Mash (L), 788.
Mashga (C), 228.
Masius (M), 71, 217 f., 220.
Matinu-ba'al (K), 228.
Mazares (Cr), 1386.
Media and Medes (Madai), 224, 247 f., 258, 294, 311, 362 f., 627, 629, 674, 758, 760, 777, 812, 823 ff., 1051, 1374, 1379, 1401.
Mediterranean Sea, 90 f., 180, 219 ; Assyrian name, 179 f. ; coast land, 71, 331 ; coast land peoples, 166.
Medo-Persian empire, 1386 ff., 1413.
Megiddo (C), 141, 145, 152, 163, 210 n., 1034.
Melchizedek (K), 37.
Melikoff (name), 1. app. 2.
Melkart (D), 59.

Melucha (D), 96, 675, 678, 755 n., 780.
Memphis (C), 313, 347, 656, 756, 767, 1030.
Menahem (K), Hebrew, 267, 306, 310, 616 ; Phœnician, 675.
Mentu (D), 144.
Merneptah (K), 166 f., 879.
Merodach (Maruduk, Marduk, D), 85, 112, 117, 123, 748 f., 818, 1054, 1383, 1393 ff., 1398.
Merodach-baladan (K), 340, 621, 637, 660 ff., 671 f., 679 ; his sons, 751.
Mesha (K), 212, 221, 235.
Meshech, see Mushkē.
Mesopotamia (L), 18, 41, 71, 75, 132, 137, 141, 145 f., 154 f., 173, 175 f., 178, 181, 188, 217 f.
Messianic ideal, 603 f., 916, 1161.
Metenna (K), II. app. 10.
Micah (the prophet), 319, 321, 354, 356, 606, 644 f., 798 n., 800, II. app. 8, 998, 1092.
Micaiah b. Gamariah, 1119.
Mice, 705, 707, II. app. 13.
Michmash (C), 196, 687.
Midianites (P), 50, 183, 189.
Mikado, as illustration, 431.
Milcom (D), 59, 855 ; cf. Molech.
Militarism (cf. Warfare), 318, 613, 889, 1261, 1420.
Militene (Milid, C), 228, 629.
Milton and Isaiah, 1406.
Minæans (P), 878 n.
Minni (P), see Mannai.
Miriam and her Song, 449 n., 890, 913.
Mitā (K), 627.
Mitāni (L), 132, 150, 154 f., 162.
Mitintī (Metintī, K), of Askalon, 332 ; of Ashdod, 675.
"Mixed multitude" (Bedawin), 453, 550.
Mizpah (C), 1240, 1242 ff.
Moab and Moabites, 18, 26, 48, 50, 138, 183, 188, 190, 201, 209, 215, 231, 233, 235, 263, 268 f., 273, 337, 550 n., 633, 675, 761, 894 f., 972, 1157, 1240, 1243, 1251.

2 G

Mohammed (cf. Islam), 567 n., 568, 965, 1328.
Molech (Moloch, D). I. app. 2, 855, 1006.
Monarchy, see King.
Monotheism (cf. Jehovah, Religion), 1338.
Monuments, see especially Assyrians, Babylonians.
Moon-worship, 856.
Morality: its evolution, 611 ff., 950, 980 ff.; Christian and Hebrew, 615 ff.; its criteria and standards, 948 ff., 964, 1258 ff.; conditions and basis, 950, 958, 962, 984 ff., 1000 f., 1016.
Moresheth-Gath (C), 356.
Moschi, see Mushkē.
Moses, the lawgiver, 183, 449 ff.; his Blessing, 935.
Motherhood, 430.
Mugheir (Ur, S). 100.
Musa ibn Nosair (Ch). 568 n.
Mushkē (Meshech, Moschi, LP). 179, 217, 627 ff., 666.
Muṣri (L), 228, 230, I. app. 5; cf. 437 n.
Mut-Adda (Cr), 152.
Mutilation of the dead, 285 n.
Myth making, 1184 ff.

Nabatæans (P). 755 n.
Nabonassar (K). 203.
Nabonidus (K). 87, 1371 f., 1392 ff., 1401.
Nabopalassar (K), 822 f., 825 f., 1042, 1370 n.
Nabopaliddin (K), 219 n.
Naboth of Jezreel, 583, 606, 981 f.
Nabû-bēl-shumi (Ch), 784.
Nadab (K), 211.
Nagītu (C), 734, 737 f.
Naharina (Mesopotamia), 132, 145, 150.
Nahr el Kelb. 1213 n.
Nahum, the prophet, 831 ff., 1129, 1138.
Naïri (L), 179, 216.
Naming, in Israel, 1040 n., 1411 n.
Namri (Namar, L), 258.

Nanā (Ishtar, D), 101, 107.
Napata (C). 347.
Naphtali (TL), 272, 275, 331, I. app. 13, 479.
Narām-Sin (K), 87 ff.
Nathan (prophet). his parable, 910, 977 f.
National literature, 915 f.
Nationalism, Hebrew (cf. Patriotism), 470 f., 515, 967 f.
Nationality. Semitic, 46 ff., 1315 f.; and religion, 61.
Natnu (Ch). 787 f.
Naturalization, see Adoption.
Nature-worship, 321, 1184 ff.
Navigation, Phœnician, 66; Babylonian, 1305 n.
Nebaioth (Nabatæans, LP), 787 f.
Nebo (D). 57, 59, 112, 117, 249, I. app. 7, 818, 820, 1054, 1056, 1063, 1392, 1394; (M), 188; (C), 235.
Neboshazban (Cr), 1233 n.
Nebuchadrezzar (K): I, 178, 1286; II, 42, 407, 825, 1042, 1052 ff., 1075 ff., 1115, 1137, 1167, 1171, 1210, 1213, 1231, 1235, 1241, 1273, 1277, 1286, 1296 f., 1337, 1364 ff., 1379, 1403, 1414.
Nebuzaradan (Cr), 1232, 1240, 1242.
Necho (K): I, 766, 768, 1029; II, 827, 1031 ff., 1043, 1207.
Negeb (L), 273.
Nēmitti-Bēl (rampart), 749, 1053.
Nergal (D), 85, 94, 228, 818.
Nergal-shar-uṣur: (1) b. Sinacherib, 744; (2) see Neriglissar.
Nergal-ushēzib (K), 739.
Neriglissar (K). 1233 n., 1370.
Nestorians, 36, I. app. 2.
New Testament and Old, 615 ff.
New Year's festival, 1392, 1394.
Nile valley, 346 f.
Nimrūd, see Kalach.
Ninā (Ishtar, D), 171 f.
Nineveh (C), 39 f., 74, 141, 171 f., 175, 247, 283, 341, 741 ff., 750, 762, 815, 824 ff.
Ninus (K), 249.
Niphates (M), 71.

Nippur (Nuffar. C), 91. 94, 101, 104 f., 108. 110, 112, 293, 1081, 1284 ff.
Nisibis (C), 75, 141, 217.
Nisroch, see Nusku.
Nobles, see Rulers.
Nomads and nomadic life (cf. Tribalism), 56, 400 ff., 416, 424 f., 438 ff., 465 ff., 1141 f., 1384.
Noph (C), see Memphis.
Nubia, see Cush.
Numbers in Old Testament. I. app. 6, 443 n., 460, II. app. 6, 13; (book), 925 f.
Nûr-Ramman (K), 108.
Nusku (D), 744, 818.

Obadiah (book). 1404 n.
Obelisks (Egyptian). 767 n., 1255 n.
Occupations. see Employments.
Old Testament, in our evolution. 611 ff.; and New, 614 ff.
Omri (K), 212, 239.
Omri-land (N. Israel), see Bit-Chumri.
On (Heliopolis, C), 657, 767, 1255 n.
Onesimus (slave), 406.
Opis (C), 1395 f.
Oracles, 488, 702 (1071), 1073, 1210, 1215. 1220. 1253, 1387.
Oratorical literature, 938 ff.
Oratory. Hebrew. 940.
Ormuzd, see Ahuramazda.
Orontes (R), 125, 141, 161, 282, 226.
Osorkon II (K). 215.
Othniel (J). 188, 550.

P, see Priestly narrative.
Padan-Aram (L). 75, I. app. 9.
Padi (K), 675, 692. 695, II. app. 14.
Pakrura (G). 766.
Palestine (collectively). 17, 54 f., 90, 125 ff., 132 f., 135 ff., 151 ff., 163 ff., 201. 291, 780.
Pallakopas (W), 100, 1293.
Panics explained, 732 n.
Parentage, 430.
Parsua (L), 224.

Parties and partisanship in Israel, 598 ff., 607, 983, 987 f., 991, 1093 ff., 1149, 1157 ff.
Pasebchanu (K), 207.
Pashhur (b. Immer), 1111; (b. Malchiah), 1215.
Pastoral life (cf. Nomads), 476, 479.
Pasture-grounds, 38. 565, 1304.
Patin, see Chattin.
Patria potestas, 408 ff.
Patriarchs of Israel, 137; in history, 442 ff.; their morality, 948 ff., 961.
Patriotism: Semitic, 61; Hebrew, 470 f., 479, 900. 915. 967. 1024, 1123, 1156, 1223; prophetic, 723, 1113 f., 1258 ff., 1409.
Pekah (K), 316 (325), 332, I. app. 13.
Pekahiah (K), 316.
Pekod (P). 339. 1103 n.
Pelusium (C), 705. 709.
Pennel (Peniel, C), 210.
Pepi (K), 134.
Perizzites (P), 127, 130.
Persia (Persis, L), 1374, 1378.
Persian Gulf, extent, 71; navigation, 737 f.
Persians (cf. Iranians), political tendencies, 56.
Pesept (L), 766.
Pestilence, 259, 261 f., 704, 707, 709, II. app. 13.
Pethor (Pitru, C), 228.
Petra (C), 254.
Pharisaism, 616 f.
Philemon (slave-owner), 406.
Philistian plain (Palastu), 139, 141, 250, 645. 684.
Philistines and their cities, 50, 51, 164, 166, 192 ff., 196 ff., 200, 203 ff., 211, 243, 248, 264. 268, 273, 302, 315, 325, 332, 371, 479, 491 f., 512. 515. 631 f., 651, 675, 677, 684. 690 ff., 761, 1240.
Phinehas (J). 490, 589.
Phœnicians. classification, 18; names. 132 f.; achievements, 66, 154, 683; colonies and government, 42 ff., I. app. 3, 772; trade and navigation, 42 ff., (97), 128, 184, 206 (209), 230, I. app. 3,

737 f., 1031, 1367; religion and deities, 137, 213; events in history, 126, 144 f., 152, 164, 166, 180, 184, 219, 230, 311, 315, 675, 680 ff., 753, 761, 772 f., 821. See especially Sidon, Tyre.
Phraortes (K), 824.
Pianchi (K), 347.
Pisgah (M), 1244.
Pisiris (K), 628.
Planet worship, 1061, 1063.
Polyandry, 417 f.
Polygamy, 206, 424, 449.
Polytheism, national, 59 f.
Poverty in Israel: its occasions, 541, 572, 575; its consequences, 573 ff., 601; the "poor" as a class, 598 ff.
Preaching, see Prophesying.
Prediction (cf. Foresight), 1147, 1367, 1410 f., 1418 f.
Priest-kings, 57, 98, 172.
Priestly narrative, 885 ff., 891 f., 923 ff.
Priests and priesthood in Israel, 488, 504 f., 570, 588 f., 642 f., 974, 1013 ff., 1101, 1170, 1344 f., 1351; as counsellors, 488 f., 1015; their achievements, 1017 f.; Babylonian, 339, 660, 1287 f., 1392.
Primogeniture, 429.
Princes (rulers), 455, 476 n., 487, 531, 592, 1002, 1221, 1312.
Professional prophets, 1093, 1103 ff.
Property (cf. Land), its influence in society and politics, 425, 563.
Prophesying, 937 ff.
Prophetic histories, 923 f., 934.
Prophets and Prophecy, 195, 214, 244, 295 ff., 313 ff., 318 ff., 382, 462, 488, 532, 546, 570, 589 n., 600, 606, 610, 725, 829, 851, 936 ff., 983, 993, 1065 ff., 1133, 1145 f., 1172, 1200, 1258 ff., 1336 ff., 1345, 1400 ff., 1418 ff.
Proverbs (book), 600, 910; their limitations, 999 ff.
Psalms, by David (?) 909; motives of composition, 605 f.; partisan, 598 ff.; "vindictive," 609 n., 1108 n.; of exile, 1363.

Psammetichus, (K) I, 768, 774 f., 812, 1029; II, 1207.
Ptah (D), 705.
Pteria (C), 150, 1387.
Ptolemy, canon of, 293, I. app. 6.
Pudu'il (K), 675.
Pûl, Pûlu, see Tiglathpileser III.
Punt (P), 145, 1089 n.
Pût (P), 770, 1089.
Pythia, the, 851 n.

Queen of Heaven, 856, 1094, 1256.
Queens, see Women.

Rabbath-Ammon (C), 204.
Rabmag (title), 1233 n.
Rabsaris (title), 609, 1233 n.
Rabshakeh (title), 290, 609 ff., II. app. 14.
Rachel bat Laban, 413.
Ramah (C), 477, 1242.
Rammân (cf. Rimmon, D), 172, 228.
Rammân-nâdin-achê (K), 177.
Rammân-nirâri (K), I. 175; II, 216; III, 248 ff., 282, I. app. 7.
Ramoth (C), 212, 215, 231, 235 f.
Ramses (K), II. 163, 165; III, 166 f., 207.
Raphia (*Rapichu, Refâ*. C), 625, 756.
Reading, public, 1117.
Rebekah bat Bethuel, 412.
Rechabites (T), 416, 1141 f.
Red Sea traffic, 97, 206, 209, 215, 236, 254, 264, 269.
Reforms in Israel, 852 ff., 1019 ff.
Regnal year, II. app. 6.
Rehob (L), 204.
Rehoboam (K), 208, 210.
Religion among the Semites: its political influence, 58 ff., 99, 290, 551, 639, 774 n., II. app. 7, 841; syncretism, 60, 290, 495, 855, 1155; religion and kinship, 397, 402 f.; bound to the soil, 61, 289 f., 495, 551, 909, 1024; its scope and motive, 495, 497 ff., 504 ff., 601, 911, 985; Hebrew religion distinctive, 62, 613; personal religion in

INDEX I 453

Israel, 607 ff., 980. 985 ff., 1009 ff., 1340, 1349; in a Gentile, 1054. For the types, see the several divisions of the Semitic race.
Representative government, 56 (29, 37).
Reshep (D), 137.
Retenu (L. Syria), 132, 145.
Reuben (T), 183, 204, 935.
Rezon (K), I, 209; II, 310, 333, 335.
Rhabdomancy. 1210 f.
Rhapsodists, 871, 894.
Rhodes (I). I. app. 3.
Rhodes, Cecil, as an historical type, 955, 1411 n.
Rib-addi (G), 152.
Riblah (C), 1038, 1213.
Riches and the public weal, 571 ff.; the "rich" as a class, 98 ff.; cf. 618.
Rimmon (Rammân, D), of Damascus, 59; of Aleppo, 228.
Rizpah bat Aiah, 972.
Roads, great, 202.
Roman social institutions cited, 408 ff., 413 f., 421, 424 f., 427.
Rulers (cf. Princes, Judges, Chiefs, Elders). 536 ff., 559, 569, 587, 642 f., 974.
Ruth (book), 476, 550 n.

Saba'a (P. North Sabæans), 334, 630.
Sabako (K), 347, I. app. 14, 625. 705.
Sabataka (K), I. app. 14, 625, 630, 632, II. app. 4.
Sabbath, 1346 f.
Sachi (L), 797.
Sacrifice and sacrifices, 738, 1006 f., 1014.
Sacrificers, 489. 505, 535, 863, 1014.
Sais (C), 766, 1030.
Salamânu (K; cf. Shalman), 337.
Samaria (C), 40, 128, 212, 254, 275 f., 289, 343, 349 ff., I. app. 16, 1247; (L) see Israel Northern; Assyrian province, 624 f., 653, 685, 799.
Sangar-Nebo (Cr), 1233 n.
Samsi (Q), 334, 630.

Samsiruna (C), 675.
Samson (J), 193, 965; his biography, 908, 917 f.
Samsu-iluna (K), 118.
Samuel (J), 195 f., 430, 595, 975 f.; (book), 908 f., 935, 1361.
Sanibu (K), 337.
Sapalel (K), 163.
Sardanapalus, see Asshurbanipal.
Sardis (C), 775, 1387 ff.
Sarepta (C), 675.
Sargon (K): I, 89 ff., 112 n., 667; II, 42, 287, 358 ff., I. app. 10, 15, 16, 620 ff., 653 ff., 660 ff., 722, II. app. 2, 4, 5.
Sarsechim (title), 1233 n.
Satarna (K), 150.
Saul (K), 196 ff., 415, 517, 521 f., 525, 975; his biography, 919, 935.
Scythians (P), 777 n., 810 ff., 821, 824, 1383 f., 1401.
Scythopolis (C), 812 n.
Seers (cf. Prophets), 937.
Seir (M), 109.
Semiramis (Q), 249, I. app. 7.
Semites (collectively), characteristics, 5 f., 1146; course of history, 9 ff., 171, 174, 1045; territory, 17 ff.; classification, 18 f.; distribution, 20 ff., 79 ff., 105 n., 223; languages, I. app. 1; religion and deities, 57 ff., 137, 164, 283, 289 f.; political tendencies, 28 ff., 289, 591, 697 n., 778, 1414 f. See the several divisions of the race.
Senir (Sanir, M), 242.
Senkereh (Larsa, C), 101.
Sepharvaim (C), 94, 349.
Seraiah b. Neriah, 1172.
Seraphim, 1176 n.
Serpent, Brazen, 854.
Servant of Jehovah, 1262, 1420.
Servants and servitude, cf. Slaves and hirelings.
Sesostris, see Ramses II.
Sethon (Seti, K), 705.
Seti I (K), 163.
Seve (K), 343, 349, I. app. 14, 625.
Sexual morality, 213, 321 f., 596, 857, 956 f., 965, 971, 1189 f., 1330,

1332 ; in law and prescription, 957, 1190, 1330 ff.
Shabara'in (C). 349.
Shagur (Pethor. C). 228.
Shallum (K), 267.
Shallum b. Josiah, see Jehoahaz.
Shalman (K), 314, I. app. 8, 681.
Shalmaneser (K), I, 175; II, 221 ff., 237 f., 240 ff., 341 ; III, 256 f. ; IV, 342 ff., 349 ; Fort, 228.
Shamash (Shamsu, D), 94.
Shamash-shum-ukin (K), 763, 778, 780 ff., II. app. 17.
Shamgar (J), 479.
Shamshi-Rammân (K): I, 172 ; IV. 247.
Shangar (K), 228.
Shaphan (O), 843, 846, 850.
Shapiya (C), 340.
"Sharezer," 744 n.
Sharludâri (K), of Askalon, 675, 691 ; of Pelusium, 766.
Sharuhen (C), 144.
Shâsu (Bedawin), 132, 135 ff.. 167.
Shatt-el-Hai (R), 95, 100.
Shatt-en-Nil (R), 94, 100 f., 1274, 1290, 1299 f.
Sheba (L), 145.
Shebna (O), 697, 699.
Shechem (C), 49, 189, 208, 210, 477, 563 n., 1247.
Shemaiah (exile), 1169 f.
Shepherd princes, see Hyksos.
Sheshbazzar (prince), 1312.
Shian (L), 228.
Shiloh (C), 186, 194, 490, 504, 1091, 1093, 1247.
Shinar (Shumer, L), 109 ff.
Shishak (Sheshonk, K), 207, 210, 345.
Shrines (cf. Temple), 490, 496, 501, 860, 994, 1060 f., 1244, 1247.
Shumer (see Sumerians). Shumer and Akkad, 102, 104, 108, 110, 175, 223, 293, 778 n., 1393.
Shushan, see Susa.
Shuzub (K), 733, 739.
Sibraim (C), 349.
Sib'u (K), see Seve.

Sidon (C), 34, 39, 43 f., 120, 152, 243, 248, I. app. 3, 675, 681 f.. 753, 772, 1157, 1213 n., 1367.
Sieges (cf. Fortresses), 236, 251, 357, 664, 675, 681, 698, 783, 824 ff., 831 f., II. app. 14, 1039 (1178), 1214 ff., 1230 f., 1388.
Sihon (K), 183.
Sil-bêl (K), 675.
Siloam (Siloah, brook and pool), 329 (cf. 326), 698 (730), 731 n.
Silver in commerce, I. app. 3 ; cf. 630.
Simeon (T), 186.
Simirra (C), 624.
Sin (D), 94, 100, 104, II. app. 4.
Sin (political), 290, 675, II. app. 11.
Sinacherib (K), 42, 55, 281 n., 635, 637, 669 ff., 718, 722 f., 732 ff., II. app. 9–14.
Sinai (M), 183, 450.
Sinaitic peninsula, 134, 450, 755 ; cf. North Arabia.
Sin-iddin (K), 108 (104).
Sinjirli inscriptions, I. app. 9, I. app. 16.
Sin-shar-ishkun (K), 820.
Sippar (C), 86 ff., 94, 293, 739, 752, 783, 1395 f.
Slavery, its occasions, 475, 539 ff., 584 f. ; its effects, 544 ff.. 1278 ; its morality, 949 ; its symbolism, 407.
Slaves in Israel, social relations, 405 ff., 507 ff., 540, 542, 544, 551 ; employments, 507 ff., 567 (1228 n.) ; emancipated, 1218 ; their lot ameliorated, 542 ff. ; their legal protection, 542 f. ; fugitive, 543, 545 ; in literature, 546 ; their unique position, 542 ff. ; Egyptian, 346, 436, 440 ; Babylonian, 749, 1279 ff.. 1326 ; Tyrian, 547.
Slave-trade, 45, 264, 406, 539.
Smintheus (D), II. app. 13.
Snefru (K), 134.
So (K), see Seve.
"Social Evolution," 614 n.
Social changes in Israel, 562 ff., 569 ff., 578, 991, 1153.

Social questions in Israel, 569 ff.; their importance, 574, 578, 607.
Society, Hebrew, its constitution, see Family, Household, Clans, Tribes, Slaves, Strangers, Clientage, and cf. Hebrews, government, religion and morals.
Sociological literature, Hebrew, 598 ff.
Sodom (C), 109.
Solomon (K), 205 ff., 519, 524 ff., 971, 1357; his poems, 904, 910; his "Acts," 1358.
Son (member of guild), 570.
Sorcery, 858.
Sparta (C), 1387.
Spelling, 876.
Spirituality, see Religion, personal.
Stone-pillars, 854.
Strangers (sojourners, guests, clients), their naturalization, 548; factors of Israel, 550 ff., 567; in literature, 552 ff.
Subject states, see Dependencies.
Sûchu (L), 219.
Suez Canal, 1031.
Sumerians (Shumer), 80 ff., 95 f.
Sun-chariots, 856.
Sun-worship, 321, 856 (1186), 1191.
Superstitions. 732, 858, 1183.
Supnat (R), 215, 218.
Surety in Israel, 584, 596.
Sûru (C), 218.
Susa (Shushan, C), 106 f., 785, 799.
Susiana (L), 106, 120.
Suzerainty, see Dependencies.
Sybil, the, 851 n.
Symbolical prophetic actions, 658, 1158 f., 1172, 1178 ff., 1197 (1243), 1255.
Synagogue, 1348.
Syria and Syrians (collectively), 17 f., 90, 125, 132 f., 135 ff., 160 ff., 201 f., 204, 230, 250, 257. 291; Northern Syrians, 123, 152, 157 ff., 219, 226, 243, 247, 294, 306, 311, 315, 624, 680; Middle and Southern Syrians, 226, 307, 311, 315, 624.

Tabal (Tibarene, LP), 217, 338, 628, 773.
Tābēl, of Damascus, 326.
Tab-Rimmon (K), 211.
Tabua (Q), 755.
Tadmor (Palmyra, C), 141.
Tahpanhes (C), 1083, 1254 f.
Talent, II. app. 11.
Tammaritu (K), 782, 784.
Tammuz (D), 1184 ff.
Tamud (P), 636.
Tanis, see Zoan.
Tarshish (C), 128.
Tarsus (Tarzi, C), 243 n., 735.
Tartān (title), I. app. 14, 690.
Taurus (M), 71.
Taxation, see Imposts.
Teispes (K), 1378.
Tekoa, the woman of, 398 n.
Tel-abūb (S), 1296, 1305.
Tel-harsha (S), 1273.
Tel Ibrahim (S), 94.
Telloh (S), 91, 95, 1291.
Tel-melach (S), 1273.
Tēma (P), 334.
Tema (C), 1371, 1392.
Temple in Jerusalem, 206, 276 f., 589, 601, 731, 796, 846 n., 904, 968, 1118 n., 1183 f., 1233; of Ezekiel, 1344; Babylonian temples. 740 n., 1060 f., 1063, 1279, 1287 f., 1371 f.
Teraphim, 413, 506, 1210 f.
Teumman (K), 779.
Teüshpā (K), 758 n.
Thapsacus (C), 737 n.
Thebes (No-Amen, C), 143 f., 207, 210 n., 345, 764, 767, 770, 831, 1030.
Theophanies, 356, 718, 909, 1410.
Thi (Q), 150.
Thothmes (K): I. 145, 346; III, 145, 162, 173. 369 n.
Tibarene, see Tubal.
Tid'al (K), 109, 117.
Tiglathpileser (K): I, 179 f.; II, 216; III., 110, 279 ff., 305 ff., 326, 331 ff., 342 ff., I. app. 8, 13, 14.
Tigris (R), 71 f., 117, 216, 218, 222, 330, 1291 f., 1387.

Til-Barsip (C). 737.
Tilshapalachi (C), 228.
Timnath (C), 675.
Tin in commerce, I. app. 3.
Tirhakah (K), 678, 756, 764 ff., II. app. 14.
Tirzah (C). 212. 267.
Titles of kings, 98, 102.
Tiyari (L), I. app. 2.
Tob (L), 204.
Togarmah (LP), 814.
Tophet (valley), 718, 855, 1095, 1110.
Tornadotos (Turnat. R), 218.
Totemism. 1183 n.
Tower of Babel, 1063.
Trade, see especially Aramæans, Babylonians, Hebrews, Phœnicians, and Caravan.
Tribal conditions in Israel. 186, 190, 200, 206, 363, 372 ff., 443, 480 ff., 530.
Tribalism (cf. Nomads), 307 ff., 458 n., 461, 510 (618), 950, 954, 964, 973, 1420.
Tribes (cf. Clans), 306 ff., 458, 500.
Tubal, see Tabal.
Tuklat-Adar (K): I. 175; II, 216.
Tunip (C), 145.
Turkish régime in Asia, 27 f., 743, 1050.
Turushpa (C), 311.
Tyre (C) and Tyrians, 34, 30, 42 ff., 126, 128, 141, 145, 152, 206, 243, 248, 264, 302, 310, 338, 077, 680 ff., 753 f., 757, 771 f., II. app. 10, 1030, 1157, 1208, 1213, 1240 n., 1365 ff.

Uaite (Ch), 788.
Ukīnzīr (K), 340.
Uknu (Choaspes, Kercha, R), 107, 339, 661.
Ulai (Eulæus, Karun, R), 107.
Ulluba (L), 307.
Ullusunu (Ch), II. app. 3.
Ululai (K), I. app. 8; see Shalmaneser IV.
Ummanaldash (K). 784 f.
Ummanigash (K), 779 f., 782.

Umman-Manda (P; cf. Scythians), 1383 f.
Umman-menanu (K), 739 f.
Universalism, prophetic, 553 f., 1420.
Ur (C), 94. 100 ff., 104, 108, 110, 1291.
Ur-Ba'u (K), 95 ff.
Urdaman (K), 767.
Ur-gur (K), 101.
Uriah, the Hittite, 520 n., 523, 550; b. Shemaiah, 1092.
Urijah (priest), 540.
Urmia (lake), 217, 248, 256.
Ur-Ninā (K). 95.
Urtaku (K), 779.
Urumilku (K). 675.
Usertesen III (K), 346.
Ushu (C), 675, 789.
Usury. see Interest.
Uzziah (Azariah, K), 261, 268 f., 306 ff., 325, I. app. 9, 1358 n.

Van (lake), 217, 256; (C), see Turushpa; (P), see Mannai.
Vassalage, see Dependencies.
Venality in Israel. 594 f.
Venus (planet). 1185.
Vergil and Isaiah, 1406.
Villages (unwalled), 38.
Virgo (constellation), 1185 n.
Virtues, their moral quality, 958 ff.

Wady Brissa, 1213 n.
Wady Halfa, 346.
Walls and gates, their significance, 1058 and n., 1233.
War, see Militarism.
Warfare: Hebrew, 512 ff., 540; Assyrian, 620, 1192, 1230 ff.
Warka (Erech, C). 101.
Warriors, see Army.
"Wars of Jehovah" (book), 894, 906, 913.
Watercourses, 72, 117, 663, 742, 1051 n., 1276, 1290 ff., 1308.
Water-wheels. 1302 n.
Weapons, 479, 484, 514, 516.
Week, cf. Sabbath.
Well. song of the. 894.
West-land, Asiatic, 125 ff.

Witch of Endor, 851 n.
Women: as rulers, 334, 423, 755; as prophetesses, 423, 851; in family relations, 417 ff., 427, 430, 1199; as property-holders, 422; emancipated, 421 ff., 426; morally and socially, 271, 322, 596, 721, 1184, 1189 f., 1256, 1332.
Words and their associations, 392 f.
Writing, by marks, 877; cuneiform, 80 ff., 104 f., 153 f., 873 ff.; Hettite, 159; alphabetic, 154, 872 ff.; among the Hebrews, 872, 877 ff.; Aramæans, 874 f.; Phœnicians (Canaanites), 872, 875, 877 f.; earliest uses, 882.
Written discourses, 939.

Xenophon, 1412 n.

Yamani ("Ionian"), II. app. 4.
"Yareb," I. app. 10.
Yatbur (L), 662.
Yatnā ("Cyprian"), II. app. 4.
Yatnan (Cyprus, etc.), 133, 682.
Ya'ubi'di (K), I. app. 9, 624.

Ya'udi (L). I. app. 9.
Yaüta (Ch.), 786.

Zab (R), Lower, 74, 123, 171; Upper, 74.
Zadok (priest), 1344.
Zahi (L), 132.
Zalzallat (W), 1395.
Zarpanit (D), 123.
Zebulun (TL), 272, 479.
Zechariah (K), 267.
"Zechariah," ix.–xi., 304, 315, I. app. 11.
Zedekiah (K), of Judah, 1148 f., 1150 ff., 1215 ff., 1247; of Askalon, 675, 691; exile, 1169.
Zelek of Ammon, 550.
Zephaniah (prophet), 814, 830, 1138; (priest), 1170, 1215.
Zerah, see Osorkon.
Zerubbabel (prince), 1147, 1312.
Zikkūrat (temple tower), 1061, 1063.
Zion (M), 204.
Zoan (Tanis, C), 137, 656, 766.
Zobah (L), 201, 204, 209, 787.
Zodiac, 856.

INDEX II

ANCIENT AUTHORITIES AND ILLUSTRATIONS

(Passages translated are marked with an asterisk.)

A. BIBLICAL

GENESIS					
		xv. 2 ff.	§ 412	xxxi. 43	§ 412
		xv. 6	932, 962	xxxi. 49 f., 53	413
i.-xi.	§ 885-888	xv. 9 ff.	1219	xxxi. 53	930 n.
ii.-iv.	932	xv. 19-21	130 n.	xxxii. 13, xxxiii. 10	594
ii.	1291 n.	xvi.	957	xxxiii. 30 f.	931
ii. 10	105 n.	xvi. 1	437 n.	xxxiv.	447 n.
ii. 13	120	xvi 12	314	xxxiv. 2	130 n.
iii. 6	1126	xvii. 19	I. app. 12	xxxiv. 12	419
iii. 15 f.	927	xviii. 19	412, 774 n., 927	xxxiv. 30	I. app. 4
iv. 7	1126	xviii. 32	1201	xxxv. 2 ff.	961
iv. 12, 14, 15	398 n.	xix. 17, 26	1395 n.	xxxv. 22	418 n.
iv. 20-22	431, 929	xx. 1 ff.	955	xxxvi. 31 ff.	306 n.
iv. 23, 24	889	xx. 3	418	xxxvi. 43	152
v. 29	927	xx. 7	928*	xxxvii. 25	238
viii. 21 f.	927	xx. 13	930 n.	xxxviii.	927, 929
ix. 13	944	xxi. 10, 14	412	xxxviii. 1 f.	447 n.
ix. 18 f.	929	xxi. 20	337 n.	xxxviii. 14 ff.	1392 n.
ix. 25-27	929	xxi. 21	430	xxxviii. 15 ff.	957
ix. 26 f.	540, 927	xxii.	412	xxxviii. 17 ff.	584
x. 2 f.	758	xxiii.	160	xxxviii. 18, 22	928*
x. 7	334	xxiii. 4	549	xxxviii. 21	1190
x. 10	101, 111 n.	xxiv. 28 ff.	405 n., 419	xxxix. 8	960
x. 11, 12	932	xxv. 3	334	xliii. 11 ff.	414, 594
x. 12	74	xxv. 4	630	xliv. 18 ff.	927
x. 13	1089 n.	xxv. 6	412, 594	xlv. 8	431
x. 15-18	130 n.	xxv. 9 f.	460	xlvi. 34	132 n.
x. 26 ff.	932	xxv. 13	334	xlviii. 14 ff.	428 n.
xi.	111, 932	xxv. 27	337 n.	xlviii. 22	514, 563 n.*
xii. 2 f.	927	xxvi. 34 f.	160, 412	xlix.	905
xii. 6	931	xxvii.	412, 428 n.	xlix. 3 f.	428 n.
xii. 10 ff.	955	xxvii. 3 ff.	337 n., 927	l. 16 f.	411
xiii. 7	I. app. 4	xxviii. 1, 5	412		
xiv.	109, 111, 153, 276,	xxviii. 13 ff.	931	EXODUS	
	732 n.	xxix. 14 f.	412	iii. 16	443
xiv. 14	447 n., 520	xxx. 14 ff.	927	iv. 22	429, 432
xiv. 18	590	xxxi. 21	I. app. 9	iv. 29	443

v. 14 ff.	§ 567	xxi. 14–18, 27–30	§ 894, 899	xxiii. 9, 14	§ 419
vi. 9	440	xxi. 15	894*	xxiii. 15 f.	543
xii. 21	443	xxii. 8	938	xxiii. 17 f.	857, 1190,
xii. 48	552	xxiii., xxiv.	895		1350
xv.	890	xxiii. 3	938	xxiii. 19 ff.	552, 576, 577
xvi. 4 f.	1346 n.	xxiii. 9	299, 466	xxiv. 1	419
xvii. 14	891	xxiii. 10	906 n.	xxiv. 6	584 n.
xviii.	36, 455 ff., 891	xxvi. 51	II. app. 13	xxiv. 7	547
xviii. 21	476 n.	xxvii. 8	427	xxiv. 10 ff.	584
xviii. 25 f.	455*	xxx. 13	419*	xxiv. 19	577
xx.–xxiii.	474 ff., 891	xxxv. 15	552	xxv. 13, 15	596
xx. 22–xxiii.	920–922	xxxvi. 2 ff.	427	xxvi. 1 ff.	461, 502, 590
xx. 10	463 n., 474 n.	xxxvi. 6	420	xxvi. 5	26, 434 n.
xx. 17	418, 1330			xxvi. 10	1024*
xxi. 1–11	541, 584 n.	**DEUTERONOMY**		xxvi. 12 f.	552, 576
xxi. 2	1217			xxvii.–xxx.	847 n.
xxi. 6	488	i.–iv. 40	847 n.	xxvii. 17	583
xxi. 7 ff.	427	i. 6, 9	462	xxviii. 64 ff.	1165
xxi. 12 ff.	906	i. 13, 15	455	xxix. 10 f.	552
xxi. 13	465, 474 n.	i. 16	552	xxix. 14	583
xxi. 16	547	iii. 9	242 n., I. app. 3	xxx. 14	1023
xxi. 20 ff.	475, 487, 542	v. 3	944	xxxi.–xxxiv.	847 n.
xxii. 3 ff.	475, 488	v. 6–21	892	xxxi. 12	552
xxii. 7 f.	1015	v. 15	547	xxxii. 6	432
xxii. 16	419	vi. 4	1335	xxxii. 9 ff.	434 n.
xxii. 21 f.	552, 921	vi. 10	503	xxxiii. 9 f.	1015
xxii. 25	576	vii. 9	1335	xxxiii. 28	299
xxii. 26 f.	584, 921	x. 18 f.	552		
xxii. 28	488 n.	xii. 1–28	860	**JOSHUA**	
xxiii. 8	595*	xii. 3	854		
xxiii. 9 ff.	475, 552, 576	xii. 9	1024*	vi. 26	498 n.
xxiii. 12	1346 n.	xii. 29–31	855	vii. 21	1064
xxiii. 16	1344 n.	xiii.	855 n.	ix. 7, 17	130 n.
xxiii. 20–23	921	xiii. 12 ff.	502	x. 12	896*
xxv.–xxxi.	891	xiv. 21	552	xi. 3	130 n.
xxxiv. 17–26	892	xiv. 28 f.	576	xv. 3	152
xxxiv. 22	1344 n.	xv. 12 ff.	584 n., 1217	xv. 41	693
xxxv. 41	891	xvi. 1–17	862	xix. 44	693
		xvi. 5	1024*	xix. 45	695
LEVITICUS		xvi. 9 ff.	547, 552, 576	xx. 4	510
		xvi. 18	455, 461, 502	xxiv. 19 f.	501
xvii.–xxvi.	1362	xvi. 19	595		
xix. 2	1362 n.	xvi. 21 f.	854	**JUDGES**	
xix. 33 f.	552	xvii. 2–7	856		
xxv. 35, 47	549	xvii. 5	34	i. 4 f.	I. app. 4
xxvi. 30	321	xvii. 8 ff.	461	i. 14 f.	563
		xviii. 1 ff.	863, 1019	i. 18	192
NUMBERS		xviii. 10–14	855, 858	i. 19	478
		xviii. 15 ff.	858	i. 26	I. app. 5
i.–x.	891	xix. 12	486, 510	i. 28 ff.	540
ii. 9, 16, 24, 31	II. app. 13	xix. 15 ff.	502	i. 34	136 n.
iv. 18	396	xxi. 1 ff.	486, 856	iii. 3	130 n.
xi. 5	440	xxi. 15–17	428	iii. 31	479, 917 n.
xi. 16 ff.	461 n.	xxii. 15 ff.	486	iv. 4	423
xiii. 33	929	xxii. 22 ff.	1331	iv. 11, 17	416, 964
xxi. 5	440	xxiii. 3 f.	550 n.	v.	479

INDEX II

v. 8	§ 188	ix. 21	§ 396	xii. 1 ff.	§ 903
v. 14	879*	x. 4	773 n.	xii. 26 ff.	57
v. 24	416, 964	x. 15 ff.	570	xii. 31	972
vi. 27 ff.	482 n.	x. 12	908 n.	xiii. 12	971
vi. 30	415	x. 26	57, 501	xiv. 7	465
vi. 34	460	x. 27	594	xiv. 14	398 n.
vii.	732 n.	xii. 3 ff.	595, 976	xv. 2	34
viii. 18 ff.	972	xiii. 2 ff.	517, 687	xv. 19	550
viii. 22 f.	51	xiii. 8 ff.	57	xv. 24	863
viii. 33 f.	482 n., 552	xiii. 19	129 n.	xv. 34	970
ix. 6 ff.	534	xiv. 1 ff.	474 n., 732 n.	xvi. 1 ff.	520
ix. 7-15	908	xiv. 44	415	xvi. 20 ff.	418 n., 971
ix. 27	1246	xiv.	152, 517	xvii. 4	971
ix. 46	33, 482 n.	xv.	975	xvii. 21 f.	520
ix. 51 ff.	33	xv. 22. 23	908	xviii. 1	518
x. 3 ff.	191	xv. 26 f.	1067	xviii. 33	902
x. 12	896*	xvii. 17	520	xix. 43	II. app. 11
xi. 35	908	xvii. 18, xviii. 13	517	xx. 1	465
xiii.-xvi.	917	xvii. 46, 51	785 n.	xxi. 2	130 n.
xiv. 2 f.	427	xviii. 7	908	xxi. 11 ff.	972
xiv. 14, 18, xv. 16		xviii. 17 ff.	427	xxii., see Ps. xviii.	
	908, 918 n.	xix. 13 ff., xx. 5 ff.	970	xxiii. 1-7	908 n.
xv. 16	908	xx. 6	484	xxiii. 37	550
xvii. 5 ff.	503, 863, 1211 n.	xx. 8-10	1248	xxiv. 3	523
xvii. 10	431	xx. 18	490 n.	xxiv. 6	130 n., 204 n.,
xviii. 7, 28	I. app. 3	xx. 25 ff.	415		I. app. 5
xviii. 19	431, 504	xxi. 6, 29	500	xxiv. 15 ff.	707
xix.-xxi.	193, 482 n., 965	xxii. 3 f.	550 n.		
xix. 16	501	xxiv. 13	908 n.	**1 KINGS**	
xix. 22	965	xxv. 5 ff.	520		
xxi. 12	396	xxv. 10	543 n.	i. 41, 45	33
xxi. 19 ff.	1246	xxv. 14 ff.	420, 542	ii. 39 f.	543 n.
xxi. 21	965	xxv. 44	427	iii. 16 ff.	590
xxi. 25	503	xxvi. 19	58	iii. 28	726
		xxvii. 6	919	iv. 25	604
RUTH		xxx. 14	192 n.	iv. 30 f.	910
i. 16	58	xxxi. 10	200 n.	iv. 32 (v. 12)	904
ii. 4	501, 508			v. 20	I. app. 3
iv. 1 ff.	477, 486	**2 SAMUEL**		viii. 41 f.	553
iv. 10 ff.	34			viii. 53	907 n.*
		i. 19-27	898	ix. 11	272
1 SAMUEL		iii. 7 f.	418 n.	ix. 18	141
		iii. 13 ff.	427	ix. 26 ff.	523
i.	430	iii. 17, v. 3	537	x. 22	524
ii. 1-10	908	iii. 33	902 n.*, 908	x. 28	230 n., I. app. 5, 519
ii. 12 ff.	589, 1248	v. 8	908 n.	xi. 41	1358
iii. 13	414*	v. 21	299 n.	xii. 1, 20	537
v. 3 f.	1406 n.	vii. 10 f.	195	xii. 16	465
vi. 4 f.	707	viii. 2	972	xiv. 23	320
vii. 14	493	viii. 3	I. app. 5	xv.	922 n.
viii. 1 ff.	595	viii. 6, 14	474	xv. 12	1190
viii. 9 ff.	534	viii. 9 ff.	202, 523	xv. 14	320
viii. 12	517	ix. 9 ff.	415, 542	xv. 19	591
viii. 19 f.	51	xi. 1	233 n.	xv. 22	1244 n.
ix. 5 ff.	542	xi. 6 ff.	520 n.	xvi. 9	520
ix. 9	937 n.	xi. 16	236 n.	xvi. 31	92, I. app. 3

xvi. 34	§ 498 n.	xiv. 4	§ 320	xix. 12		§ 227
xviii. 25	732	xiv. 7	254	xix. 13		349*
xviii. 40	1067	xiv. 8–14	260	xix. 32 f.	II. app. 14
xix. 3	930	xiv. 22	269	xix. 35	II. app. 13
xix. 15	241	xiv. 25	262	xix. 37	744 n., 746 f.*
xix. 18	983	xiv. 28	I. app. 9	xx.		635, 637
xx.	231, 233	xv. 1–7	1358 n.	xx. 9 ff.		640
xx. 14 ff.	531	xv. 4	320	xxi. 5, 6		799, 855
xx. 23 ff.	58, 520 n.	xv. 5	308	xxi. 7		1182
xx. 34	34, 212, 231 f.	xv. 10	267 n.*	xxi. 19, 23 ff.		806
xxi. 3, 7	981	xv. 13	315	xxii.–xxiii. 3	846–852
xxi. 10–16	239, 583	xv. 16	306	xxii. 10 f.		1039*
xxii. 1 f.	231, 234	xv. 19 f.	280, 310*	xxii. 20		698
xxii. 43	320		I. app. 8	xxiii. 4–20	855–858
xxii. 46	1190	xv. 29 f.	272, 280, 331*	xxiii. 4, 7, 11	846 n.
xxii. 48	236		I. app. 13	xxiii. 8 f.		1019
		xv. 35	118 n.	xxiii. 12		640
2 KINGS		xvi. 2	635	xxiii. 14		321
i.	978	xvi. 3 f.	319, 320	xxiii. 15 ff.		840
i. 8	584 n.	xvi. 5 ff.	325, 335	xxiii. 24		1211 n.
i. 9	518	xvi. 6	1360 n.	xxiii. 29		827
ii. 12	431	xvi. 7	280, 286, 326, 540	xxiii. 30	1039
iii.	235	xvi. 8	594	xxiii. 31		1039 n.
iii. 2	321	xvi. 9	697 n., II. app. 7	xxiii. 33	1040
iii. 27	1233 n.	xvi. 10	280, 336	xxiii. 34		1039
iv. 1 ff.	541, 585	xvi. 18	II. app. 7	xxiii. 36		1039 n.
iv. 8 ff.	420	xvii. 3	540	xxiv. 1	540, 1075 n.
iv. 23	1346 n.	xvii. 4–6	343*, 362,	xxiv. 2		1078
iv. 42	577 n.		I. app. 6, 823 n.	xxiv. 3 f.	1122 n.
v. 2	233	xvii. 24, 30	94, 761 n.	xxiv. 6		1078
v. 15	701	xvii. 26 ff.	58, 61	xxiv. 8	1039, 1079
v. 17	61	xviii. 13–xix. 35	II. app.	xxiv. 13 ff.	1080, 1234 n.,
vi., vii.	236		14			1275, 1306
vi. 8, 24	231	xviii. 2	635	xxiv. 18	II. app. 6
vi. 21–23	129 n, 233, 431,	xviii. 4	321, 854	xxiv. 19		1155
	612*	xviii. 8	651, 700, 792	xxv. 1		1214
vii. 6	I. app. 5	xviii. 9–11	343, 362*, 635	xxv. 2	II. app. 6
vii. 13	519	xviii. 9–13	I. app. 6, 501 n.	xxv. 3–10	1230–1233
viii. 12	244	xviii. 13	635, 686	xxv. 7		1197
viii. 13 ff.	241	xviii. 14–16	287, 290,	xxv. 18 ff.	1170, 1192 n.,
viii. 22	1360 n.		688*, 693, II. app.			1235
ix. 14	236 n.		11*, 14	xxv. 22		843
ix. 24 ff.	583	xviii. 17	696, 1233 n.	xxv. 23		1243 n.
x. 15 ff.	416	xviii. 20 f.	696	xxv. 27 ff.	1081, 1360,
x. 26 f.	321	xviii. 21	II. app. 4			1369
x. 32 f.	236, 243	xviii. 22	58, 290, 700			
xi., xii.	254	xviii. 23	519	**1 CHRONICLES**	
xi. 4, 19	518	xviii. 25	1036, 1029 n.			
xi. 29 ff.	979	xviii. 26–35	701	i. 12		166 n.
xii. 3	320	xviii. 27	1179 n.	ii. 55	416, 1275 n.
xii. 4 ff.	846	xviii. 32	74, 353	iii. 17 f.	1039 n., 1081,
xii. 17 f.	243 and n.	xviii. 34	94, 349, 680			1147
xiii. 4 f.	246*, 252	xix.	702–704	iv. 12		1275 n.
xiii. 7	245*, 519	xix. 3–37	741 n.	v. 6		280
xiii. 14	431	xix. 8 ff.	678, 693,	v. 26		280
xiii. 24 f.	251 f.		II. app. 14	xv. 17		337 n.

xxvi. 18	§ 856	xxii. 5 ff., xxiv. 2 ff.		lxviii. 5	§ 132
xxvii. 25 ff.	540 n.		§ 584, 599	lxviii. 29	286 n.
xxix. 15	549	xxix. 7 ff.	34, 600 n.	lxix.	1363
		xxxi.	600	lxxi.	1363
2 CHRONICLES		xxxi. 11	592	lxxii.	600 n.
		xxxi. 13 ff.	406, 543*	lxxii. 4, 10 ff.	604*
i. 16	230 n.	xxxii. 7	560	lxxii. 10	286 n.
viii. 4	141	xxxviii. 28	432 n.	lxxiii.	598, 608, 986
xiv. 4	321	xlii. 10	301	lxxiv. 8, 10	796 n., 1239
xvi. 14	1216 n.	xlii. 15	430	lxxvi.	731 n.
xx.	215			lxxviii. 60	490
xxi. 19	1216 n.	**PSALMS**		lxxix.	1239
xxiv. 23 f.	243 n.	i. 5	601	lxxx. 8 ff.	434 n.
xxv. 7	275 n.	ii. 6 f.	432	lxxxi. 6	434 n.
xxvi.	268 f., 540 n.	iv. 7	991*	lxxxii. 16	598
xxvii. 5	269 n.	v. 4 ff.	601	lxxxiii.	215
xxviii. 5 ff., 18	325	x. 3	598	lxxxiv.	1363
xxviii. 20	280	xi. 5	320	lxxxvi. 9, lxxxvii.	554
xxviii. 23	640	xii. 5	602	lxxxix. 14	457
xxxii. 3-5	698	xiv.	598, 608	lxxxix. 26 f.	429, 432
xxxii. 27 f.	651	xiv. 20	785 n.	xc. 2	432
xxxii. 30	698 n.*	xv.	595, 601	xci. 5 f.	II. app. 13
xxxiii. 10	790*	xvii.	598	xciv. 20	598
xxxiii. 11	798	xviii.	718, 908 f., 1410	xcvii. 2	457
xxxiv. 4, 7	321	xx.	1073, 1211 n.	ci.	600 n.
xxxv. 21, 23	1034*	xxii.	1363	cii. 19 ff.	554
xxxv. 24 f.	1035*, 1237	xxii. 25 ff.	554, 601	ciii. 13	433
xxxvi. 13	1148	xxiv.-xxvi.	595, 601	ciii. 20 f.	407
xxxvi. 17	1232 n.	xxvii. 11	1054 n.	cv. 11 ff.	434 n.
		xxviii. 2 ff.	601	cxix. 19	549
EZRA		xxxi. 19 f.	601	cxxvi.	1263, 1363
i. 2 ff.	1416 n.	xxxv. 15	896 n.	cxxxvii.	1263, 1348*
i. 8, etc.	1312	xxxv. 16	598	cxxxvii. 7	1078 n.,
ii. 59 f.	1273	xxxvi.	609 n.		1240 n.
iii. 3	61	xxxvii.	598, 601, 609	cxxxix.	609 n.
iii. 7	45, 67	xxxviii.	609	cxli. 6	598
iv. 2	761 n., 799	xxxix.	549, 609	cxlvi. 7	546
iv. 9	101 n., 799	xl. 12 ff.	609	cxlvi. 9	554
iv. 12 ff.	1241	xli.-xliii.	601	cxlvii. 2-4	1406 n.
		xlii., xliii.	607 n., 609, 1011		
NEHEMIAH		xliii. 3 f.	1340*	**PROVERBS**	
v. 3 ff.	541, 585	xlv. 12	286 n., 594	iii. 12	433
v. 9	606	xlvi.	731	vi. 1 ff.	596
vi. 14	851 n.	xlvi. 4	731 n.*	vi. 20	430
vi. 15	1185	xlvi. 9	746 n.	vi. 35	594
vii. 61 f.	1273	xlviii. 3	1402 n.	viii. 15	879 n.
viii. 1 ff.	34	xlviii. 12 ff.	1233 n.	x. 3, 7	601
viii. 17	1273 n.	xlix. 6 ff.	598, 601	xi. 1, 15, 26	596
xii. 27, 30	1233 n.	l.	909	xiii. 22 f.	601
		l. 11		xiv. 1	420
JOB		li.	I. app. 7 718, 1363	xiv. 21, 31	601
i. 15	334	lii.	598, 601	xv. 27	594, 595
iii. 2 ff.	1112	lv., lvi.	598, 601	xvi. 11	596
vi. 19	334	lviii.	598	xvii. 8, 23	594, 595
ix. 24	600	lxiii. 1, 5	609	xviii. 16	594, 595

xix. 1, 17, 22	§ 601	viii. 23	§ 272	xxxi. 7		§ 321
xx. 10, 23	596	ix. 5 ff.	I. app. 12,	xxxii. 1 ff.		603
xx. 16	584, 596		431 n.*, 603, 726	xxxiii.		728–730
xxi. 12, 13	601	ix. 8–x. 4	325 n.	xxxiii. 7		703
xxi. 14	594, 595	ix. 12	325	xxxiii. 8		696 n.
xxi. 27	601	x. 1	595, 879 n.	xxxiii. 13–16		729*
xxii. 22 f.	34, 601	x. 5–xi. 16	722–727	xxxiii. 15		595, 601
xxii. 26 f.	596	x. 5	3, 297, 725	xxxiii. 18		729*
xxiii. 10 f.	583*	x. 7	78	xxxiii. 20		485
xxiv. 15 ff.	601	x. 8	1312 n.	xxxiii. 21 f.		730*
xxv. 14	595	x. 9	111 n.	xxxvi. 12		717
xxviii. 8, 27	601	x. 14	292	xxxvii. 7		709
xxix. 4	595	x. 28–32	687	xxxvii. 18		723
xxix. 7	601	x. 33 f.	725*, 730	xxxvii. 25		708
xxix. 18	1260*	xi. 2 f.	720	xxxvii. 29		718
xxx. 10 ff.	420	xiii.–xix.	324	xxxvii. 30		721 n.
xxx., xxxi.	910	xiii.–xiv. 23	1401 f.	xxxvii. 36		704*
xxx. 10 f.	420	xiii. 19	1056	xxxviii.		635
xxxi. 1, 10 ff.	420 (910)	xiv. 4 ff.	290, 1402*	xxxviii. 6		637
		xv., xvi.,	273 n.	xxxviii. 10–20		909
		xvi. 1 ff.	269	xxxix. 1		594, 679
ECCLESIASTES		xvii. 1–11	330, 355	xxxix. 7		798 n.
v. 8	592*	xvii. 8	321	xl.–lv.		1405 ff.
vii. 7	594	xviii.–xx.	655–659	xl. 3–5		1410*
		xix. 1–13	769	xl. 20 f.		1338
ISAIAH		xix. 18	153, 879 f.	xl. 29 f.		1406 n.
i.	309	xix. 19, 20	860 n.	xli. 2 ff.		1403 n., 1409,
i. 6	213	xix. 24	129 n.			1411 n.
i. 8	236 n., 309	xx.	631, 634, 658 f., 711	xli. 7		1405
i. 9	546	xx. 1	II. app. 4	xli. 8 f.		1313
i. 11	1011	xxi. 1–10	1404	xli. 14		1409
i. 13	940	xxi. 2	1401 n.	xli. 17 ff.		1406 n.
i. 17	604*	xxii.	697 f., 722	xlii. 6		1411 n.
i. 21	33	xxii. 6 f.	696	xlii. 7		1406 n.
i. 23	595	xxii. 15 ff.	559	xlii. 15		72
i. 29	321, 860 n.	xxiii.	772	xlii. 21		298
ii. 1	318 n.	xxv. 6 ff.	554	xliii. 3, 7		1313, 1405
ii. 1–8	318, 321, 553	xxvi. 1	1233 n.	xliii. 14		1405
ii. 6	643	xxvii. 9	321	xliii. 27		431
ii. 16	67, 269	xxviii.	995	xliv. 1 f.		1313
ii. 18, 20	321	xxviii. 1–4	212, 355, 596	xliv. 5		407*, 553
iii. 2 f.	321	xxviii. 5–29	580, 596,	xliv. 12–20		1338, 1406 n.
iii. 4, 12	317, 420		642 f., 646 f.	xliv. 28		1411 n.*
iii. 16 f.	321, 596	xxviii. 7	1200	xlv. 3		310
v. 8 ff.	583, 596	xxviii. 28	475 n.	xlv. 4		1409
v. 25	309	xxix.–xxxii.	711–721	xlv. 6		1411
vi. 9 f.	319, 938	xxix. 10	720	xlv. 13		1411 n.
vii.	325 ff.	xxx. 3–7	286 n., 700,	xlv. 20		1406 n.
vii. 3	698		II. app. 15	xlv. 22 f.		553
vii. 14 ff.	I. app. 12	xxx. 7	II. app. 15*,	xlvi. 1 ff.		299 n., 1405,
viii. 1 ff.	329, 640		1336 n.			1406 n.
viii. 6	698 n., 995	xxx. 9 ff.	420, 596, 721	xlvi. 11		1403 n., 1409
viii. 6 f.	730 n., 1308 n.	xxx. 15 f.	716*	xlvii. 2		1405
viii. 8 f.	I. app. 12*	xxx. 22	321	xlvii. 12 ff.		858, 1211,
viii. 19	321	xxx. 27 f.	730			1405
viii. 22	329	xxxi. 1	520	xlviii. 18		1296 n.

xlix. 5 ff.	§ 1405, 1418	vii. 21 ff.	§ 1068, 1094*	xxvi. 10	§ 1118 n.
xlix. 12	1418	vii. 29–33	1095*	xxvi. 18	644, 11. app. 8,
xlix. 16	1233 n.	viii. 1–16	1096 f.*		998
xlix. 19	1296 n., 1418	viii. 2	856	xxvi. 22 f.	1121 n.
xlix. 23	1418	viii. 10	589	xxvii. 3 f.	1154, 1156 f.
li.	419, 541, 585	viii. 18–22	1098	xxvii. 5–22	1157
li. 1 f.	434 n.	ix. 1	1098*	xxvii. 16	1157*
li. 3, 11	1418	ix. 22 f.	1099*	xxviii. 1 ff.	1106, 1155 f.,
li. 13 f.	1406 n.	ix. 24	1114		1158 f.*
li. 14	1221, 1415*	xi. 1–8	1065 n.	xxviii. 11, 13	1159 n.*
liii. 3 f.	1145	xi. 1–xii. 6	1100 f.	xxix.	1167–1170
liii. 9	601	xi. 2	1341	xxix. 2	1275
liv. 2	465	xi. 21	1066 n., 1069	xxix. 5, 28	1194 n.
liv. 4–6	426	xii. 5	1109*	xxix. 21 ff.	1268
liv. 11 f.	1233 n.	xii. 7–14	1140	xxix. 26	1066
lvi. 6 f.	553	xii. 14	1078 n.	xxx.–xxxiii.	1173 n.
lviii. 11 f.	1296 n.	xiii. 1–7	1255 n.	xxxi. 9	429
lix. 19	1296 n.	xiii. 1–27	1143	xxxi. 15	1242
lx. 3 ff.	553	xiii. 15–18	1143*	xxxi. 20	432
lx. 6	630 n.	xiv.–xvii.	1124–1127	xxxi. 29 f.	1204
lx. 7	787 n.	xiv. 8	1125*	xxxi. 30 ff.	1341*
lx. 8 f.	66	xiv. 13	1125*	xxxi. 32	426
lx. 18	1058 n.	xv. 1–9	1126*	xxxi. 34	554 n.
lxii. 4	418, 426 n.	xv. 10–21	1242 n.	xxxii. 3–5	1221 n.
lxiii. 16	432	xv. 19–21	1126*	xxxii. 6–44	1225 f., 1321
lxiv. 8	432	xvi. 13	955	xxxii. 7 ff.	1069
lxv. 21	1194 n.	xvi. 19	553	xxxii. 9–14	1225 n.
lxvi. 3, 17	1183 n.	xvii. 5–13	1127 n.	xxxii. 24	1230
lxvi. 12	1296 n.	xvii. 14–18	1127	xxxiv.	1216–1219
lxvi. 18 ff.	553	xviii.	1102–1104	xxxiv. 13 f.	584 n., 1219
		xix. 1–15	1110	xxxv.	416, 465, 1141 f.
		xx. 2	1066, 1118 n.	xxxv. 19	1275 n.
JEREMIAH		xx. 7–13	1112*	xxxvi. 1 ff.	829 n.
i. 6	1069	xx. 7–18	1150 n.	xxxvi. 4	1082 n., 1116 f.
i. 15	813*	xx. 9 ff.	1109	xxxvi. 9 f.	940, 1082 n.*,
ii. 1–iv. 4	1086 f.	xx. 14–18	1112		1118 f.
ii. 3	1087*	xxi. 1–10	1215*	xxxvi. 11–24	843, 1119 f.
ii. 10 f.	1086*	xxii. 1–9	1161	xxxvi. 32	1082
ii. 15 f.	1083*	xxii. 10, 27	301, 1082,	xxxvii.	1220–1224
ii. 18	1083*		1145	xxxvii. 5	1034 n., 1218*
ii. 28	1087*	xxii. 15 ff.	1069	xxxvii. 7	1222
ii. 36	1083, 1087*	xxii. 20–30	1144–1147*	xxxvii. 14 f.	1221
iii. 1	419	xxii. 24 ff.	1079, 1081	xxxvii. 15 ff.	559
iii. 6–18	1086 n.	xxiii. 1–8	1161*, 1263	xxxvii. 21	34, 851 n.
iii. 17	553	xxiii. 9 ff.	1162	xxxviii.	1227–1229
iv.–vi.	813, 1091	xxiv. 1 ff.	1166, 1275	xxxviii. 4	1216
iv. 7	1115	xxv. 1, 2	1115	xxxviii. 5	1151, 1221
v. 15, 17	813	xxv. 3	813	xxxviii. 19	1221 n.
v. 31	1017 n.	xxv. 8, 9	1115*	xxxviii. 20	1216 n.
vi. 13	589	xxv. 9	1054, 1091,	xxxviii. 25	559
vi. 22 f.	813		1115 n.	xxxix. 2–8	1230–1233
vii.–x.	1093–1099	xxv. 20	1032 n.	xxxix. 3	1232 n.,
vii. 4–11	1093*	xxv. 25	1163		1233 n.*, 1370
vii. 14	490	xxv. 26	1403 n.	xxxix. 11–14	1212 n.
vii. 16 ff.	856, 1068,	xxvi. 6	490	xl.	1242–1246
	1094*	xxvi. 7–24	1092	xl. 14	1213

xli.	§ 1246–1249	vii. 27	§ 1312 n.	xxvii. 13, 17		§ 45
xli. 9	1247 n.*	viii. 1–4	1176	xxvii. 18		1213 n.
xlii.	1252 f.	viii. 1 1176 n., 1185, 1311		xxviii. 3		1201 n.
xliii.	1254 f.	viii. 3	1118 n.	xxviii. 20–24		1213 n.*
xliii. 10 ff.	1366	viii. 3–14	1182–1190	xxviii. 26		1194 n.
xliv.	1256 f.	viii. 10	1183 n.*	xxix.–xxxii.		1366
xliv. 1	1254	viii. 15 f.	1191	xxix. 17 ff.	1345, 1366
xliv. 17 ff.	856, 1256	viii. 17	1191 n.*	xxx. 14 ff.		770 n.
xlv.	1212	ix.	1191 f.	xxxi. 3 ff.		833*
xlvi. 2	827, 1043, 1084	ix. 2 ff.	1272	xxxii. 17–32		1366 n.
xlvi. 3–12	1088 f.	x.	1193	xxxii. 24 f.		1163
xlvi. 9	1089 n.	xi.	1194–1196	xxxiii.		1342
xlvi. 13 ff.	1366	xi. 16, 18 f.	1195*	xxxiii. 2 ff.		1337
xlvi. 17	1366 n.*	xii.	1197 f.	xxxiii. 15		584
xlvi. 25	770 n.	xii. 10	1312 n.	xxxiii. 24		1243
xlvii. ff.	324	xiii.–xvi.	1198–1202	xxxiii. 26		1330
xlvii. 1	1034 n., 1222	xiii. 10 ff.	1154	xxxiii. 30 f.		1336 n.
xlvii. 4	166 n.	xiii. 17 ff.	851 n.	xxxv. 5 ff.		1240 n.
xlviii.	273 n.	xiv. 1	1176 n., 1311	xxxvii. 27		399
xlviii. 11	1156 n.	xvi. 3	160*, 434 n.	xxxviii.		814
xlix. 1 ff.	273 n., 274, 1213	xvi. 53	301	xl.–xlviii.	1178 n., 1344, 1362
		xvii.	1209			
xlix. 19	1109 n.	xvii. 13 f.	1152, 1156*	xlv. 7 ff.		1312 n.
xlix. 34 ff.	1163	xvii. 16, 19	1209 n.	xlv. 18 f.		1344
l. 1–li. 58	1403	xvii. 18 ff.	1148	xlv. 22 ff.		1346 n.
l. 21	339, 1403 n.	xvii. 20	1197	xlvi. 2 ff.		1312 n.
l. 23	1088	xviii.	1204	xlvii. 1–12		1294 n.
li. 1	1403 n.	xviii. 6	1344	xlvii. 16		349
li. 41	1403 n.	xviii. 7, 12, 16	584			
li. 44	1109 n.	xix. 4	718, 1039	**DANIEL**		
li. 59 ff.	1171 f.	xix. 5–9	1143			
lii. 5–14, 17–24	1230–1233	xix. 6	1039	i. 1		1075 n.
lii. 28–30	1234, 1250	xix. 10 ff.	1209	ii. 1, 48		1201 n.
		xx. 1–44	1206	iii. 16 ff.		1169 n.
LAMENTATIONS		xx. 1	1176 n., 1311	viii. 2, 16		106
		xx. 12	1344	x. 5		1192
i. 4 etc.	1238	xx. 49	1336 n.			
ii. 9	1259	xxi.	1210	**HOSEA**		
ii. 18	896 n.	xxi. 3	1039	i. 4		240, 312
ii. 20	1230	xxi. 21 f.	1210*	i. 7		320
iv. 10	1230	xxii.	1212	i. 11		315
iv. 22	1240 n.	xxii. 12 f.	595	ii. 2 ff.		426
v. 7	1205	xxii. 26	1017 n.	ii. 11	940, 994, 1346 n.
		xxii. 30	1154	ii. 16		418
EZEKIEL		xxiii.	1212	iii. 2		427
i. 2	1174	xxiii. 14	1183 n.	iii. 4 f.	312, 1211 n.
i. 4–28	1176	xxiii. 23	339	iv.–xiv.		312
i. 4	1402 n.	xxiii. 38	1344	iv. 4 f.		589
ii. 17 ff.	1337	xxiv. 1 f.	1214	iv. 13 ff.		1190
iii. 7 ff.	1176	xxv. ff.	324	iv. 15		320
iii. 15	1296*, 1336 n.	xxv. 1 ff.	1213	iv. 16 f.		275 n.
iii. 22–27	1176 n., 1178 n.	xxv. 16	192 n.	v. 1 ff.		1017
iv.–vii.	1178–1180	xxvi.–xxviii.	1367	v. 1		1244
iv. 4 ff.	1179*, 1344	xxvi. 1 ff.	1240 n.	v. 3		275 n.
v. 11	1344	xxvii.	l. app. 3	v. 9		275 n.
vi. 4, 6	321	xxvii. 7	66	v. 10		320

INDEX II 467

v. 11	§ 314	vi. 5	§ 909	iii. 8-10		§ 770
v. 13	314*	vi. 6	275 n., 596	iii. 10 f.		78
v. 18	941	vi. 7	302	iii. 18		731 n.
vi. 4	320	vi. 14	262 n., 302, 1137*			
vi. 6	1011	vii. 7 ff.	646	**HABAKKUK**		
vi. 10	275 n.	vii. 10	940			
vi. 11	320	vii. 14	570	i. 2-ii. 4		1130-1132*
vii. 3	538, 587	vii. 15	938	i. 6		1137 n.
vii. 8 ff.	313 f.	vii. 16	940 n.	ii. 5		1135*
vii. 12	1197	vii. 17	302 f.	ii. 6-20		1135
viii. 8-10	314*	viii. 5	596, 1346 n.	iii.	718, 909, 1136, 1410
viii. 14	320	viii. 6	541, 596			
ix. 3 f.	303, 314*	viii. 14	930	**ZEPHANIAH**		
ix. 6	313	ix. 4	302			
ix. 13, 17	314	ix. 7	3, 166 n., 297	i., ii.		830
x. 5 f.	299 n.*, 355			ii.		324, 814
x. 14 f.	314*	**OBADIAH**		ii. 5		192 n.
xi. 1	165, 432			ii. 8 ff.		273 n.
xi. 8	275 n.	10 ff.	1078 n., 1240 n.	ii. 13-15		830*
xi. 10	I. app. 11			iii. 4		589, 1017 n.
xi. 12	320	**MICAH**				
xii. 1	313			**ZECHARIAH**		
xii. 2	320	i.	718, 1403			
xii. 7	596	i.-iii.	II. app. 8	ii. 11		553
xiii. 1	275 n.	i. 3 f.	356*, 909	viii. 20 ff.		553
xiii. 10 f.	314*	i. 5, 9, 13	319	ix.-xi.		324
xiii. 15 f.	355	i. 10-16	645	ix. 1 ff.	258 n., 315
		i. 14 ff.	798 n.	ix. 6		II. app. 4
JOEL		ii., iii.	798 n.	ix. 13	I. app. 11, II. app. 4
iii. 6	II. app. 4	ii. 1 ff.	583, 644	x. 6		315
		ii. 9	585	x. 11		760
		iii. 2 f.	644	xi. 1-17		315
AMOS		iii. 5	595	xi. 3		1109 n.
i. f.	324	iii. 6-11	321, 589, 644	xii. 11		I. app. 5
i. 1	II. app. 6		1017	xiii. 11		1411 n.
i. 3 ff.	244, 254, 264, 274	iii. 12	II. app. 8, 1236	xiv. 5		265
i. 6-8	689	iv. 1 ff.	553, 604			
i. 9	1213 n.	v. 3-5	I. app. 12, 603	**MALACHI**		
ii. 4	320	v. 12 f.	321, 644			
ii. 6 f.	541, 1190	vi. 5	895	i. 6		326, 435*
ii. 8	584, 596, 1017	vi. 6-8	1006	ii. 6 f.		1015
iii. 2	774 n.	vi. 7	855	ii. 10		432 and n.
iii. 9 ff.	355	vi. 8	601, 1419			
iv. 1	596	vi. 9 ff.	798 n.	**2 MACCABEES**		
iv. 2 f.	302, 355	vi. 10 f.	596			
iv. 6 ff.	264, 541	vi. 16	319	ii. 1 ff.		1244
iv. 10 ff.	34, 264, 265, 596, 707	vii. 2	601	**MATTHEW**		
v. 3	264, 518	vii. 3	595*, 1200			
v. 5	930	vii. 8	1078 n.	i. 12 ff.		1147
v. 8, 18, 20	265			iii. 4		584 n.
v. 11 f.	541, 595, 596	**NAHUM**		v. 8		1009
v. 15	275 n.			v. 31		419
v. 16 f.	355	i.-iii.	831-833	vi. 9		435
v. 21 ff.	1011	ii. 3-5	832 n.	vii. 12		619
v. 27	302	ii. 6	827 n.*	vii. 15		584 n.
vi. 2 ff.	111 n., 355	ii. 11 f.	78, 833*, 1032			

INDEX II

viii. 28	§ 130 n.	**ROMANS**		**HEBREWS**	
xi. 8	384 n.				
xvi. 18	1233 n.	vii. 1 f.	§ 419	ii. 19 ff.	§ 429
xxv. 44	1415 n.	viii. 29	429	x. 38	1133 n.
				xi. 1	1133 n.
		2 CORINTHIANS		xi. 32	929 n.
MARK				xi. 37	805 n.
vii. 13	1097 n.	v. 1	465	xii. 23	429
		GALATIANS		**1 PETER**	
LUKE					
vii. 9	1008 n.	iv. 1	428 n.*	iii. 6	418
vii. 25	584 n.	vi. 10	407		
xii. 13 f.	486 n.	vi. 14	1099	**2 PETER**	
xv. 11 ff.	433			i. 13 f.	465
xviii. 2 ff.	599	**EPHESIANS**			
		ii. 19	407	**1 JOHN**	
		iii. 15	399*	iii. 3	1009
JOHN		v. 22 ff.	426		
ix. 7	1308 n.			**REVELATION**	
xi. 39	785 n.			v. 2	713
xiv. 6	1008 n.			vii. 3	1192
		PHILIPPIANS		xvi. 16	145
		i. 1	407	xx. 7 ff.	814
ACTS				xxi. 3	399
ix. 11	34 n.	**COLOSSIANS**		xxi. 12 ff.	1233 n.
xii. 20	45	i. 15, 18	429	xxii. 3 f.	407*

B. INSCRIPTIONAL

Amarna tablets:		IV, 5	§ 755*	46, 1–9	§ 229
Br. M.:		IV, 16, 23 ff.	756	63, 13	673
2	§ 149	IV, 2	759	66–68	311, 331 f., 334,
8, 9	154, 162	IV, 29	761*		I. app. 13
28, 30	154 n.			72 f.	331 f., 334 f.
64	152	C^b.:		98, 2	242*
AN:		258 n., 293 n., 311, 341 n.			
(I R, 17–26)	217 ff.	C¹8:		Mesha stone:	
1, 4	57*	II. i. pl. 1–14, 15 ff.,		lines 9 ff.	235, 274
1, 25	57	73 ff.	875 n.	Mon. (III R, 7 f.):	
III, 17 ff.	219 n.			29–75	227
III, 23 f.	223	Deluge Story:		78 ff.	228*
		line 108	748 n.		
BA:				Nab. *Annals*:	
II, 257 (Cyrus)	1393 n.*	"Gudea":		II, III	1392 n.
II, 258 ff. (Merodach-		B, VI, 64	98	II, 1 ff.	1382
baladan)	665 n.			II, 15–18	1387 n.*,
Bab. Chr.:		K:			1388 n.
I, 23–28	342	2801	172	III, 12–18	1395*
II, 39 ff.	739	3082, 3086	756	III, 19 f.,	1397*
III, 18 ff.	739 n.	4378, col. v, vi	757 n.	III, 21 f.	1398 n.
III, 28	740 n.	4668	758	III, 22 f.	1396 n.
III, 34 ff.	744, 746*			III, 24 ff.	1397 n.
III, 39 ff.	751	Lay.:		Neb.:	
IV, 9, 17 f.	752	17, 4–7	293	I, 55 ff.	1054*
IV, 3, 6	753	29	331 f., 334 f.	II, 12 ff.	1053

INDEX II

VIII, 29-44	§ 1062*	II R:		2, 126-326	§ 777	
VIII, 64 f.	1062 n.*	16, 32	§ 1346 n.*	3, 27 ff.	779	
		45, 11, 29	1403 n.	3, 96 ff.	780	
		50, 20 f.	1058 n.	3, 128 ff. -4, 41	782	
Obel. (Lay, 87 ff.):		50, 28 f.	1285 n.	4, 97 ff.	781 n.	
26-49	227	53. 39. 57. 59	250	5, 34 f.	784	
54-66	229	67, 5, 42	293, 340, 311	5, 36-7, 81	785	
83 ff.	237	52-55	334	6, 107 ff. 88, 107, 785 n.		
96 ff.	242	60	314 n.	7, 82-10, 5	786-789	
138	243 n.	67, 57-66	336-338	8, 27 ff., 9, 42 ff.,		
		III R:		9, 103 ff., 9,		
		3, nr. 6	178 n.	115 ff.	788 n.	
PCT (OBT):		4, nr. 2	175	25, 1-7	1331 n.	
I		4, nr. 7	89	25, 7 ff.	1332 n.	
pl. 2	92	5, nr. 6	242*	29, nr. 1, 6	1185	
pl. 4.	92	9, nr. 2	307 n.	33	123	
pl. 9-13	104	9, 30 ff. (nr. 3)	307,	35, 6	1398 n.	
pl. 32. 1051 n., 1054*			311*	35, 7-15	1383*	
IX:		10, nr. 2, 1. 6-15	331 f.,	35, 16-19	1395*	
nr. 48 1308 n., 1324 n.			I. app. 13*	35, 20-22	1378 n.	
nr. 49	1324 n.	10, 30-38	334	35. 27. 35	1397 n.	
		12 f. II. app. 9, 97, 738		35, 31 f.	94, 1399*	
		12, 18. 21 ff. 682, 691 f.		35, 32 f.	1398	
		14, 6 ff.	742	55-57	178	
I R:		14, 43 ff.	740 n.	62, 5 ff.	778 n.	
2, nr. III, IV	104, 108	14, 48 ff.	180	64, I, 18-33	1383*	
3, nr. VII	91	15, I, 2 ff.	746*	64, I, 32	825 n.	
5	104	15, II, 1 ff.	751	64, I, 41	125 n.	
7, VIII, 1	II. app. 12*	15, IV, 1 ff.	760	64, II, 56 ff.	87	
8, nr. 3	820 n.	16, V, 13 ff.	761	66, II, 7	117 n.	
28	180	16, nr. 2	820 n.			
29-31	247	30. 31, col. iii., iv.	777			
29, 39-53	247	31-33, col. iv.-vi.	779 f.	S:		
35, nrs. 1-4	248 ff.	34, col. vii.	786	2005	758	
35, nr. 4, 21 ff.	172	46	875 n.	2027	756	
38, 34-39, 41	675 ff.*	49, col. i., ii.	748*	Sargon:		
39, 42 ff.	733	IV R:		Annals:		
39, 50-61	734*	7, I, 17 ff.	112	1. 55-57, 76, 77		
40, 26	97	31	1185 n.		II. app. 3	
41, 1 ff.	1192	32	1346 n.*	1. 94-99	630*	
41, 21 ff.	739 n.	33	1185 n.	1. 207 f.	630	
41, 47-42, 23	739	34	90, 92, 93 n.	1. 215-228	II. app. 4*	
42, 33 ff.	742	36¹, nr. 21	113	1. 235 f.	II. app. 6	
43, 8 f.	743 n.*	36¹, nr. 45	118 n.	Cyl.:		
43, 23 ff.	97	39(44 f.)	175	20	630	
44, 55 ff.	742	V R:		64	757 n.	
45, 1, 10 ff.	753.	1, 2	756, 764 ff.	ST:		
45, II. 6 758 n.*, 759 n.		1, 8 ff.	763	pl. 1, 1. 10 ff.		
45, II, 32 ff.	751	1, 31 ff.	816		I. app. 16*	
46, III, 25	755*	1, 45 ff.	763	pl. 30 f., 1. 23-25		
46, IV, 8 ff.	760	1, 52	755 n.		I. app. 16*	
47, V, 11	761	2, 7	766 n.	pl. 33 f.	II. app. 4*	
49, col. i., ii. 740, 748*		2, 41 ff.	767 n.	pl. 38, 1. 31 f.		
49, col. iii., iv.	749*	2, 58	771*		I. app. 16	
67, col. i. 14	1370 n.*	2, 63-94	773	pl. 44 f.	631₁	
69, II, 29; III, 27	94 n.	2, 95-125	774*		II. app. 4*	
69, II, 48; III, 28	95 n.					

pl. 48, l. 8		VII:		p. 148-152 (II R,
	II. app. 5	43 f.	§ 178 n.	66, III R, 4) § 175
TP:		60-70	172	
(I R. 1-16)	§ 179	TSBA:		
I, 62 ff.	176 n.	V, 422	91	ZA:
VI:				II, 69 ff. 1051 n.
39-48	179*	UAG:		IV, 406 92
58-84	180 n.	p. 145-147	113	

C. JOSEPHUS

Ant.:		X, 11, 2	1369 n.	I, 20	1059 n., 1369 n.
VIII, 5, 3	42 n.	XI, 2	1416 n.	I, 21	1365 n.
IX, 4, 3	681	Apion:			
IX, 11, 2	42 n.	I, 14	136		
X, 6, 1	1075 n.*	I, 19	1056 n., 1057*		

D. GREEK AND ROMAN

Herodotus:		I, 195	§ 1064	Iliad:	
I, 15, 104	§ 758	I, 199	1332 n.	I, 37	II. app. 13
I, 87	1388 n.	II, 141	705*	xii, 299 ff., xviii.	
I, 105	812	II, 157	812, 1032	161 f.	§ 719
I, 107-124	1384 n.	II, 158, 159	1031	Odyssey, xi. 14	758 n.
I, 125, 127	1385	II, 161, 163, 169	1365 n.	Eneid, i. 628 ff.	547
I, 178 ff.	1056 n., 1058 ff.	IV, 11, 12	758	Ovid, Met. i, 85	1009 n.
		IV, 42	1031	Diodorus, II. 26	827 n.
I, 180	34 n., 1059 n.	VII, 11	1378 n.	Pliny, Hist. Nat.	
I, 181	1062 n., 1063 n.	Xenophon, Anab.		V, 11, 65	787 n.
I, 183	1332 n.	III, 4, 9	827 n.	Lucian, Charon, ch. 23	
I, 194	1305 n.				827 n.

www.ingramcontent.com/pod-product-compliance
Lightning Source LLC
Chambersburg PA
CBHW020831020526
44114CB00040B/545